FREUD

THE MIND
OF THE MORALIST

FREUD

THE MIND
OF THE MORALIST

Third Edition

Philip Rieff

THE UNIVERSITY OF CHICAGO PRESS
CHICAGO AND LONDON

TO MY PARENTS
AND TO MY SON

The University of Chicago Press, Chicago 60637
The University of Chicago Press, Ltd., London

© 1959, 1961, 1979 by Philip Rieff
All rights reserved. Published 1959
Third Edition 1979
Printed in the United States of America
00 99 98 97 96 95 94 93 92   5 6 7 8 9

ISBN: 0-226-71640-6 (cloth)
0-226-71639-2 (paper)
Library of Congress Catalog Card Number: 78-69967

CONTENTS

PREFACE TO THE
FIRST EDITION

In the double title of this book lies its motive and main point. I have tried to show the mind of Freud, not the man or the movement he founded, as it derives lessons on the right conduct of life from the misery of living it.

Freud is perhaps the most eminent recent example of the advantages and disadvantages of founding a movement: the chief advantage being that a movement, however small, gives its founder a favorable environment in which to carry on his work, and the disadvantage that all movements learn to speak more in the name of than with the voice of the founder. The battle to remain orthodox is always lost. Orthodoxy, as a shrewd Huguenot pastor observed long ago, is successful heresy. Contemporary psychoanalysis, even that part which claims to be most orthodox, is a very successful heresy. Not that it should be otherwise; the founder is dead; his word should be used, not merely invoked to legitimate fresh departures from his positions. Whatever the balance of piety and alienation among Freudians in relation to Freud, psychoanalysis is not, I am aware, just a body of cold print, examinable as any other by mortician professors expert chiefly in letting the blood out of ideas. Freud's writings are the canon of what was once a great movement and is now an influential profession. It is appropriate to examine the canon in one book, reserving an examination of the movement to another. Ernest Jones has done the man. Future biographers, as I have occasion to say later in this preface, will have to revise the work of Jones, but that essential book has been done.

From 1900 onward, in a series of essays and larger works that will fill twenty-three volumes when they at length appear complete in a definitive English edition, Freud created the masterwork of the century, a psychology that counsels mothers and fathers, lovers and haters, sick and less sick, the arts and sciences, that unriddles—to use Emerson's prophetic catalogue of subjects considered inexplicable in his day—"language, sleep, madness, dreams, beasts, sex." Freud's doctrine, created piecemeal and fortunately never integrated into one systematic statement, has changed the course of Western intellectual history; moreover, it has contributed as much as doctrine possibly can to the correction of our standards of conduct.

Freud is the least confused of modern minds because he has no message; he accepts contradiction and builds his psychology on it. But if he has no message, in the old sense of something positive and constructive to offer, nevertheless his doctrine contains intellectual and moral implications that, when drawn, constitute a message. My object in this book is so to probe the doctrine as to bare these intellectual and moral implications.

What we can learn in reading through what is perhaps the most important body of thought committed to paper in the twentieth century is never comforting. None of the consolations of philosophy or the hopes of religion are to be found in Freud. There are truths in these texts, but no truth; helps but no help. The succession of profound and original insights leaves us more than ever strangers to ourselves. We know more, but we are made to realize how little our knowledge matters. No ultimate advice may be expected from Freud. His is a very intimate wisdom, tailored to this patient and that occasion. Yet he made it clear that we are all, despite the variety of symptoms, very much alike. Therefore, the implications to be drawn from his thought refer to that populous world, made up entirely of latent and manifest patients, in which we all live. No prophet of our destiny, neither Marx nor Darwin nor any other, has spoken with greater import to the human condition in general and yet spoken to it more intimately. Unlike Marx, Freud did not have a religious temperament. He looked forward to no salvations. He was more a statesman of the inner life, aiming at shrewd compromises with the human condition, not at its basic transformation. It stands to his credit that he is a prophet nonetheless. Smashing up the past, denying any meaningful future and yet leaving that question reasonably open, Freud concentrated entirely on the present. Posterity will revere him as the first prophet of a time that is simply each man's own, the first visionary to look neither forward nor backward except to stare down projections and to penetrate fixations.

A culture in which Freud is the presiding figure appears very different from any that have preceded it. He is not only the first completely irreligious moralist, he is a moralist without even a moralizing message. Man is tied to the weight of his own past, and even by a great therapeutic labor little more can be accomplished than a shifting of the burden. Freud's case histories are apologues that teach nothing; every case is different—or, what amounts to the same thing, could have been interpreted differently. It is exhilarating and yet terrifying to read Freud as a moralist, to see how compelling can be the judgment of a man who never preaches, leads us nowhere, assures us of nothing except perhaps that, having learned from him, the burden of misery we must find strength to carry will be somewhat lighter. To be less vulnerable to the arrows of sickness that fortune inevitably shoots at us, and that we, by virtue of our particular constitution, invite—this is as much good health as any one of us educated by Freud can wish for.

In America today, Freud's intellectual influence is greater than that of any other modern thinker. He presides over the mass media, the college classroom, the chatter at parties, the playgrounds of the middle classes where child-rearing is a prominent and somewhat anxious topic of conversation; he has bequeathed to many couples a new self-consciousness about their marriages and the temperature of their social enthusiasms. It is a good omen that he is being treated as a culture hero. The days of liberal culture are numbered, its true life over, when it can incorporate no new and hostile insights. Freud's ascendancy among the American educated classes indicates further that our culture still has some use for its critics. Freud was a very ambiguous critic at that. The monsters and grotesques that he slew, in the deepest and darkest interior of our civilization, have many lives. Some of these lives he himself declared to be immortal. This critic of the very foundations of our culture has at the same time done as much as any apologist to generate new respect for that culture. and he may be remembered by posterity as a saving critic rather than a damning one. The issue is far from settled. I hope that this book will serve to stake out the ground upon which any settling of the issue has to take place.

In conducting the reader through the labyrinth of implication Freud left behind, in search of the pattern that may provide a clue to the way out, I have had no choice but constantly to risk carrying an overload of detail. Without such expository loading, critical generalization is especially difficult. For Freud plunges us into an incredible world: fantastic realities beneath reasonable appearances; worlds composed of absurd conjunctions—events that never happened and yet control those that do; cure coming through a stranger who aims to know another more intimately than his intimates have ever known him; thoughts that wander in an overdetermined way. Consider alone the absurdity, and yet the demonstrated inevitability, of that faith the patient develops in his analyst—there you have a hint of the profound and true absurdity of psychoanalysis.

Freud's one small hope, reason, is closely and properly linked to his mixed vision, half longing and half repugnance, of the force of death. Reason cannot save us, nothing can; but reason can mitigate the cruelty of living, or give sufficient reasons for not living. Beyond the training in lucidity, no healing is honest. Freud was not the first angry old man to protest against every romance and against the enthusiasms that accompany each stage of life—the id illusions of dependence, love, happiness, union; the super-ego illusions of the good society, progress, brotherhood, fatherhood, finally even of health; the ego illusion of reason, energetic, independent, and purposeful in a purposeless and meaningless universe. It is the message of a very severe moralist. Western culture in the twentieth century has produced no other equally severe, equally able to forgo ideal convictions and analytic simplicities in the quest for the ordered life. Freud was not gulled by any of the false hopes or ego satisfactions in which all of us are educated; somehow he re-educated himself to avoid them and thereafter did not invent new hopes. Least of all did he hope for the sexual revolution with which some misinformed people have linked his name.

The word "fate" recurs in Freud's formulations perhaps as significantly as the word "sexuality." Because he considered that fate had done so much to shape his life, there is something tragic about Freud's image of himself. He is neither guilty nor innocent of the charges brought against him; upon him the terms can no longer enforce their old meanings. Fate had shaped his life and he placed himself in the service of fate. The most he could do, in order to raise himself a little above fate, to choice, was to become a student of both guilt and innocence.

Clearly no one so unsentimental as Freud can be accused of loving humanity, at least not in the ways encouraged by our religions and their political derivatives. He is no Marx, raising the proletariat to an embodiment of the reason of history. He has not idolized the instincts nor simply debunked conscience. He was interested in problems not patients, in the mechanisms of civilization not in programs of mental health. If he has achieved a kind of secular sainthood, if he can be used by the practical as well as invoked by the dedicated, it is because he taught us in a unique and subtle way how to grow unsentimental about ourselves. That he has been sentimentalized as a critic, reformer, doctor, merely indicates how rigid are the ways in which our culture must respond to this strange new attitude that is slowly overtaking our established ones, and which I have called in this book, in a tentative and exploratory way, the attitude of "psychological man." Freud's own unsentimental attitude toward himself, as the first out-patient of the hospital culture in which we live, is an attitude desired by every thoughtful person nowadays, not as an end in itself but to assure that person that he is himself alone and not merely acting out various roles —now physician, now patient, now curious bystander—in the unending series of accidents and emergencies that constitute life, both private and public.

ACKNOWLEDGMENTS

Any commentator on the mind of Freud must begin with an acknowledgment of the debt he owes to the biography of the man by Ernest Jones. *The Life and Work of Sigmund Freud* * will need cor-

---

* 3 vols. (New York: Basic Books, 1953–1957).

rection, for the writer of it was too near his subject. Nevertheless Freud has wanted this increase in stature, a memorial erected by a close associate. Great masters need great disciples; it is a prerequisite of greatness among those who found movements. Calvin had his Beza, Luther his Melancthon, Marx his Engels. Each disciple himself was great, not in his own right, but in relation to his master, whom he interpreted to the world. Paul is the greatest example of discipleship in the history of our culture, for it is the Jesus of his imagination that lives, not the historical one.

That master is fortunate who does not see, among his disciples, the closest fall away, jealous at being so near to greatness and yet not the greatest. Inevitably Luther had his Carlstadt, Freud had not merely his Jung but also his Rank and that constant near-schismatic Ferenczi. Fortunately for him, Freud retained his Jones. Of the original "Committee"—founded by Jones in 1912 to create a "bodyguard around Freud" and at the same time to carry his message out into the world —some died and others departed; Ernest Jones remained. Just before his death, with the completion of the biography, Jones took his rightful place as the greatest of Freud's disciples. For with this work he has fulfilled, better than in any of his scientific writing or practical therapy, the historic function of the great disciple: he has dispelled the loneliness and isolation of the master and has compelled the reader to venerate the man as well as respect the ideas. At the very end of his life, Freud saw that the world was coming to him. Jones has completed the task of reconciliation; he has brought Freud to the world.

I have used the Jones volumes even though I cannot entirely believe them. Clearly, master and disciple grow to resemble each other. In the process of writing, the portrait of the master may be transformed into an uncanny likeness of the disciple; but we shall not know that for many years to come.

Being honest and pious at the same time, Jones has imposed his own interpretation not merely upon those curious about a great man's life but upon all future honest biographers of Freud. There is enough raw material in the three parent volumes for a dozen Oedipal offspring. Any man with talent and daring enough can begin to write a different interpretation of Freud's life with nothing more at his elbow than Jones. But he cannot be so daring as wholly to reject the *Life* Jones has created.

It cannot be pure accident that this model *Life* was written by the most sensible and well-balanced of Freud's disciples, the steadiest and longest lived, the one who outlasted all the others and brought the master to the attention of a posterity that is moved as much by great lives as by great ideas. The achievement of Jones is the more striking because Freud's life was in no sense great. He behaved well, married late, died in his own time full of honors and years. It is Jones's interpretation of the *inner* life of Freud that so increases the stature of the man. Anything written hereafter can only tip the interpretation one way or the other. For Jones has created the *Life* of a man in perfect balance. To destroy that balance would be to destroy the entire interpretation, and this would be a task more difficult than is at first apparent. Add something to Freud's pessimism and an equivalent optimism can be cited. Subtract something from Freud's kindliness, and utter kindness can be cited.

There is something very English about the Freud that lives and dies so equably, in England, land of his inner affinity. All that antinomian imagination is hedged off neatly by an unimpeachable private life; all that passion countered by stoic calm; all that friendship muted by reserve; all that desire to lead tempered by encouragement to epigones striking out on their own—if not too far. No doubt Jones's interpretation is the true one. Freud must have been a giant of common sense and a character in perfect equilibrium to have led, amicably and for so long, such erratic and scheming followers in a highly moral intellectual movement to scrape clean the encrusted moral intelligence of Western culture. On the other hand, he must have felt the need for disciples desperately. The Freud that has emerged into popular consciousness, because of the Jones volumes, is in fact the ideal product of psychoanalytic therapy, the long-sought physician who, if he has not cured himself, arriving at peace of mind, has achieved a truce within himself.

There are friends and colleagues to thank for services that only friendly colleagues can render—criticism, correction, and encouragement. During my year at the Center for Advanced Study in the Behavioral Sciences I had these benefits from Marcus Cunliffe, John Bowlby, Fritz Stern, and Guy Swanson. They have saved me from a number of errors of judgment, fact, and taste. For this congenial company, in the most favorable scholarly climate in America, I have to thank Ralph Tyler, Director of the Center, and his staff.

Philip Rieff
*Center for Advanced Study
in the Behavioral Sciences*
June 1958

PREFACE TO THE
SECOND EDITION

I have revised some passages and augmented a few others for this edition. In the main, the book stands as it first appeared in 1959. Since that time, however, another selection of Freud's letters, even more personal than those to Wilhelm Fliess, has been published.* Freud's intimate correspondence reveals an emotional life remarkably consonant with the intellectual life examined in the chapters that follow.

Freud wrote letters in huge quantities; only now can we see that he was supremely talented at it. On the evidence, I think, Freud is entitled to a place among the great letter writers of this century; only D. H. Lawrence and William James emerge from their personal correspondence anywhere near as man-size as Freud.

Freud's greatness of character comes through his letters swiftly, and particularly in his love letters to Martha Bernays, during the four long years between their engagement and their marriage. Great letters are written by great characters; they must be intensely personal and revealing, yet make us feel that, however familiarly we lean across the shoulder of the writer, we are in the presence of greatness. Freud's letters show that presence already there in his early twenties. Only great characters can survive this test of intimacy. Marx, for example, does not survive; his letters do not move us to respect him more as we get to know him better. How rarely do great men retain their presence when we get close to them, in the one way possible across the distance of history—in their personal correspondence. Freud survives, and grows in stature.

That Freud was a great old man can be denied only by denying his achievement. Now, from his letters, we see that if he had greatness, it

* See *Letters of Sigmund Freud*, selected and edited by Ernst L. Freud: translated by Tania and James Stern (New York: Basic Books, 1960).

was in his person long before his achievement set it at large. As more of these autobiographical materials appear, Ernest Jones's biography becomes less and less adequate. In his lack of feeling for the intensity of his subject, and despite occasional efforts at depth of penetration, Jones put together a portrait that is almost Byzantine in its flatness. Given Jones's intention, to record the life of Freud, the flatness could not be avoided. It is the mind of Freud that gave his life a depth quite beyond the range Jones evidently set for himself as a biographer.

There is nothing flat about Freud's own self-portrait, as given informally in his letters. Told from the inside, Freud's life takes on depth, even heroic proportion, not because of the external pace of events, which is in fact steady, but, rather, because of the heavy burden of knowingness about life that Freud carried from the beginning, on his back, as it were. Yet he never bent over in defeat; difficult as he found the task, he forced himself to remain emotionally and morally upright to the last, "defiant" of his corrupting knowledge—although as he himself admitted, in a letter splendid with modesty, he did not know quite why he thus maintained his integrity. All he knew, at the end of his life, was that, as a moral man, he could not be otherwise.

The famous old Freud and his obscure young predecessor bear a resemblance to one another so close that, taken together, they challenge the sacred canon of development. Age did not alter Freud in any essential way; it merely gave him time to polish the intellectual instrument with which he expressed the greatness of his character. Psychoanalysis was the perfect instrument of that character. When at last he found himself, after searching around systematically in various established disciplines, Freud established a new discipline, first of all for himself. Later, as psychoanalysis became more adaptable, the hidden force of Freud's character operated through the discipline, detached from his person. Psychoanalysis became a transferable art, and therefore something like a science; others could be taught what Freud knew for himself.

The young Freud was one of those rare unlucky ones, burdened in youth with the wisdom of age. He was never really young. When, at twenty-three, he remarks to Martha on "the absurdity of this world," this is no passing adolescent sadness; it carries the full poignancy of full comprehension, and only deepens with time. Such strokes of wisdom often left him in one of his "wretched moods." But his gift of understanding the world, as it is, was, and will be, did not leave him completely exposed and vulnerable. Guarded by his self-image as a scientist, Freud's personal wisdom hardened him just enough to permit him to remain wise without ever falling over into the jeopardy of demanding an end of wisdom—some synthesis of his analytic attitude that must, as he knew, take him beyond the specific gravity of his intelligence. The perfect nonsense of the artist, or of the religious genius, never appealed to Freud; he chose, rather, to make imperfect sense. One letter concludes, with final accuracy, "In short, I am evidently an analyst."

To compel his imagination to stay put, short of synthesis, was admittedly a severe limitation upon it. But the absurdity of this world could not be balanced, in his opinion, by absurd ideas. To be religious is to be sick, by definition: it is the effort to find a cure where none can possibly exist. For Freud, religion can be only a symptom of what it seeks to cure. Psychoanalysis does not cure; it merely reconciles. Therefore it works best for healthy men, who are willing to sacrifice their precious first sons of thought on the altar of reality. For those who seek, through analysis, to avoid the sacrifice, therapy must inevitably fail. Psychoanalysis is a therapy for the healthy, not a solution for the sick—except so far as the sick themselves become analysts, and find in this therapeutic their personal solution, as Freud did. In his science, Freud overcame the "tiredness" from which he suffered. His recurrent fatigue was, he explained to Martha, a "kind of minor illness; neurasthenia, it is called." Work was the one way out of this tiredness. Thus Freud turned necessity into therapy; there was no other way out, before death. In a sense we can now better understand, there is something to the gross charge that psychoanalysis is the perfect profession for neurotics—but only for extremely intelligent neurotics, those who can learn to inhibit successfully their religious impulse. "The moment a man questions the meaning and value of life," Freud wrote to Marie Bonaparte, "he is sick, since objectively neither has any existence." The analyst proudly needed no synthesis.

But Freud needed no synthesis because it was already there, built into his character. More easily than most, if they are truly analytical, Freud could avoid asking the essential question, for within him he had an answer that he guarded and cherished, although toward the end of his life his own ambivalence toward that answer increased so much that he could not resist both analyzing and justifying it. Finally, but with extreme reluctance, he published *Moses and Monotheism,* his own private answer. He discovered that although he was not a believing Jew, he remained a psychological one. It was, in fact, Freud's *mystique* of membership in the Jewish community that protected him from asking too obviously the sickest of questions. His letters are full of obedience to the authority of his ancestry. When Freud goes "every day for three lonely weeks" to contemplate the Moses of Michelangelo, in a Roman church, it is an act of piety—which must eventuate in a psychoanalytic exercise, of course.

Following in Freud's steps, not long ago, I went to that same church in Rome. But, having had the American experience of detachment from all communities, it was Michelangelo's Moses that I saw, not Freud's. Being still attached to his community, the Jew Freud could afford to be merely what he was—an analyst, and that long before psychoanalysis permitted him to cosset his sense of despair in the professionalism of his analytic attitude. At times, before his wish for genius came true, Freud experienced "something like attacks of despondency and faintheartedness." At other times, he grudgingly admits to Martha his "gray, grim despair," does nothing all day, except perhaps browse in Russian history or some other subject equally remote from his work. On one occasion, he reaches for a passage in Milton, as if it were a shield behind which he can advance again on the unconquerable enemy realities. That passage, cited by the early Freud, is appropriate in theme for Freud in his later years.

> Let us consult
> What reinforcement we may gain from hope;
> If not, what resolution from despair.

But immediately he says to Martha that he has "no use for this mood." Paradise never has been lost, and therefore cannot be regained. But what of those who are not members of Milton's mysterious community of the elect by desperate resolution? Or of Freud's even more mysterious one? Pity the poor Gentile, or, if not, pity the half-Gentiles of American intellectual Jewry. Freud was not long on pity, and certainly had none for the Gentiles. There is an early letter in which he fans his envy, suggesting to Martha that perhaps he will "try and live more like the Gentiles—modestly, learning and practicing the usual things and not striving after discoveries and delving too deep." The mood did not persist. Freud was his own ideal Jew—not a half-Gentile of the real Jewish world but a fantasy Moses, lonely and estranged as he leads the large remainder of himself, resisting, through the "magic world of intellect and unhappiness," from one small oasis of rational insight to another, with no promises of a promised land this time around. Such a powerfully useful self-image, once deeply buried, is not easily given up.

Being, in youth and age, a lonely man, Freud sought love and loyal company with an ardor that his letters express in a permanently readable way. Martha Bernays became his first chosen person. (Later, there was Fliess.) In his love letters, the young Freud is engaged in the training of his bride-to-be. Martha did not understand him; Sigmund was determined that she should. After all, the circumstances were strained. He had proposed before he really knew her. He was twenty-three, and he had decided to marry. In the four years of their affianced courtship, he educated her to him, so that, despite the revolutions brewing in his mind, he could enjoy the safety of marriage. He "picks her to peices," so finely that at times she must have protested; he then promises to restrain his analytic thrust. But, through all the pedagogy of his letters, he is grateful to her: the promise of her lifelong company and confidence has saved him from "the worst fate," loneliness. His gratitude permits him to unbend with her; otherwise he is never deprived of his pride in being alone.

Freud needed a standard Jewish marriage, in which the wife is queen and keeper of a standard Jewish household. From this bridgehead of tradition, Freud the theoretician invaded the whole rotten empire of the family, without running the ultimate risk of cutting himself off from the devout practice of its creed. No more compulsively moral man ever has explored the compulsiveness of morality. This prince of the modern moral quandary needed a princess remote precisely from that quandary, completely untouched by it. Not that the courtship, following the engagement and conducted through the mails, was easy. Freud was no tame Jewish doctor; he did not want his wife so tamed that she would not have an idea of what he was about. His letters to Martha function as deliberate revelations of himself, a first playing-out of his tremendous intelligence upon the special case of their own relation. Freud's love letters serve a double purpose: They prepare her for marriage to him; he prepares himself for his long, tenacious contest with life, one in which he knew he could not become an old-style hero, winning through in one decisive battle with himself, but, rather, holding his own and learning how to give better than he got.

Freud was lucky the first time. Desperate loneliness can lead to errors in judgment. But when he decided to fall in love, and did so with Martha, promptly, at first sight, his gamble succeeded. His later, secondary to break through his loneliness were not as fortunate. First-rate disciples can be trained, but they do not easily compose themselves into members of an intellectual family, even when that family is fathered by a Freud. That he tried, hard and genuinely, to avoid his inevitable role is evident in the patience of his relations with Jung, Rank, Ferenczi, Jones, and others. Max Eitingon actually insisted on symbolic adoption, as a son, into Freud's family. But definitive assessment of Freud's character can be attempted only as part of a history of the psychoanalytic movement. When that history is written, I suspect that Freud's personal stature will grow rather than diminish. The greatness of the man is beyond question, complementing the greatness of his mind.

PHILIP RIEFF
University of California, Berkeley

PREFACE TO THE
THIRD EDITION

Being mainly a photographic reproduction of the first edition (New York, 1959), this third incorporates the less extensive revisions made in the second (New York, 1961). The economics of transferring thirteen longer revisions outnumbered regrets at not making them.

The main difference between this and the two preceding editions is in the Epilogue. In the new chapter, I have intended to show readers beyond the emergence of psychological man, whose passion in life has been for lowering what is high and raising what is low. This stripping of concealments, this tipping too far forward the delicate balances of reticence and candor that play the imperative part in making any society civilized, was no part of Freud's mind. His own aspirations could not have been higher. His therapeutic aim was in no way lowering. The pity of it is that neither was Freud's therapy raising; its aim was moral in a way that this book was intended to work through, to see what is put at stake in such a morality. Freud prepares us to live in a world of spent sacred forces—a world made easy for profanations, all grievances sticking out and every sense of limit challenged.

Some part of Freud admired the earlier healthy, though delicate, balances implicit in forces that later spent themselves and were transformed, as Freud saw them, into diseases of authority. Freud's genius was to see that higher authority was recreated precisely out of the rebel wish to lower it. Neuroses are that rebel wish, ill concealed. Having turned his own neurosis into a triumph of superior concealment, Freud continued to admire others before him who had recreated those authorizing concealments, at once directively deep and superficial, that constitute the history of Western culture. That Freud's triumph has been subject to Nemesis, even more than others before his, shows how little there is in his authority to resist the present lowering manner of its defeat. As a rule, every creator of authorizing concealments must suffer them to succeed in shallow, more transparent versions. The statics of vulgar piety overcome the dynamics of subtle revelation. Vulgar Freudianism has buried Freud. But the living Freud said nothing to declare a moratorium on *must;* he sponsored none of our present resexualizations of remissiveness. Who then, or what, has talked Freud's sacred reticences into the prevailing profanation of candor?

Lacking direction, with no culture of commands from which to draw hostile inferences toward the right conduct of life, psychological man seems determined to try talking his way into a moral void. This type lives by elaborate reflections of and on the fact of having nothing to say. For moralizing visions, psychological man has substituted a policy of keeping both eyes open to his deeper motives, so to challenge the old possibility that something is always hidden down there worth being ashamed of. By comparison, underground man was no less an adept in the arts of lowering himself to a depth at which no conceit of superiority can survive. Nevertheless, that earlier rebel, against the authority vested in every self by sacred order, lived on the hope of rising above the humiliations of self-knowledge to cultivate the graces, as humans must, on the surfaces of life.

It is evident that psychological man has had enough of *must*—excepting Hamlet's "Must, like a whore, unpack my heart with words." He believes himself free at last to cultivate gracelessness and see unblinking through to the indifferent heart of things. To think life is no longer a question of making right responses to inescapable answers already given is our commanding conceit. This escape into a conceit of freedom, as if there were nothing sacred, poses a nice contrast with the fact that every great revealer, Freud included, must depend for his creative power upon the concealing character of his vision, the blindly obedient eye of it. As each freedom at every moment depends upon the one thing forbidden to it, so all true visions take their direction from the turning of a blind eye. Before the unsighted object of a vision so true as Freud's, we must, like him, close one eye at least to all but its dimmest glimmer. The final truth of Freud's vision is in the one thing he will not see, except in delicately balanced distortions and at safe distances, hidden behind newly acceptable surrogates. In short, what I have had to say in the added chapter, following Freud faithfully through his own resistances, is how "repression" cannot be abolished; and why not.

I am grateful to Professor Samuel Heilman for his corrective readings of the Epilogue. The phrase "repressive imperative" (see page 367) is Professor Heilman's coinage. Of course, the freedom to correct is forbidden the moment it threatens to correct completely. Professor Heilman is not responsible for what has remained uncorrected in the Epilogue. Martha Pamplin Rosso, with her usual patience and precision, has turned into perfectly clean copy each relentless rewriting of every last thing I have written. Mrs. Rosso made new entries in the index and has been the chief proofreader of this edition.

University of Pennsylvania
Philadelphia
October 1978

FREUD

THE MIND
OF THE MORALIST

CHAPTER ONE

SCIENCE AND MORAL PSYCHOLOGY

*This immense and almost new domain of dangerous knowl-
edge . . . Never yet did a profounder world of insight reveal itself to daring travellers and adventurers, and the
psychologists who thus "make a sacrifice"—it is not the
sacrificio dell' intelleto, on the contrary!—will at least be
entitled to demand in return that psychology shall once
more be recognized as the Queen of the sciences, for whose
service and equipment the other sciences exist. For psychology is once more the path to the fundamental problems.*
                                                    —NIETZSCHE

THERE is a tantalizing remark early in Freud's *Autobiographical
Study* (1925) to the effect that he had never really wanted to be a
physician, that his entire scientific career was a detour leading away
from his original interest in "human concerns" and "cultural problems." [1] * The excitement for us of Freud's thought is increased by
our awareness that he is in fact trespassing on territory outside that
assigned to medicine. An irrepressible moral earnestness colors his
attitude of scrupulous scientific neutrality. Though he began as a
neurologist and never ceased to look for the neurological truth underlying the psychological appearance, he could not avoid drawing morals
from his diagnoses and influencing attitudes by his interpretations. In
psychoanalysis, Freud found a way of being the philosopher he desired to be, and of applying his philosophy to himself, humanity, the
cosmos—to everything, visible and invisible, which as a scientist and
physician he observed.

---

* Numbered reference notes begin on page 363.

Freud has been rebuked for this; members of the profession he founded have held that his permanent contribution lies in his unimpeachable clinical data on dreams and symptomatic behavior, and in the valuable inferences on the importance of sexuality which he drew from these data. When he gave in to his overwhelming urge to speculate, it is argued, he blurred the sharp empirical outlines of his early research. But psychoanalysts continue to generalize, despite the professional modesty that has overcome the movement. And it is precisely its combination of strict medical judgments with a sweeping criticism of the contemporary moral climate that has elevated Freudianism to its present position of intellectual affluence. Psychology in our time has become, as Nietzsche prophesied, "the Queen of the sciences."

Freud was not the first to attempt to re-establish the unity of all the sciences through the elaboration of a new, all-embracing secular dogma: Comte, and later Spencer, had tried it with sociology; Marx effected a combination of classical economics and revolutionary political science. But where we now discount Marxism as idealism or ideology, as well as in its larger claims to being a universal science of society, we cannot do the same with Freudianism; even when we deny that it provides a master key to all social and ethical behavior, we cannot disavow the magnitude of Freud's insight into what he termed "human concerns."

Freud saw himself as an intellectual conquistador,[2] the leader of a movement to extend the vision of science, by rational means, beyond the limits the empiricists had set for it. The range of psychoanalysis is due, however, not only to its founder's sense of his mission to civilization, but to a logic inherent within the doctrine itself. The "fundamental problems" to which Nietzsche alludes in the passage quoted above are personal—even intimate—problems. They are the preoccupations of psychological man, who in our time has succeeded economic man as the dominant moral type of Western culture. Once again, history has produced a type specially adapted to endure his own period: the trained egoist, the private man, who turns away from the arenas of public failure to re-examine himself and his own emotions. A new discipline was needed to fit this introversion of interest, and Freudian psychology, with its ingenious interpretations of politics, religion, and culture in terms of the inner life of the individual and his immediate family experiences, exactly filled the bill.

I

Freud's decision to enter private medical practice, where he found at last—and to his surprise—the "great cause" [3] that he sought, was reluctant and unpremeditated. Throughout a restless and prolonged academic career, his ambitions were all centered in the laboratory. After studying zoology and chemistry for three years, he went through a stable and satisfying apprenticeship in animal physiology, working for six years (1876–1882) under Ernst Brücke. No one stays at a university for nine years unless he means to stay forever. But the professional climb at the University of Vienna was apparently too steep for a young theoretician who had the added handicap of being a Jew. It was due to financial hardship that Freud took the advice of his kind mentor, Brücke, to make use of the physician's license for which he had, like most would-be laboratory researchers, perfunctorily qualified. (Freud considered his delay in taking the M.D. examinations a measure of his distaste for a career in any branch of "medicine proper.")[4] The reasons that dictated his choice of a medical specialty were also more practical than theoretical. Concluding that the field of brain anatomy in which he had been engrossed during the three years of his internship (1882–1885) was too well staffed to allow an ambitious man to rise quickly in it, he turned to a less crowded field—that of nervous diseases.

Though expediency had forced him to abandon a career in the laboratory, Freud continued to feel most secure when working in physiology. In his early correspondence with his medical friend Fliess, he expressed not only his dissatisfactions with the medical profession but his theoretical uncertainties. The materialist bias of his early work, in which he aimed at correlating neurophysiological hypotheses with physical concepts, is clear from these letters. In 1895 he sent

Fliess the draft of a treatise, subsequently abandoned, entitled "Psychology for Neurologists",* in which, reformulating neurological theory, he proposed "to represent physical processes as quantitatively determined states of specifiable material particles" and assumed that "the material particles in question are the neurones."

The uncertainty was to remain with him a long time. Much later, when his psychoanalytic theory had matured and he could proclaim confidently (in "The Unconscious," 1915) that "every attempt to deduce a localization of mental processes, every endeavor to think of ideas as stored up in nerve cells and of excitations as passing along nerve fibers has completely miscarried"—even then, he did not discard the hope that psychological explanations might eventually be replaced by physiological ones. It is only "for the present," he continued in the same essay, that "our psychical topography has . . . nothing to do with anatomy." [5] Again, in the boldly speculative *Beyond the Pleasure Principle* (1920), Freud affirmed that "the deficiencies in our description would probably vanish if we were already in a position to replace the psychological terms by physiological or chemical ones." [6] Psychoanalysts never forget, he assures his readers in another place, "that the mental is based on the organic." [7] There are only organic processes, he maintains, whose consequences manifest themselves in a manner it is convenient to describe by means of psychic terminology.†

---

* Contained in the letters to Fliess, *The Origins of Psychoanalysis*, pp. 349–445. The numerous manuscripts, of which this (in some versions titled "Project for a Scientific Psychology") is the most important, that he sent Fliess in the years from 1887 to 1902 show the persistence of Freud's materialist inclinations.

† This remains a common interpretation of psychoanalysis, utilized by writers of the most diverse polemical intentions. A. Wohlgemuth, desiring to discredit Freud, says that "all the phenomena of memory . . . on forgetting are quite explicable by 'neural disposition'; and the existence of ideas in the 'Unconscious,' or the 'Preconscious,' are gratuitous and unwarranted assumptions of the mythopaeist" (*A Critical Examination of Psycho-Analysis*, New York, 1923, p. 53). The English philosopher Stephen Toulmin uses the same point to defend the "logical status of psychoanalysis." He argues, rather circularly, that: (a) Freud does not claim to investigate (efficient) *causes* but rather the *motives* of action; (b) the motive is not a cause because it is not "substantial"; (c) therefore, a psychological event (such as Freud studies) cannot be a cause; it is a motive. The causes of action can be given only by neurophysiology. (See "The Logical Status of Psychoanalysis," *Analysis*, October 1949.) As

Freud's unwillingness to abandon his physiological presuppositions was partly due to the influence of personal friends such as Fliess, and Freud's early collaborator, Josef Breuer, whom he used up, emotionally and intellectually, in tutelary relationships. One of the chief ways in which he depended on Fliess was to keep him abreast of the latest physiological research. Such requests for information, coming from one who had himself done notable and exacting research in physiology, may be partly discounted as a token of regard. But the dependence was also genuine: through his exchanges with Fliess, Freud hoped to work his way back to the safe ground of physiology.* With his severance from this mentor and confidant, Freud was cut off from his last immediate source of materialist counsel. After the Fliess period one notices a diminishing tendency on Freud's part to physiologize—or, at any rate, to promise eventually to physiologize—the new discoveries.†

Even while he was making these gestures of deference to neuro-physiology, Freud's conclusions were leading him progressively farther away from his former field. By 1900, in *The Interpretation of Dreams,* he was saying that the dream has a symbolic or expressive function, even where it has a physiological occasion. Though unaware at first of his own daring, he had turned the old philosophical concept of the unconscious on its head by arguing that, far from being (as in the materialist view) a convenient fiction, it was every bit as much a part

we shall see, both this typical attack on and this typical defense of psycho-analysis are gratuitous.

* He wrote, in the letter to Fliess of June 30, 1896: "Anxiety, chemical factors, etc.—perhaps you may supply me with solid ground on which I shall be able to give up explaining things psychologically and start finding a firm basis in physiology!" (*The Origins of Psychoanalysis,* p. 169; see also the letter on p. 264; and Jones, *Life and Work,* I, 299).

† Freud did not feel as great a need for exchanges of confidences and erudition in the new field of psychology which he was entering. Jones reports that he was "ill-informed in the field of contemporary psychology and seems to have derived only from hearsay any knowledge he had of it" (*Life and Work,* I, 371). Although his knowledge was vague, Freud's bibliomania probably supplemented to some extent mere hearsay. (See his self-reproaches for his book-collecting habits in the "dream of a botanical monograph," *The Interpretation of Dreams,* SE IV, 172–73.) Like most bibliophiles, he probably did not read anywhere near all he bought or was given, but it is worth noting that Ebbinghaus and two editions of that early and esoteric psychologist of the unconscious, Carl-Gustav Carus, were on Freud's shelves.

of experienced reality as consciousness—and causally of far greater importance to the history of mind. In the materialist conception, mind is the agent of body; in the Freudian conception, as it gradually emerged through these early years of uncertainty, the body exists as a symptom of mental demands.

It required a certain courage to urge such a view, for the fresh clues Freud got to the psychological—as opposed to physiological—realities of neurosis came from suspect or, at the least, foreign sources. In Germany psychological inquiry was concentrated in the laboratory study of mensurable aptitudes of the mind, chiefly the measurement of neural sensation. The psychologists from whom Freud felt he had most to learn were almost all French; but psychology—or psychiatry —in France was connected with the rediscovery and legitimation by French physicians of the hitherto disreputable art of hypnosis.* Following the pioneer James Braid, a Scotsman, the French physician Liébault had taken up the study of hypnotism in 1860.† By the late 1870s, when Freud was a student, there were two centers of research into hypnosis: Paris, where the neurologist Charcot worked, and Nancy, where Liébault's pupil, Hippolyte Bernheim, was. Both of these places Freud visited. However, neither Charcot nor Bernheim offered a satisfactory explanation for the unruly facts they had observed—facts such as the existence of male hysterics (when hysteria was commonly thought to be a female affliction only), or that hysterical symptoms could be produced artificially, under hypnosis (when no cause other than the physiological had previously been considered). The very report of such facts by Freud to his superiors in Vienna was received with hostile incredulity. In order to annex for science this

---

* Of course, hypnosis had its partisans among the literati in the nineteenth century (Harriet Martineau was successfully treated by mesmerism after a nervous breakdown); and, among other pseudo-sciences, phrenology was taken seriously by Poe and Whitman. But both were, in most scientific circles, held in disrepute, although during the lifetime of its founder, Gall, phrenology was a serious attempt to develop a scientific study of the functions of the brain— and widely respected as such.

† There is a reference to Liébault in *The Interpretation of Dreams;* Freud says (p. 570 fn.) it is Liébault "to whom is due the revival in modern times of research into hypnotism."

domain penetrated by the mysterious technique of hypnosis, heretofore mainly the province of charlatans and faith healers, Freud had to challenge the ruling scientific conventions of his time.

Later, when he acquired a movement of his own to address, Freud's consciousness of his radical break with the medicine of his time became explicit and confident. By 1925, in the essay "The Resistances to Psychoanalysis," he was noting that

> the contemporary generation of doctors . . . had been brought up to respect only anatomical, physical and chemical factors. . . . They were not prepared for taking psychical ones into account and therefore met them with indifference or antipathy. . . . As an excessive reaction against an early phase during which medicine had been dominated by . . . the "philosophy of Nature," they regarded abstractions, such as those with which psychology is obliged to work, as nebulous, fantastic and mystical. . . . The symptoms of hysterical neuroses were looked upon as shamming and the phenomena of hypnotism as a hoax. Even the psychiatrists, upon whose attention the most unusual and astonishing mental phenomena were constantly being forced, showed no inclination to examine their details or inquire into their connections. They were content to classify the variegated array of symptoms and trace them back, as far as they could manage, to somatic, anatomical or chemical aetiological disturbances.
>
> It is easy to understand why doctors, with an attitude of this kind towards the mind, should have had no liking for psychoanalysis.[8]

At the beginning, however, aware that he was dealing with materials hitherto treated by the quack side of science or by art, Freud evinced discomfort about their possibly sensational quality. He apologized, in the *Studies on Hysteria,* because his cases read so much like novels that, "as one might say, they lack the serious stamp of science." [9] But the apologetic tone was not his most serious or personal one. It passed, and a certain defensive daring remained. Freud had an image of himself as a Joseph, a new dream-interpreter, or a Prospero, engaging in battle "the most evil of those half-tamed demons that inhabit the human breast." [10] The possible threat to his scientific respectability did not keep him from trespassing even on such suspect problems as mental telepathy. A member of both the English and American branches of the Society for Psychical Research, he wrote several papers on telepathic phenomena.* It was evidence of intellectual courage that he was willing to extend his theory of the unconscious and his therapeutic method even into areas of speculation where misunderstanding is especially likely.

II

In making my case for his theoretic daring, I do not want to slight Freud's contribution as a therapist, exemplified first of all by his interest in what was in his time, among physicians, the most despised of patient types, the neurotic. Freud was consistently attracted to the undervalued aspects of reality: sex, which society had tried to ignore; dreams, which science had tried to ignore; the patient, whom medicine had tried to ignore. No humanity could have been more practical and at the same time more utopian than his. It is true that in his late essay, "Analysis Terminable and Interminable" (1938), he rebuked those analysts seeking therapeutic shortcuts by underscoring the difficulties of getting an unambiguous diagnosis and of effecting a truly permanent cure.[11] But such arguments cannot disguise the generous sympathies of his view. By its program of extended and painstaking attention to the intangibles of a person's entire life and thought, psychoanalysis pays rare tribute to the interest of the individual and to the rich ambiguity of human character.

At least a minimum recognition of the patient's state of mind as a factor in his condition is so much more common today among all kinds of physicians, except perhaps surgeons, that it is hard to appreciate how fundamental was the break which Freud's emphasis inaugurated with the accepted medical practice of his time. In the school in which Freud trained, the physician addressed himself only to the disease, as an alien which had somehow insinuated itself into the body of the patient. Talk between the physician and patient re-

---

* "A Premonitory Dream Fulfilled" (1899); "Psychoanalysis and Telepathy (1921); "Dreams and Telepathy" (1922); "The Occult Significance of Dreams" (1925); and a chapter in the *New Introductory Lectures* (1932), "Dreams and the Occult." Telepathy "may be the original archaic method by which individuals understood one another," Freud conjectures, "which had been pushed into the background in the course of phylogenetic development."

mained an extra-professional amenity, having little to do with the mechanics of cure. The pathos of the patient was only a distraction, and the physician, to guard against it, trained himself in a bedside manner, a standard mask of geniality and aloofness assumed for the benefit of patients and their friends and relatives alike. The patient, for his part, was merely obliged to be docile. Like a feudal lady, he was a spectator at the tournament for which he had engaged the physician as his champion. He was the accidental host of his disease, and the treatment—like the disease, once contracted—was something to which he could only submit.

It may seem odd that Freud, with his training in physiology, should eventually have devised the nonphysical method of treating disease which psychoanalysis relies on. Yet we may see this not so much as an abandoning of the exact standards of physiology as an extension of his native dislike of materialist medicine, in which the devotion to scientific procedure excluded human sympathy. During his student days, Freud had declared that if he must choose as a profession either "mutilating animals or tormenting human beings" he preferred "the former alternative." [12] His reported aversion to shedding blood [13] was another intimation of the new considerateness for the patient which he introduced into medicine.

This considerateness did not stem from any great or personally felt sympathy with the neglected class of patients, the neurotics, to whom he addressed himself. Freud's older colleague, Breuer, who first attempted to care for a neurotic through the use of an unprecedented technique of solicitous inquiry, seems to have felt such a personal concern. Breuer had, at the time of treating "Anna O.," the ur-patient of psychoanalysis, no new explanation for the enigma of hysteria. He simply tried replacing contempt with lengthy observation, indifference with sympathy—so much genuine sympathy that the patient responded with aggressive gestures of transference; Breuer became frightened, his wife made a scene, and the whole case was dropped with much embarrassment.[14] Freud was apparently more detached in his work with neurotics. One cannot be certain, but partial clues—reproaches addressed to himself in his own case histories for his lack of overt sympathy,[15] the haughty way in which patients are mentioned in the letters to Fliess—lead me to doubt that Freud was much involved in the pathos of those he treated.* His interest was from the beginning mainly investigative, and he was not without a measure of contempt for his patients—comfortably off women, many of them. Yet one of the ironies of Freud's scientific aloofness is that it resulted in such an essentially humane method of treatment. However impersonal his own couch-side manner, his sympathy for the patient did nevertheless express itself: in a *theory* which focused on the personal factors in disease and cure, rather than on professional skill in treating the illness.

Freud's entire training inclined him toward impersonal explanations. Like Breuer, he had accepted the familiar picture of the mind as a machine (or, alternatively, as an electrical circuit) whose parts fall into disequilibrium with one another. Thus mental sickness was the breakdown of physical processes unknown to the patient, whose repair, as first attempted under hypnosis, also proceeded without the patient's knowledge or aid. But what Freud uncovered, as he went beyond the original cathartic technique, were the numerous volitional elements in each case history. He traced the patient's illness to a desire to be sick, to a will to forget painful memories—not to organic causes or to the theoretic assumption of them. Consequently, he reasoned, the patient's conscious cooperation is required as a necessary part of the cure; he must be taught to renounce his symptoms, rather than to harbor them as a (mistaken) way of resolving his difficulties. The technique of therapy evolved by Breuer, in which a cure was effected on a semi-conscious and passive patient, preserved the mechanistic assumption of the disease as an alien entity within the patient. For Freud, however, neurosis was no intruder, ruining the happy life of the emotions; it was not simply the objective symptoms manifested by the patient but was, beyond that, an element of *character,* identical with the patient himself. It was the host himself—or rather, his moral character—that must be treated. In thus conceiving psychoanalysis as addressing itself not to diagnostic categories but to moral agents, each with its own special developmental history and each in need of an almost permanent analysis, Freud restored an

* This may be one explanation for his strict disavowal of counter-transference.

ethical, and therefore a social, conception of human sickness. The patient becomes important not generically but as an individual; the physical symptom becomes interesting only as a symbol of memories and motives. Symptoms are dubiously useful errors, with which a sufferer hides some truth from himself.

From a Freudian perspective, sickness is the way a patient speaks even when he is mute. What psychoanalysis demonstrates in its attendance on the seemingly trivial symptom is just this idea of the patient as an infinitely expressive, though often reluctantly communicative, subject. The emotional tensions which a healthy individual is supposed to turn outward onto the world are instead painfully incarnated in the body. All sickness may be viewed as ingrown gesture, whose effect is to displace those outgoing gestures by which the self achieves a healthy momentum of development, and such recurrent but ephemeral moments of identity as social life allows. The neurotic has great trouble identifying self and not-self.* Like the hyena in Hemingway's "The Green Hills of Africa," devouring its own entrails out of a misdirected hunger, the neurotic symptom may come to devour the person. The energy thus "introverted," to use Jung's term, will eventually express itself—possibly in eccentricities of speech, obsessive thoughts, compulsive patterns of behavior. Later, if not somehow drained off, it may threaten not merely to change behavior but to end existence. Freud could understand even death psychologically. Death is more than a bodily event; death is willed. This is the road he took with the "death instinct," first enunciated in *Beyond the Pleasure Principle* (1920). In 1938, a year before he died of cancer, he suspected that we die not merely of disease but of the death-wish, locked forever in conflict with Eros. Finally the balance of power shifts. Eros ages; ageless Thanatos asserts itself "until it at length succeeds in doing the individual to death." [16]

III

During his lifetime and in the years since his death, Freud's work has been criticized for dismissing physiological realities in favor of

---

* So far as a civilization encourages problems of self-identity, it may be fairly labeled "neurotic."

impalpables—wishes, attitudes, emotions. Compare the Freudian view of the emotions with, for instance, that offered by William James in his masterpiece, *The Principles of Psychology* (1890). "The emotion," James declared, "is nothing but the feeling of a bodily state, and it has a purely bodily cause." His account of the emotion "dread" may serve to illustrate:

> If inability to draw deep breath, fluttering of the heart, and that peculiar epigastric change felt as "precordial anxiety" with an irresistible tendency to take a somewhat crouching attitude and to sit still, and with perhaps other visceral processes not now known, all spontaneously occur together in a certain person; his feeling of the combination *is* the emotion of dread.[17]

For James, and for physiological psychology since, the emotional is our experience of the organic: we are sad because we cry, happy because we laugh. For Freud, the common-sense view—that we cry because we are sad, laugh because we are happy—sufficed. What physiological psychology had to say about the emotions, he wrote in 1917, "the James-Lange theory, for instance—is utterly incomprehensible to us psychoanalysts and impossible for us to discuss." [18]

Perhaps the most cogent among the revisionist attempts within the psychoanalytic movement is that of "psychosomatic" medicine, which has grown up, under the leadership of Franz Alexander, at the Institute for Psychoanalysis in Chicago. Alexander and his followers aim at coordinating the psychological factor with the somatic, claiming it is no longer necessary to choose between opposing methods of treatment, the psychiatric and the organic. Their research has chiefly been conducted on asthma or similar complaints, chronic constipation, hypertension, peptic ulcers, and colitis; but even infectious diseases such as tuberculosis have been studied. In the latter disease, according to Alexander, the physiological factor (e.g., contamination by bacilli) and the emotionally produced factor (e.g., the default of the organism's resistance) may be causally of equal importance.[19]

Some support can be found for this attempt in Freud's own thought, specifically in his statement that "symptoms are invariably 'over-determined.' " [20] It is not a simple matter, however, to draw the line between psyche and soma; indeed, in the attempt to bisect the two, flaws appear in the pluralist psychosomatic concept. Alexander sees two kinds of illness: "conversion neurosis" and "organic neurosis," each affecting a different part of the nervous system. The conversion symptom, he says, is "a symbolic expression" of a psychological content, having as its purpose the discharge of emotional tension by means of the voluntary neuro-muscular or the sensory-perceptive system. An organic neurosis, on the other hand, is "the physiological response of the . . . organs to constant or to periodically returning emotional states." [21] But the criteria Alexander uses—symbolic expressiveness and physiological response—actually belong to two different provinces of logical inquiry, two different methods, either of which is capable of engrossing the *entire* problem of disease.*

To render thus arbitrarily unto the body what is the body's and unto the mind what is the mind's is to ignore the imperial prerogatives of both sides of the psychosomatic division. On the one hand, physiological explanations need not halt at the threshold of the voluntary neuro-muscular system. Conceivably, the physiologist could record differing brain waves and metabolic variations in all the afflictions treated by the psychoanalyst. On the other hand, the psychoanalyst, once having inquired what hysteria *means,* need not stop there. The question of meaning (the psychological question) may be asked of any disorder, organic or otherwise.

Mind may be studied in purely physiological terms. Or it can be treated, in Dewey's words, as "the body of organized meaning by which events of the present have significance for us." Each method studies, from an equivalent metaphoric distance, a different subject; no choice between them is necessary. But neither is there any possibility of a compromise between them. The exact correlation between thoughts and neurons is still unknown; in consequence, it is the "mental datum" (the thought, which we experience) that is the fact, the "neural datum" that is the inference.† But even if neurology were

---

* In this discussion, I have followed mainly Jean Starobinski, "Le Médecine psychosomatique," *Critique,* February 1954.
† John Crowe Ransom's phrase.
A notable early disciple of Freud's, the Hungarian psychoanalyst Sandor Ferenczi, formulated a criticism of the materialist view in 1908, which still applies: "Psycho-physical parallelism . . . is certainly a possible but really a

to make advances far beyond the expectations of the neurologists, the logical autonomy of both methods would still prohibit their merger. The difference between physiology and psychology is absolute—which is but a specific way of reaffirming the independence of the moral sciences from the physical.

The history of the study of the human mind, from the Greeks to our own time, may be traced through these alternative methods. In his *De Anima* Aristotle calls the two "dialectical" and "physical." A dialectical psychologist would define, say, anger "as the appetite for returning pain for pain, or something like that." A physical psychologist "would define it as a boiling of the blood or warm substance surrounding the heart." * It is the former which makes possible a moral science; the latter style of definition excludes the moral—that is, human—questions altogether.

Much of the ostensibly physical research in the pre-scientific era (as the studies of medieval alchemy by C. G. Jung have shown) is a covert form of psychological speculation, and therefore dependent on dialectical presuppositions. But in the nineteenth century science was entirely identified with the "physical" method; "dialectical" explanations were consigned to religion and philosophy. Freud gave a new impetus to the dialectical tradition, but psychoanalytic doctrine owes

---

very improbable philosophic theorem by which we need not let ourselves be misled in our observations. . . . If it is a fallacy to speak of 'molecular movements' of the brain cells instead simply of feeling, thinking, and willing, then it is no less disingenuous to throw anatomical, physiological, physical, and chemical expressions about when describing the so-called functional neuroses." Unlike Freud, Ferenczi conceded nothing to the hope that some day we will know the neural facts behind the mental experiences. Even if these endeavors had not so far failed, Ferenczi argued, psychology would be in no better position with respect to its specific tasks than it was before. "It is useless to attempt to palliate facts . . . we can analyze one set of phenomena only physically and another set only psychologically." Psychology would still have to use psychological (introspective) categories, even if it knew the facts "behind" them. "Analysis of direct inner perception" is the source of psychological knowledge (Sandor Ferenczi, *Further Contributions to the Theory and Technique of Psycho-Analysis,* London, 1926, pp. 16–18).

* The difference, continues Aristotle, is the same as defining a house as "a shelter against destruction by wind, rain, and heat" or instead as "stones, bricks, and timbers" (*De Anima,* 403 [b]). By the "dialectical" method, Aristotle was no doubt alluding to the purely mentalist psychology of Plato, while he, ever the intransigent meliorist, aspired to a compromise between the two methods, engrossing both the "material" and the "formulatable" essence.

nothing to the older religious psychologies. Indeed, it is just the Christian connection between sin and sickness, between certain prohibited thoughts and emotions and bodily suffering, that psychoanalysis rejects. Christian apologists, skilled at incorporating even the most hostile attacks into their own religious defenses, may detect a certain formal agreement between psychoanalysis and polite extremes of modern religious optimism—for example, Christian Science, whose retreat from the body is so complete that disease is not acknowledged except as a disorder of mind. But the basic attitude of Freudian medicine is a realism about the body and its demands which challenges all the various cures of souls offered by our religious tradition.

Psychoanalysis is much closer to the Stoic view, another form of dialectical explanation, which recognized the influence of mind without repudiating the body. Seneca's idea that certain emotions, if repeated, may cause sickness, suggests Freud's notion of the conversion of hysterical emotion into physical symptoms.[22] And the Stoic imagination, when after the Renaissance it sloughed off its overlay of Christian asceticism, produced a number of psychologists—Montaigne, Burton, Hobbes, La Rochefoucauld—with whom it would be apt and even historically sound to compare Freud. To be sure, the Stoic list of correspondences between physical illness and mental passion is incomplete. Shame, fear, sexual frustration, anger, ambition, and envy are understood to cause insomnia, fever, lethargy, paralysis, and the like; but what inspires these passions themselves we are never told. Lacking a dynamic theory of the passions, the Stoic psychologists left them largely unexplained and autonomous. Nevertheless the connection is partly made, and from it issued that great body of pathographic writing in the drama and novel from which Freud professes to have learned far more than from academic psychology. His taste for Shakespeare—whose characters and situations embody many of the precepts of the Stoic psychology—is further evidence of an indirect but genuine affinity between psychoanalysis and the psychological theories of Stoicism.

IV

More serious than the charge that Freud undervalued the physiological basis of mind is one brought against him on his own, entirely psychological, grounds: namely, that psychoanalysis ignores basic functions of mind in its ordinary activities. Ernest Jones reports that Freud "was apt to be careless and imprecise in his use of terms, using, for instance, 'perception' as interchangeable with 'idea,' and the like." [23] The admission is sweeping, for this is no matter (as Jones seems to think) of linguistic imprecision; it cuts off a vast area of psychological investigation. Seeing, hearing, touching, speaking, and such compound activities as perceiving and learning, are in themselves a suitable topic for the psychologist.* But by making "perception" interchangeable with "idea," Freud showed that he was interested only in the *contents* of mind, in intrapsychic rather than perceptual functions. Yet he treated the psyche, as we shall see, largely as the theater for conflicts taking place in the external, social world—in character development and family relations. Both society and the individual psyche depend for their formation, in his account, on the characteristic actions of individuals engaged first, and thereafter by symbolic repetition, in family life. Concerning such a fundamental topic of investigation as the powers of reasoning (e.g., of deducing similarity, sequence, number, abstraction) he has no theory at all.

By focusing so exclusively on the human subject in a state of recovering its capacity for decision, Freud breaks the bonds between psychology and natural science. What human beings share with animals, which perceive and learn in ways that elucidate the human, is entirely outside his interest, for, though animals have impulses, they have no beliefs and thus cannot be moral agents—or subjects for psychoanalysis. It is as a *social* science that Freudian psychology must be dealt with.

Those who like their psychologies neat, in the popular image of natural science, have, however, continued to subject psychoanalysis

---

* Freud wrote a long monograph on aphasia (a species of muteness). But this belongs to his pre-psychoanalytic period, and aphasia is considered from the neurologist's point of view.

to the techniques of experiment and statistical testing developed by
the natural sciences. Analogues to the situations of stress—such as
hunger and sexual frustration—considered crucial by Freudian
thought, have been most ingeniously constructed with that favorite
experimental character the rat. But of all the attempts to support or
discredit psychoanalysis by the application of experimental criteria,
such tests with animal subjects seem particularly futile. To what
extent does the experimental, or gown, rat resemble the town variety?
More seriously, to what extent do laboratory rats resemble human
beings? There are no strictly definable personality types among rats,
but humans can be so typed. Further, Freudian psychology, as I hope
to show, refers basically to a definite historical situation: it deals with
a certain type of individual in intrapsychic and social tension. For
this reason the tenets of psychoanalysis continue to resist verification
with infrahuman subjects. Methods of research change, however. The
study of "personality" in animals now being conducted by ethologists
may ultimately build a bridge from animal to human psychology, in
particular through the elaboration of instinct theory, in ways thus far
closed to "rat psychology." [24]

There have also been attempts to verify Freudian concepts empiri-
cally on human subjects. Of the many examples that could be cited, I
shall mention only one, which seems to me among the most expert—
that designed by Kurt Lewin and his followers. Lewin ingeniously
devised contrasting "democratic" and "authoritarian" situations
among two groups of school children, to test their emotional relation
to figures of authority. Freud's ideas were repeatedly confirmed. But
the confirmation offered by such experiments, however ingenious, is
shallow—precisely because they are experiments, in which experience
is manipulable.* Whether applied to human or animal subjects, labo-

---

* A further caution, when empirical tests are taken to "confirm" the Freudian theory. A sharper distinction than that usually drawn between "theory"
or "concepts," on the one hand, and "facts," on the other, is necessary. Concepts cannot be observed, only facts. And, in a strict sense, facts cannot be
made to speak positively for a theory; they either disprove it or, what is
usually taken as confirmation, they remain neutral. Certainly the facts which
contradict a concept may be used as evidence against it. But the facts which
do not contradict a concept or may be absorbed under its heading do not
thereby establish the truth of the concept. Concepts are on a different methodo-

ratory techniques remain at cross purposes with human experience, which, as Freud rightly sees, is individual and historical. All his cases are recorded, significantly, as *historical*. The techniques of natural science, however, can measure only routine and repeatable events. The laboratory is not society, and its tests cannot reproduce the spontaneity of human action; indeed, they negate it. Only in a live historical context do even the delicate methods of direct interviewing and indirect testing developed by psychology give us anything usable as a check on the hidden motives Freud describes.

Some of Freud's contentions are of course factually verifiable. Others can be discounted so far as they reflect prejudices that, since Freud's time, have receded into the historical distance. For instance, such ostensibly clinical phenomena as penis envy, along with Freud's general conjectures on the female character, have undergone what is to my mind a just repudiation by Adler and, among neo-Freudian analysts, notably by Karen Horney. But the confirmation or discounting of Freud's ideas requires an amalgam of perspectives; the skills of the anthropologist and social historian are needed to cue those of the psychologist. For the passions with which Freud concerned himself display such elusive modulations and reversals, express themselves so ingeniously, and are at the same time (this is in no way contradictory) so gross, so morally fraught, so unwieldy, that experimental science cannot encompass them.

It is perhaps to a recognition of this that we owe the heavily metaphoric cast of Freud's thought. He translated somewhat too easily into metaphors the literally intended concepts of physical psychology. Where Helmholtz and his school had talked of "neurological energy," Freud talked of "psychic energy," using the quantitative term "energy" at first without any metaphoric reservations. In his first major theoretical paper (1894), Freud defined emotion as a

> sum of excitation . . . having all the attributes of a quantity—although we possess no means of measuring it—a something which is

___

logical level, and can be confuted only by other, more inclusive and more acute, concepts. Again, here, the ethological study of animals in their natural settings promises a way out of this methodological dilemma.

capable of increase, decrease, displacement and discharge, and which extends itself over the memory-traces of an idea like an electric charge over the surface of the body.[25]

Throughout the theoretical chapter in *Studies on Hysteria,* the nervous system is compared to an electric system. When some excitation overloads the apparatus, Freud says, the resulting disequilibrium is "converted" into hysterical symptoms. Normally, it is supposed, "energy," or tension, strives to remain constant within the nervous system, a tendency he at first referred to as "the law of constancy." * Gradually, however, his Helmholtzian vocabulary of forces and their conservation became merely metaphoric or illustrative, and a term such as "energy" only a rhetorical mask for the ethical direction of his thought. The tendency of nervous energy to remain constant reappears under more personalized names: the "pleasure principle," and the "Nirvana principle." Later, too, he speaks of the mind not in its familiar guise as a machine but as a suite of connecting rooms: between "the large ante-room" of the unconscious, "in which the various mental excitations are crowding upon one another, like individual beings" and the adjoining smaller room "in which consciousness resides," stands a "doorkeeper" with the power to censor some ideas and admit others.[27] Or, in another metaphor, Freud explains the workings of mind as a trio of inner voices like the good and bad counselors of the old morality plays, each with its intimate persuasive claim: the id desiring, the ego steering, the super-ego exhorting.

---

* The English analyst John Rickman has suggested that psychoanalysis would have taken a quite different course had Freud been, say, a rheologist. "In place of the concept of a reflex mechanism for maintaining a low and constant state of tensions, he might have pictured mind as a plastic mass with certain mensurable degrees of resilience which, under some analogues of temperature and pressure, suffered irreversible changes into rigidity." [26] But I doubt whether psychoanalytic concepts would have altered seriously by such a switch in models. Freud's imagery is not consistently mechanistic. He did in fact resort in later writings to the image of mental rigidity, but he also appended such biological notions as growth and development to his picture of mind as a machine, and he even invoked a related image, of mind as a pressure system, with the unconscious seething and straining beneath the lid of consciousness. Beneath the mechanist trappings of hydraulics (as of electricity), Freud's metaphors of mental activity are always reliably dialectical and dynamic.

Despite the criticisms that can validly be made * of such a ready use of metaphor, there is a good deal to be said for using such language to convey facts. It is not true that in analysis we stick to the fact itself, while in metaphor we substitute for the fact to be described some quite different fact which is connected with it only by a more or less remote analogy.† The impersonal quantitative abstractions sought by scientific psychology are no less remote from the fact than are other styles of metaphor; what quantification may gain in precision it loses again because of its greater formalism and distance from the human subject.

Freud's metaphors are not, in any case, simply a correctible extravagance in an otherwise sound and scientific method. His animistic imagery is fundamental to his thought. Every technical label he applies to the impalpable and mysterious forces of the psyche carries animistic overtones, and even (his own disclaimers notwithstanding) what appear to be mechanist images have animistic contents. Thus he writes of "the sexual substances, which are saturated conductors, so to speak, of the erotic tensions." [28] Freud's concept of the libido, which begins in the image of electrical energy, eventually emerges as —*élan vital*. It was Jung who ventured explicitly to identify libido with *élan vital*,[29] but the identification is clearly foreshadowed in Freud's early usage of terms such as "libidinal charge." For another instance: Freud explained hysteria as caused by a "certain quantity of excitation" spilling over the psychic threshold. But surely this is to say nothing less qualitative than that, under specific conditions, psychic tension inscribes itself in physical symptoms. The traumatic

---

* It has often been objected that Freud's metaphoric usage is imprecise, the noun, "the unconscious," being used interchangeably with an adjective, "unconscious," when the word properly denotes a quality of, not a place inside, the mind. He has also been reproved for reifying his concepts, as with those voices within the self: id, ego, and super-ego. Cf. Wohlgemuth; William McDougall, in his valuable *Psychoanalysis and Social Psychology* (1936), pp. 56–61; Patrick Mullahy, *Oedipus Myth and Complex* (1948), p. 321. Jastrow calls it the "fallacy of attribution" in *The House That Freud Built* (1932), pp. 220–23.

† For a searching defense of metaphor, as opposed to abstractions, in science and philosophy, see Karin Stephen's first book (written before she became a psychoanalyst), a study of Bergson entitled *The Misuse of Mind* (London: 1922), especially pp. 15–46.

detail, the entire case history needed to understand an individual through his symptoms, renders a satisfactory quantifying of the "mechanisms" of mental life theoretically impossible. To grasp his subject Freud had not to quantify and measure but rather to intuit, to interpret, and—as I shall be concerned to show in detail in the course of later chapters—to evaluate.

V

Regardless of how far he ranged outside the recognized boundaries of experimental science, Freud was anxious to preserve the image of himself as a solid scientist rather than a free-lance explorer poking around savage hinterlands of the civilized mind. His professional career shows none of the eclecticism or intellectual restlessness of, say, his first host in America, G. Stanley Hall; Hall began as a theological student, meandered through philosophy and a chain of interests (pursued along the circuit of German universities in the same decade, the seventies, that Freud spent as a student in Vienna) before gravitating into teaching and clinical work in psychiatry. The first generation of psychoanalysts was drawn heavily from among just such maverick intellectuals; they are a type which invariably fills the ranks of a new discipline until it becomes economically respectable. A number of Freud's earliest disciples—Otto Rank, Hanns Sachs, and, somewhat later, Gèza Ròheim and Siegfried Bernfeld, were not doctors at all; others, if they had M.D.'s, had originally aspired to music (Dorian Feigenbaum), law (Victor Tausk), or letters (Karl Abraham). Freud, however, endeavored to keep his own interest in fields outside psychoanalysis out of his work.

His reported omnivorousness as a reader—for ten years, he read nothing for recreation but English books [30]—is efficiently suppressed in his writings. Where erudition, or personal culture, serves no scientific purpose it is excluded from his early prose style. In the close intellectual weave of *The Interpretation of Dreams,* for example, few literary references slip through, except those detected in his own dreams. (The dreams of his own that Freud relates invariably seem more erudite than base: in one dream alone, "the dream of Count

Thun," he finds direct references to Mozart, Beaumarchais, the revolution of 1848, Tennyson, Shakespeare, Zola, Grillparzer, the Spanish Armada, and Rabelais.) [31] How much the apparent restriction of erudition owes to calculation is hard to decide. From the *Autobiographical Study* we learn that he had deliberately abstained from reading Nietzsche for fear of becoming less original.[32] Privately he admitted to remote intellectual connections—with Kant, Voltaire, Feuerbach; more than once he classed himself with Copernicus and Darwin;[33] in his last writings he added Empedocles and Plato to his genealogy.[34] Yet in his major works Freud kept his humanist literacy under wraps. Erudition could not serve his rhetorical purpose. Perhaps he surmised that his ideas would be more attractive coming from a dogged insular scientist than from the voracious book-browser and idea-fancier he also was.

Whatever Freud's motives for isolating himself intellectually, the result seems salutary. Compare him with Jung, whose best book, *Psychological Types,* is a work as much in the intellectual history of German Romanticism as in psychology. The analytic edge of Jung's thought has been blunted by a characteristically German ambition to hand down his message from a magic mountain of erudition. Much of the slack, analogical quality of his argument may be ascribed to a hyper-awareness of his own affinities with the Romantic poets and philosophers. Jung cannot help showing that he has read too much. He empties his notes into his books. Freud, however, does not disclose, at least publicly, his many connections with Romantic literature and philosophy. He is rigorous and searching in argument, elegant and precise in style.* Above all, his work has qualities of intellectual patience and thoroughness that might have been undermined by a more developed self-consciousness about his intellectual ancestry.

For this successfully guarded originality, however, Freud paid with a corresponding limitation. His historical sense, compared with Jung's,

---

* Freud wrote tight, lucid, elegant German, and he was extremely sensitive to these matters. See the memorial essay he wrote on Charcot (1893), in which he singles out the great neurologist's lecturing and writing style as a major cause for praise (*Coll. Papers* I, 14, 17). Also, the letters to Fliess (see *The Origins of Psychoanalysis,* pp. 289–90) give evidence of the stylistic anxieties that went into the writing of *The Interpretation of Dreams.*

is weak. His quick sweep of interest, his easy catholicity, resembles that of his mentor and patron, the physiologist Brücke. Along with his many writings on animal psychology, Brücke—son of a near-great painter and himself aspiring to art before turning to science —published papers on music, social psychology, and language. But these humane subjects were treated in accordance with the physicalist (Helmholtzian) doctrines to which Brücke adhered; he could not abandon his materialist preconceptions in approaching them. Something of the narrowness and aggressiveness of late-nineteenth-century materialism characterizes Freud's ambition for the scope of psychoanalysis. He asserts in his "On the History of the Psychoanalytic Movement" (1914) that "psychoanalysis explains not only pathological phenomena but reveals their connection with normal life and discloses unsuspected relationships between psychiatry and the most various other sciences dealing with activities of the mind." At different times and places he mentions mythology and "the abstractions of religion," history, philology, aesthetics (interpretation of works of art through the "sources of artistic production"), philosophy, politics —even sociology "can be nothing other than applied psychology." [35] * But his claim that psychoanalysis was indispensable to the understanding of all that "man makes or does," [36] was based not on its comprehending new areas of subject matter, but rather on its providing a new and unifying approach to the established ones. By offering to every subject the improvement, and the humiliation, of a new method, psychoanalysis brings together under one roof the most disparate subjects; they all, examined by the psychological method, become fairly similar.

Freud was sensitive from the beginning about his unorthodox catholicity of interest; to compensate for it, he met objections from

* Of course much of this ambitious program was never attempted by Freud himself; but it provided theoretical support for the work of immediate disciples —the gifted "second generation" of Freudians which included Sandor Ferenczi, Otto Rank, Theodore Reik, Ernest Jones, and others—during the decade and a half before and after World War I. Ferenczi added criminology, sociology, and jurisprudence to Freud's list of "applied mental sciences." See his *Further Contributions to the Theory and Teaching of Psychoanalysis* (1926), p. 424; and Otto Rank and Hanns Sachs, *The Significance of Psychoanalysis for the Mental Sciences* (1916).

the world of strict science with his own gestures of strictness. Though privately, in the letters to Fliess, he used the word "speculative" pridefully, to convey his sense of his own theoretic daring, publicly he stood against speculation. Too often in his early papers he assures us that everything is founded on patient and direct observation. So anxious was he to establish the legitimacy of his movement that the complaint of "unscientific" is made again and again * of critics and renegades alike. It is his errant followers (i.e., Jung, Adler) who are speculative, while he himself claims to have "learned to restrain speculative tendencies." [37]

Despite these disclaimers, the label of "unscientific" was affixed to Freud by his very first academic reviewers †—not wholly without cause. Psychoanalysis, as I have indicated in this chapter, cannot meet the rigid standards of scientific theory. Yet I am concerned lest this label "unscientific" be used to condemn Freud or, worse, to praise him condescendingly for just those rare qualities in him that we do not

---

* Freud's protestations of solidarity with the community of science occurred when the community itself was changing too rapidly to permit such generalized patriotism. He was in fact not very knowledgeable about modern science. When he encountered the speculativeness of the new physics in a figure like Ernst Mach, his contemporary and fellow Viennese, he read him out of science as an "intellectual nihilist" (New Introductory Lectures, pp. 224–26). Mach's view, which Freud found intolerable—that all scientific statements concern sense observation, and do not necessarily describe an actual physical world or refer to a hidden truth behind appearances—has since become the main methodological platitude of modern science. Cf. Coll. Papers V, 301; when Freud came to explain why he never personally sought out a contemporary social philosopher he deeply admired and considered himself influenced by, Josef Popper-Lynkeus, his best reason was: Popper-Lynkeus was also a physicist and a "friend of Ernst Mach. . . . I was anxious that the happy impression of our agreement" on psychological matters "should not be spoilt."

† Ernest Jones (Life and Work, I, 361) reports that when The Interpretation of Dreams was published in 1900, one eminent reviewer, the psychologist Wilhelm Stern, suggested that "un-critical minds would be delighted to join in this play with ideas and would end up in complete mysticism and chaotic arbitrariness." A Professor Leipmann of Berlin regretted that "the imaginative thoughts of an artist had triumphed over the scientific investigator." This last is a slur that was to recur throughout Freud's career—see his reply to the same charge made by Havelock Ellis, in "A Note on the Prehistory of the Technique of Psychoanalysis" (1920), in SE XVIII, 263–65—and is still influential today. Jones adds that The Interpretation of Dreams made so little stir, critical or uncritical, when it was first published, that it took eight years to sell out the edition of six hundred copies.

encourage among ourselves: his wide range and subtlety, his unsurpassed brilliance as an exegete of the universal language of pain and suffering, his willingness to pronounce judgments and draw out the evidence for them from his own life as well as from clinical data. His scientific motives are of a piece with the ethical implications of his thought, whose catch phrases have seeped down from the conversations of the educated into the popular consciousness of the age. It would be an impertinence, into which no received notion of the boundary between science and ethics should lead us, to judge one of Freud's faces authentic and dismiss the other. For humanists in science, and for scientists of the human, Freud should be the model of a concern with the distinctively human that is truly scientific.

CHAPTER TWO

CONFLICT AND CHARACTER

The carnal man . . . though he may work good, yet he has no taste for it . . . always having the contrary desire.
—LUTHER

No small part of Freud's impact upon the contemporary moral imagination derives from his idea of the self in conflict. He conceives of the self not as an abstract entity, uniting experience and cognition, but as the subject of a struggle between two objective forces—unregenerate instincts and overbearing culture. Between these two forces there may be compromise but no resolution. Since the individual can neither extirpate his instincts nor wholly reject the demands of society, his character expresses the way in which he organizes and appeases the conflict between the two.

Retaining the method of the mechanist psychology in which he trained, Freud at the same time transformed the mechanist notion of impersonal objective forces within the individual; he made these forces, the instincts, the individual's chief mode of defense against the world, by defining the individual as the agent of his instincts, seeking a means of expression for them. His concept of the unconscious, as attempting to break through the denials of consciousness and the superficies of civilization, has a similarly polemical intent; the unconscious, as he saw it, serves as the individual's defense against a repressive culture.

I

To have a psychology at all requires, I believe, an understanding of the mind in terms of social and moral behavior. Neither the primitive's notion of the soul (*anima*) as the principle of the body's preservation and locomotion, nor the modern physiologist's dispassionate model of the brain as an intricate communications switchboard is a psychological conception. It is only when psychic life is segregated conceptually from the rest of biological nature that psychology proper may be said to exist, and that the idea of the individual can become, as it was for Freud, the unit of analysis. Freud's entire psychological nomenclature reflects, as I have suggested in Chapter I, his attempt to share in the prestige of positivist science, with its dissolution of the individual into a unit of the larger natural process; at the same time he tried to reinfuse some of the characteristic vocabulary of nineteenth-century materialist science with meanings that would make it feasible to examine our human natures as distinct from the rest of nature. The way in which he stated his instinct theory, through which he broached the whole question of conflict as it affects the individual, reflects this ambivalence.

Freud's critics have been quick to point out the looseness and equivocation of his language in discussing the instincts, without understanding the reasons for it. His use of the term "instinct" (*Trieb*) seems, on the one hand, biological: instinct is pictured as a quantity of bodily energy forcing its way in a certain direction. It is, moreover, impersonal: the "instincts are all qualitatively alike and owe the effect they make only to the amount of excitation they carry." [1] On the other hand, Freud allows instinct a most ambiguous relation to the body. In the first of the *Three Essays on Sexuality* (1905), an instinct is understood as

> the psychical representative of an endosomatic, continuously flowing source of stimulation, as contrasted with a "stimulus," which is set up by single excitations coming from without. The concept of instinct is thus one of those lying on the frontier between the mental and the physical.[2]

We cannot know the body, Freud implies, but only its "psychical representatives"—its instincts. Freud seems to discount the biological value of instincts, as the means toward procreation, as too obvious to need discussion. He is not interested in connecting them with visceral feelings, as did his brilliant English contemporary William McDougall; fear, rage, hunger, and the others among the fourteen enumerated by McDougall are not instincts in Freud's sense. Nor does "sexual instinct" for him carry a wholly pragmatic connotation of something restricted to genital sensation. An instinct, for Freud, is a purely formal quantity—a varied and highly attenuated ensemble of psychic aims.*

The most penetrating critique of Freud's instinct theory, though it is not aimed at Freud alone, remains John Dewey's *Human Nature and Conduct* (1921), which not only is the seminal work of American social psychology and still the most widely read book in the field, but has also had a strong influence on a large number of those professionally affiliated with the Freudian movement.

Dewey rejects any such metabiological entity as that which Freud calls "instinct." There is no "separate psychic realm" [3] or force,† no "original individual consciousness," [4] Dewey argues, but only a neutral potentiality, without effect until it becomes an element in social habits. For "instinct" Dewey would substitute the term "impulse." Both terms imply the formal necessity of social response, and some measure of inhibition. But Dewey's term is far less dialectical. He treats the failure of response, or the lag in it, as quite apart from the

---

* In a footnote, written three decades later to a new edition of the *Three Essays*, Freud remarks that "the science of the instincts is the most incomplete part of the psychoanalytic theory" (SE VII, 168). In this exposition I am dealing with his concept of instinct before 1920. In late writings, such as the *New Introductory Lectures*, the term "instinct" includes the empirical fact of individual drives—and goes beyond them; his Eros and Thanatos are veritable "cosmic" instincts, which Freud posited as macroscopic versions of individual libido and aggression. In the *Outline of Psychoanalysis*, his last book, instincts are defined as "the somatic demands upon mental life" (p. 5), while organic instincts "are themselves composed of fusions of two primal forces . . ." (p. 67). In short, there is good reason for confusion about Freud's theory of instinct.

† Actually, Freud posited none. Nor is his use of instinct falsely concrete, as Dewey charges.

content of impulse. Indeed, impulse becomes merely a reservoir of vitality, upon which each new attempt at self-satisfaction or social reformation must draw.

Freud's instinct theory is more dynamic and critical. Instinct is to him just that element which makes any response inadequate. The failure of response can be traced not merely to societal rigidities (as Dewey would have it) but farther back—to the ambivalent structure of instinct itself, which continually prepares the ground for conflicts. On the one hand, Freud warns us that the instincts exert a positive threatening pressure; if they are dammed up, they will explode. On the other hand, he gives the instincts their own built-in "vicissitudes," so that simple animal expressiveness is never even theoretically possible, let alone finally satisfactory.

Dewey sees the conversion of impulse to culture as a process of integration, the setting of impulse in a new controlling situation which he calls "habit." For Freud, however, residues of instinctual contradiction persist, crude and threatening, beneath the surface of socially acceptable behavior; there is always the hazard of a renewal of conflict. Freud explains such upheavals genetically, progress being interrupted when the sublimatory achievements of culture are dissolved back into their archaic instinctual elements. Dewey, however, explains them without reference to time, seeing them merely as the "disintegration" of present modes of behavior into others equally contemporaneous. He admits that these disintegrated modes of behavior strikingly resemble those of children and primitives,* but he insists that the resemblance tells us little. He refuses to call such behavior, as Freud does, "regressive." For Dewey the individual is not, as in Freud's conception,

---

* Notice that, for all his disdain of the metabiological notion of instinct, Dewey cannot answer the question Freud has raised—not how, but *why* a character or an activity "disintegrates." Freud wishes to account for misleading resemblances between "disintegrated" behavior and behavior on genetically prior levels, like that of children and primitives. Dewey can only say, circularly, that such behavior results from a disturbance of "psychic equilibrium." (I exclude here all organic causation, such as that treated by Kurt Goldstein, an influential psychologist who, incidentally, talks in terms very similar to Dewey's. [See Goldstein's *The Organism*, 1939.] Freud is interested in ordinary psychic life, *not* in deviations caused by physiological crises like brain injuries.) Freud's genetic position may be overstated, but Dewey's position suffers from a worse fault: it is tautological.

under a constant threat from the instincts lying in wait below the surface of consciousness, ready at any moment to claim their original
autonomy.

Terms such as "organization," "integration," "interaction," prominent in the vocabulary of current American social science, are expressive of the liberal belief, to which Dewey contributed more sub-
stantially than any other American philosopher, that we can turn
conflicts to advantage and progressively fulfill our boundless wants
and desires. Freud was not so optimistic. His term "sublimation"
would seem to serve the same function as "adaptation" for Dewey:
sublimation is the successful adaptation of a given instinct—sexual
or aggressive—to the repressive social process. But there is a large
difference. Sublimation implies a cost to the individual which Dewey's
idea of adaptation does not. Freud, while favoring sublimation, emphasizes the limited human capacity for enduring it—being, he says,
the real thing, the instincts will not easily tolerate substitutes for the
real gratifications of life. Dewey, on the other hand, attributes imperfect adaptation to social habit's being inadequate to its task of organiz-
ing impulse suitably to control the gratifications available at the
moment. Which view is more acceptable depends on which version
—Dewey's or Freud's—of the real thing, striving to liberate itself in
man's self-seeking behavior, appeals more to the reader.

Thus Dewey locates in society the critical principle that Freud assigns to human nature, and this divergence accounts for a difference
of ethical vision. Dewey sees the impulses as capable of rescuing a
society in which habits in institutional structures (i.e., collective
habit) have become petrified and therefore impediments to progress,
where Freud sees the instincts as themselves the force which limits
progress by threatening a renewal of conflict; by their very existence,
the instincts serve notice of the inadequacies of all social arrangements. Thus Dewey and Freud meet back-to-back. It becomes clear
why the meliorist Dewey accused Freud of reducing "social results"
to "psychic causes." [5] But with equal justification Dewey may be accused of reducing psychic results to social causes; for his analysis
traces all failures of personality back to their faulty social context,

thereby shoring up the liberal hope for progressively more intelligent fusions of impulse and situation.

Rejecting two of Freud's principal categories of concern—the problem of origins and the operation of goals other than contemporaneous—Dewey holds that the present contains factors sufficient to account for both itself and the past. The person, he says, acts in a continuum of response to social and biological stimuli. Present experience is the explicit criterion Dewey employs to measure the success (health) or failure (sickness) of an individual or social institution, thus advancing a masterly variation on the argument canonical with liberalism since Bentham: that human nature may be comprehended by its strivings to obtain pleasure and avoid pain. In liberal psychology as it has evolved from Bentham to Dewey, social organization, not instinct, has become the source of and the limitation upon the perfectability of human nature. Indeed, human nature can be discussed only in terms of social conduct.

No doubt many of Freud's personal biases are frozen into his instinct theory—for example, as I shall discuss in a later chapter, that concerning women. But his instinctualism is chiefly what gives an admirable sharpness to his estimate of human nature, and makes it more valuable as a defense of the individual than the critique of his position theoretically prefigured by Dewey and carried out by such neo-Freudians as Karen Horney and Erich Fromm, or than the present-centered psychology of Adler, which blames society for the characteristic frustrations of the individual. The liberal revisers of Freud, in their efforts to avoid the pessimistic implications of his genetic reasoning, tend to let the idea of the individual be absorbed into the social, or at best to permit it a vague and harried existence. Freud himself— through his mythology of the instincts—kept some part of character safe from society, restoring to the idea of human nature a hard core, not easily warped or reshaped by social experience.

In Freud's definition, instinct is desiring, intention, drive, carrying with it an implication not only of will but of resistance. Human relations are seen in terms of clashing intentions, which society at best can regulate but can never suppress. Far from being a residual idea left over from his biological training, as the neo-Freudians have maintained, Freud's theory of instinct is the basis for his insight into the painful snare of contradiction in which nature and culture, individual and society, are forever fixed.

II

Freud designated as " 'unconscious' any mental process the existence of which we are obliged to assume—because, for instance, we infer it in some way from its effects—but of which we are not directly aware." [6] Here, even more radically than in his biologistic concept of instinct, his doctrine goes against the traditions of empirical science. The unconscious functions for Freud as a "god-term," to use Kenneth Burke's suggestive epithet; it is Freud's conceptual ultimate, a First Cause, to be believed in precisely because it is both fundamental to and inaccessible to experience.

Philosophy cannot do without god-terms. Positivist science, however rationalist and empirical its pretensions, similarly divinized "society." But it makes a difference whether such an ultimate is a notion of "form" or "structure," from which one is led to infer that every form must form "something," and thence to imagining some fundamental substrate—as in the ontology of the Greek philosophers—or whether one puts the substrate first, as one's ultimate term, and imagines the controlling or shaping agency as secondary. Freud follows the latter course. His god-term, the unconscious, is allied not to classical ontology but to the more recent German idealist notion of creative eruption and subsequent repression. Freud's concept is another version of the idea of primitive Chaos that supplied Romanticism with its first cause and last resort.* The unconscious is fertile "nature," the womb of darkness, the identity in which every distinction fades and all things reunite. Just as his concept of instinct is based on the sameness of instinctual life, Freud's notion of the unconscious

---

* Schlegel writes in *Lucinde:* the essence of Romanticism is "that which cannot be described." Thus, a Romantic science—in Freud—was the product of German Romantic and religious aestheticism, which began in part as a protest against science.

stresses the lack of differentiation in feeling: all unconscious desires are impersonal, as all persons are creatures of a vaguely instinctual demiurge. The Romantic conception of the unconscious may originally have contributed to the anti-democratic idea of genius (as in Schelling), but Freud democratized genius by giving everyone a creative unconscious. Though hardly so leveling a psychology as Pavlov's, which credits everybody, including animals, with the same instincts, psychoanalysis at least supposes a radical democracy among human beings in their possession of an impersonal force—the "instincts," the "unconscious mind," or (as Freud later called it) the "it" or "id."

Freud thought of the unconscious as somewhat like a hidden god —indifferent, impersonal, unconcerned about the life of its creation. It is inferred always in negative terms. While for Jung the unconscious is all that consciousness can become, for Freud it is, more simply, all that consciousness is not. Consciousness is discriminating and selective. The unconscious never says *No.* Consciousness can learn from reality and is capable of indecision or the postponement of gratification. The unconscious can only strive blindly "to gratify its instincts in complete disregard of the superior strength of outside forces." Consciousness is alterable. Unconscious forces are "indestructible." [7] Instincts fill the unconscious with energy, "but it has no organization, no unified will . . . the laws of logic—above all the laws of contradiction" do not apply to it; it knows "no values, no good and evil, no morality." [8] Yet it is something upon which civilization must draw for the sake of its life, something which contains "the true psychic reality." [9] The unconscious is the "larger sphere," Freud writes, "which includes within it the smaller sphere of the conscious." [10] There is a circularity in this way of conceiving the mind, with the unknown part becoming that through which the known takes on meaning. It is actually through consciousness that we form an idea of our unconscious drives and motivations. Yet at the same time we are invited to understand consciousness from what it appears to be if compared with what it is not.

Before Freud, the term "unconscious" had gone through a long evolution of meaning. Leibniz used it to describe the appetitive intentions of a transcendental nature installed in the self. But later philosophers—Fichte, Schelling, Hegel, Schopenhauer, von Hartmann, Nietzsche—broached the meaning Freud finally gave to the term, by seeing the unconscious as blind, natural will. Will in this sense is not actual, of course, but metaphoric, and implies desires of which the mind is ignorant, or which the conscious mind rejects. Like the mainspring in a watch, the whole potency of mind—in this conception—lies coiled up within the self and unwinds inexorably in the course of time. In Schopenhauer the unconscious as Will is the source of all that happens—of character, of the whole of life, of all that we repudiate and, like our nightmares, do not (consciously) will.* Thus, from being a locus of subjective intention, the unconscious, in the psychologizing philosophies of the nineteenth century, became the expression of an objective force, of fixed contents and developments.

It is this meaning which Freud absorbs, adding to it chiefly a more explicit opposition between consciousness and the unconscious. Freud's unconscious is not simply—as in the philosophic concept— mind burdened with meanings waiting to be discharged. Those merely latent elements of mind Freud called "pre-conscious," to distinguish them from his critical conception of the unconscious as repressed—consisting of contents which are incapable of "becoming conscious in the ordinary way." [11] I use the word "critical" in this connection because Freud's theory of the unconscious is mainly a critique of the repressions. The term "pre-conscious" is purely descriptive, for Freud, but the "unconscious" he used critically. "While in the descriptive sense there are two kinds of unconscious," he wrote, "in the dynamic sense there is only one." [12] The word "dynamic" refers here, as wherever else Freud used it, to the basic modes of conflict by which character develops. It is because the pre-conscious is not a critical category—it has no quarrel, in principle, with consciousness—that he permits it so small a role in his theory.

Had Freud settled for a concept of the pre-conscious, rather than going on to distinguish an unconscious as existing beyond—or below —it, his psychoanalytic doctrine might have met with less resistance. That there is a depth and a dormant unhappiness in our present lives,

---

* Freud acknowledges that Schopenhauer's "unconscious 'Will' is equivalent to the instincts in the mind as seen by psychoanalysis" (*Coll. Papers* IV, 355).

no one would deny. But that this depth, this immense fund of unacknowledged contents, exists so far out of the reach of consciousness that it must be lodged, metaphorically, in another part of the psyche, is just the extremity upon which Freud insisted—to the uneasiness of his meliorist critics. I would hazard a guess that the cause of widespread hostility to the idea of the unconscious among non-Freudian psychologists, and the reason for its current repudiation by influential neo-Freudian revisers of psychoanalysis, is not simply the philosophic and even metaphysical flavor of the term as Freud used it, but something else—its critical implications, and, moreover, Freud's resigned modesty about just how much any man can do to alter the fates working themselves out of the unconscious. The idea of the unconscious, which forms the cornerstone for Freud's historical conception of sickness, must be got out of the way before the situational or contextual control of sickness, given its most subtle formulation by Dewey and now dominant, in adulterated form, in American social and individual psychology, can prevail.

III

Without gauging the critical function of repression in the Freudian scheme, we cannot perceive either the hidden weight of Freud's moralizing or his appeal to modern minds, suspicious of all moralizing.

It was his appraisal of the determining power of the past that led Freud to distinguish what is unconscious from what is merely preconscious. The unconscious contains not simply what is not conscious, or that of which we are at the moment unaware, it contains, he insisted, our forgotten origins. Yet to forget them is not to abolish them. On the contrary, to forget an event or motive is to conserve and even augment its importance. The stretches of the past stored up in the unconscious only *seem* empty; in reality, they are burdened with the present.

Mechanistic psychology conceived of the human memory as a receptacle, divided into compartments according to the divisions of chronological time. Memory-testing experiments, from William James, who began them, to Ebbinghaus, who brought them to their pinnacle, have all been based on this conception. For Ebbinghaus, "pure memory" was represented as a container of rote-learned nonsense syllables whose rate of assimilation could be measured. But such a conception ignores the individual's capacity to make decisions; the information gained by such experiments is relevant chiefly to workers engaged in automatic tasks not requiring a choice. Freud's psychology begins more realistically, with the eruptive and contradictory occurrences in human behavior.

Memory, for Freud, is not a passive receiver whose performance can be measured quantitatively; it embodies a moral choice, a sequence of acceptances and rejections. Forgetting is active; it is not the absence of an action, something dropped out of the container mind. Freud felt his way down into the container until he found its false bottom, repression; below this memory really begins. Certain crucial events of the past may, at the behest of the ego, which does not want to remember them, be at some time repressed. Repression thus becomes an infallible index of ethical import. What is too imperative to be remembered suffers the compliment of being forgotten.

Briefly, Freud may be understood to say that, because the patient has chosen to forget his painful past, he is ill. Neurotic symptoms are a mask for memory, "a substitute"—made necessary by repression—for things the patient has forgotten.[13] There are, to be sure, cases of successful repression.[14] It is not amnesia as such, but the sad fact that amnesia is incomplete, that causes the past to erupt into present symptoms. If only repression could be total, no one would be ill. Short of this, Freud saw no alternative to substituting another control device for the repressions. Since neurosis arises through the partial leakage of painful memories, the job of the analyst is to decipher entirely the palimpsest of the patient's mind, to illuminate all, not merely part, of the obscure script. Only this could dissolve the "abnormal attachment to the past" by which Freud defined neurosis.[15]

Freud's general thesis—sickness conceived of as historical—does not in itself entail his also believing that the *earliest* events of childhood fester and multiply in the unconscious until, unless excised with the aid of analysis, they overwhelm us. In the case history that initiated Freud's therapeutic struggle to lift the weight of the past, that of the youthful hysteric known as "Anna O.," Breuer, the girl's physician, found no reason to extend his therapy so far back into his patient's past.* He placed Anna under deep hypnosis and repeated to her the words she mumbled during her delirium; she responded with elaborate fantasies and daydreams recalling the recent crisis which had precipitated her hysterical attack—the fatal illness of her father. By relating a number of these, Anna was relieved of her crippling somatic afflictions, though for only a few hours at a time.

Breuer was able to make the "talking cure" (as his patient named it) less temporary only when he required her to do more than "associate." He instructed Anna, while still hypnotized, to describe the exact scene at which each of her symptoms had appeared and to express not only her random thoughts about that scene but to vent freely the emotions it aroused. For instance, during a summer of intense heat, Anna suddenly became unable to drink a single glass of water. After this had been true for six weeks, she was talking one day in hypnosis about her English governess, whom she disliked, and recounted "with every sign of disgust" how she had once seen the lady's dog, which she abhorred, drinking out of a glass.

> The patient had said nothing, as she had wanted to be polite. [Now] after giving further energetic expression to the anger she had held back, she asked for something to drink, drank a large quantity of water without any difficulty and woke from her hypnosis with the glass at her lips; thereupon the disturbance vanished, never to return.[16]

Like this neurotic incapacity to drink, Anna's symptoms were all explained as precipitates of painful experiences toward which she had been emotionally too passive, too conventional in response. As her memories and especially her suppressed emotional reactions were evoked, her symptoms disappeared one by one; and a permanent cure

---

* Breuer treated "Anna O." from 1880 to 1882, while Freud was still engaged in desultory physiological research. Hers is the first case in their collaborative volume, *Studies on Hysteria* (1895). Freud discusses the case in the "Clark Lectures," SE XI, 10–15; *Introductory Lectures*, p. 243; and in his *Autobiographical Study*, pp. 34–36.

was achieved with a rapidity that was to become suspect, by Freudian standards. That the wholesale discharge of pent-up emotion has a calming effect is hardly a novel idea. But Breuer's was a new and more specifically therapeutic adaptation of the principle of catharsis: he effected a cure directly by the release of inhibited rage within the permissive meeting presided over by the physician.

The idea of cure Freud developed was, by contrast, more rational. He came increasingly to play down the role of emotional catharsis as such and to consider therapy as a purely recollective act. What cures the patient, he thought, is not the expressing of suppressed emotions in the relaxed state of hypnosis, but the act of dealing with the forgotten past, the repressed emotions, while in conscious control of and thereby superior to them.

"Our hysterical patients suffer from reminiscences." [17] Freud italicized the passage. The unique misery of man he ascribed to the discontinuous development of his memory—not instinctual as among other animals, yet almost as inaccessible to reason as the instincts. Among the animals a protective device, in human beings memory was a prison, but one the unenlightened presumably do not know they inhabit. The neurotic, like a habitually incarcerated person, a criminal or an invalid, may learn to feel more comfortable in his prison than outside it.

Freud's momentous enlargement of Breuer's technique—to drive the patient's recollective effort behind the occasion of the first appearance of his symptom, back through his entire life history—emphasizes the importance of memory in his conception. Breuer had found it sufficient to have his patient recall only those scenes the recollection of which her symptoms embodied or "represented" as "residues," [18] but Freud thought it necessary to trace his patients' symptoms back to more remote memories, to the early and seemingly normal amnesia which overlays early childhood up to the age of five, six, or even eight. He discovered that

the analysis of each single hysterical symptom leads to a whole chain of former impressions [which] reaches . . . back into the earliest years of childhood, so that the hysterical amnesia is seen to be a direct continuation of the infantile amnesia which hides the earliest impressions of our mental life from all of us.[19]

These early experiences, Freud reasoned, just because they are invariably forgotten, must have been the decisive ones.

Though we may question his playing down of the impact of later years upon character, Freud's genetic overstatement is more than justified by his brilliant insight—arrived at through subtle distinctions regarding the function of memory—into the continuum between sickness and health. He defines sickness as a particular kind of failure of memory: it is ignorance asserting itself, a positive "fixation" upon some past event or situation, an "unprofitable attitude towards life" which is the "universal trait common to every neurosis." [20] But, by driving the task of recall beyond the occasion of the symptoms back to childhood—in other words, by turning from symptom-analysis to character-analysis—Freud discovered that everyone, not just the neurotic, suffers from decisive failures of memory. By deepening it to include the unconscious, he made memory more of a clue to the human condition than it had been since Plato's theory of anamnesis.[21] Anyone, he said, may recover lost memories. And since "in forgetting, there can really be no question of a direct function of time"— or, as he put it metaphorically, since the unconscious "knows no time limit"—Freud presumes that the repressed traces of memory suffer no change even over the longest periods.*

Freud's belief in the continued existence of the past, and in the perennial hazards of its revival, links him with the Romantic poets, for whom the whole of experience, and especially childhood, survives in a mental underworld. Fortunately we are permitted only occasional glimpses of this world, for should we gain the power of total recall,

---

* *Psychopathology of Everyday Life,* pp. 174–75 fn. See this passage especially: "The most important, as well as the most peculiar character of psychic fixation consists in the fact that all impressions are, on the one hand, retained in the same form as they were received, and also in the forms they have assumed in their further development. . . . By virtue of this theory, every former state of memory content may thus be restored, even though all original relations have long been replaced by newer ones."

the result would be delirium—which is nothing other than uncontrolled memory, time gone mad. In his *Biographia Literaria* (1817), Coleridge illustrates this with a clinical anecdote concerning an illiterate young woman who, during a seizure of what he calls "nervous fever," could recite at length in Latin, Greek, and Hebrew. Her physicians were baffled, until it was discovered that, years before, she had been a servant in the household of an elderly Protestant pastor, whose custom it was to pace up and down a hallway adjoining the kitchen, reading aloud to himself out of his favorite books. Apparently the girl had absorbed these sounds, which were without meaning for her; and under the stress of mental illness they came to the surface of her mind. Of course, the question of which Freud has made us aware—what was the relation of the servant girl to her elderly employer that led her to this particular feat of rote recall and not to another?—did not occur to Coleridge. His interest in the case was only in the support it gave to his general thesis that "all thoughts are in themselves imperishable," and that, if our mental faculties were somehow more comprehensive, it would be feasible to restore to every mind "the collective experience of its whole past existence." Not "a single act, a single thought" can be "loosened or lost from that living chain of causes" among whose "links" Coleridge includes what is "conscious or unconscious." [22]

Freud assumed no less, with regard to the limitless powers of memory, than did Coleridge. The therapeutic task which psychoanalysis sets itself, "to repair all the damages to the patient's memories," [23] can be carried out because even the impressions of infancy "have never really been forgotten" but are "only inaccessible and latent, having become part of the unconscious." [24] But Freud's concern with memory, unlike Coleridge's, carried an animus. "Past," for him, is a pejorative term; neurotics "cannot get free of the past." [25] To have a repressed past is to be sick of it, to be healthy is to live more fully in the present. It is in this sense that the analytic effort differs from the labors of the archaeologist, to which it is often compared.* The

---

* Freud himself used the archaeological image to describe the respect the analyst shows for the patient's mental relics, and his caution and tentativeness in piecing together a picture of the total past ("Constructions in Analysis,"

archaeologist is neither for nor against what he digs up, but the analyst is necessarily arrayed against the patient's past, since he sees it as an incubus on the present.

The comparison of analyst with archaeologist is invalidated on another count as well—that psychological history cannot be represented spatially. Freud likens that "ancient edifice," the mind, to the eternal city, Rome, upon which new layers of buildings have been erected. But since, unlike the material Rome, no part of the buried mind can "really be the victim of total destruction," [26] it is as if, in Rome

the palaces of the Caesars were still standing on the Palatine and . . . where the Palazzo Caffarelli stands there would also be, without this being removed, the Temple of Jupiter Capitolinus, not merely in its latest form moreover, as the Romans of the Caesars saw it, but also in its earliest shape, when it still wore an Etruscan design and was adorned with terra-cotta antefixae. . . . On the Piazza of the Pantheon we should find not only the Pantheon of today as bequeathed to us by Hadrian, but on the same site also Agrippa's original edifice. . . .[27]

Beneath the mild exercise of classical erudition a major issue of Freud's psychological theory is involved. When "we try to represent historical sequence in spatial terms," [28] we face an apparent absurdity: that of envisaging several contents occupying the same space. But, psychologically speaking, two or more contents *can* occupy the same "space" at the same time—past and present *do* coexist in the mind. Freud's implication is that psychology had better avoid, as misleading and simplifying, any sustained recourse to spatial metaphors.*

Collected Papers V, 360). The first use (so far as I know) that he makes of the image is where he announces to his friend Fliess his discovery of the Oedipus Complex. Freud writes: "It is as if Schliemann had dug up another Troy which had hitherto been believed to be mythical" (p. 305). He reminded Fliess of his "predilection for the prehistoric in all its human forms" (*The Origins of Psycho-Analysis*, p. 275). Here, of course, the archaeological image has none of the aggressive overtones it was to gather as a strategy used upon patients. It is an image of *self*-discovery.

* Freud's likening of the mind to an impossibly four-dimensional Rome can be used to remonstrate against the current attempts to remold psychoanalysis and general psychological theory according to the imagery of physics, using metaphors of "life-space" and "power-fields." The pioneer, and perhaps the most influential of these attempts was made by the late Kurt Lewin (see his book, *The Principles of Topological Psychology*, New York, 1936; and two

In principle, Freud's method is indirect, seeking causes and contents far outside the patient's current psychological condition. But his preoccupation with origins leads him to simplify that current condition, collapsing present into past, as it were, in order to explain the production of symptoms. Present emotional crises are all traced back to some original one, and take on a certain aspect of inevitability. In this sense Freud's method is unhistorical: present irregularities of neurotic behavior are shown to be entirely determined by past; and that this love, that hate, such a conflict persists is not accidental, once the genetic strands are untangled.

It is not so paradoxical as it at first appears that psychoanalysis encourages its subjects to live with a reduced burden of memory, closer to the surface of life, where tensions cannot take root and feed off the accumulated energies of the past. Though Freud is commonly thought to have measured neurosis against the ideal of an unimpaired sexual efficiency, it would be more accurate to say that he measured it against an ideal contemporaneity. No current difficulties can impair one's sexuality, he implies, except as they are vivified by memories which persist inappropriately, too emphatically, in the present. Consequently, the lengthy and minute investigation of the patient's past, in the analysis, is not meant to enhance its importance, but rather—by an introspective lingering—to divest it of psychological resonance.

IV

Freud's geneticism may be usefully viewed in terms of his recourse to certain rhetorical devices. He was particularly fond of the trope known as synecdoche, in which the name of a part or adjunct or attribute is made to stand for the whole, and relied on it heavily—to

---

papers: "Field Theory and Experiment in Social Psychology," 1939, and "Defining the 'field at a given time,' " 1943) and more recently by the Chicago psychoanalyst Thomas French.

Spatial models in psychology—as Lewin's topological diagrams, for instance, clearly show—presume an enclosure, a locatable limit to relations of consciousness. Despite the metaphoric ornament of "vectors" (replacing the dynamic of instinct or impulse), spatial psychologies can show only a cross-section of life-history, and must approach behavior through the narrows of existing person-environment relations.

the detriment, as I shall attempt to show, of his argument—in expressing his bias against the past.

His contention that sexual experience prefigures the adult character supplies perhaps the clearest instance of his use of synecdoche. He has been understood as saying that only the neurotic character is fixated on the past, that it is typically the neurotic (presumably in contrast to the normal character) who clings to "an infantile state" [29] of sexuality. Actually Freud said much more: that we all do the same. The understanding of normal character through the neurotic character, of health through sickness, is indeed his master trope. Among the specific synecdochal accusations he made against us all are the following: that the first sexual object, the parent, is the model of later love experiences—"there is no love that does not reproduce infantile prototypes"; [30] that infantile sexual sensation prefigures later aesthetic sensation; [31] that infantile sexual curiosity is the model for all later intellectual work, and that the first rebuff of sexual curiosity "has a crippling effect for ever after"; [32] that sexual confidence is the model of self-confidence; [33] that fear of castration is the model of all later fears, such as fear of death [34] and fear of conscience.[35]

Freud's habit of naming character traits in terms of specific bodily organs similarly relies on the synecdochal style. He tells us that generosity arises out of fixation on early erotic sensation in the mouth, stubbornness out of a certain arrestment of interest in excrement,[36] "burning" ambition in earlier enuresis.[37] Since the oral stage means compliancy, Freud can speak of "oral generosity." The anal stage means stinginess; therefore "anal stubbornness," hoarding, avarice, pedantry, and the like. Because the urethral stage evokes a period of childhood exhibitionism and rivalry, adults may suffer from "urethral ambition." Or, in a related set of examples, notice Freud's coupling of basic sentiments with bodily objects and feelings, so that he speaks of "fecal" renunciation, "penis" envy, "castration" fear.

Not only did Freud assume that certain parts of organically locatable experience can be taken for the whole; he further assumed that there is a defining tension between part and whole, between biological and moral component. A given character trait results from the contradiction of some organic drive. Here "contradiction" ought not to be confused with "renunciation." One does not, as in the conventional, ascetic tradition of moral psychology, renounce an organic drive in order to achieve a higher development of character. Freud's notion is more modest: a character trait is a function or sign of "displacement" of a bodily (broadly speaking, sexual) interest. Thus, it is by the repression of fecal interest that the traits of stinginess and pedantry (negative) or cleanliness and insight (positive) are reached.

Freud's general view that character is built through an interlocking system of repressions promises a dialectical specification which he does not really give it. The sequence of bodily stresses and phases hardens, instead, into a law of progressive development: the individual moves from oral stage through anal stage to genital stage. Though Freud does not mean "mouth," "anus," "genitals" in an entirely literal sense in these stages, but rather sees the body as a complex of needs and emotional imperatives, the psychoanalytic dialectic of character does have a direct and concrete reference. The body metaphors were never discarded: first come the genetic energies of the instincts; and, specifying these, motives are collated with "erogenous zones," each with its peremptory and shaping demands upon the organism. Character forms and re-forms in a sequence of acceptances and rejections of the primary sequence of demands.

Freud's law of erotic development follows the familiar positivist sequence: the evolution of man's conceptions of the universe, from animistic, through metaphysical or religious, to scientific. What had been for the great nineteenth-century philosophers of history a theory of the intellectual evolution of society thus becomes for Freud a theory of "the *libidinous* development of the individual." * Where

---

* Freud's synecdoche of intellectual development as libidinal has had enormous influence, especially among the "British school" of psychoanalysts with their related, superior synecdochal theory of the *introjection* (Ferenczi's coinage) of "good" and "bad" objects as a way of explaining thought. To cite only one choice passage representative of this school: "At bottom," the English analyst Edward Glover wrote, "mental function is and continues to be valued in terms of concrete experience. . . . For the unconscious a thought is a substance . . . [and] the nature of the substance depends upon the system of libidinal and aggressive interest in vogue during the formation of a particular layer of psychic organization. . . . During the primacy of oral interest and aggression, all the world's a breast and all that's in it good or bad milk. During the predominance of excretory interest and mental organization, the world

the positivists had moved from the social to the individual, Freud moved from the individual to the social, inferring that

> the *animistic* phase would correspond to narcissism both chronologically and in its content; the *religious* phase would correspond to the stage of object-choice of which the characteristic is a child's attachment to his parents; while the *scientific* phase would have an exact counterpart in the stage at which an individual has reached maturity, has renounced the pleasure principle, adjusted himself to reality and turned to the external world for the object of his desires.[38]

Thus Freud not only correlates mental development with particular phases of sexual development, he sees libido, turned outward upon the world of action, as a goad to progress.

In his elaborate somatography, at once erotic and moral, Freud may be said to have dramatized the body and naturalized the mind. His conception of the moral as attached to a biological function may appear optimistic and progressive, as did the thinking of Cabanis, Prosper Enfantin, and other Utopian bio-moralists of an earlier generation.* But actually, in revealing instances, Freud's method bears him away from optimism. His tropes of genetic development have a singularly reductive effect upon the terminal phase of certain emotions. To assert, as he does, that infantile helplessness is the model of religious feeling [39] hardly leaves the latter feeling uncompromised. To say that intellectual impulses derive from infantile sexual curiosity [40] puts the autonomy of reason in question. To find a common denomi-

---

at one time is a genital cloaca, at other times a phallus. The overlappings and interdependence of these main systems give rise to the multiplicity and variety of fantasy formations. One element is however common to all phases . . . and all varieties of fantasies . . . the element of aggression, direct or inverted. So all the substances in the world are benign or malignant, creative or destructive, good or bad" (*International Journal of Psychoanalysis*, 1931). See also Melanie Klein, "Personification in the Play of Children" (1929), "A Contribution to the Psychogenesis of Manic-Depressive States" (1934), and other papers in *Contributions to Psychoanalysis, 1921–1945* (London: 1948).

* Freud's method of offering organic parts for moral wholes suggests resemblances with the writings of Carl-Gustav Carus, whose daring books at the borderland uniting physiology and psychology Freud kept in his library. Another beginning at a synecdochal system, using organs of the body to represent states of mind, is evident in the *"physiologie réligieuse"* of Prosper Enfantin, the important disciple of Saint-Simon. See his collection of essays, *Le Science de l'homme*, published in 1858, which depends, in turn, on the work of Cabanis.

nator for bravery and cowardice, cruelty and tenderness, all in their sexual origins thins the line separating virtue from vice and, therefore, alters our attitude toward both.

Freud's use of the analytical tool of synecdoche takes on a significance that is more than rhetorical in his theory of the prototype. A prototype may be defined as an event which is (1) prefigurative, (2) prior in time, and (3) causally related to later behavior. Freud illustrates the concept in an essay "The Dynamics of the Transference" (1912). The childhood capacity to love, he declares there, "forms a cliché or stereotype" in the person "which perpetually repeats and reproduces itself as life goes on." [41] Therapy works by soliciting the patient's libidinal clichés: as all present loves reanimate the affections of the past, so the patient's emotions toward the analyst (the "transference") revive emotions originally felt toward one or the other parent. This transference, necessary to successful therapy, is but one instance of the power of protoypes. Prosaic and even trivial events of the past, as well as the images of authoritative persons (imagoes), have the same power to shape the present. What Freud called the traumatic event, usually an instance of sexual shock—e.g., a threat of castration, seduction (real or imaginary) by an adult—may be understood as a special case of the prototype. His theory of normality—which includes his theory of infantile sexuality—connects, by way of the prototype, with his psychopathology, with its search for the trauma, the past injury to the emotions which produces an obsessional rite or a hysterical symptom. Not all prototypical experiences are traumatic, but all traumas are, by definition, prototypical—that is, prefigurative of later experience.

Even when the term "prototype" is understood in this general sense, however, there is still no warrant for believing that early experiences necessarily provide the motive power for later experiences of the same kind—and even for later experiences of a different kind. Indeed, to decide what are experiences of the same kind constitutes a dilemma, in logic and in life, unresolved even by Freud's unsurpassed explanations of the sameness of life. An experience normally originating through one motive may, if it persists, take on successive overlays of contemporary and independent motivation. Freud would seem to have committed the genetic fallacy: while an oak does originate in an acorn, the mature tree cannot be held to be still "essentially" acorn-ish.

The psychoanalytic ideal of normalcy is to be guided by motives which have freed themselves from their prototypes. But most people are not so guided and, therefore, not normal. It is because Freud took normalcy as an ideal, not as a statistical average, that he found sickness—the failure to become emancipated from one's past—far more prevalent in the world than do his anti-geneticist critics. Those who read Freud as urging the reduction of every experience to its earliest source are mistaken. He neither reduced the prototype to fixed elements nor dissolved it in a dynamic developmental notion. It was, rather, the prototype as a superfluous emotion operating dynamically in the present that provided him with his therapeutic target.

Freud's doctrine of the past as it is embodied in the prototype suffers by his repudiation of the distinction expressed in Aristotle's contrast between *ethos,* disposition of character, and *pathos,* emotion in a given situation. If, for analytical purposes, a choice had to be made, mine would be for the more concrete pathos; this was the choice of Stoic psychologists in their conception of "passions"—forces which could, in certain circumstances, overthrow a person's native disposition. Freud loses in psychological delicacy by making ethos pre-eminent, so that a person's natural bent, the trajectory of development in his character, is held to influence and, in fact, overwhelm any action in the present. To equate character with destiny, as Freud does, is familiar and profound. But familiar profundities may obscure those decisive idiosyncracies that preserve the possibility of surprise in every life. Mental constitution and experience combine in more arbitrary ways than Freud admits. Destiny may transform itself into character, rather than character into destiny. Later events in a life-history may stamp themselves on motive, twisting it out of its original shape.

However, Freud's view of the power of the past retains its pertinence and cogency when read in a more limited way, as a psychology of childhood. Though he surely never intends to say that childhood events absolutely determine later behavior, the time of childhood does bear the greatest emotional weight, and its habits do involve the greatest effort of self-overcoming. Prefigurative events, embedded in the psychological system, *can* rise up and buckle the surfaces of character in later years.

Early in his therapeutic work Freud made the discovery that these early events which shape later life may be either actual or symbolic. He learned this from hearing the tales of childhood seduction, or of witnessing parental coitus, recounted by so many of his patients. These were not, as he first thought, actual experiences he heard related but fantasy: when actual experience is insufficient, he realized, the primal imagination steps in to supply the trauma. From this he came to view the imagined as having no less power than the actual. Such a judgment shows his preference for verbal analysis and his genius for assimilating the category of fact to the category of interpretation. The nearest Freud thought he could come to an event was in the patient's statement about it. Indeed, event is thus dissolved into attitude, and whether it ever actually occurred becomes of secondary importance.

This notion of a superior psychological reality, lodged securely in the imagination, became essential to Freud's theory and gave his therapy its peculiarly generous interpretative sanctions. Given the personification of the Mother as experienced by infants not actually deprived of the mother-relation, or the actual idiosyncratic mother-relation as an event experienced differently in each different life, analytic reasoning has a tendency to force the latter into the mold of the former. Cavils against such over-interpreting of the concrete emotional fact in the light of the prototype are legitimate but, used with restraint, this rediscovery of experience as a function of the imagination can be put to remarkable uses. The prototype of one's later relations to women may well be an after-impression of one's mother, while false to the reality of that person. Kings and fathers mean far more to subjects and sons than their actual personal qualities warrant. The conception of the prototype turns our attention to the true fictions of the interior life. In particular, it makes us aware of the extent to which human relations consist in the playing of roles: we are not our individual selves but merely stock characters in the perennial dramatization of the family quarrel.

Freud's habit of synecdoche, valuable as the insights it yields sometimes are, puts a grave limit on his theory of knowing. So far as he may be said to acknowledge the epistemological process at all, it is as a process of taking parts for wholes. Psychoanalysis thus avoids the main problems of human perception.

Perception, in the Freudian canon, may be (1) reductionist, through spatial analogies: the example offered in Freud's dream symbolism, where a variety of elongated objects indicate the male genital; or it may be (2) projectionist, through prototypes: thus present perceptions are interpreted in the light of past images and emotions. What is missing is that whole span of psychic tasks lying between the two extremes of reduction and projection, tasks such as those investigated by Gestalt theory, which finds an ineradicable and completely contemporaneous constructiveness in mental activity. To perceive, in Gestalt terms, is neither to project nor to reduce but to grasp in wholes (even when this grasp, in its zeal, goes beyond realistic indications), thus demonstrating the orderliness and formality of perception.

Freud was not interested in straightforward contemporaneous slices of experience; he refused to treat mind except as a historical process. Therefore the notion of perceptions analyzable in themselves, referable not to past events but to the ever-present aptitudes of mind, is unhappily missing from psychoanalysis. Despite a casual admission that his own work had continued and completed Kant's epistemology,[42] Freud is radically anti-Kantian: he has no theory of *forms* of the mind. On the contrary, his theory of cognition in service to the emotions, the egoistic self, the will, completes the psychologizing of philosophy initiated by Schopenhauer and Nietzsche. Freud begins with the proposition toward which the psychologizing philosophers worked: that mental activity must be explained by a motivation outside itself. With the one notable exception of sexual drives, no thought or feeling is self-explainable to Freud, but must be referred to something earlier or simpler which is being symbolized.

This effort to trace perception back to original and unchanging motives entangled Freud in a net of dubious evolutionist conjecture. Thus he explained dreaming historically—using "historical" in a special sense. The common symbolism of dreams, he said, is a vestige of a "racial heritage" from the language of primitive times.[43] As Erich Fromm has pointed out in *The Forgotten Language* (1951), this assumption is gratuitous.[44] It suffices to say, simply, that dream symbols are a form of the mind. Freudian analysis, in its synecdochal attempt to view all the different stages of a person's life simultaneously, as unified by certain recurring themes, is thematic rather than historical.

V

Freud has been judged a fatalist about character, and with reason. His "laws" of character development are based on certain immutable elements. Sexuality for him is a relatively fixed datum—especially for women, whom Freud conceives as ethically and intellectually limited by their complex libidinal development.[45] Constitutional elements— heredity, organic dispositions—also present a "fixed datum in the problem," one which "sets a limit to our efforts." [46] Moreover, there are the fixed instinctual demands—not malleable, but forming a hard core of character—and the basic eruptive threat of the unconscious. Also fixed are the terrible weights of the individual's past, the bondages to past affections, the burdens of "silence, solitude, and darkness" that even in childhood recreate "infantile anxiety." [47] Finally, the repressive process is seen by Freud as preordained: the determinative sequence of organ interest is fixed, as therefore are the correlative stages of development. Thus, for example, when the interest attached to body wastes (which have some of the value of the self) is diverted onto other objects, like money or possessions, an "anal character" inevitably develops.[48]

We do not find Freud's sense of inevitability congenial. The myth of democratic culture is one of self-confidence and consolation; it is only by accident, we believe, that we are prevented from realizing our fullest selves. Such a belief probably accounts for the popularity in America, especially among nursery-school teachers and psychiatric social workers, of Adlerian versions of Freud. Adler's notion of socially imposed traumas—as evidenced in his substitution of the term "masculine protest" for Freud's biologically grounded "penis envy"— gives promise that through rational education (accompanied by changes in the social order) we may avoid the worst, if not create the best. Psychological theories generally undergo such a softening-up process in the course of being translated into pedagogic cautions and maxims. But Freud's theory does not lend itself to popular homeopathy, despite his insight—upon which the sedulous optimism of many American followers is based—that our injuries are mainly historical, occurring unfortunately in early childhood, before we attain the age of competence in playing the subtle game of seeking pleasure and avoiding pain. This did not mean to Freud that such injuries were accidental, and therefore preventable. On the contrary, he saw them as unavoidable. We are forced to participate in the games of life before we can possibly learn how to use the options in the rules governing them.

Nevertheless, Freud did see free-moving elements in character. Even as an instinct psychology, Freudianism is not static. His insistence on a duality of instincts* means that, although certain definite tendencies accompany each instinct (as specific traits are allied with special bodily interests), characters of opposite kinds may arise out of the same instinct or organ-fixation. An "oral" character may be either too compliant or prone to aggressions and envy. An overdose

---

* At different periods Freud called his two instincts by different names. First he posited a conflict between "ego-instincts" and "sexual instincts"; that is, between instincts preserving the self and those preserving the race. An important work of his middle period, the *Introductory Lectures* (1917), is based on the distinction between sexual instincts, whose motive force is libido, and ego instincts, whose characteristic act is "appropriation" (p. 359).

In later writings (cf. "Analysis Terminable and Interminable," *Coll. Papers* V, 347–50), to emphasize that his meaning of "instinct" was far larger than that of bodily sensation, Freud self-consciously appended to his instinct theory the grand idea which had permeated the physical speculations of the ancient Greeks, of the two opposed principles of solidarity and repulsion, called Eros and Thanatos, Love and Death, out of whose unjust but not entirely destructive antagonism life and the whole world of things are generated.

of the aggressive component may come to the fore as cowardice as well as bullying. By thus making each instinct convertible into its contradiction, Freudianism gains an advantage over less dialectical psychologies: one has both the certainty of instinct and the blank check of ambivalence. Aggressive feelings can issue in a caress, or tender feelings in an act of violence.* Indeed, because the instincts are supposed to exist only in a mixed state, paradoxical emotions become the basis of the Freudian psycho-logic. Love is somewhat predatory, predation is partly an act of love. Freud's analytic taste was attracted, within the relatively harmless pathology of everyday life, to the exotic blends of character, the walking contradictions— the honest liar, the lascivious ascetic, the tender murderer, the pious iconoclast—relished by the sensibilities of such nineteenth-century writers as Dostoevski and Browning.†

Freud's concept of ambivalence complicates his idea that the mind is definitely molded during the first five years of childhood, by introducing into it a subtle and perennial hazard of reversibility. Once laid down by an infantile prototype, a sentiment or trait is difficult to annul; but any character, however fixed, can always be overturned by the sudden emergence of the opposite, "repressed" sentiment or trait. And even beyond the ambivalence installed to begin with in the prototype, Freud acknowledges ways of evading psychic fixity. Despite the overwhelming impact of infantile traumas and the childhood frustrations, there is an inner logic of development by which character emerges from the interstices of family oppression. True, as we have already noted, events may lag behind fantasy: a child need not suffer an actual castration threat in order to develop the appropriate anxiety. Some of the historical inevitabilities of childhood in which Freud believed seemed questionable: is, say, the actual threat of castration as universal as he imagined? Yet, even accepting the darkest psycho-

---

* As, for example, Freud found characteristic in obsessional neurosis, where "regression of the libido to the antecedent stage of sadistic-anal organization is the most conspicuous factor. . . . The impulse to love must then mask itself under the sadistic impulse. The obsessive thought, 'I should like to murder you,' means (when it has been detached from certain superimposed elements . . .) nothing else but 'I should like to enjoy love of you' " (*Introductory Lectures*, p. 301).
† The interest of Poe, Baudelaire, Rimbard, Nietzsche is all in what Browning called "the dangerous edge of things" (*Bishop Bloughram's Apology*, 395–400).

analytic reading of child-life as an incubus upon adulthood, Freud continues to put before us a prospect of growth, however wry.

To be sure, even if fixation is avoided in traversing the stages of the oral-anal-phallic-genital sequence, the chance of regression in maturity remains. If, in maturing, a person can ascend such a ladder, he can descend again; a stage theory of development implies regression as well as fixation and advance.* Only in the last of Freud's characterological stages, the genital, is the threat of regression overcome. If that stage can be reached without too long a delay on the way, the personality becomes relatively invulnerable.

The genital character is characterized, for Freud, by achieved harmony, efficiently deployed energy, directness, and fully employed libido.† So qualitatively different is this final bio-moral type from its predecessors that "genital" becomes a tendentious term, describing the whole man, the normal man in an abnormal society. Although Freud saw it as the terminal stage, genitality is not so much another stage as the abolition of stages. The genital character is an ideal.

What kind of an ideal? A lack of concreteness on Freud's part has allowed critics to accuse him of supporting a conception of the well-adjusted personality. He might indeed have supplied a rationale for the deeply American rage for conformity—the necessary complement to our particular brand of individualism—except for a certain inner reservation which he never abandoned. At most he can be accused of providing the outline for such a conformist ideal, not filling in its specific American content: by genital character he implied, I think, no more than an antonym to the threats of fixity located conceptually in his other character stages.

Nevertheless, there is a fatal lack of commitment about Freud's ideal type. To be busy, spirited, and self-confident is a goal that will inspire only those who have resigned the ghosts of older and nobler inspirations. Freud never understood the ethic of self-sacrifice. The

---

* Of course, as we shall see, Freud did not always condemn regression. The goal of progressive integration is explicit in psychoanalytic theory, but the way is hazardous; and regression may sometimes be wise, a defense in depth—to turn Freud's own military metaphor, a securing of positions on which we may fall back from our cultural overextensions.

† Reacting against Freud's synecdochal use of the word "genital," Karen Horney uses the phrase "the sincere character"; Thomas French, the "integrated" character; Erich Fromm, the "productive" orientation.

omission leaves his humane doctrine a little cold, and capable of sinister applications.

VI

Given his dialectic of progress and regress in character, Freud has been viewed as being on the whole pessimistic about the chances of human improvement. The neo-Freudians accuse him of denying, through his mainly biological orientation, the importance of the individual's positive powers of growth and maturity. But his "instinctualism" or "biologism" is his way of expressing the more fundamental idea, sacrificed by his revisers, of human behavior conceived as *conflict*. By uncompromisingly posing instinct against those forces, within the self as well as in society, which block its development, Freud preserves the most vital function of the individual. His dark vision of the embattled self seems to me truer than the cheery platitudes of his revisers, who assure us that what we need to solve our problems is "genuine warmth and affection" from parents, or better living through a cessation of "excessive demands on the environment" (Horney), or learning to cooperate with "rational authority" while rejecting "irrational authority" (Fromm).* The goals set by the neo-Freudians—the goals of "actualizing" or "realizing" our full potentialities for "productiveness," "maturity," "freedom," "spontaneity" —conceal a wholesale sacrifice of what is challenging and serious in the Freudian insights.

Freud himself does not frequently employ the word "conflict"; oc-

---

* In his statement that "every neurosis is the result of a conflict between man's inherent powers and those forces which block their development" (*Man for Himself*, p. 220), Fromm might seem to be in agreement with Freud. But conflict is for him a secondary phenomenon, since man is fortunately endowed also with "an inherent drive for growth and integration" (ibid., p. 219). And compare the temporizing phrase, "inherent powers," with Freud's unequivocal "instinct."

Fromm argues, moreover, that every person has the capacity to "be alive," which means we are all capable of "productive and integrated living." And here the whole system of neo-Freudian tautologies is exposed. See *Man for Himself*, p. 49: "The mature, productive, rational person will choose a system [of belief] which permits him to be mature, productive, and rational."

casionally he soothes us with the word "dynamic," * much as contemporary American sociology uses the term "interaction" to mask and soften the notion of conflict. The conceptual term "ambivalence" is not a synonym for "conflict." On the contrary, in the concept of ambivalence Freud found the basis for understanding the dialectic whereby conflicts may resolve themselves. His notion of conflict is twofold: the instincts strain not merely against the repressive demands of culture but against the equally repressive demands of other instincts, in fundamental expression of the original "ambivalence of human emotions."[49]

Take, for example, his reinterpretation of family life. Experience begins with a trauma, birth, and the child's unwonted separation from the mother; brothers and sisters do not welcome the newcomer, and there is a chance its parents, consciously or unconsciously, did not want the child either. How constricting, as well as protecting, is the family circle around the child. All family relations are competitive: the children are originally bound by mutual hatred, which is only later repudiated as a sacrifice to parental love. "Being in love with one parent and hating the other" forms part of the permanent "stock of psychical impulses" [50] which arise in early childhood. The child lives in a world of frustration, goaded by unappeasable desires and envies. Childhood neurosis, Freud tells us, "is not the exception but the rule"; it is "unavoidable." [51]

No idea of individuality occurs in Freud—nor, I should say, in any critical psychology—without this prior conception of conflict, both social and intrapsychic. The miseries of childhood are inseparable from the inner logic of character development, for only from within the narrow confines of family tension does character emerge. With the aging, if not the resolution, of the Oedipal conflict, a mature individual finally emerges. So far as individuality is possible, in the

---

* Cf. his conception of psychoanalysis in 1910 as a "dynamic one, which traces mental life back to an interplay between forces that favor or inhibit one another" (SE XI, 213; cf. also *Introductory Lectures*, p. 60). "Dynamics" appears as the positive term; "conflict" is the implicit negative. Fenichel reveals this clearly when he writes: "Psychoanalysis is essentially a *dynamic* discipline. It evaluates given phenomena as a result of conflicts" (*The Psycho-Analytic Theory of Neuroses*, New York, 1945, p. 526).

Freudian conception, it is a complication and a disguise of the conflict between present strivings for independence and past emotional dependencies.

Freud's idea of conflict is central to the various schemes he developed for describing the psychic apparatus. His earliest conception of mental conflict is that contained in the opposition between a conscious and an unconscious mind. This antithesis was never discarded. But relatively late he outlined a new anatomy of the psyche, which is of considerably greater range and subtlety. Here mind is seen as consisting of *three* parts in conflict and balance: an id, an ego, and a super-ego.

The evident excellence of this late tripartite scheme is that it does not simplify the functioning of mind into a conflict between rational and irrational, as modern writers have tended to do. A favorite beginning for treatises on social science—say, Hans Kelsen's *Nature and Society* or Pareto's *Mind and Society*—is first to distinguish between rational (conscious) and irrational (unconscious) motives, and then to proclaim the supremacy of the irrational. But such a proclamation is too easy. To polarize conscious and unconscious, as Freud himself did in his early work, or reason and unreason, as Plato did in the preliminary formula in Book IV of the *Republic* ("The forbidding principle is derived from reason, and that which bids and attracts proceeds from passion and disease," IV, 439), is to give everything to passion and disease, for the passions—Viennese or Greek—are obviously more powerful than reason. To give reason a chance, it is necessary to create a mediator between it and unreason, one which can take the side of either, and which, moreover, has some of the energy which in two-part divisions is assigned entirely to the irrational.

Thus it was that Plato, in his final formulation in Book IV of the *Republic*, divided the mind in three rather than two parts. His word for the mediator which holds the balance of power, the volitional agency that acts on behalf of *either* reason or the appetites, is *thymoiedes*, usually rendered as "spirit" but best translated, I think, as the "personal emotions."

Freud proceeds in a similar way, depicting the psyche in three "parts" or "agencies," each of which has its "special function" with "a fixed spatial relationship between them." [52] * Superficially the three terms, discriminated according to function, recall Plato's; here is the agency of bodily appetite (id), the mediating function (ego), and the guardian of moral prohibitions (super-ego). Moreover, as I have implied, Freud's is, like Plato's, a conflict conception. Thus Freud writes: "Our mind . . . is no peacefully self-contained unity. It is rather to be compared to a modern State in which a mob, eager for enjoyment and destruction, has to be held down forcibly by a prudent superior class." [53]

But there is a difference: for Plato the ruling principle, reason (*logistikon*), is also the source of moral judgment. Freud, however, locates reason in the ego, in the middle position separating appetite (id) from conscience (super-ego). Twice he uses the same image for the ego that Plato uses in the *Phaedrus* for reason. The ego, Freud says, "in relation to the id . . . is like a man on horseback, who has to hold in check the superior strength of the horse." [54] In Plato's image, the rider is at once rational and moral; in Freud's, Greek reason is still the rider, but is disengaged from any moral commitments. Freud insisted that we "keep firmly to the . . . separation of the ego from an observing, critical, punishing agency"; [55] in other words, that we preserve reason from what he considered the tyranny of moral principles embodied in the super-ego.

By awarding the moral impulse "a name of its own" separate from the ego, Freud meant to imply how alien is the social personality (super-ego) from the genuine self (ego). Nevertheless, morality, so far as it is internalized by libidinal coercion ("identification"), draws upon the natural resources of the id. Further, it is a purely "natural" stage in the evolution of character, the Oedipus Complex, which the super-ego replaces.[56] Implicitly Freud presumes that the decisions of

---

* Of course this spatial relation is not meant literally. Freud posits certain "ideal localities or places," carefully avoiding "the temptation to determine the psychic locality in any anatomical sense." The tripartite topography is clearly a moral metaphor, employing the self-evident genetic implications of the spatial values "higher" and "lower." Cf. "A Difficulty in the Path of Psycho-Analysis," SE XVII, 141: "This mind is not a simple thing; on the contrary, it is a hierarchy of superordinated and subordinated agencies."

conscience are invariably irrational; indeed conscience is defined as being—it is a powerful rhetorical affront—no less irrational than the instinctual id. The ego is the real "I"—the Latin word *ego* tends to blur that *—to which the chaos of the "psychological underworld" [57] is less akin than it is to the spurious proprieties dictated by a social conscience.

Genetically, to be sure, Freud views the mind as of a piece. The ego is but an outer portion of the id—crystallizing independently as soon as the infant becomes aware of a physical world different from the self. Then, onto this acceptance of reality lodged in the perceptual system, are superimposed the exhortations of society: first embodied in the figures of the parents and later constituted as a part of the personality, the super-ego. It follows that the super-ego is part of the ego; threaten the former, and the latter is involved, in its own defense. Logically, however, these functions of the mind are distinct. One of the ego's jobs is to subdue the unsociable chaos of the id's desires; another is to keep its own perceptual responses uncontaminated by the super-individual constraints of morality.

This last is not to say that Freud entirely avoids an ethical conception of the ego.† In its task of mediating between the conflicting drives of super-ego and id on the one hand, and the realistic prompt-

---

* Freud's own terms were not "id," "ego," "super-ego"; this is only how *es, ich,* and *überich* have been rendered in translation. When coining the set in 1923, he requested in particular that the "psychical agencies" be called by "simple pronouns" rather than "high-sounding Greek names." Freud preferred to "make use of everyday conceptions rather than throw them away" (*The Question of Lay Analysis,* p. 15). May we not assume that neither would Freud have preferred high-sounding Latin names? The use by English translators of Latin instead of common English pronouns has made the psychoanalytic rhetoric more difficult to appreciate. It should be the "I" (or the "me," as E. M. Forster has proposed) instead of the ego, as it is *le moi* and *el yo* in the French and Spanish translations, respectively; the Latin usage obscures an important significance which the common pronoun directly suggests.

† The link between Freud's perceptual and ethical ideas of the ego is, as we might expect, a genetic one. He posits a "primitive" ego in the infant, which wholly identifies itself with the world (a regression to this state of the ego is how Freud accounts, in *Civilization and Its Discontents,* for the "oceanic feeling" described by mystics). Subsequently, however, this natural ego is beaten down by the external world; the "reality principle" impinges on it, and the ego comes to acknowledge its limitations. It is this mature ego, the order of realistic perceptivity and awareness, with which I am concerned here. Of course Freud presumes that in adults the primitive ego does not disappear, but is conserved, in the unconscious, along with the rest of one's past.

ings of the outer world on the other, the conscious role of the ego becomes representative of the character values of prudence and rationality. The chaotic id and the "rigid" super-ego are the areas of psychic vulnerability; the ego, having flexibility and craft, is Freud's category of resolution.

Notice the pragmatic scope of this ego-control. Freud does not disapprove of the attempt of morality (the super-ego) to prevent the "dangerous instinctual wishes" from being gratified or allowed to enter consciousness. But such impulses, while repressed "from the point of view of consciousness," do survive in the unconscious.* If "the severity of our internal police-force" is too harsh, the psychic equilibrium is upset and "what is repressed contrives somehow to force its way into consciousness or into movement or into both." Then "we are no longer normal: at that point the whole range of neurotic and psychotic symptoms arise." [58] It is not the moral dictates promulgated by the super-ego as such to which Freud objects, but rather that they have failed to integrate the psyche as a going concern. The ego is able to provide a more sophisticated dictatorship, conceding much to the instincts, because it is by definition that part of the mind which receives stimuli and controls the paths of access to motility.

But the "procrastinating factor of thought" which the ego "interpolates between desire and action" [59] is a bureaucratic function. In describing the ego's task as the formal and integrative one of "reducing the forces and influences which work in it and upon it to some kind of harmony," [60] Freud renounces for it all substantive claims. In his view, the ego has no independent source of energy. Thus, while one of its jobs is to curb "the pretensions of the id," [61] Freud insisted that, "from a dynamic point of view," the ego is entirely indebted to

---

* The doctrine of repression is another way of stating the Freudian idea of conflict. (In Freud's earliest papers what he was later to term "repression" was called "defense.") And here at this concept Freud's individual and social psychology are joined, for the fact of repression constantly poses the doubt as to whether society is possible without it. Note that repression is for Freud a function of the ego; it is not society which directly represses, but the ego which employs repression to mediate between the demands of instinct and society. For, ruled by instinct, life would be a nightmare scramble of insatiable desire. This points to the positive function of the repressive process and to its necessity for our preservation.

the id and must use "tricks" to draw "further amounts of energy from the id." The ego, "weak" but crafty, "recommends itself to the id" in place of the id's natural objects, and "seeks to attract the libido of the id onto itself." [62]

Members of the school of "ego psychology" have qualified particularly this weakling conception of the ego, and their revisions should be welcomed so far as they further elaborate the dynamic conception of the ego in psychoanalytic doctrine. If the ego can accomplish all Freud said it can—the sober ego "saves" the foolish id, which, "blindly striving to gratify its instincts in complete disregard of the superior strength of outside forces, could not otherwise escape annihilation" [63]—it cannot also be so passive. On the other hand, it may be charged that the ego-psychology wing of psychoanalysis overestimates the parliamentary capacities of the mind and discounts the negative, conflictual elements which Freud saw in it.

Freud tended to envisage the ego in permanent crisis. He saw its proper—largely arbitrative—activity as "goaded on by the id, hemmed in by the super-ego, and rebuffed by reality." [64] As he sees it, neurosis means a "neurotic ego." * To be ill is to have an ego which "has no single-minded purpose" and "has lost its unity." [65]

There is no neurosis, Freud wrote, without signs of "conflict" between "contradictory and opposed wishes. . . . One side of the personality stands for certain wishes, while another part struggles against them and fends them off." [66] The illness *is* this conflict, characteristically "between the libido and the sexual repression," and the compromises of meaning (the symptoms) generated by the struggle between "these two mental currents." [67] The entire notion of the ego's various "mechanisms of defense," such as repression, as well as of symptom formation, presupposes the idea of conflict.

What hope is allowed for the ego when it "is no longer capable of any proper synthesis" and is torn apart by "discordant impulses, un-

---

* When the ego is forced to acknowledge its weakness, it breaks out into anxiety: reality anxiety in face of the external world, moral anxiety in face of the super-ego, and neurotic anxiety in face of the strength of the passions in the id" (*New Introductory Lectures*, p. 104).

appeased conflicts, and unsolved doubts"? [68] While refusing to minimize the ego's inherent weakness and its triple burden, Freud was not fatalistic. He used a military metaphor. The ego is an army besieged on three fronts. "We must come to its aid." The "civil war" which is neurosis may be resolved. The siege of the ego may be lifted by the analyst who is the ego's "ally from without." [69]

That this notion of a civil war within the mind broaches a deeply serious, even passionate view of life, and that it gives Freud's psychology an essential value over those of his numerous revisers, I do not doubt; yet I cannot agree with those who have found in psychoanalysis a genuinely tragic view of personality. The submission to fate of which tragedy consisted, in preceding ages, means something very different in the age of science. A tragic view does not put an emphasis such as Freud put on the control and manipulation of everyday life, the care and deployment of one's psychological forces. The undertone of tragedy in his doctrine of immutable conflict has superimposed upon it the comic solvent, therapy.

Freud once likened the course of psychoanalytic treatment to the play *Oedipus Rex*—in which a deed long accomplished is slowly brought to light "by skilfully prolonged inquiry, constantly fed by new evidence." [70] But *Oedipus Rex* is the story of a man whose tragedy is that he desired to know too much; the Freudian drama ultimately develops into a comedy of knowledge. A more apt parallel could be drawn with *The Cocktail Party,* in which the conflict between husband and wife ends neither in suicide nor in separation. The psychiatrist, Dr. Harcourt-Reilly, reconciles them; he teaches them to tolerate their mutual tepid unhappiness; and since each character may receive what he desires, in Eliot's play, for Celia, who really desires a martyr's agony, Africa and crucifixion on an ant-hill are prescribed.* So, too, with Freud, who characteristically transforms the tragic themes into comic arrangements, in which guilt and aspiration are to be appeased and placated.

Conflict, Freud thought, need not necessarily issue in neurosis. The privations endured by the libido may be constructive—a possibility

---

* Eliot's play is the unsuccessful attempt of an ironist to reconcile a declining religious ethic with an emerging psychological one.

which allows for unremitting sublimatory ventures on the part of those few, among whom Freud included himself, so irrevocably civilized that their conflicts and repressions can no longer be described as neurotic. And further, he acknowledged that there are cases "in which the physician himself must admit that the solution of a conflict by neurosis is one most harmless and most tolerable socially." The physician is not to be a "fanatic about health." [71] Equally meliorist and practical in spirit are his prescriptions for health, when health is in order—for aiding and strengthening the mismanaged ego by a detailed inventory-taking, the staking out of an area of calm reasonableness within the realm of frenetic emotions generated by the id and the super-ego. Mitigating the gravity of Freud's view of human nature is a hardy confidence in the chances for technological self-mastery, a self-mastery which proceeds through rational interrogations of the past and is nowhere chastened (as was Oedipus) by what is discovered.

Socrates (in Nietzsche's account) fascinated the contest-craving Greeks by offering them a new kind of spiritualized dialectical contest; [72] the psychoanalytic resolutions of conflict are embodied in a dialectical therapy which is itself a kind of sublimation, a transferring of the patient's conflicts to "higher levels," a new "battlefield" where the forces contending for his mind must meet. [73] The untragic promise in Freudianism is this curative use of the ideal of scientific neutrality, embodied in the ostensibly amoral knowledge of the ego. Overtly there is the claim that we may become reconciled to our diseases by becoming engrossed in their symptoms: a kind of theoretic hypochondriasis, as Rivers calls it in *Instinct and the Unconscious*. Covertly, more is expected: that by such knowledge the mismanagements of the past may be not only understood but ameliorated. The therapist's "knowledge" is to compensate for the patient's "ignorance," in order to give the patient's "ego once more mastery over the lost provinces of his mental life." [74]

CHAPTER THREE

THE HIDDEN SELF

One's own self is well hidden from one's own self; of all
mines of treasure one's own is the last to be dug up.
—NIETZSCHE

AMONG Freudians, Freud's self-analysis remains singular. Psycho-analysis begins with a heroic exception to the rule that the self may not know the self, the subject not be its own object. Freud apparently suffered from neurotic crises throughout the decade of the nineties; in the summer of 1897, at the age of forty-one, he embarked upon an epic exploration of himself. "It is hard for us nowadays," exclaims Ernest Jones, "to imagine how momentous this achievement was, that difficulty being the fate of most pioneering exploits." [1] Freud's self-analysis stands outside the tests of his own science; it is like the mystery of the unmoved mover. ". . . uniqueness of the feat remains. Once done it is done forever. For no one again can be the first to explore those depths." [2] The amount of deference to Freud's singularity which analysts (minds, after all, trained to suspect father-images) allow themselves is perhaps warranted. Yet in effect, despite an overlay of belief in the impersonality of science, psycho-analysis is thus linked with Freud's personal development in a way in which scientific doctrines rarely are with the intimate lives of their founders.

What justly gives *The Interpretation of Dreams*—his first psycho-analytic book, for which much of the material is taken from his self-analysis—its high place in the literature of self-reflection lies not so much in the energy and daring of the interpretations as in Freud's preponderantly theoretic interests and equable, detached mood. *The*

Interpretation of Dreams is a great, undisturbed book about a most disturbing subject. While exposing the undignified sources of this or that dream, Freud is neither contrite nor defensive. Though the literature of didactic or Romantic confession yields insights perhaps as commanding, what is distinctive about Freud's writing is its dispassionate attitude toward the self, and especially toward illness, sex, the body. Freud is free from that egoism which improves on honesty. Rousseau, and, following him, many poets of the nineteenth century, laid the ground for the understanding of emotional ambivalence. But the assertive, intrusive ego of Rousseau's *Confessions*—as of confessional poetry in general—makes no claim to tell home truths in so calm a voice. Prior to the Romantic literature of the self, I know of only one writer who, in a mood of urbanity not unlike Freud's, may be said to have resolved the problem of being honest about himself: Montaigne. For their disinterested and pragmatic self-analysis,[3] Montaigne's *Essays* deserve a prominent place among the predecessors of *The Interpretation of Dreams.* Freud's science completes Montaigne's humanism. It continues the strategic retreat of knowing men from a civilization of public authority to a civilized inspection of the private life.

With Montaigne begins the modern distrust of civilization; in Freud that distrust found its theoretician. Our civilization does not encourage introspection. Its emphasis falls on practical success, its popular manuals of self-examination are characteristically tools of trade; in a market economy, emotions too can become exchangeable commodities. Only as Science, made impersonal, does introspection still share the prestige of its older solitary or religious forms. It is as scientific research that Freud validates his own reflectiveness. Scientific good manners require that he apologize, cursorily, for exposing "so many intimate facts" of his own private life in *The Interpretation of Dreams;* the self-exposure is, after all, for the sake of throwing light on previously obscure scientific problems.[4] In the earlier traditions of introspection, the value of such exposures was entirely personal; only thus did they become exemplary. Freud's self-exposure becomes exemplary only as it becomes impersonal. Here is a 180-degree divergence between the moral perspectives of religion and science. Until Ernest Jones wrote his biography, the public at large had little idea of the magnitude of Freud's personal achievement. If, after Jones, there is a tendency to overestimate what had been previously underestimated, this vacillation expresses both the indifference and respect of a culture which has exchanged introspective ideals for various programs of adjustment and action, toward its last great (though defensive) exponent of the introspective art. With Freud, this art takes on some of the qualities of science, and loses its merely personal voice.

I

Freud himself laid out the possible uniqueness of his self-analysis, with reasons more closely related to the technical character of his science. His effort was different both from the religious attempt to know the self as the body's restive tenant, and from the Cartesian construction of mind as exercising proprietorship over the body, as an extension of its substance. For Freud the mind is not so much that which dwells inside the body, speaking metaphorically, as that which forms a sheath for the body. It is mind—by means of its basic unit, the "wish"—which first defines the body's needs. The unconscious, or "primary system," as Freud sometimes calls it, "is unable to do anything but wish." [5] But between the wish and its enactment lies a whole set of psychic snares—repression, partial amnesia, displacement, sublimation. Consequently not merely the neurotic but everyone suffers from "a sort of ignorance." [6] As an *object* of the mind, the body is misunderstood and simplified in a variety of projective and symbolic ways. The complex schemes of mental anatomy which Freud first drew in Chapter 7 of *The Interpretation of Dreams*—and later redrew in *The Ego and the Id*—assert at least this: the instinctual forces are "obscure," [7] and an extensive portion of the unconscious, "the core of our being," will always remain inaccessible to consciousness.[8] Only in his highly metaphoric notion of the "censor" does Freud suggest that there is a portion of the mind which can survey the psychic apparatus in its entirety, responsive to the commands from above yet privy to the permanent revolution below. Generally he stresses the mystery of the unconscious and the futility of trying to penetrate its depths.

Here is a passage Freud italicized to make his point:

> The unconscious is the true psychical reality; *in its innermost nature it is as much unknown to us as the reality of the external world, and it is as incompletely presented by the data of consciousness as is the external world by the communications of our sense organs.*[9]

Freud is hardly so naïve as to think that the senses are primarily conveyors of a message about the external world—a notion heavily qualified even in the eighteenth-century springtime of British empiricism. His notion was not of bodily sensation as a primary datum of experience. The message of bodily drives and sensations is never received directly but comes as an instinctual "idea," and in this form is more or less imperfectly transmitted.* All messages, from inner as well as outer reality, become obscure and need decoding. Although Freud would have regarded a solipsistic attitude about the reality of other selves as neurotic, he does seem to sponsor a provisional and casuistical moral solipsism about inner reality; this provisional solipsism holds good until the mind of the analyst, acting as a supplement to the patient's own, aids the patient in decoding himself.

Psychoanalysis is the triumph in ethical form of the modern scientific idea. It is characteristic of modern science that nature, the object of knowledge, is seen as withdrawn and definitely unlike the way we experience it—this in contrast to ancient and medieval science, which presumed no disjunction between experience and the truth of nature. Freud carried the scientific suspicion of nature into ethics. It was as if, after all the pronouncements of theology and philosophy, after all the indications of experience, we had scarcely begun to under-

---

* From "The Unconscious" (1915), SE XIV, 177: "The antithesis of conscious and unconscious is not applicable to instincts. An instinct can never become an object of consciousness—only the idea that represents the instinct can. Even in the unconscious, moreover, an instinct cannot be represented otherwise than by an idea. If the instinct did not attach itself to an idea or manifest itself as an affective state, we could know nothing about it. When we nevertheless speak of an unconscious instinctual impulse or a repressed instinctual impulse . . . we can only mean an instinctual impulse the ideational presentation of which is unconscious, for nothing else comes into consideration."

stand ourselves. Not only is the external nature examined by the physical sciences basically deceptive, but even more so, Freud insists, our inner nature—the ultimate subject studied by all the moral sciences—lies hidden.

Against the conventional assumption that each knows himself best in his own heart, Freud supports the Nietzschean assumption that each is farthest from his own self and must journey through experience in search of it. He surpasses even the Romantics in his deprecation of mere intellect. He calls into question all self-insight, intuitive as well as intellectual. Not only does Freud anticipate that, when a patient offers a seemly account of his conduct, the analyst will be able to detect aggressive or erotic motives which the patient's account has concealed.* More damaging to the pride of self-insight is the fact that, even as he charges that real motives are generally hidden behind some rationalization, Freud denies the importance of the conscious lie, the deliberate deception of others. It is for its continual self-deceptions that he reproves the ego:

> In every case . . . the news that reaches your consciousness is incomplete and often not to be relied on. Often enough, too, it happens that you get news of events only when they are over and when you can no longer do anything to change them. Even if you are not ill, who can tell all that is stirring in your mind of which you know nothing or are falsely informed? You behave like an absolute ruler who is content with the information supplied him by his highest officials and never goes among the people to hear their voice. Turn your eyes inward, look into your own depths, learn first to know yourself! [10]

The Freudian solution to the ego's fallibilities was to permit the self's knowledge to be directed by the professional acumen of an analytic "other." Despite Freud's own unaided introspective success, a physician is generally needed to play policy adviser to the overdignified sovereign ego, and with his knowledge to correct the ego's ignorance.

To "know thyself" is to be known by another. This was Freud's

---

* But given another theory of motives, as Kenneth Burke points out, one can construct an equally airtight theory of self-deception. The sexual rationalizations and individualistic neuroses of Freudian theory can in turn be discounted by Marxists as ideology, a retreat or escape from the economic facts that are "really" at the heart of our motives.

powerful revision of the Delphic injunction, and by which he intended to make psychoanalysis the most disenchanting of sciences. What Copernicus had done to man's universe, what Darwin had done to man's ancestry, Freud claimed to have done to man's ultimate resource—his reason.[11] Yet no more than Darwin was misanthropic was Freud anti-rationalist. Rather, he was a cautious advocate of the rationalist tradition, registering a very modest claim on behalf of reason for its own sake: only understood as the frailest of mental powers does reason stand an outside chance of hegemony.

Freud appears as a defender of the beleaguered power of reason. Therapeutic intervention is defined as "an instrument to enable the ego to push its conquest of the id further still" [12]—in other words, the rationalist aim of reason vanquishing the passions. Elsewhere Freud describes the "struggle between physician and patient" as a conflict "between intellect and the forces of instinct." [13] No champion of instinctual pugnacity, Freud was rather a critic of the passions. Yet, for the most part, his discounting of self-knowledge was due less to the muffled claims of instinct than to the sharp directives of conscience. He recommends that rational criteria replace, as far as possible, *both* the irrational indulgences of the id and the equally irrational aspirations of the super-ego. But according to his scheme of mental topography, only the super-ego, the moral faculty, is therapeutically accessible. The id is defined negatively, as the inaccessible portion of the psyche,[14] for which nothing can be done except by indirection. By thus implicitly making the id not available to rational admonishment, Freud's therapy takes on a more anti-moral address than he may have intended.

The aim of reason may be either (1) to introduce or to buttress super-ego controls for purposes of efficiency, or (2) to break down rigid and superfluous moral controls. Freud's patients were invariably assigned aims of the second type. These patients were mostly bourgeois women, miserably ascetic, or bourgeois men, imperfectly libertine. They were evidently late Victorians, in the still pejorative sense of the word. Unsuccessfully repressed, they suffered under moral laws in which they still half believed, their neuroses resulting from a genuine punishment by the frayed taboos of conscience. Freud thus concentrates his criticism mainly on the burdens of conscience, not on the hindrances of desire. The first aim, to work toward greater rather than lesser moral engagement, seems therapeutically more common now than in Freud's time. Warnings sounded in recent psychoanalytic literature against the analyst's being too "moralistic" indicates that patients are no longer so ascetic—perhaps a little too free with their desires. In the case of either aim, however, reason's assigned task is to revise the moral faculty, the super-ego.

Far from being wholly a burden, conscience can become a means of self-approval. No doubt in many instances Freud's patients, even as they confessed their moral shortcomings, were ready to discount them. He could not, however, foresee the final twist of the dialectic—that the criticism of criticism could itself become complacent. Freud was wary of the competence of his literate and cooperative patients when they inclined to prove psychological theories instead of themselves.[15] But he seems unresponsive to the ways in which the jargon of a doctrine criticizing self-criticism might itself be used apologetically or aggressively to protect cherished new illusions about the self—indeed, that psychological explanation is peculiarly liable to such uses.

Freud's critique of conscience derives from his conception of it as a deposit of inhibitions and ideals expressive of authority, originally located in the parents. This he formulated in the proposition that the super-ego is the heir of the Oedipus Complex.[16] As his term implies, Freud sees super-ego as imposed or superinduced on the real individual (ego). Given the disparity between the aims of conscience and the instinctual realities disclosed in dreams, all disapproval of the self stands revealed as the blind defensiveness of the super-ego. "Like Oedipus, we live in ignorance of these wishes, repugnant to morality, which have been forced upon us by Nature." [17] Even after their unveiling, the super-ego tries to avert our gaze from the harsh facts of the self. Conscience, not passion, emerges as the last enemy of reason. True self-awareness is impossible until the moralizing voice is retrained, or at least controlled. Freud presumes it is impossible otherwise to be truly self-aware. By destroying what he thought to be the illusion of self-knowledge, he particularly criticized self-criticism, thus defining the scope of analytic intervention. The analyst must teach the patient, product of an ascetic culture, how to keep from censoring himself. Against the rigid moralizing tyranny of conscience, Freud posed a flexible but highly limited administration by the rational ego.

Thus narrowly defined, reason makes a weak champion. Because reason exists at the modifiable superficies of the psyche, at the same time that the psychoanalyst seeks to encourage it his science aims to expose its limits. The kind of intelligence the ego would ideally manifest is modest and practical, not prideful and aspiring. Equipped with a Freudian sagacity about ourselves, we do not hope to abolish the constraints from which we suffer; such hopes are moralizing and utopian, not rational and realistic.

Because it must inevitably criticize the source of super-ego restraints (the parents and, behind them, society), psychoanalysis is compelled, by the turns of its genetic analysis, to be a reformist doctrine. But Freud, the critic of Victorian hypocrisy, is not identical with Freud, the therapeutic pedagogue. Granting an occasional opportunity for opposing reality, the Freudian therapy remains mainly a tutorial in the managerial virtues of prudence and compromise. Healing, in Freud's view, is an empiric art, not a dogmatic one. The psychological expert, whom he proposed as the ego's ally in the world outside, may define for each case that point at which the dangerous variety of drives and impulses can be combined in efficient balance—even as the task of reason itself is to be reasonable, to avoid conflict by compromise.

II

If Freud's theoretic contraction of reason is initially patronizing, his therapeutic use is rich and enthusiastic. How vigorously intellectual are the Freudian case histories in their labors of extracting "the pure metal of valuable unconscious thoughts" from "the raw material of the patient's associations." [18] Even including the didactic analyses of his later years, when he sometimes exhorted his student-patient, rapping on the couch if the right associations were not forthcoming,[19] Freud's therapies could be brilliant intellectual encounters.

A quality of intellectuality is already present in the cases Freud contributed to the volume written with Breuer, *Studies on Hysteria*. The third of these cases, that of an English governess in the family of a widowed Viennese factory superintendent, is characteristic. Besides the usual depression and lassitude, "Lucy R." suffered from delicate but concrete symptoms: recurrent nasal catarrh (with total analgesia) and tormenting subjective sensations of smell. Freud decided these symptoms commemorated the occasion when the patient's employer had severely rebuked her for a trivial leniency with his children. "Lucy R." had, it was plain, a Jane Eyre complex. Freud's aim in treating her was to advance toward the explanation that the girl herself needed to admit to consciousness: her infatuation with her employer. Light dawned on "Lucy R." more quickly than Freud had anticipated. After only nine weeks' treatment, the patient arrived one day, looking

as though transfigured. She was smiling and carried her head high. I thought for a moment that after all I had been wrong about the situation, and that the children's governess had become the Director's fiancée. But she dispelled my notion. "Nothing has happened. It's just that you don't know me. You have only seen me ill and depressed. I'm always cheerful as a rule. When I woke yesterday morning the weight was no longer on my mind, and since then I have felt well."— "And what do you think of your prospects in the house?"—"I am quite clear on the subject. I know I have none, and I shan't make myself unhappy over it."—"And will you get on all right with the servants now?"—"I think my own oversensitiveness was responsible for most of that."—"And are you still in love with your employer?" —"Yes, I certainly am, but that makes no difference. After all, I can have thoughts and feelings to myself."

I then examined her nose and found that its sensitivity to pain and reflex excitability had been almost completely restored. . . .[20]

The confrontation of the matter-of-fact patient and the too sympathetic analyst is a paradigmatic comedy of the Freudian encounter, with reconciliation to things as they are as its classic final scene.

All four of Freud's cases in this volume differ significantly from Breuer's case of "Anna O." Freud's patients were not dramatically disabled by their symptoms. The severest torment of "Lucy R." was a persistent imagining of the odor of burnt pastry; Freud interpreted it as a "memory symbol" of an event which she had forgotten because it was painful. Moreover, while Freud considered himself as still following Breuer's method, his cure proceeded less by the venting of emotion than by the patient's coming to acknowledged the hopelessness of her life-situation. The difference is clear in the most intricate of Freud's early clinical studies, the case of "Dora." (Her analysis occurred at the end of 1900, though not published until 1905.) None of the extreme symptoms of hysteria—cutaneous insensitivities, partial paralysis, impairment of vision—such as had afflicted Anna O., trouble Dora. Hers is the symptomology of a more recent psychoanalytic clientele: a *tedium vitae* attributable to the wearing disorder of her family life, a nervous cough, some fainting spells, and fits of crying. Further, while Breuer had diagnosed the sickness of Anna O. as a failure to express her emotions, Freud diagnosed the sickness of Dora as her failure to understand her emotions.

From the beginning Freud's word—"analysis"—carried a rationalist promise that distinguished it from cathartic procedures. To this was added the precaution of recommending analysis only to especially able minds,[21] as they would have to engage in intellectual combat with Freud. As the case of Dora took its course, Dora would propose explanations of her wretchedness which Freud criticized, countering with his own; or Freud would spin out his arguments, ending with a fair challenge to his patient—"And now, what have your recollections to say to this?"[22] But it was not just Dora's intellectual gifts, remarked by Freud, that made disputation possible. The discursive web of treatment was spun to suit not merely this precocious girl. It characterized the method long after Freud's own stated preference for intelligent patients dropped out of the canon. Regardless of the intellectual facility of the patient, psychoanalysis makes a procedural assumption which necessarily exaggerates the import of the patient's present talk and her understanding of it: that is, it equates the events of the patient's life with her verbal account of them, precisely by treating the verbalisms as telling distortions of the truth. Freud himself does not listen to what the brute symptom might be trying to say. Because he saw *all* behavior as symptomatic, he could concentrate entirely on Dora's statement. To track down a dream, or any actual event, was inessential. As evidence, the recollection of the dream seemed to

Freud relevant as the dream itself, since it was, however distorted, merely a *further* distortion. A dream, the further twist of recollection —these were equally valid documents, forgeries published by the motivations lurking in the background. Thus, in the analytic setting, the event reported is assimilated into its narration. Any point of recall —a day, a year, ten years after—is as good as any other.* Old dream thoughts are anyway included among the new.

By its indiscriminate acceptance of the relevance of every statement,† the Freudian technique of interpretation shows itself to be based on a logic of the coherence behind contradiction to which we are perhaps more accustomed in modern art. Take, for example, the *Merz* paintings put together by the Dadaist Kurt Schwitters during the early twenties. In the attempt to shed conventional aesthetic restraints, Schwitters selected deliberately unartistic materials. One collage of his, of extraordinary brilliance, is assembled from the gutter-pickings in a single city block; I am reminded of Freud's stricture that his method divines things from "the rubbish-heap . . . of our observations," [23] from the collation of the most insignificant details.‡ Schwitters made another collage by tearing up a sheet of heavy blue paper, then dealing out the pieces at random on a sheet of white, pasting these where they fell. In these efforts he meant to demonstrate—and was successful, I think, in doing so—that there is nothing necessarily unartistic within the arbitrary and unplanned.

A similar assumption supports Freudian therapy. As a time limit

---

* For the idea that all dreams may be treated contemporaneously, see *The Interpretation of Dreams*, SE V, 522: "I had long been in the habit of getting my patients, who sometimes tell me dreams dating from earlier years, to interpret them—by the same procedure and with the same success—as though they had dreamt them the night before."

† At least, theoretically. For obvious practical reasons, of course, all elements of the patient's account cannot be subjected to an equally intense scrutiny; although all are equally *relevant,* those which are stressed by the analyst are hardly selected indiscriminately. Cf. Otto Fenichel, *Collected Papers: First Series*, p. 324.

‡ Freud found no contradiction between his assertion that "dreams are never occupied with minor details" and the equally acceptable "contrary view that dreams pick up indifferent refuse left over from the previous day" (*Interpretation of Dreams*, SE V, 589). Cf. also (same page) where Freud explains how, because of "censorship," the dream process finds it easier to transfer psychic intensity to "indifferent ideational material."

the analyst's daily hour is no less arbitrary than the space limit of one block from whose gutter the rubbish was collected. If "Dora" had come for treatment in the afternoon hour between 3:00 and 4:00 instead of between 10:30 and 11:30 every morning, the matter of her associations would have varied somewhat; so would the analyst's interpretations. But the likelihood of such discrepancies left Freud unperturbed. As I have shown in the previous chapter, only in the earliest period of his thinking—when he accepted tales of childhood seduction as literally true—did he assume that some actual event behind the associations and memories was properly within the therapist's grasp. After the initial dismay of recognizing that these seduction anecdotes were mere fantasies, Freud ingeniously put this recognition near the center of his interpretative scheme. Fantasy became psychologically real and therefore as legitimate an invitation to analytic exertion as any actual event. The patient's associations, not the event around which the associations may be woven; the memory of the dream, not the dream remembered—these are the subjects of therapeutic scrutiny.

As certain modern artists have found any combination of materials aesthetically serviceable, so Freud discovered that for a depth psychology the most trivial event, the blankest nonsense has a discoverable, often a profound, meaning. Everywhere motives lie embedded, true meanings are necessarily hidden. Judged by its fanatic search behind all statements for a hidden and therefore truer meaning, the Freudian technique of introspection may be said to measure all communication from the standpoint of pathology. Dada dissolved the line between art and non-art; Freud's determinism merges what is normal, straightforward, to be taken at the surface, with the pathological event whose hallmark it is to conceal and be concealed. The very title, *The Psychopathology of Everyday Life,* reports Freud's annulment of the distinction between normal and pathological. Slips of the tongue, pen, memory; mislaying of objects; fiddling or doodling; random naming and numbering—the most ordinary trivialities may become symptomatic, meaningful, according to Freud's interest in meanings that both conceal and betray some deeper motive. *The Psychopathology of Everyday Life* is actually a study in the psychopathology of communication, in the "double meaning" [24] by which we transmit both what we have to say and what we would like to say.

By dissolving this distinction, Freud broke through the established barriers of intelligibility into rich and largely unworked veins. At the same time, however, his achievement encourages an excess of digging, in which what is significant becomes simply what is underneath. The psychoanalytic expectation is of the sinister; the signposts all point downward, into the dark. Though Freud enriched our conception of what is pathological by allowing the "manifest content" to serve merely as a pointer to what is underneath, he narrows his idea of the meaningful to that which is hidden and dynamic. Yet meaning may not be always coiled and ready to unwind, under analytic probing or at the stronger touch of time. Motives easily and directly expressed, lying on the conscious surface of the mind, may be still more revealing.

Even where manifest content fails to do justice to latent sense, there are, conceivably, explanations other than that the latent sense has been forcibly suppressed. Freud nowhere gives a proper estimate of the liabilities of purely verbal analysis. Yet therapy takes place entirely through the verbal medium; the classical couch posture is designed to deny the patient the distracting sight of the analyst [25] and to confine their interchange to words. But thought is notoriously richer, more various, less distinct than words—especially those mental experiences most highly prized by psychoanalysis, the recollection of dreams and of the events of early childhood. The incompleteness of the manifest account may testify not only to the specialized psychic censorship but, more generally, to the unavoidable lag between sensations and thoughts as experienced and their transaction on the verbal level.* For Freud, however, it is "resistance" to specific ele-

---

* After writing this passage, I came across a similar formulation by the Marxist critic Christopher Caudwell in *Illusion and Reality* (London: 1937), p. 211. Caudwell's extended discussion of Freud is very much worth reading.

In *The Interpretation of Dreams,* Freud declares that the "forgetting of dreams depends far more on the resistance [to the dream thoughts] than on the mutually alien character of the waking and sleeping states." But these are not contradictory explanations for why we forget, or for why, when we do remember, it is with such distortions. One may posit a "resistance" operative in the person awake, not only against this or that socially proscribed intention as expressed in dreams and other symptoms, but an intractability inherent in

ments in the dream that produces a distortion or ellipsis on the manifest level; hence the meaning of their symptoms is beyond even the most intellectually skillful patients. In fact, resistance itself may be a major intellectual skill.

Freud's definition of meaning may be partly discounted as one of the preconditions of therapeutic effectiveness. What he himself characterized as the "heads I win, tails you lose" method [26] wins arguments. And the patient needs to be convinced if he is to be cured. Defeat in the analytic encounter may lessen defeat in life. Scarcely a foundation for objective inquiry, Freud's method is justified by the fact that he aimed, first, not to inquire but to cure. Moreover, his appeal to a dialectical and reconciliatory notion of language (both yes and no, either and or, true and false) ought to be taken seriously. Though, as a logic, it rehabilitates the ambivalences of the primitive mind, as a therapy it claims to cure them.

Primitives, Freud noted, may use the same word for opposites— the same word for strong and weak, young and old, sacred and profane. He gave an example borrowed from philology:

> Since the concept of strength could not be formed except as a contrary to weakness, the word denoting "strong" contained a simultaneous recollection of "weak," as the thing by means of which it first came into existence. In reality this word denoted neither "strong" nor "weak," but the relation and difference between the two, which created both of them equally.*

Put genetically: our ideas arise through comparison, and language retains this burden of double meaning. Put logically: every word, univocal at the superficies, actually combines two emotional valences.† Therefore, the ostensible meaning for a word would indicate to the

---

language itself to the whole quality and complexity of our intimate feelings. Cf. Ernest G. Schachtel, "On Memory and Childhood Amnesia," *Psychiatry,* Vol. 10, 1947, pp. 1–26.

* From Freud's review-discussion of Karl Abel's "The Antithetical Sense of Primal Words" (1910), SE XI, 157–58.

† Freud cites the Scots philosopher Alexander Bain (quoted by Abel): "The essential relativity of all knowledge, thought, or consciousness cannot but show itself in language. If everything that we can know is viewed as a transition from something else, every experience must have two sides; and either every name must have a double meaning, or else for every meaning there must be two names" (SE XI, 159).

trained observer that its complementary other had remained latent and must be ferreted out. Linguistic ambiguity is transformed into the inevitable fact of ambivalence. Language is the prison of feeling, Freud implies. It is impossible to avoid thinking in emotional pairs, for our language and our feeling merely refine ur-words and ur-opposites.[27]

Because treatment is administered entirely through the linguistic medium, the ambience of language becomes a main clue to the contrasts which lurk in the psychic depths. Freud is less than convincing when he claims it is the dreams themselves,[28] not his interpretations, that are witty and ingenious, even playful, in their manipulation of verbal tones. No one who has sampled the unrelenting brilliance of *The Interpretation of Dreams* can doubt that much of Freud's analysis of dreams and other symptoms reflects his own, not merely his patients', intellectual virtuosity. In search of the means utilized by the dream to express its "hidden meaning," [29] he constructs the dream itself as a kind of word pun. He could infer a hidden sexual meaning from the apparently quite asexual "violets" which figured in the dream of a woman acquaintance, on the basis of the "chance similarity" of "violets" with the English word "violate," which was one of the dreamer's associations.[30] An entire neurosis can take the form of an elaborate pun. This was the case with the patient known in the psychoanalytic literature as the "Rat Man," so called because one of his symptoms was an obsessive fantasy that a horrible Chinese punishment, in which the person is tied down and rats allowed to bore their way into the anus, was being carried out on his father and on a lady whom he admired. Freud solved the enigma of his patient's sadistic obsession by "unpacking" the word rat—i.e., amplifying it by means of a number of words allied to "rat" in sound which the patient produced, associating *Ratten* (rats) with *Spielratte* (gambler), with *Raten* (installments, money), with *heiraten* (to marry), etc.[31]

This recognition of the ambiguity of language leads, it is true, to a rather one-sided expansiveness. Thus, in the "violets-violates" example, Freud sees the dream as employing a guileless word to express a sexually weighted thought; it is never the reverse. This view of language, which so constrains the patient's emotional ambience, protects the analyst's interpretative venturesomeness. Such dialectics of emotion and language make it hard to pin Freud down to a single, sexual sense. Even in his most questionable venture in rendering the meaningless intelligible—the dictionary of dream symbols—he always maintained an escape clause. On the principle of verbal ambivalence, he refused to claim that symbolic equations are altogether invariant.[32]

In exposing the underside of the obvious, the Freudian strategy assumes that what is hidden *contradicts* the obvious; in order to save time it can, therefore, be "inferred" rather than "detected." Freud loved the dialectical Jewish joke with its arrogance of inferring. Psychoanalysis itself has much of the cerebrally playful temper of the Middle-European Jew, which Freud evokes in his *Jokes and Their Relation to the Unconscious.* In this book, with its store of Jewish jokes,* we get sharp exemplifications of the personal encounter and struggle for intellectual supremacy sublimated in the logic of Freud's therapy. The model analytic dialogue is between those two Jews who meet on a train. "Where are you going?" one asks. "I'm going to Pinsk," the other replies. To which the first answers, "You say you are going to Pinsk, because you want me to think you are going to Minsk. But I know you are going to Pinsk. So why are you lying to me?"[33]

Ingenuity of inference, however, can lead into crude errors as well as refined truths. In the case of "Dora," one piece of evidence indicating the nature of her neurosis was the girl's unresponsiveness to the sexual advances of "Herr K." Freud assumed that, despite her refusal, Dora *wanted* to accept K. "We never discover a 'No' in the unconscious."[34] Sexual distaste, like other forms of rejection, may be a dishonest emotion, a defensive tactic of conscience against desire. Negation is for Freud (Bergson held a view very similar) a purely "psychological" fact. A denial expresses that revision which follows the disappointment of some expectation. Because a "negative judgement" is simply the "intellectual substitute for repression,"[35] each denial masks an affirmation. A "No" from the patient is "confirma-

---

* Of the two kinds of jokes which Freud tells, the Jewish and the non-Jewish, notice that the Jewish jokes are the non-sexual ones—mostly about food, or forms of social evasion (begging, traveling free, not bathing, laziness), or the comedy of marriage.

tion" of what the analyst has proposed.[36] Thus, when an explanation of his "was met by Dora with a most emphatic negative," he could consider that this "No"

> does no more than register the existence of a repression and its severity. . . . If this "No," instead of being regarded as the expression of an impartial judgement (of which, indeed, the patient is incapable), is ignored, and if work is continued, the first evidence soon begins to appear that in such a case "No" signifies the desired "Yes." [37]

By presuming the patient incapable of an impartial judgment, the therapist is empowered to disregard the patient's denials, substituting a positive feeling for the subject matter of the association. A patient says: "You may think I meant to say something insulting but I've no such intention"; or: "The woman in my dream was not my mother." From this the analyst must conclude: So, she does mean to say something insulting; So, it was his mother.[38] This suspicion of dislikes can sweep dislike away. We are urged to attend to all cases of vehement moral reproof, what people despise and what they loathe. As Georg Groddeck wrote: "You will never go wrong in concluding that a man has once loved deeply whatever he hates, and loves it yet, that he once admired and still admires what he scorns, that he once greedily desired what now disgusts him." [39] But to charge that all aversions betray their opposite is as misleading as to accept all aversions at face value. Rejection is a proper activity of the super-ego. To uncover an acceptance beneath every rejection is to be incredulous of human goodness.

It encourages too easy a cynicism, this principled suspicion of our dislikes. Dora could have turned down Herr K. for several good reasons. Perhaps, at fourteen, she had not yet quite the aplomb to relish an affair with the man who was, after all, the husband of her father's mistress. Possibly she did not find him attractive. What Freud saw was that this female did not respond to the sexual advances of an attractive male; he had seen Herr K. and noted that he was "prepossessing." [40] But, if argued to its conclusion, this logic could make neurosis a sort of *hubris* of distaste; the neurotic makes too many rejections. In rare moments of libertarian sentimentality Freud arrives at such conclusions; mainly, however, he never confuses the sovereignty of personal taste, in love or work, with the slavery of neurotic rejection.

As a therapist Freud had to suspect Dora's prudish objections to erotic games; they had offended her too deeply. Thus, at one time, "the sharp-sighted Dora" was overcome by the idea that she had been virtually handed over to Herr K., her middle-aged admirer, as the price of tolerating the relations between her father and Frau K.[41] Freud admired Dora's insight into this over-intricate affair. He countered with his own more intricate researches into the tangle of her motives. He insisted that, unknown to herself, Dora had got her libido engaged on all the possible levels: that she was at once in love with (of course) her mother, her father, the would-be seducer Herr K., and, at the deepest level, even with Frau K., her father's mistress; this last Freud called "the strongest unconscious current in her mental life" [42] because it was not in any way overt. Dora expressed disbelief. Freud applauds his own persistence; he speaks of using facts against the patient [43] and reports how he overwhelmed Dora with interpretations, pounding away at her argument, until "Dora disputed the facts no longer." [44] But, despite this victory, Freud still had to face the difficulty that if the patient has spun her own "sound and incontestable train of argument . . . the physician is liable to feel a moment's embarrassment." Dora was a brilliant detective too, parrying Freud's own brilliance. Her interpretation of her situation was often so acute that Freud could not help asking himself why his was superior.

In this earnest debate Freud's tactic was not to dispute Dora's logic but to suspect her motives. "The patient is using thoughts of this kind, which the analysis cannot attack, for the purpose of cloaking others which are anxious to escape from criticism and from consciousness." [45] Dora reproaches her father and Herr K. because she wishes to conceal self-reproaches. Her logic covers a deeper passion. Thus Freud by-passed the patient's insight into her environment as part of the misleading obvious; he suspected her reasonableness as an ideological instrument of her neurosis. Years later Freud was to call this the most tenacious of all forms of resistance—"intellectual opposition." [46]

To relax Dora's intellectual tenacity, Freud's tactic was to insinuate a set of self-suspicions until he managed to convince her that she was too logical and reasoned too closely for her own good. Here his skepticism toward intellectual self-understanding is most apparent: let there be insight, yes, but not too much or too soon, for this endangers the credulity basic to cure. He made more allowances than usual for Dora's insight acting as a hedge around her emotions; as it turned out, it was just her intellectual verve that threatened and upset her. Dora's acumen was obsessive. She could not let go of her interpretations; she persisted too much in them, while "a normal train of thought, however intense it may be, can be disposed of." [47] Her exaggeration of rationality was no longer rational.

For the patient Freud advocated a balanced, flexible standard of reason; persisting too long in any train of thought, one resigns "omnipotence" to it. In a curiously exact way, Freud's own therapeutic habits—spinning out beautiful and complicated lines of argument—meet all the requirements of neurotic brilliance; he had, therefore, to exempt at least himself from his critique of obsessive ratiocination.* Esoterically, he approved a self-insight which would be tolerant even of its own conclusions. But these liberal virtues disappear before his own intellectual zealotry. Freud detected meaning in everything, even in the fact that the florin notes with which an obsessional patient paid for his consultations "were invariably clean and smooth." [48]

He saw little contradiction in his double standard of reason. He derogated conventional insight for tending to suppress unauthorized trains of thought—in sum, for harboring all sorts of discriminatory

---

* The relentless quality of their "Freudian labors" upon themselves is reported by Freud's early disciples. Cf. A. A. Brill, *Basic Principles of Psychoanalysis* (New York: Doubleday and Co., 1949), p. 48. In an interpolation in his English translation of *The Psychopathology of Everyday Life* (Modern Library edition, p. 57), Brill reports the flavor of "the pioneer days of Freud among psychiatrists. . . . We made no scruples, for instance, of asking a man at table why he did not use his spoon in the proper way, or why he did such and such a thing in such and such a manner. It was impossible for one to show any degree of hesitation or make some abrupt pause in speaking without being at once called to account. We had to keep ourselves well in hand, ever ready and alert, for there was no telling when and where there would be a new attack. We had to explain why we whistled or hummed some particular tune or why we made some slip in talking or some mistake in writing. But we were glad to do this if for no other reason than to learn to face the truth."

refinements that confused the burdens of conscience with the burdens of consciousness. Whatever the intensities of reasoning allowed the analyst, among his patients Freud discouraged speculative excess as an analogue to paranoia.[49] Reason is championed as the chief "mechanism of defense," to recall the conceptual equivalence suggested in the title of Anna Freud's important book, *Ego and the Mechanisms of Defense* (1936). Reason aspires to no final solutions, but is capable of engineering a judicious easing of overwrought moral—and intellectual—demands. The daily therapeutic session is designed as a uniquely permissive oasis in the patient's life, and part of its liberating intent, as we have seen in the case of Dora, is aimed at the fanaticism of reason itself.

III

From the limited and special kinds of rationality that Freud encouraged in his patients, diverse implications may be drawn. They were to be relaxed and self-permissive intellectually—what he called his "fundamental technical rule." [50] The frame of mind which Freud wished his patients to suppress is that of the "man who is reflecting" and exercising "his critical faculty." A critical temper does not help cure a sick psyche. On the contrary, it leads a patient

> to reject some of the ideas that occur to him after perceiving them, to cut short others without following the trains of thought which they would open up to him, and to behave in such a way towards still others that they never become conscious at all and are accordingly suppressed before being perceived.

The patient is to replace such a self-critical attitude, stemming from the agency of the super-ego, with the self-explorations conducted by the ego, exchange the sort of insight Freud called "reflection" for a more impartial sort he called "observation."

> The self-observer on the other hand need only take the trouble to suppress his critical faculty. If he succeeds in doing that, innumerable ideas come into his consciousness of which he could otherwise never have got hold.[51]

This implicit contrast between the "effort" or "exertion" of conscious-ness and the ease of mind receptive to the "play" of unconscious thoughts [52] may, however, be exaggerated. Freud charges the patient not to "hold back any idea from communication, even if . . . he feels that it is too disagreeable . . . nonsensical . . . unimportant or . . . irrelevant to what is being looked for." [53] But can one ever renounce selective thinking spontaneously? To abandon the restric-tions of logic and theme, the patient must learn an arduous technique. Therapy is both an effort of will and an effort to relax the will. Here is a paradox of the Freudian re-education: only by a strict introspec-tive discipline can the capacity for instinctual pleasure be restored. Freud's program for the recovery of instinctual aptitudes is oddly cerebral. The recovery of the natural proceeds through an intellectual-ization of nature itself.

The relaxed state which Freud commends is said to be analogous, as regards the "distribution of psychical energy," to "the state before falling asleep." [54] The patient's thoughts are to be as involuntary and unpremeditated as the images which tangle in the mind before sleep. To help approximate this state, Freud advised that the patient be literally, mimetically "restful." The patient was to recline comfortably on a couch, so that he would be free from distracting visual sensa-tions and fully "to concentrate his attention on his self-observa-tion." [55] * Here Freud suggests solicitude for the patient's uninter-rupted thoughtfulness. But there are other meanings implicit in the rules of treatment. Posture has been an essential strategy of all spiritual exercises. To be prone (even face up) also suggests sub-mission, a postural analogue to the demand that the patient become intellectually "completely passive." [56] The analytic rule against the

---

* Freud also says that it is "an advantage" for the patient to "shut his eyes," but, as his editors say, "the stress upon the advisability of shutting the eyes (a remnant of the old hypnotic procedure) was very soon dropped." See also "Further Recommendations in the Technique of Psychoanalysis," *Collected Papers* II, p. 354. Also the paper "Freud's Psycho-Analytic Method," from Löwenfeld, *Psychische Zwangserscheinungen Collected Papers* I, p. 266: by reclining, the concentrating patient is to be "spared every muscular exertion and every distracting sensory impression which might draw his attention from his own mental activity."

patient's exercising his critical faculty greatly augments the physician's authority to shape the patient's raw verbal profusion.

I do not mean to overstate Freud's claim for the analyst's authority. A successful analyst must not press his creative aims too hard; the material easily becomes recalcitrant. Freud had occasion to reproach himself for just such excess of intellectual zeal when Dora abruptly broke off treatment after only three months, while his "hopes of a successful termination . . . were at their highest." Coming at a time when he lacked confidence that he could cure his patients at all, Dora's "unmistakable act of vengeance" needed explaining, for he knew the failure was his perhaps more than Dora's. Freud could accept therapeutic failure with the hauteur of a new Prospero ruling unthanked over the old anarchic human nature. "No one," he writes, "who, like me, has conjured up the most evil of those half-tamed demons that inhabit the human breast and seeks to wrestle with them, can expect to come through the struggle unscathed." In this case, however, the half-tamed demon was not evil, but only Dora's neurotically overdeveloped sense of good. The fact that it escaped, only half tamed, evidently rankled. Freud asked himself whether he had been too exacting, too coldly scientific, whether a show of "warm personal interest" might have thawed Dora's resistances, and avoided an abortive ending to the case.[57] A regrettable miscalculation. He had thought he "had ample time. . . and the material for the analysis had not yet run dry." [58]

If excessive argumentation had been the difficulty in the case of Dora, Freud took the lesson to heart. Gradually he closed the gap, open since the period of the hypnotic and abreactive techniques, between such rational standards as he authorized for the patient and those for the analyst. In papers on technique written between 1912 and 1915, two decades after the Dora case, he warned analysts, as they must warn their patients, against intellectualizing the encounter. Both were to let their minds wander in conscientious illogicality. Despite the didactic tendencies of his own therapeutic habits,* Freud

---

* Cf. the interpretative forcing of Dora's two dreams, and his later, hortatory training analyses as reported by Joseph Wortis, in *Fragments of an Analysis with Freud* (New York: 1954).

warned his physicians against the strict application of reason. The analyst must not only urge the patient "to communicate everything that occurs to him without criticism or selection," but also Freud suggests he

> surrender himself to his own unconscious mental activity, in a state of *evenly suspended attention,* to avoid so far as possible reflection and the construction of conscious expectations, not to try to fix anything that he heard particularly in his memory, and by these means to catch the drift of the patient's unconscious with his own unconscious.[59]

In another passage, Freud says that the analyst "must bend his own unconscious like a receptive organ towards the emerging unconscious of the patient, be as the receiver of the telephone to the disc." [60] Forbidden any intellectual aids, "even of note-taking," [61] the analyst is to learn, like the patient, the high intuitive art of concentrating on nothing in particular. (Freud tells us his own memory was so acute —actually photographic during his school years—that he never needed to take notes.)[62] The required feeling tone for this pedagogy is not a "deliberate attentiveness," which might induce an unbearably professional "strain." It is the "calm," "quiet," "evenly-hovering" awareness best suited to the pursuit of one unconscious by another.* Baudelaire's demand that the poet should be hypnotist and somnambulist combined translates perfectly into Freud's demands upon the psychoanalyst.

Freud's rules for procedural calm issue from a tension made familiar by historians of the Romantic movement—that between reason

---

* *Collected Papers* II, 325, 327: "A conscious effort to retain a recollection of the point would probably have resulted in nothing. . . . The most successful cases are those in which one proceeds, as it were, aimlessly, and allows oneself to be overtaken by any surprises, always presenting to them an open mind, free from any expectations." The analyst must avoid "speculation or brooding" during the analysis itself, although, after the case is concluded, he can of course submit it to conscious examination and scientific formulation.

Ibid., p. 324: "The principle of evenly-distributed attention is the necessary corollary to the demand on the patient to communicate everything that occurs to him without criticism or selection." Attentiveness only creates expectations, and then "there is the danger of never finding anything but what is already known."

and spontaneity. It puts us onto something important about Freud's thought to recall that the opposition of reason and spontaneity gained currency as a notion explaining artistic genius. In England the idea appears as early as Addison (see the *Spectator,* Number 160) and is definitively set forth in Young's "Conjectures on Original Composition" (1759). In France related formulae occurred to Rousseau and, earlier, to Diderot. In Germany the tension appeared in the *Critique of Judgment,* underlying Kant's distinction between scientific and artistic imagination, again in Schiller's *Aesthetic Letters,* and especially in his famous essay "On Naïve and Sentimental Poetry" (1769), this last a document which sheds an immense light on the critical nerve of Freudianism. All these various constructions unite in extolling true art as original and spontaneous, and condemning art practiced by mere intellection. Though the argument flourished first in the arts, in reaction to the strait jacket of neo-classical decorum imposed by critics during the eighteenth century, it can be and has been used against the activity of intellect as such.

After a suggestive passage in Schiller's correspondence with Körner was pointed out to him, Freud explicitly likened "the essential condition of poetical creation" to the regimen of mental relaxation necessary for psychiatric treatment. Freud quoted the passage at unusual length in the second edition of *The Interpretation of Dreams:*

Schiller (writing on December 1, 1788) replies to his friend's complaint of insufficient productivity: "The ground for your complaint seems to me to lie in the constraint imposed by your reason upon your imagination. . . . It seems a bad thing and detrimental to the creative work of the mind if Reason makes too close an examination of the ideas as they come pouring in—at the very gateway, as it were. Looked at in isolation, a thought may seem very trivial or very fantastic; but it may be made important by another thought that comes after it, and, in conjunction with other thoughts that may seem equally absurd, it may turn out to form a most effective link. Reason cannot form any opinion upon all this unless it retains the thought long enough to look at it in connection with the others. On the other hand, where there is a creative mind, Reason—so it seems to me—relaxes its watch upon the gates, and the ideas rush in pell-mell, and only then does it look them through and examine them in a mass. . . . You complain of your unfruitfulness because you reject too soon and discriminate too severely."

The relaxation of meddling reason which Schiller recommends, "the adoption of an attitude of uncritical self-observation," Freud comments, "is by no means difficult." Revived as science, the poet's advice need no longer be limited to a few unusually gifted, if unproductive, creative writers; it describes a state of mind to be sought by everyone. "Most of my patients," Freud adds, "achieve it after their first instructions." [63] Thus the aesthetic attitude of the eighteenth century is rationalized in the psychological attitude of the twentieth.

Of course Freud did not arrive at his own techniques through the study of aesthetics. Even more revealing than the citation of Schiller is a paper which Freud published anonymously, "A Note on the Pre-History of the Technique of Analysis" (1920),* in which he named for free association a more immediate forerunner than Schiller. A volume of essays by the German-Jewish essayist and short-story writer Ludwig Börne was the only book from his childhood that survived in Freud's library. Until it was pointed out to him in 1920, he did not remember the satiric essay in question, "The Art of Becoming an Original Writer in Three Days," nor Börne's specific instructions:

> Take a few sheets of paper and for three days on end write down, without fabrication or hypocrisy, everything that comes into your head . . . what you think of yourself, of your wife, of the Turkish War, of Goethe, of Fonk's trial, of the Last Judgment, of your superiors—and when three days have passed you will be quite out of your senses with astonishment at the new and unheard-of thoughts you have had.[64]

Freud notes, as if to make a scientific point about his lack of originality, that other essays in the same volume kept recurring to his mind, apparently "for no particular reason," over the years. Having acknowledged elsewhere his well-known scientific predecessors in free-

---

* The occasion of the paper was to answer an uncharitably intended comparison, made by Havelock Ellis, between Freud and the Swedenborgian poet and physician C. J. Garth Wilkinson, who had composed (in 1857) a volume of mystic doggerel. Answering Ellis, Freud disclaimed any pretense of originality; the merit of discovery went to him who saw how to use what others had merely handled.

association techniques—Vives, Wundt, Kraepelin, Bleuler, Jung *—
here Freud recalls his older debt to a man of letters; before he was
aware of it, he had become heir to the Romantic insight that equated
artistic creativeness with the process of unconscious truth-telling in
general.

Free association is one technique, among others familiar in the arts,
for inducing spontaneity. As the mantic poets of primitive communities needed to put themselves in a state of possession, modern secular
poets have tried in all sorts of ways to dull the watchfulness of the
conscious mind and to entice upward, as art, the suppressed powers
of the unconscious. De Quincey, for example, used opium. He wanted
to show there is no such thing as forgetting, that "traces once impressed upon the memory are indestructible," † and to prove the existence of a kind of hyper-creativity which would dissolve the line
between art and dream. The self-imposed task which ostensibly led to
his taking up the opium habit—that of becoming a talented dreamer
—sounds very Freudian. Elsewhere De Quincey remarks that he had
heard that Dryden ate raw meat "for the purpose of obtaining splendid dreams: how much better, for such a purpose, to have eaten
opium." ‡ On how to manipulate the creating mind, few artists in the

---

* For brief notices of the scientific precursors of free-association techniques,
cf. *Introductory Lectures*, p. 98; SE XIV, 28.

† Thomas De Quincey, *Selected Writings* (New York: The Modern Library, 1937), p. 847. *The Confessions of an English Opium Eater* were published in 1822; in a sequel (1845), De Quincey insists they were written "to
reveal something of the grandeur which belongs *potentially* to human dreams,"
and only with the "slight secondary purpose of exposing this specific power of
opium upon the faculty of dreaming" (pp. 870, 872).

‡ Ibid., 851. It does not matter that the claim of De Quincey, as well as that
of Coleridge, to open through opium a whole new world of experience for
literary treatment may be disproved. (Elizabeth Schneider has shown, for instance, that Coleridge's "literary 'opium dreams' . . . actually differ little,
save in elaborateness, from an entry made in his diary in 1803 before his use
of opium began . . ." See René Wellek and Austin Warren, *Theory of Literature;* New York: 1948, p. 81.) The analogue with psychological techniques
best explains why this is so. The technique of free association—which Freud
took over from its limited use by Bleuler and Jung—has also opened up a
whole new world of experience for psychological investigation. But no one
contends that it is the technique, free association, which produces these contents. Free association is not itself (any more than the artist's drugs or alcohol
need be) a means of psychic derangement. It is a tool for laying bare already
existent, conventionally deranged expressions of the mind.

last century and a half have not ventured an opinion. Creating under the influence of drugs, twilight states of consciousness, the aesthetics of chance ("the creative accident"), have been intensively discussed as well as practiced. It remained for Freud systematically to translate techniques for eliciting aesthetic sincerity and the free flow of poetic images into a technique of eliciting psychological sincerity and the free flow of therapeutic insight.

IV

One special quality in Freud's posing of the Romantic antipode of reason and spontaneity ought to be noted. In an earlier view, children, more accessible to daily observation than other primitives, were hailed as representing authenticity amid the artificialities of culture. Spontaneity in the child was held superior to the gray deliberateness of the mature individual. On this Freud differed: his opposing of reason and spontaneity belongs to our century and not to the nineteenth, and reflects a change that can be seen in adult art itself. The stress on spontaneity, the mistrust of intellect, persists in contemporary art. But special homage to the child, in the manner of Wordsworth and Coleridge, has plainly waned. Modern prophets of the irrational—from D. H. Lawrence to Henry Miller—are uninterested in the irrational as a regressive capacity. On the contrary, modern primitivism is for adults only, and among adults for only the tough-minded and unnostalgic. Freud is similarly tough-minded. He no more renews the cult of the child than he encourages primitivism in painting. While psychoanalysis has helped democratize art, admitting the art of primitives, children, and even the insane, Freud had no Rousseauian reverence for the irrational and childlike. He did not rediscover the noble savage in the nursery. Thanks to him, we are in fact kinder to children and far less sentimental about them than earlier generations. In contrast with the wistful earlier view of childhood as a golden age of innocence and happiness, psychoanalysis has disclosed in childlife an adult-sized fierceness of sexual desire and frustration. In Freud's transcription of the romantic polarities, the child becomes the problem of the adult, no longer his exemplar.

Freud's great case study of infantile sexuality, "Little Hans," seems as much a study of infantile intellectuality. There is clever Hans tracking down the mystery of how babies are born, despite the frustrating lies of his parents and the baffling intrusions of a professor who likes to collect his stories. Hans's mother and father, determined to bring up their son in the light of psychoanalytic doctrines, had a stolid respect for the traumatic sequence. Freud describes scenes in which "our young investigator" was confused with the conventional lies— stork, God, and all—regarding the sexual facts of life. Apparently the parents (whom Freud reports as among his "closest adherents" [65]) felt duty bound to give Hans the benefit of normal traumas, lest their special know-how untie too quickly the requisite knots in his line of development. This pedant's respect for the inevitability of the traumatic sequence Freud himself shared—if one may surmise from a comment which he made on an incident Hans's father reported. (The "analysis" was conducted by correspondence.) When Hans's mother found the child fondling his penis she dutifully threatened, "If you do that, I shall send for Dr. A. to cut off your widdler. And then what'll you widdle with?" Hans's unregenerate reply was, "With my bottom." On this Freud comments heavily: "He made this reply without having any sense of guilt as yet. But this was the occasion of his acquiring the 'castration complex,' the presence of which we are so often obliged to infer in analysing neurotics, though they one and all struggle violently against recognizing it." [66]

The boy did what he could to help. When his parents appeared to falter, little Hans manfully shouldered the burden of their analytic labor. "We'll write to the Professor," he announced. Dictating some excremental fantasy, he interrupted himself to explain, "I say, I *am* glad. I'm always so glad when I can write to the Professor." [67] Having grasped the principle that the Professor collected sex stories, Hans took to analysis as an intriguing game complete with rules. When his father gave him a cue with some moralizing reproof ("A good boy doesn't wish that sort of thing"), Hans retorted with theoretic exactitude, *"But he may THINK it."* To his father's counter-thrust, "But that isn't good," Hans offered, more ingenuously, a new rule: *"If he thinks it, it IS good all the same, because you can write it to the*

Professor." [68] It was fine sport, this: "Let's write something down for the Professor." [69] The entire case history has an unintended droll effect, partly because Freud himself seems unaware of the drollery.

Little Hans's cure followed the rationalist Freudian pattern. Remission of his difficulty (a phobic fear of horses) followed upon "enlightenment," as Freud calls it. All Hans's anxieties and questions—except the one about the female genital—were evaded, his fears allowed to ripen until the case reached its peripety: the brief single consultation in which child and father sat before Freud and "the Professor" revealed to the long-prepared Hans that *Horse* stood in his mind for *Father*. Directly after the visit with Freud, Hans's father noted the first real improvement: the child played in front of the house for an hour, even though horses were passing by. Henceforth Hans's anxiety steadily abated. When, in their trained incapacity, Hans's parents still hesitated to supply the long-overdue information about the mechanics of birth, Hans took "the analysis into his own hands" by means of the "brilliant symptomatic act" of ripping open a doll.[70] Thereupon his parents were ready to enlighten him. As the case ended, the father wrote, there was just one "unsolved residue." Hans kept "cudgelling his brains to discover what a father has to do with his child, since it is the mother who brings it into the world." [71] On this Freud comments that, had he had full charge, he would have explained the father's sexual task to the child, and thus completed the resolution.

V

While upsetting the Romantic valuations of childhood, Freud maintained the Romantic view of reason. To think of him as a Romantic despite his ardent faith in science involves no contradiction, for though he insisted on the pre-rational core of human nature, Freud remained a rationalist. Indeed, there is a peculiar convergence of the two notions—of the scientific ideal of rational neutrality and the romantic debunking of reason.

Yet Freudianism is not a brand of Romanticism that repudiates mindfulness. Instead, Freud transformed what the Romantics had held as the vice of reason—its power to blight spontaneity—into a therapeutic virtue. Anna O. was wrongly if completely cured by venting her emotions. Little Hans was correctly cured—by rational enlightenment. When he was enlightened as to his real motives, his emotions were checked. No attitude could be farther from the Romantic regard for consciousness as a necessary "disease" (to use Carlyle's word), stunting the neutral instincts, stifling the voice of the blood. With the Romantics, Freud agrees this far: made conscious, the unconscious wish is irremediably tamed.[72] Simply by the act of being brought to consciousness, Freud presumes, the spontaneity of desire will be weakened. On just this Romantic pessimism Freud based the curative hope of his therapy. "After all," he writes, defending the sexual enlightenment of the young Dora,

> the whole effectiveness of the treatment is based upon our knowledge that the affect attached to an unconscious idea operates more strongly and, since it cannot be inhibited, more injuriously than the affect attached to a conscious one.[73]

Psychoanalysis has not sullied Dora's "innocence of mind," Freud protests. Sexuality is far more dangerous when it is seething below the floor of consciousness, out of the regulative reach of conscious judgment. But when the patient is made conscious of her fantasies "to their fullest extent," then she can "obtain command of the interest which is attached to them." [74] Exposed to consciousness, the contradictions of sexual desire lose force. They may be sorted out and, when necessary, prudently conciliated by the ego.

In the *Introductory Lectures,* Freud writes: "Symptoms are not produced by conscious processes; as soon as the unconscious processes involved are made conscious the symptom must vanish." [75] And, a few pages later: "The task of the psycho-analytic treatment can be summed up in this formula: everything pathogenic in the unconscious must be transferred into consciousness." [76] Thus did Freud formally preserve—in his idea that the goal of therapy is consciousness *—a

---

* The crux of the therapeutic process, even for the revisionist schools of Adler, Horney, Fromm, Sullivan, etc., remains this development of insight, though of course it is added that this does not mean "mere intellectual appreciation of the complex of conscious and unconscious patterns operating in one's personality" but an "actual *experiencing* of them." Frieda Fromm-Reich-

strain of Platonic-Enlightenment optimism concerning rational insight: that, knowing what is right, one will do it. But the strain is a faint one. It is conceivable that a patient might make a rational decision for a neurotic value, even after gaining insight into his neurosis and its sources. A patient who is a businessman, after coming to understand that he is "anal" and "compulsive," might decide that these neurotic trends are responsible for his success, and that therefore he would prefer to stay the way he is. Freud never discusses such a possibility, but he implicitly recognizes it by making analysis more than insight—rather, an intellectual conversion, an erotic acceptance. Insight is so personal, so necessarily laden with confirmative emotion that it cannot be called rational.

For yet another reason the psychoanalytic view of insight is only superficially Socratean. To Freud, reason is without content, a technical instrument. Psychoanalytic therapy proposes no substantive program to the ego. The ego's aim is exploration itself, without any set policy except self-consciousness.* Indeed, since reason is a mediating aptitude and not an inclusive end, Freud even intimates that, so long

---

mann has described the process in these words ("Recent Advances in Psychoanalytic Therapy," in P. Mullahy, ed., *A Study of Interpersonal Relations;* New York: 1949, p. 122 f.): "The aim of psychoanalytic therapy is to bring these rejected drives and wishes, together with the patient's individual and environmental moral standards, which are the instruments for his rejections, into consciousness and in this way place them at his free disposal. In doing this the conscious self becomes strengthened, since it is no longer involved in the continuous job of repressing mental content from his own awareness. The patient can then decide independently which desires he wants to accept and which he wishes to reject, his personality no longer being warped or dominated by uncontrollable drives and moral standards. This process permits growth and maturation."

* I am aware that, throughout this chapter, I have been equating analogous parts from schemes of mental anatomy which Freud worked out at different stages of his thought. The "ego" is, of course, not identical with "consciousness," according to Freud—although that part of the ego which is conscious is all there is of consciousness (cf. Chapter Two, p. 61). Freud makes it clear that a large part of the ego is unconscious (*The Ego and the Id,* pp. 15–17). Nevertheless, I think the present equation justified. Cf. Freud's remark in the *Introductory Lectures,* p. 315: "Notice how closely connected the libido and the unconscious, on the one hand, and the ego, consciousness, and reality, on the other, show themselves to be, although there were no such connections between them originally."

as it is of equal intensity, any rational commitment can be as healing as any other.*

Freud presumed there was something more therapeutic than belief itself—he proposed a self-canceling conviction, a therapeutic unbelief. To insist on the tentativeness of reason and the modest gratification of needs is not to install a substitute conviction but to advance unbelief to its logical conclusion. Reason remains a peculiarly instrumental category in the psychoanalytic scheme. Abhorring psychic chaos, Freud does tend to advocate control for the sake of control, its validity confirmed by neurosis—the failure of control. The gain in consciousness and self-control thus becomes its own justification. For rational self-consciousness prohibits self-reproach; if it neutralizes the more violent emotions, and achieves "the restful expression of a self-observer," [79] the powers of reason have been exercised in the best possible way.

Psychoanalysis—at least programmatically—does not aim at achieving a more critical view of the self, as does existentialism, for example, which has sponsored a heightened introspection in order to validate a more negative and critical view of both self and world. Rather psychoanalysis seeks to ease the burden of responsibility and engagement. "Hence arose the technique of educating the patient to give up the whole of his critical attitude," Freud says.[80] Self-criticism is to be replaced by neutral probings. But is this what actually happens? I think not. Here we are at the paradoxical heart of Freud's therapeutic pessimism about the limits of self-knowledge, and his dubious strategies for freeing the self from tyrannies of which it is ignorant. Due to the emphatic setting in which they are placed, all the Freudian liberations tend to be at odds with themselves. The command to let the mind wander must be at odds with the painstaking *technique* (free association) on which this command is modeled. Similarly, the desire to emancipate the patient from painful memories,

---

* This position was later explicitly developed by Freud's student Otto Rank in his idea of a "will therapy." Rank frankly proposed to cure by replacing neurotic belief with the authority of analytic conviction.[77] In a similar argument the English analyst Edward Glover has urged the high curative value of deliberately inexact interpretations as offering artificial substitute symptoms, which may make the spontaneous symptoms superfluous.[78]

obsessive symbolizings, neurotic anxieties, may be undermined by the vivid concentration upon them. While enjoining a person to be less severe with himself, Freudian analysis may also develop in the patient new qualities of self-suspicion. This medicinal self-knowledge was not intended to serve an ambition higher than the decorous one of psychic harmony or balance. Nevertheless, while aiming to annul the discriminatory powers of conscience, analysis may itself hurt and excoriate. The therapy manufactures a new sort of conscience, one which demands a more accurate and yet more scrupulous self-centeredness.

VI

That the self cannot fully know itself appears, on the one hand, to display a laudable modesty, a new respect for the unfathomable depths of personality. On the other hand, from this deprecation of the possibilities of self-insight issues whatever we might term authoritarian in Freud's own therapeutic posture. Freudianism involves analyst and patient in a cooperative search for insight. But there is every theoretic encouragement for the analyst to assume a monopoly of insight and responsibility for moral direction.

Although he began with an austerely intellectual aim for his therapy —to exhibit to patients their errors and unacknowledged feelings, leaving the life-decisions up to them—in time Freud became convinced of the need for more authority on the analyst's part.[81] In the important papers on therapeutic technique published between 1912 and 1915, a main theme is that analysis may *not* be thought of as a colloquy between equals; it "presupposes . . . a superior and a subordinate." [82] Here Freud projects an image of the analyst as a figure of authority—indeed a rather old-fashioned figure, definitely aristocratic and ascetic. He must fulfill "very exacting requirements"; [83] a "long and severe discipline and training in self-discipline" is necessary; he must have "courage"; [84] his character must be "irreproachable." [85] Even more important than what the analyst really is as a person are the emblems necessary to his office. Before patients he is never to let down his guard. He must appear "impenetrable to the patient." He must cultivate "coldness in feeling." He is to show nothing, except as a "mirror." [86] There is a place for Socratic irony in the analytic encounter. Although Freud did not recommend that analysts feign equality with the patient, they may begin modestly, as if they did not already know where the talk will lead. In classical Freudian pedagogy, the analyst knows all almost before he begins. He is the relentless detective, with the main outlines of the crime already in his dossier before the victim comes in to lodge his complaint.

As an explanation for patients' not accepting the details which in time fill out the dossier, Freud offers the important concept of "resistance." Built into the therapy, through this notion of resistance, is disavowal of the patient's critical judgment. Indeed, the concept of resistance is itself a mode of attack for the therapist. The entire success of the treatment, Freud declared, rests on breaking down the resistances. Because "the discovery of the unconscious and the introduction of it into consciousness is performed in the face of a continuous *resistance* on the part of the patient," the psychoanalytic therapy may in general be conceived of as "a *re-education in overcoming internal resistances.*" [87] It is the presence of resistance that is the test of significance, the best clue to the importance of the material under consideration. Whatever was important, the patient "resisted." Whatever the patient "resisted" was important.[88] Freud applied his theory of resistance not only to the strategies and compliances of patients, but to the general public's reception of his science. Time has weakened this invincible explanation Freud gave of why his ideas meet objection. It is at least debatable that "no one wants to get to know his unconscious and that the most convenient plan is to deny its possibility altogether." [89] * Nowadays significant numbers of Americans are

---

* Freud's rhetoric when addressing congresses of psychoanalysts contains, as addresses to professional conventions must, some advice to the profession. See the address of 1910, "The Future Prospects of Psychoanalytic Therapy," where a major theme is: everyone resists us with objections that are ostensibly intellectual but really shield emotional objections (SE XI, 141–151). Many "lonely discoverers," Freud wrote, are "tormented by the need to account for the lack of sympathy or the aversion of their contemporaries, and feel this attitude as a distressing contradiction to the security of their own sense of conviction. There was no need for me to feel so; for psychoanalytic theory enabled me to understand this attitude in my contemporaries and to see it as a necessary consequence of fundamental analytic premises. If it was true that the set of facts I had discovered were kept from the knowledge of patients

willing to make the acquaintance of their unconscious. The waiting lists of psychoanalysts are not composed exclusively of desperate cases, nor is the interest of persons on these lists to be dismissed as specious curiosity. Freud has made definite progress in his mission of re-education. But he did not take his popularity more seriously than the antagonism which his doctrines aroused. Nor did he treat serious intellectual objections to his work as essentially emotional resistance.[90] Since he held that psychoanalytic theories, just because they refuse to flatter human nature, *must* be received with hostility, he could repudiate assent to his theories when it was merely "intellectual" as yet another form of resistance. Very properly, he feared detached or partial praise as a resistance even more difficult to overcome than quick blame. No patient is more elusive than the overcooperative one, who would gladly agree with the analyst than lose the argument against him.

Such a tight connection between insight and conviction explains some of the considerable antipathy psychoanalysis has aroused among champions of differing psychologies. While respecting Freud's insistence that his therapeutic method remained unmodified, practitioners of other methods have understandably balked at his suggestion that his theory is somehow exempt from the sort of rational criticism and partial incorporations all theory invites. Psychoanalysis holds itself apart from other theories of the mind, which can be judged impartially; these statements are about *you,* and you are bound to "resist" because you don't want to admit them. Only someone who has been analyzed—i.e., has undergone the extra-intellectual process of learning that comprises analysis—is considered even potentially fit to judge and report the theory.[91] Neither objections nor assent to psychoanalysis are recognized as valid, made from outside the analytic conversion experience.

It is mainly Freud's conception of memory that adds further authority to the role of the analytic pedagogue, already powerfully enhanced by the transference. Memory is, in the most significant sense,

---

themselves by internal resistances of an affective kind, then these resistances would be bound to appear in healthy people too, as soon as some external source confronted them with what was repressed. It was not surprising that they should be able to justify this rejection of my ideas on intellectual grounds though it was actually affective in origin. The same thing happened equally often with patients . . ." (SE XIV, 23–24).

not in the possession of its carrier. While not instinctual as among other animals, human memory is nearly as inaccessible to reason as are the instincts. Indeed, Freud insisted, it is the significant memories which tend to sink below the surface of consciousness.* But even if Freud is right to say that much of our past is shielded by amnesia, there is no reason to assume that what is forgotten and presently unknown is therefore more relevant to the present.

Freud's attack on the veracity of memory took in not only what was *not* remembered. The analyst gains tremendous interpretative latitude through Freud's insistence that memories need not be literal to express psychic reality. To him, as we have seen, the emotion that accompanies the thing remembered gives false memories, fantasies, imagined relations an equal share of psychological truth. Nowhere more than in his consideration of memory does Freud's genius for interpretation lead him toward the danger of overinterpretation. The events he discerned were always curiously ideal: his case histories relate not to an objective past, as in history commonly understood, but to consensus arrived at through an interpretative decision.

Freud acknowledged the suggestive potency of the interpretation in his remarks on dreams which "as it were, lag after the analysis." Sometimes, even with competent patients, "these are the only dreams that one obtains." That is, what has been forgotten is reproduced only after one has constructed the dreams from symptomatic, associational, and other materials. After the interpretation has been "propounded" to the patient, "then follow the confirmatory dreams." [92]

Thus Freud had the courage to understand the cure as possibly circular. Confirmatory dreams, he admits, may well be "imagined in compliance with the physician's words instead of having been brought to light from the dreamer's unconscious." The "very latent dream thoughts that have to be arrived at by interpretation" may be suggested by the analyst. "This ambiguous position cannot be escaped in the analysis," Freud concluded. After all, "unless one interprets, constructs, and propounds, one never obtains access to what is re-

---

* Thus Freud says "those pieces of a dream which are at first forgotten and are only subsequently remembered are invariably the most important from the point of view of understanding the dream" (*Collected Papers* III, p. 121).

pressed." [93] Elsewhere he remarks: "The reconstruction of forgotten experience always results in a tremendous therapeutic effect, no matter whether such reconstructions may be objectively confirmed or not." [94]

If what matters is chiefly the subjective confirmation, does not analysis become a self-confirming process? What defenses against "the suggestive influence . . . inevitably exercised by the physician" can shield both patient and physician from the power of suggestion intrinsic to the analytic situation? Though adhering to the rationalist faith in science as truth, Freud had no illusions about the emancipative power of truth unaided by emotional conviction, or what Newman called the "illative sense." It is through an emotional bond with the physician—the "transference"—that the patient submits himself to the physician's findings about his own life.

The procedural powers of suggestion granted the psychoanalyst should not be overstressed. Although he believed the patient needed to feel the full weight of the emotional authority of the analyst, Freud presumed this necessary and implicit coercion would gradually fade away. Ideally, the suggestive authority incarnated in the transference would spend itself in interpretative self-insight. In therapy, interpretation is chiefly a weapon of ideological reconstitution. Yet, as we shall see, interpretation has a wider validity for Freud than is suggested by its curative task. Even in therapy, interpretation is not merely an agency of suggestion. The analyst's interpretation, although administered authoritatively, acts as a rational counterbalance to the less controllable, irrational procedure of transference. The personality of the physician will fade; the interpretation must remain.

CHAPTER FOUR

THE TACTICS
OF INTERPRETATION

It is only through representation that a thing becomes plain. There is no easier way of understanding it than by seeing it represented. Thus the Ego is understood only as represented by the Non-Ego. The Non-Ego is the symbol of the Ego and serves only to give the Ego an understanding of itself. . . . Vice versa, the Non-Ego cannot be understood except as represented by the Ego and through the Ego as its symbol.

—NOVALIS

A S A STRATEGIST in the wars of truth, Freud habitually insisted that theory and therapy are really the same. Thus truth is identified with its therapeutic and didactic use. Yet the psychoanalytic method of interpretation can scarcely be confined to its use in reinforcing the suggestive authority of the analyst, or as a technique of explanation for the benefit of patients. Freud's methods of interpretation press beyond merely therapeutic uses. His insistence that the unconscious has its own laws, and that no psychic product is without meaning, tends to make analysts of us all. The method of interpretation ranges everywhere. Just as Freud put so much of himself to account—his childhood memories and adult vanities, his amusements and trips, disciples (e.g., little Hans's father), conjugal resentments, observations on his infant daughter's nightmare and his nephew's play—so the psychologically trained man (in or out of the therapeutic regimen) lives alert to the interpretative opportunity; his whole life becomes a source of material for interpretation. Self-conscious about our inner constraints, we are, in that degree, liberated from them, and the analyst's tool, interpretation, broadens out to include modes of insight available to all.

Indeed the patient may even be dispensed with. Freud held that no dream could be interpreted without possessing the free associations of the patient,[1] yet we are also told that the dreamer's associations are unnecessary when one can interpret the dream symbolically.[2] When the important dreams analyzed at length are Freud's own, as in *The Interpretation of Dreams,* this contradiction may pass unnoticed. But in Freud's psychoanalytic study of Leonardo da Vinci (1910) and the essay on Jensen's novel *Gradiva* (1910) it shows plainly. The dead painter Leonardo, and the fictional neurotic Norbert Hanold (the hero of the novel), could not offer their associations, yet an interpretation of their dreams was confidently proffered. And in Chapter Ten of the *Introductory Lectures* (1917), the best discussion of the theory of symbolism after its introduction in 1900, Freud stated that, by means of symbols, the dream may be interpreted "without questioning the dreamer," [3] whom it revealed in spite of his conscious intent—just as the work of art revealed the artist's character, whatever his aesthetic intent.

The same contradiction qualified Freud's deprecation of the patient's capacities for self-understanding. He thought he could interpret his own dreams even better than those of others.[4] Yet elsewhere he says that the dreamer never knows the meaning of his own dream.[5] Even when his patients, whose testimony he offers in evidence, "used one of the common phrases of speech in which . . . symbolism is crystallized," the fact remained "that its true meaning . . . escaped [them]." [6] More is involved here than the assertion that no dream can be interpreted completely.[7] Freud insisted, for reasons noted in the previous chapter, that the dreamer *cannot* know the meaning of his own dream. Even with clever patients and after therapeutic tutelage, there are always resistances which block self-knowledge. Elaborating his dichotomy of conscious- and unconscious-ness, self-knowledge and unknowability, he was led to ordain a quasi-elite (the analysts) able to read the dreams of others (the patients) while they themselves, like Calvinist saints who are still human and are therefore sinners, undergo regular scrutiny at one another's hands as patients. Freud reserved to himself, as he who first found the way, the skill to dismantle his own dreams accurately without another's aid. Nobody psychoanalyzed the first psychoanalyst. Nevertheless, he says in one place that "everyone can submit his own dreams to analytic examination, and the technique of interpreting dreams may be easily learnt from the instructions and examples which I have given." [8] The contradiction here could hardly be more open. Suppose he had proposed that the interpretative method could be practiced by patients upon themselves, without dependence upon an analytic translator in the context of treatment? If the style of interpretation could be learned, patients could know in advance what the symbolism was, could themselves speak (and know they spoke) symbolically.[9] But, as Freud defines it, symbolism is unconscious language. The "dreamer's knowledge of symbolism" is, therefore, "unconscious and belongs to his unconscious mental life." [10] Thus, if the patient held the key to symbolic meanings, a withering away of the unconscious itself would take place.

This paradox returns us to the previous issue: the limits of Freud's analysis. He insists that interpretation can be properly administered only in the setting of therapy. Yet nothing falls outside the range of the "meaningful and interpretable." Whether the dreams of Norbert Hanold were fictitious or represented repressed knowledge on the part of his creator, the novelist Jensen, in no way affected Freud's discussion. "Those dreams which have never been dreamed," Freud wrote, "those created by authors and attributed to fictitious characters in the context of their stories," reveal as much, to the psychoanalytic view, as the dreams of real patients.[11] Freud's interpretative method thus reaches out to embrace all subjects, including those that have not given their consents. In moving from the analysis of persons to the analysis of certain precipitates of psychic life—whether in the special conditions of therapy, ordinary observation, art, or historical record—Freud often strained to combine both interpretative endeavors. But where data or consent from a subject were not available, or in Freud's judgment unnecessary, he did not hesitate to open public worlds like art and religion to a new criticism, at once unremittingly personal and yet able to ignore the person as an impediment to analysis.

The interpretation of dreams was Freud's first and most fruitful discovery. Subsequently he decided that all behavior—not just dreams ("our normal psychosis") but as well a joke or piece of nonsense, a senseless compulsion, a trivial error or slip of the tongue—invites similar treatment. However, all the presuppositions of Freud's technique were embedded first in statements about the dream. It is extraordinary how much this first psychoanalytic book—with the word "interpretation" carefully chosen for its title [12]—can be made to explain. For the originality of psychoanalysis lies chiefly in its hermeneutic skill. This, I believe, is how we should read Freud's insistence that dream-interpretation is the keystone of the entire psychoanalytic structure.[13]

I

What does it mean to "interpret" a dream, a novel, a joke, an event, a life-history, even the history of a whole people? "Why should it have needed any interpretation at all?" Freud asks rhetorically in the early pages of *The Interpretation of Dreams*. "Why did it not say what it meant straight out?" [14]

Freud remarked that it is the peculiarity of dreams—of all symptoms, of which the dream is one—that they need to be elucidated. But this is no explanation. What first needs to be made clear in Freud's method is this: it is not the thing itself, but a representation of it, that is being interpreted. We do not possess the dream in its original form but only as it is recounted, say, in the therapeutic session.* Interpretation cannot approach the emotions directly, but must wait until they are clothed in some representation or statement. Even memory is not enough, until composed in a symptomatic paraphrase

---

* One consequence of this is Freud's basic distinction between the *idea* and its *technique* of expression—a distinction which, as we shall see, had a shaping effect on the Freudian idea of art. So, for example, Freud begins his *Jokes and Their Relation to the Unconscious* (SE VIII, 16) by distinguishing two possible causes of joking: "either the thought expressed . . . possesses in itself the character of being a joke or the joke resides in the expression which the thought has been given."

like the dream. In this light, the endless stream of talk on which psychoanalytic treatment is carried becomes the opposite of a liability, as some have urged; the value of therapy is just its prolonged opportunity for the patient to *formulate* his emotion. Mediated as talk, emotion may be brought before the tribunal of interpretation and appeased. Hence Freud's primary interest in the discursive by-products of emotion—wit, speech errors, dreams, art.

In this tactic of interpretation, the psychoanalytic procedure is not unique but rather branches off from ancient precedent. The text has changed, but the procedure and moralizing intent of psychoanalytic interpretation are better understood when compared with the tradition of religious hermeneutics, which psychoanalysis parodies. As neurosis declares itself by its concrete presence in a symptom,* so it is proper to speak of religion only when religion has emerged from its beginnings in religiosity, undefined feelings such as awe and fear or a diffused apprehension of power, and has been fashioned into more or less definite beliefs, rites, and creeds. (In a parallel way anxiety, or instinctual protest, not yet objectified in symbols but remaining in the unconscious, is inaccessible to the Freudian analyst.) The problem of "interpretation" in religion properly arises only when the vague fact of sentiment hardens into statement. Portions of a religion's canon, appearing at different historical moments, may, as time passes, become a yoke to the culture, a burden from the past—inviting revision, through new interpretations, to accord with notions adopted at a later period of a religion's development.

This notion of interpretation imputes a large measure of sophistication to the religious commentators. In many cases, no doubt, commentaries are written out of the desire to explicate or exhibit the sacred text, with no thought of qualifying it. Thus the Rabbinic scholars kept *Midrash* quite separate from the work of the Hebrew Scriptures, in order to show clearly the work of expansion. Their aim was to remain faithful to the canon while expounding it. However, the exegetical motive does invariably pass over into another—we

---

* The inclusiveness of Freud's idea of a symptom should be kept in mind: ultimately all action is symptomatic. There are "normal" symptoms, like the dream, as well as somatic symptoms like a facial tic or a paralyzed leg.

shall call it the reconciliatory—which is inspired by the perception of some discrepancy within the text, or between it and some other text. Here the problem of the interpreter is no longer one of remaining faithful to the text; the interpreter must alter the literal emphases of that text to conform with some new challenge of document or dogma. Thus we have the subsequent spiritualizing of the Olympian religion by philosophers of a later period in ancient Greek history who refused to ascribe to a deity traits so grossly human as those recorded in Homer and Hesiod. Again, where the Jewish faith came in contact with Greek culture at Alexandria, the philosophic task was reconciliation, and the favorite means (cf. Philo) was to transmute into allegory the literal historical narrative of the Old Testament.

Freud's method is clearly allied to the second of these two styles; it is reconciliatory rather than exegetical. He has little of the modesty of the exegete. His aim is not to bring out literal meaning; the literal meaning, if there is one, becomes a disguise for more significant contents. Trained in the Freudian suspicion of the obvious, no psychiatric interpreter is willing to stay within the limits of a symptomatic text all of whose metaphors and meanings are pressing outward. Psychiatric interpretation always goes beyond exegesis.

As a technique of interpretation, psychoanalysis displays two concerns which stamp it as reconciliatory. First, Freud regularly examines the symptomatic text for disproportionate emphases. Characteristically he will begin the interpretation of, say, a dream, by specifying incongruities within the dream itself: differences in the sensory intensity of single images and in the distinctness of various parts, lacunae or interruptions or partial forgetting, and, above all, absurdity of content. Once granted that the dream, however meager and laconic, is a meaningful text, the interpreter's work is to make sense out of these discrepancies, to order them in a logical translation.

This leads to Freud's second concern: what is authentic? He is able to interpret the dream—or rather, the patient's memory of it—only by "stratifying" it,[15] by constructing a "bottom" layer upon which the discrepancies are presumed to be "superimposed." [16] The genuine part of the dream Freud calls the "latent content"; the dream itself, with all its nonsense, is the "manifest content." The dream (that is, the "manifest" dream) thus substitutes for some other, more genuine, content.[17] The dream is conceived as a complex of assertions taken from different time layers of the dreamer's development. Those originating at an earlier stage are more likely to be covered over, repressed. Lodged in the unconscious, and therefore, in the dynamic sense, unforgotten, the repressed thought continues to participate covertly in the utterance. Repressions both conceal and betray.[18] The psychoanalytic interpreter looks for tell-tale ways in which repressed material manifests itself: in dreams, by the eruption of symbols, distortions of logic and sentiment; in the pathology of daytime, by an unusual arrangement of the patient's words, a forced expression or gesture, an accidental clumsiness.

In traditional hermeneutics, the discrepancies which inspire the interpretative effort are attributed either to accidental mutilation or to secret intention. In psychic texts, discrepancies—breaks in continuity, distortions of content—are always presumed to disclose intention. Mutilations to the psychic life do not occur by chance. More than once in Freud the dreamer's situation is likened to that of a journalist who, in order to evade political censorship, supplies ingenious hints to put the reader on the track of the message which he cannot declare straightforwardly.[19] The political metaphor is particularly apt because the censor, the super-ego, acts not for itself but as deputy for the culture outside it. Freud reads discrepancies between the layers in the dream as a compromise between the demands of nature and the denials of culture. Just as an ethical substrate was discerned by theological or philosophical interpreters beneath the events of the Homeric poems or the Old Testament or the Koran, an instinctual— or, as Freud says in *The Interpretation of Dreams,* the universally "egoistic"—essence of personality is unmasked by the psychiatric interpreter beneath the inconsistencies and civilities of the dream, poem, fantasy, or any symptomatic act.

The reconciliatory mode of religious hermeneutics presupposes a discrepancy between literal text and ethical sense. Even if held to be divinely dictated, the sacred document is recorded at a particular historical moment. But faith discerns in the text a stable meaning which transcends the limitations of its history. The reconciliatory mode of psychiatric interpretation also presupposes a discrepancy—between the literal ("manifest") text and the basic, instinctual meaning. But here ends the analogy between the two hermeneutic styles. The polarity in religion between the manifest literal and the latent ethical exactly reverses the Freudian. What is hidden by the religious text is "high" (or at least "higher"), while what is hidden by the psychic symptom—even a normal symptom like the dream—is "low."

Yet the Freudian interpretation need not invariably oppose the religious. No theologian nowadays abstracts the Bible into sublimities only. The historical method has established that some of the sacred narratives represent untransformed quite worldly, even sensual motives. (See, for example, the long debate about the Song of Solomon.) We have learned to detect the inflation of motives behind religious hermeneutics. Equally, we must learn to detect the deflation of motives behind the inverse Freudian hermeneutics. It is no more true of a psychiatric symptom that its implicit meaning is invariably "low" than it is of a religious text that its explicit content is always "high." *

The location of dreams which express amiable impulses under the debunking category of "hypocritical dreams" † is one example of the inverse Freudian piety toward the sinister. Dreams do not invariably expose those impulses which are suppressed by culture. What is found in nature, below culture, is not invariably egoistic. I would agree with Erich Fromm that dreams express both high and low impulses. Yet undeniably dreams do *primarily* express our irrational and asocial natures; this has been the testimony of moral psychologists since Plato. Fromm's contention that "we often are wiser and more decent in our sleep than in our waking life," suggests, unless it is the darkest irony, the confidence in the fundamental goodness of human nature which characterizes the American view and marks it off from Freud's European perspective—according to which, to produce wis-

---

* To a certain extent, Jung has revived the religious polarity. In opposition to Freud's view that what is to be found in the "nature" below culture is invariably egoistic, Jung interprets dreams as expressing not only a "lower" but also a "higher" nature.

† Thus, in interpreting one of his own dreams, Freud insists that what *appears* in the dream as affection for "my friend R" is really envy, and feelings of rivalry. See *The Interpretation of Dreams*, SE IV, 145 f.

dom and decency there must be a regulative imposition of culture upon human nature. In contending that "the influences we are submitted to in our waking life have in many respects a stultifying effect on our intellectual and moral accomplishments," [20] Fromm, like the other Americanizers of Freud, imputes to the individual that innate morality Freud thought belonged to culture. Freud's view seems closer to the truth. While criticizing culture for its burdensomeness, he respects it as being necessary. Being American, the neo-Freudians have no such conservative respect for culture; they are all too ready to tinker with its machinery of repression in the name of individual fulfillment.

In other ways, however, the neo-Freudians have correctly amended Freud. Fromm is right to accent the amount of intellectual "work" (as Freud called it) in the dream. To Freud's view of the dreamer as a natural poet, one might add that we are all as dreamers naturally intellectual. The effort expended, in dreaming, to outwit the forces of culture is the one recurrent intellectual as well as artistic activity most people perform.* The chief quality of the dream *as interpreted* is not so much its meaning as the elaborateness of its meaningful disguises.

II

By his interpretative method, Freud brought the dream into a continuum with other psychic acts. No longer a special phenomenon of sleep, the dream becomes a basic mode of thinking, revived in waking life whenever the controls of consciousness are relaxed. This reaching out of interpretation into waking life is, I think, even more of a contribution than the discovery of the meaningfulness of dreams. Here is the impressive list of waking acts having significance, as offered in Freud's second psychoanalytic book, *The Psychopathology of Everyday Life:* forgetting proper names, foreign words, the order of words; "concealing memories" (of childhood incidents, etc.); speech blunders and accidental utterances; mistakes in reading and writing; forgetting of impressions and resolutions; mislaying of ob-

---

* See Emerson's comment upon the superior rational character of mental processes in sleep.

jects; erroneously carried out actions; acts of physical clumsiness; chance actions; and intellectual errors.*

It is impossible, Freud tells us, to compose nonsense nonsensically. Every combination of words, even a single name or a number that we "apparently conjure up quite arbitrarily . . . has a definite meaning." [21] Take, as an example, one Freud relates from his own experience. He wrote to a friend (Fliess) that he had finished reading proof sheets of *The Interpretation of Dreams,* and that he intended to make no further changes in the book "even if it contained 2,467 mistakes." Immediately after making this jocose and apparently arbitrary estimate of the number of errors that might be found in his book, Freud took note of what he had said, delivered a brief version of his *obiter dictum* about there being "nothing arbitrary or undetermined in the psychic life," and appended the following account of the determination behind his choice of this number.

Just previous to writing his letter, he explains:

I had read in the paper that General E. M. had been retired as Inspector-General of Ordnance. You must know that I am interested in this man. While I was serving as military medical student, he, then a Colonel, once came into the hospital and said to the physician: "You must make me well in eight days, as I have some work to do for which the Emperor is waiting." At that time, I decided to follow this man's career, and just think, today (1899) he is at the end of it. . . . I wished to figure out in what time he had covered this road, and assumed that I had seen him in the hospital in 1882. That would make 17 years. I related this to my wife, and she remarked, "Then you, too, should be retired." And I protested, "The Lord forbid!" After this conversation, I seated myself at the table to write to you. The previous train of thought continued, and for good reason. The figuring was incorrect; I had a definite recollection of the circumstances in my mind. I had celebrated my . . . *24th* birthday in the military prison (for being absent without permission). Therefore [Freud served one year's com-

---

* Among other involuntary gestures interpreted by Freud as meaningful are: aimless humming, repeated winding of one's watch (*Psychopathology of Everyday Life,* 139). Freudian workers in the field of symptomatic gestures have added others to Freud's list—for example: uncontrollable laughter (Feigenbaum); twitching, cracking of knuckles, and other involuntary gestures (Feldman); use of slang, recourse to special adjectives (Sharpe).

pulsory service], I must have seen him in 1880, which makes it 19 years ago. You then have the number 24 in 2,467. Now take the number that represents my age, 43, and add 24 years to it and you have 67! That is, to the question whether I wished to retire, I had expressed the wish to work 24 years more. Obviously, I am annoyed that in the interval during which I followed Colonel M., I have not accomplished much myself, and still there is a sort of triumph in the fact that he is already finished, while I still have all before me. Thus we may justly say that not even the unintentionally thrownout number 2,467 lacks its determination from the unconscious.[22]

Besides the flavor of the real man it conveys, this little piece of selfanalysis is interesting because it is typical of the Freudian method. While Freud's explanation of the "thrown-out number" may be correct, an alternative explanation suggests itself—the alternative always lurking at the edge of every psychoanalytic interpretation. In this variant explanation, less information comes into play: one need employ only the fact that Freud read in the paper of the general's retirement and tried to recall when he met him. He told his wife that it was in 1882 (when he was 26) but then recalled that it was actually in 1880 (when he was 24). This accounts for the 2 (doubled), the 4, and the 6. It was then 19 years since he had seen General E. M., not 17. And the sum of 2, 4, 6, and 7 is 19. Hence the number 2,467.

Freud's interpretation may be more likely than mine. Nevertheless, it bears two dubious characteristics scarcely ever absent from his interpretative pattern. First, it is very complicated; it includes all sorts of forced motives (resolutions one doubts ever were made, at least not at the age of 24) and is even more arithmetic than the one I have offered (Freud's interpretation involves his present age as well). Second, it assumes as a matter of course that he was hiding something from himself—in this case, the accurate memory of his age. Now, even granting that his failure to recall correctly the year that he saw General E. M. means something, more likely motivations occur. It seems significant that Freud forgot while telling his wife, remembering immediately after. Here is a plausible connection: 1882 was the year in which he met and became affianced to Martha Bernays, and also the year in which he was forced, because of financial difficulties, to abandon a theoretical career in neurology and prepare himself for medical practice.

As a paradigm of the Freudian method on dreams, everyday acts, wit, and art, the example is of course extreme. The Freudian numerology—and, ultimately, large parts of his dream interpretation—suffers from a misplaced effort of logical finesse.*

What Freud's thoughts were when he set down at random the number 2,467, interpretation cannot disclose—not only because of the ever-present hazard of plural meanings but, more fundamentally, because interpretation always *follows,* often at great distance, the event. Freud's technique hooks, say, a dream to associations occurring after—sometimes years after—the dream experience itself.[23] Incontestably, the associations garnered after the dream reveal multiple and genuine linkages within the patient's thoughts. But the claim that these thoughts disclosed by associations are those which originally produced the dream † remains, I think, unreliable. Freud constantly "historicizes" the thought connections of the patient during the analytic session in this way, but his method undercuts any genuinely historical approach. While he presumes that he has disinterred the determinant thoughts of the past, actually his method fundamentally alters the sense of the past and its reality. When he speaks of the dream, he ad-

---

* Freud's scorn for the interest in numbers of his highly speculative friend Fliess might well be applied to himself. Ernest Jones has reported a conversation with Freud, soon after the publication of Fliess's *magnum opus* on physiological periodicity, *Der Ablauf des Lebens* (The Rhythm of Life, 1906). (The close intellectual and personal friendship between Fliess and Freud ended about 1901.)

"I asked him how Fliess managed when one attack of appendicitis occurred an irregular number of days after a previous one. Freud looked at me half quizzically and said: 'That wouldn't have bothered Fliess. He was an expert mathematician, and by multiplying 23 and 28 by the difference between them and adding or subtracting the results, or by even more complicated arithmetic, he would always arrive at the number he wanted' " (Ernest Jones, *Life and Work,* I, 291).

† As Ernest Jones formulates it (*Psychoanalysis,* 4th edition, p. 11). Through the principle of determinism, Freud "maintains that, when a subject is asked to make free associations from a given theme to which he is attending, and wholly to suspend the active selective criticism that under such circumstances is instinctively exercised toward the incoming thoughts, the associations *must* be directly or indirectly related, in a causative manner, to the initial theme." Cf. Freud, "Clark Lectures," SE XI, 32.

mittedly does not mean the dream as such, as it "really" happened, but only the dream as constructed afterward with the aid of the interpreter.* Of *this* dream the associations of the patient are indeed determinative.

Plainly applicable in the case of dreams, the same argument applies also to the minute acts under scrutiny in *The Psychopathology of Everyday Life.* The number analyzed is not the same as the number spoken, any more than the dream dreamed is identical with the dream interpreted. Because reporting the dream itself presents such problems and is invariably incomplete, the latter distinction—between the dream dreamed and the dream interpreted—is patent, while the fidelity with which the brief symptomatic act can be recounted may mislead one into presuming a closer relation, even an identity, between the account in therapy and the original. There is no more warrant for presuming that the motives unearthed by associations to 2,467 are those which *caused* Freud to write down that number than for presuming that the associations recovered in analysis caused a certain dream. Just as it is possible to "reconstruct from a single remaining fragment not, it is true, the dream—which is in any case a matter of no importance—but all the dream-thoughts," [24] so it is possible, from a fragmentary name or number thrown out, to discover *not* the past motivations which produced that number at that time—which, after all, are of no importance to Freud—but an important slab of current daytime thought. Anything can be proved by numbers; witness the example of Freud's friend Fliess's numerology of 23 and 28. Anything can be proved by words; witness the plethora of anagrammatic "proofs" of the real identity of Shakespeare. If the Freudian hermeneutic cannot be applied causally, the fact would seem to deal a serious blow to a science which ostensibly claims insight into historical memory as well as into its psychological forms, and, secondly,

---

* In *The Interpretation of Dreams,* SE V, Ch. 7, Freud freely acknowledges that it is the dream report which is analyzed, not the dream. And he adds that, if the dream report is not "the dream," the dream as dreamed is not either. For they are both distorted under the influence of the censor, and have recourse to the same guises, "dream work," secondary elaboration. Freud even suggests that, when there is less remembered than dreamed—something of which one is often directly aware—this assists the interpreter rather than hinders him.

to give an unlimited license to the suggestive powers of the Freudian interpretation.

Indisputably, all that happens in the mind has, if not "causes," then, say, "meaningful antecedents." But there is no necessary passage from this to an assumption such as Freud made with regard to dream-interpretation: that an explanation can be found for "each sign"—as if "each sign can be translated into another sign having a known meaning, in accordance with a fixed key." [25] Though he did, by conceding that the elements of a dream (like all other symptoms) are "over-determined," avoid part of the practically impossible task of finding a distinct cause for each of these elements, Freud's basic zealotry persists; he dared to assume that everything can be explained.

Like any other model that lies behind scientific explanation, a determinist one can quickly gain independent authority: a model too easily becomes a law. It was once hoped to carry out determinist explanation in physics on a scale comparable to that Freud attempted in psychology; by observing the size and motion of the most minute particles of matter, a new dimension of predictability was to emerge. But then it appeared that the sheer fact of *observing* atomic phenomena changed their velocities, and therefore the relations observed. This ruled out the possibility of perfect prediction. And if determinism and the hope of perfect prediction must be qualified in physics, with all the precision of its quantitative data, how much more likely are they to prove impossible in the case of the physician observing the intangibles dredged up by human self-scrutiny.*

---

* The lesson to psychoanalysis of the failure of physics to execute completely the determinist hypothesis was formulated by Markus Reiner, in the *Psycho-analytic Quarterly,* Vol. I, Nos. 3–4 (October 1932), and repeated briefly by Roland Dalbiez in his *Psychoanalytic Method and the Doctrine of Freud* (1941), II, 298–300.

Freud's one-time follower, the brilliant Otto Rank, was the only one among major writing Freudians of one persuasion or another with an awareness of this problem. In the book whose English title is *Will Therapy* (1929), Rank discusses the objective reality of what the psychoanalyst thinks he observes and treats. He concludes that the substance of neurotic conflict does not inhere in the conflict itself. Rather, he argues, it is constructed under the conditions of psychoanalytic investigation and treatment—an attitude to one's materials which verges on the Machian relativism to which Freud himself was so unsympathetic.

The limits of any model involve its applicability to data. It may be argued that the aggregate of causes active in human behavior is so complex and manifold that there is a categorical difference between this and inanimate causation. If Freud could have extirpated every vestige of his early model of the mind as a machine—mind assimilated to an object in which everything has its place—he might not have been drawn to exceed the logical warrant of the determinist thesis. Possibly he might then have acknowledged that not only do most mental events issue from an *irrational* cause, but also they may owe something to sheer fallibility, accident, spontaneity, play—some motive not to be formulated rationally or assigned a precise equivalent. It seems likely that at least some mental events are better explained not by a motive but by a default of motive. Freud verges on this idea in supposing that certain contents of the mind may become conscious through a "failure of repression." But since he assigns the body's interference with the mind to a secondary place,[26] and thinks of the "accidental" as an unscientific category, repression and its failure become equally determined. Science does not necessarily imply determinism. To be scientific, Freud need not have held that everything must have its explainable equivalent. He seized on the fact that minute equivalents could be offered for irrational acts as making these acts a legitimate subject for scientific study, as if the interior world can be scientifically comprehensible only if it is closed to accident or chance.

Freud's disavowal of the idea of chance may be supported by examples dealing with inanimate objects. The toss of a coin, for instance, involves no element of chance. The way it is held when tossed, the velocity with which it is thrown, the height to which it ascends and from which it returns to the palm, determine the way in which it lands. What we call chance, in such an event, refers to the ordinary inability of our senses to gauge these determining conditions; it is shared ignorance which makes coin-tossing feasible as a way of arbitration. But when we transfer determinism to the psychic world, all that remains of the thesis that mental events are determined is the truism that they can be related systematically to antecedent acts and thoughts. It is possible to estimate, with a certain amount of confidence, the variables which create this temperament or that neurotic disposition—but so far and no farther, in a science of human psychology. Machines can be constructed which will regularize the conditions of coin-tossing so that either heads or tails will appear every time. Happily, nothing like coin-tossing machines yet exists to confirm or artificially reproduce our guesses about the inner life. Therefore, as Freud explains in one of his case studies, the psychoanalyst can reason only *after* the event.

> So long as we trace the development from its final outcome backwards, the chain of events appears continuous, and we feel we have gained an insight which is completely satisfactory or even exhaustive. But if we proceed the reverse way, if we start from the premises inferred from the analysis and try to follow these up to the final result, then we no longer get the impression of an inevitable sequence of events which could not have been otherwise determined. We notice at once that there might have been another result, and that we might have been just as well able to understand and explain the latter.[27]

Freud never made for psychoanalysis the fundamental claim of modern science: the power of prediction. Psychoanalysis, he maintained, is a retrospective science, never a predictive one. While "the chain of causation can always be recognized with certainty if we follow the line of analysis . . . to predict it along the line of synthesis is impossible." [28] One cannot foretell the adult sexual disposition of a five-year-old, even though, according to Freud's belief, the determining factors of health and neurosis are already present in the young child. The fact that however deep the psychoanalysis of character goes, it can never make predictions need in no way impair our confidence in the determinist principle, modestly applied. Neurotic states of mind are systematically meaningful—which is what Freud meant by causation—whether we can predict them or not. Nevertheless, Freud's honest stop, short of the predictive claim, suggests a general caution with respect to his style of explanation. The merely *post hoc* version of the determinist thesis does not support, though neither does it contradict, the total explanatory ambitions of psychoanalysis, in particular the goal of minute explanations for each and every element of a verbal lapse, an error, or a dream.

Still, we need not dismiss the *Psychopathology of Everyday Life* as merely a set of brilliant inferences cemented together by the ingenuity of the analyst. The two-step symbols of waking life and dreams do have meaning, even in the sense Freud assigned. The meaning is imposed, not exposed; to be precise, only after the meaning is imposed does it expose itself. The number 2,467 can mean many things to many people, depending on their ingenuity. It does not become "symptomatic" until it is invested with interpretative interest; then it does reveal a certain angle of the psychological structure. So understood, we may grant Freud's claim for the constant meaningfulness of everyday life.

III

If we consider art, Freud's hermeneutic works less awkwardly. A note Hawthorne added to a sketch for a short story in his journal—"the whole to be symbolical of something"—no more impugns Hawthorne's integrity as an artist than my analysis of psychiatric interpretation impugns Freud's integrity as a psychologist. To create meaning for the patient's random acts indeed resembles literary creation. In both cases, meaning does not emerge out of the raw material of incident and language in a piece, at once. As first the experience is offered, then its larger meanings are inferred by the shaping power of the artist's intellect; so, in the therapeutic bargain, the patient offers the dream (or fantasy or random number or name), and is then asked by the analyst to associate around it, and thereby make it symptomatic. The patient having, so to speak, engendered a symbol, that symbol does tell us a great deal about him—as Freud claims.

Appropriately, psychoanalysis assumes some of the prerogatives of art. For in the Freudian view man is an aesthetic animal, and his symptoms may be comprehended as the artfulness of his will. Illuminated by psychoanalysis, everyday life takes on the appearance of a backstage cluttered with old scenery, every piece symbolic of something. The trained actor picks his way through life, aware of the strange old plots all this detritus still might serve. Untrained, we are nevertheless artful, engaged in a continuous act of deception before the naïve audience of our own consciousness. Freud would have agreed with Emerson that we are greatly more poetic than we know —"poets in our drudgery, poets in our eyes, and ears, and skin." The psychoanalytic view transforms all men into poets—incurable symbolists, betraying unknown secrets with every word. Even as Freud exposes the work of art as little more than an elaborate symptomatic appeal, in a compensatory fashion he dignifies the trivial acts and objects of ordinary psychic life to something meaningful in almost the artistic sense. The likeness of dreamer to artist, as Freud suggested in *The Interpretation of Dreams,* where the dream work is analogized to the craft of the poet,[29] reveals us all at bottom as seekers after everything. When "hard reality" frustrates our wishes, the mind can play Faust safely in its sleep, having recourse to an aesthetic catharsis. By installing in each of us—not just in a privileged class of the talented —a psychic agency for dramatizing motive, Freud democratized art. Art becomes, in his view, a public dream. Equally, the dream becomes an inward artistry lacking the power to communicate * until released

---

* Of course Freud had his forerunners in this conjecture. For one of the few pre-Freudian contributions to the explanation of dreams which still stands up under the weight and detail of the Freudian inferences, see the essay by Frances Power Cobbe, "Dreams as Illustrations of Involuntary Cerebration," in her *Darwinism in Morals and Other Essays* (London: 1872), and especially this passage (pp. 337–38):

"We have been accustomed to consider the myth-creating power of the human mind as one especially belonging to the earlier stages of growth of society and of the individual. [But] this instinct exists in every one of us, and exerts itself with more or less energy through the whole of our lives. In hours of waking consciousness, indeed, it is suppressed, or has only the narrowest range of exercise." But the daytime "play of the myth-making faculty is nothing compared to its achievements during sleep . . . at the very least half our dreams (unless I greatly err) are nothing else than myths formed by unconscious cerebration on the same approved principles, whereby Greece and India and Scandinavia gave to us the stories which we were once pleased to set apart as 'mythology' proper. Have we not here, then, evidence that there is a real law of the human mind causing us constantly to compose ingenious fables explanatory of the phenomena around us—a law which only sinks into abeyance in the waking hours of persons in whom the reason has been highly cultivated, but which resumes its sway even over their well-tutored brains when they sleep?"

It is, I think, a remarkable passage, documenting the early confluence of a rising science of mythology with a rising new psychology. Miss Cobbe was one of that company of first-rate minds, now forgotten, who wrote for the leading quarterly journals of nineteenth-century England and kept at least their section of the public superbly educated.

Otto Rank, in various supplements to Freud's *Interpretation of Dreams* (see

into the public domain by the psychoanalytic method. Although the extension of educated interest beyond the poetry and art of professionals to that of children, primitives, and the insane—the art latent in everyone—antedates Freud's writing, it is mainly under the impact of his ideas that art has become, after dreams, the *via regia* into the depths. The status which Freud awards art has been even more fully exploited by Jung and his followers, who have often taken works of the literary and religious imagination as their chief psychological documents.

The tendency of Freud's theory to normalize art—his idea that we are all artists informally, in the dream, the symptomatic act, the joke —should be balanced against his inclination to retract art into neurosis. He inherited a good deal of that hostility to art which has accompanied the scientific attitude so long as it has been empirical in pretension and practical in orientation. I refer not only to his assumption that the artist is prey to some special weakness from which hard-headed scientists who deal with "reality" are free.[30] Art itself is seen as a distortion of reality, a dangerous incitement against reason. It is as if, in the words of Bentham, "between poetry and truth there is a natural opposition. [The] business [of the poet] consists in stimulating our passions, and exciting our prejudices. Truth, exactitude of every kind, is fatal to poetry." [31] Bentham was, to be sure, more explicitly philistine than Freud. But the utilitarian approach to art need not be overtly disparaging, as Bentham's was, to remain utilitarian. Whenever art is prized for its revelatory value or its usefulness as a cathartic, it is fair to detect the unspoken presence of this same utilitarian divorce between "truth" and "poetry." Even the private tastes of so cultivated a man as Freud express his concern with the usable. At least, so one might explain the fact that he took pleasure in novels, the drama, painting, sculpture—but not in music, the most formal of all the arts and the one least easily mined for nuggets of discursive statement.[32] With the possible exception of music, however, all the arts can be converted into emblems of truth.

"Traum and Dichtung," "Traum and Mythus") and in *Der Kunstler,* draws attention to passages in Wagner's *Meistersinger,* in Schopenhauer and Kant, which suggest this intimate relation of the dream with poetry and myth.

The usable truth Freud acknowledged in art was, of course, of a lower order than that in science. It was hardly an intuitive truth, a truth beyond sense, such as is claimed by champions of art, but rather a special case of scientific truth—of a testamentary kind. Art is, for Freud, alike the material of and testimony to scientific psychological truth.

For the work of art as such, Freud cared very little. He sometimes badly misconstrued a work in his eagerness to use it illustratively. But once we have understood that to Freud the criticism of art promised more than the practice of it, we can no longer fairly read his aesthetic commentary on a particular work with an eye toward its accuracy of assessment. The work of art is something to see through; it is presumably best explained by something other than—even contradicting—itself. Every work of art is to Freud a museum piece of the unconscious, an occasion to contemplate the unconscious frozen into one of its possible gestures.

To be sure, Freud does not merely dismiss the artist after seeing through his art; neither does he merely psychoanalyze him. The artist is gifted in a rare manner for which Freud demands respect and attention. Though lacking the kind of knowledge scientists and men of affairs use, the artist has something better: "psychological insights." Being endowed with capacities to exploit his creative unconscious, the artist can "draw from sources that have not *yet* been made accessible to science." [33] It is indeed the function of psychoanalysis to penetrate the atavistic capacity, to bring it into the orbit of science. But what will happen to the artist when the sources of his inspiration are opened up for study and scientific exploitation? The poet Rilke, for one, when importuned by Lou Andreas-Salome, a friend of his and of Freud, declined to undergo analysis for fear it might sap his creative powers. Probably he was right. Freud implied that science, to the degree to which it is successful, renders art that much less necessary. The great rationalist slogan of psychoanalysis—*Where id was, there shall ego be* [34]—implicitly offers science as the successor not only to religion but to its original handmaiden, art. So far as he takes Freud's rationalist psychology seriously, every artist must face Rilke's option: whether or not to return through psychoanalysis to a grammar school of science in order to learn the sub-artistic meanings of his personal language.

Mediating between Freud's conceptions of art as an escape from reality and art endorsed as a source of psychological insight is the fact of interpretation itself. Because the "depths" from which art is presumed to emerge cannot be expressed directly, a transparent, straightforward, literal art is a contradiction in Freudian terms. As the broadest way into the unconscious, art demands interpretation. Here one thinks of the characteristic modern claim that the literary critic's job is coextensive with that of the creative writer—a claim frequently influenced by psychoanalytic prepossessions. When art is presumed to be generally intelligible in itself—whatever the actual variance in practice—criticism is confined to historical and descriptive tasks. But once it is acknowledged that art can never be directly intelligible, but always conceals meanings and motives that must be dug out, then critical interpretation becomes not a supplementary but an integral and even superior aspect of creativity. Freud provides a model instance of the work of the imagination, the dream. Given "the usual ambiguity of dreams, as of all other psychopathological formations," [35] each dream becomes susceptible to more than one interpretation. Interpretation, Freud concludes, is needed in order to complete the dream; indeed, some "over-interpretation" is always necessary.[36] The present efflorescence of academic literary criticism —which surely has been influenced by the psychoanalytic style of interpretation—follows closely this model relation of neurotic symptom and medicinal interpretation. Works of art are esteemed for their ambiguity, or richness of texture; and some of the great modern pieces of fiction seem deliberately unfinished (*vide* the novels of Kafka), as if inviting the completion of an interpretation, or are themselves constructed as many-layered conundrums, inviting (as James Joyce said of his own works) a lifetime of interpretative meditation to decipher them.

Psychoanalysis, as a science of the emotions, must proceed by indirection. For the Freudian psychology contends that the emotions are prevented from being expressed directly, not only by the weight of authority represented in the culture but by a self-canceling relation among the emotions themselves. Therefore our inner lives are not simply or directly embodied in actions, but become expressive, "symbolic," as the emotions are given distorted and partial discharge. Literature is the guile some personalities develop in exhibiting their deeper emotions. In a more cohesive society the exhibition may take place within the added safety of collective fantasy: religion, myth, superstition. When social enforcements have become frayed—when, as in Kafka's memorable description, all religions have dissolved into sects of one—this drive toward expressiveness takes the form of outright neurosis. Shared expressions fragment into personal aberration, becoming subject to the same sort of analysis that Freud imposed on symptomatic actions. Thus art, as well as religion, is transformed into varieties of emotive statement.

Of course Freud recognized that the emotive statements of art and neurosis differ fundamentally. Within the necessity of interpretation, it is possible to distinguish between art and other psychopathological formations. Although irrational and revelatory, art differs from symptom in the essential that the artist's decision to communicate publicly his fantasies entails a partial grafting of the interpretative function onto the work of art itself. For this reason art is more independent of interpretative mediation than are private neurotic symptoms, such as the dream or the error, which are not meant to be understood. Having shaped and ordered aesthetically his psychic burden, the artist has already acted therapeutically upon himself. In order to make himself understood, the artist must effect at least a primitive kind of interpretative synthesis, and this gives the work of art a special status—as compared with a dream or piece of nonsense.

In the essay "The Relation of the Poet to Daydreaming" (1908) Freud offers this difference, of communicative intent, as a way of setting apart the dream and daydream from more controlled fictions. A work of art is a system of shareable meanings, as a dream or daydream is not; a dream is merely expressive, not art but artistic, while the daydream is of no interest to others.[37] These distinctions imply stages of psychopathological statement with respect to communicative intent—climaxing in art. Thus the dream, even though (as Freud says) not designed to be understood,[38] has a purposiveness and complexity which indicate a degree of immanent meaning not contained in the nonsense word or accidental number; the work of art carries such immanent meaning to an even higher degree, although in no case is the aesthetic production completely meaningful without the capstone of interpretation. Something of the same is implied in the language of the "ego psychology" school of psychoanalysis. According to the late Ernst Kris, a leading theorist of this school, the artist during creation is, like the neurotic, subject to "ego regression." But, in contrast to the neurotic,

> . . . it is a partial and temporary ego regression, one controlled by the ego which retains the function of establishing contact with an audience. The artist identifies himself with his public in order to invite their participation, a participation postulating their subsequent identification with him. No such intention prevails in our patient; . . . basically his speech is soliloquy.[39]

The step from soliloquy to public address is therefore the step from neurosis to art. The artist, unlike the neurotic, has succeeded in inviting an audience to share his emotional prepossessions with him. Only if the neurotic can evoke credence and emotional response in others does he become in this general sense an artist—or perhaps a religious virtuoso.

Surely this makes a difference, and Freud acknowledged it. But the difference is not so great as may appear. Freud continued to assume that the artist, however trimmed and acceptable the public utterance with which he ends, begins at the same sore point as the neurotic. It thus becomes legitimate for the analytic interpreter to cancel out the publicly shareable meanings which distinguish art from fantasy or dream. His job is to transpose public statement back into private intention. Indeed, the successful patient, who makes an identification with a representative public of one, the analyst, himself becomes something of an artist. His art is also a form of catering to his public; he invites it to participate in his emotional life.

On creativity as an intellectual process Freud suggests nothing positive. He conceives of art in the Romantic sense, as evocative of an emotional response through the identification of the artist and his public, not as an expression of detached and thoughtful interest. Literary works, along with religion, supply significant data for Freud's moral science—data to be cross-sectioned so as to get at those stratified deposits of aggressive energy and unsocial wish from which moralities grow. But in Freud's opinion artists, like the pious, cannot really have insight into what they do. No more than religion is art a final resource of judgment; it merely diverts as expression what must be recovered as rational understanding.

A sharp distinction between the expressive and the purposive is missing from Freud's view. One can picture a continuum moving from the most strictly expressive (e.g., nonsense words, arbitrary choice of numbers), toward acts both expressive and purposive (e.g., play, dream, art), toward the almost purely purposive (e.g., an act of physical self-defense). But Freud tended to dismiss as superficial the expressive in itself. Thus he could not accept some dreams, or parts of them, as simply play, spontaneity. In one passage in *Jokes and Their Relation to the Unconscious,* he does suggest that some psychic products might be deemed adequately motivated by the relaxed pleasure which accompanies the playful or spontaneous exertion of the mind. When the psychic apparatus is not employed in seeking some urgently needed gratification, Freud writes, we let this apparatus itself work for the gain of pleasure. "We seek to derive pleasure from its own activity." Freud suspected that "this is in general the condition that governs all aesthetic ideation."[40] But this valuable thought was not followed up.* Characteristically, Freud insisted on the element of utility in mental exertion: thus the dream functions to protect sleep, as a defense against the threat of waking.[41] His tendency to read a maximum purposiveness into every psychic act, as well as his presumption of consistent immanent meanings, assumes too rational a reality behind the irrationalities of psychic appearance.

What characterizes Freudian technique is just this imputation of rationality, this enterprise of recovering the irrational for the rational —beginning with the reduction of behavior to emotive statement, and

---

* Recently the "ego psychologists" have made some use of this idea to broaden Freud's aesthetic view. Cf. Ernst Kris, *Psychoanalytic Explorations in Art* (New York: 1952), p. 315; Thomas M. French, *The Integration of Behavior* (Chicago: 1952), I, 152–53.

proceeding through a more or less set sequence of ingeniously rational interpretations. As Freud says of the dream, it is "only a substitute for a rational process of thought"; it can always be "interpreted—that is to say, translated into a rational process." [42] From its eighteenth-century beginnings in the study of comparative religion, when a universal substrate of natural belief was uncovered beneath the formulas of orthodoxy; through the positivist period in the middle of the last century, when the mythic and metaphysical were reduced to forerunners of the scientific attitude; to the psychological age in which we now live, the main effort of the modern intelligence has been to rationalize not only the production of goods but also our literary and imaginative productions. In this tradition, science characteristically treats works of the imagination as, so to speak, a primitive level of truth—which, uninterpreted, is false.

All the terms—"distortion," "projection," "displacement," "condensation"—which Freud uses in interpreting psychological artifacts such as dreams, errors, art, myth, refer to this double level of truth. The "work" of the imagination is to distort, complicate, individualize, and thereby conceal the potent sub-individual wishes and desires. Exactly the same adaptations to reality prevail in the special kind of symptomatic statement which is art. There is the platitude of motive, and the individual level at which motive is specified in the work of art. From being creative, the artist becomes, in the psychological sense, "recreative." The highest task of psychoanalytic interpretation is to work back through expressive statements to the repressed motive thus hidden especially from its carrier. Art, by Freudian definition, is not only a mode of fulfilling tabooed wishes, of enacting them in fantasy. Perhaps the superior work of the imagination is self-concealment, keeping us at a safe distance from ourselves and from each other. For its power, art depends on an appeal that is hidden from the artist as well as from the audience. Freud can take it for granted that the novelist Jensen could not have understood what he was saying in *Gradiva,* or Leonardo da Vinci what he was painting in "The Virgin and Saint Anne"; otherwise, the appeal of the novel and the painting, first to the artists themselves and then to their audiences, would have been dissipated.

IV

When we turn to the specific techniques of interpretation which Freud proposed, both directly and indirectly, there is one misconception that ought immediately to be dispelled. To solve the enigma of a work of art, Freud bids us look at the artist's "intention." But to stress "intention" (rather than, say, "effect") does not mean that the ⌐rtist's biography is needed to understand his work—the criticism commonly offered against the psychoanalytic view of art—any more than Freud found it necessary to have the associations of the dreamer in order to understand the dream. Freud's term "intention" may be read as something quite impersonal—as when he defined the "meaning" of any mental process as "nothing else but the intention which it serves and its place in a mental sequence." [43] With such a teleological mechanism built into his system, Freud scarcely needs biography to arrive at an appropriate interpretative destination. He no more required a case history of Jensen in order to understand *Gradiva* than he needed to interrogate Jensen's character, Norbert Hanold, in order to understand his dreams. All he needed was to find out "the meaning and content of what is represented in [a] work; I must, in other words, be able to *interpret* it." [44]

The essay on Michelangelo's "Moses," published anonymously in 1914, exemplifies the full range of Freud's hermeneutic techniques. Nothing concerning the personal motives of the sculptor is presumed. Freud goes straight to the statue itself, to establish an exact description of it. Previous critics had assumed that the figure's strained posture and wrathful expression indicate Michelangelo's intent to show Moses about to spring to his feet and hurl the Tables of the Law to the ground. Freud rejects this view.* The Moses figure, for him,

---

* Here Freud introduces somewhat lax aesthetic considerations into his otherwise rigorous interpretation of the statue. I, for one, find unconvincing his point that "Moses" is "part of a whole"—the group of figures on the tomb of "the powerful" Pope Julius II—and it would break "the state of mind which the tomb is meant to induce in us" if one of the six figures appeared to be "on the point of leaping up from its seat and rushing away to create a disturbance on its own account" (SE XIII, 213, 220).

is a man who will remain "sitting like this in his wrath forever." But then, how is one to explain the peculiar contortions of Moses' body? Freud stares the statue into life. He lingers over minute details: the marked turn to the left of Moses' head and eyes while his body faces forward, his lifted foot; but none of these solve the enigma. Finally he locates the right bit of detail: what are the fingers of Moses' right hand doing in the "mighty beard" with which they are in contact? The answer transforms Freud's argument into a paradigm of psychoanalytic procedure. Since he has begun by assuming that the statue does not represent a movement to come, it must represent movements completed in the past. Visualizing the figure as the terminal posture of a series, his case-historian's eye sees a narrative in the detail of Moses' stance. Freud supposes him to have been in three successive postures, which he reconstructs with the aid of drawings. In the first, Moses is calm, his face and body turned to the front. In the second, Moses has just glimpsed the furor around the Golden Calf and passionately prepares to rise; the Tables slip downward between his elbow and right side; he clutches at his beard "as though to turn his violence against his own body." [45] But then, he remembers the Tables and, to prevent them from falling, his right hand retreats and lets go the beard. In position three, the one depicted by the sculptor, we see a Moses frozen in the tension between his wish to preserve the Law and his wish to express his wrath. It is a brilliant iconographic account of Moses' physical posture, leading to a psychological account of his moral posture.

From Freud's analysis of the "motive forces" behind the making of the statue, points of technique can be adduced. One is, as I have shown, the alertness to detail—precisely the ignored detail. At the end of the Moses essay, Freud asks himself:

> What if we have taken too serious and profound a view of details which were nothing to the artist, details which he had introduced quite arbitrarily or for some purely formal reasons with no hidden intention behind? [46]

These are doubts about psychoanalysis itself. But Freud overcame them by a second and supporting point of technique; I shall call it the *temporal* explanation. The insignificant details which supplied the unexpected unraveling of the whole—the anomalies of Moses' hand in beard, the precarious position in which the Tables are held—these must be interpreted "as indicating a preceding movement." [47] This technique of temporal explanation—accounting for the present by referring to a movement which has gone before—seems invariably to have been absorbed into Freud's propensity to explain the present by its remote origins. In my view, however, the temporal strategy of Freud's hermeneutics is more widely applicable than his geneticism.

By the temporal explanation, I mean the manner in which Freud applies a basically dramatic reading to psychic acts. He is concerned with conflicting motives, temporally articulated. Plainly the method of understanding a psychic text as it unfolds character suits the analysis of a dream, a literary narrative, even a joke. But Freud's method can as easily dramatize relatively condensed and immediate acts—an instance of forgetting, the misplacing of an object, a mistake in speaking—by arranging these into a pattern of emotional antagonism and development. Freud's open formal and arbitrary sifting of "manifest" from "latent" contents in, say, a dream, becomes more comprehensible, I think, thus considered: it is the primary device which he employs to make this dramatic, or conflictual, analysis possible everywhere. By this distinction, even the most compact of events—the utterance of a single word—can be stratified into levels of meanings, some of which are laid down prior to and in conflict with others.[48] The spoken word, the performed act or gesture become final terms in a series, not units to be analyzed in themselves.

By this method Freud is able to dissolve all possible genre distinctions between temporal and spatial, visual and verbal forms. Surely psychoanalysis better penetrates events which occur over a stretch of time, especially those which employ language or at least can be narrated; these can with little forcing be stretched onto an agonistic frame. Nevertheless Freud worked his dramaturgic explanation ingeniously for the visual arts as well: as in his analysis of the Michelangelo Moses as actualizing one moment in a series of three pantomimic acts, so, in the *Introductory Lectures* (1917), he shows the small figures surrounding the prisoner in Schwind's painting, "The Prisoner's Dream," as representing "the successive positions" the prisoner would have to assume in making his escape.[49] Here the subject of the painting is the temporal dream.

The work on Leonardo da Vinci (1910) uses the interpretative strategy for which Freud is best known;* by means of the constructed drama of the artist, Freud finds in "The Virgin and Saint Anne" and other paintings a clue to Leonardo's psychosexual aberrations. A second temporal strategy moves within the constructed drama of the art work itself. The psychography is directed more at the object created than at its creator. Freud may discuss "Moses" without ever mentioning the personality of Michelangelo; *Hamlet* may be examined, as it was by Ernest Jones in his famous essay, with no clues from the private life of Shakespeare helping the interpretation. Freud is scarcely limited to reducing a work of art to the character problems of its creator, though he may with more justice be charged with reducing, say, a play to the character problems of the persons represented in it. But whether direct or through the fiction of the artist's motives, the same basic dramatic, or temporal, style prevails.

In fact, the modes of character dissection in therapy and in art become interchangeable. Freud's naming of the basic character problem of human life after the hero of the ancient tragedy *Oedipus Rex* was not an isolated gesture to show erudition. As models for the understanding of character, the dramas of Shakespeare and Ibsen fascinated Freud only slightly less than the Greek. Take, for example, his discussion of the character "wrecked by success" (1916), persons who collapse just upon attaining an aim for which they have worked with single-minded energy. To explain the psychological problem of two such patients, one a mistress at last legitimized and the other a professor appointed to a long-coveted chair, both of whom find it impossible to enjoy what they have now that it is theirs, Freud cites as models two characters from the drama, Lady Macbeth and Rebecca in *Rosmersholm*.

Indeed his conception of human sickness *is* dramatic, for Freud sought to understand character precisely by the reversals embedded in it. As the greatest dramatists—Sophocles, Shakespeare, Ibsen—had pursued "the problems of psychological responsibility with unrelenting rigor," [50] so the great psychologist will pursue unrelentingly a dra-

---

* Leonardo includes Freud's best known, and most trivial, overinterpretation: his acceptance of Pfister's notion that the vulture symbol for motherhood appears in one of Leonardo's paintings. (SE XI, 115–116)

matic understanding of character. Freud's dramaturgy is more technical than tragic. By showing that all character develops not in a straight line but through a series of crises by which certain attitudes or roles are exchanged, Freud exhibits at once the commonplace element in tragic character and the tragic element in everyday character. Reversal explains how anal characters become so fastidious, as well as how, at the close of Shakespeare's play, Lady Macbeth has acquired the early remorse of her husband while Macbeth has taken on the early strength of his wife.

In Freud's dramatic reading of Michelangelo's "Moses," the reversal of character is ascribed to conscious will. The novelty of Freud's interpretation is that he treats the statue as a hitherto unperceived representation of a "change of mind":

> The Moses we have reconstructed will neither leap up nor cast the Tables from him [as he desired to do]. . . . In giving way to his rage and indignation, he had to neglect the Tables, and the hand which upheld them was withdrawn. They began to slide down and were in danger of being broken. This brought him to himself. He remembered his mission and for its sake renounced an indulgence of his feelings.[51]

In his heroic self-control, Moses becomes an exception to Freud's general rule: that important reversal of intention and character are not the product of conscious will. In most cases Freud insists that character does not change deliberately, through taking thought or through decision; our character is, so to speak, changed for us, by returns from oblivion.

Even the admired Leonardo is depicted as subject to reversals of character quite out of his control. The problem dealt with in Freud's brief book on Leonardo is the gradual eclipse of the artist's aesthetic interests by scientific ones. Unexpectedly enough, Freud finds the artistic interests healthier and finds Leonardo's scientific curiosity "regressive" and definitely linked with the onset of neurotic traits. Leonardo's changing intellectual enthusiasm and conscious choices are discounted as mere façade; when Leonardo abandoned art for science, Freud tells us, it was because "his infantile past had gained control over him." [52] The famous essay on Dostoevski is unified by a similar inquiry into what Freud considered the determining reversal of attitude that guided the great novelist's creative life—Dostoevski's conversion from politically liberal beliefs to "the retrograde position of submission both to temporal and spiritual authority . . . and of a narrow Russian nationalism—a position which lesser minds have reached with smaller effort." [53] Freud performs a literary autopsy upon Dostoevski. As we might expect, Dostoveski's political and religious decisions are shown to be consubstantial with the features of his personal life—his hysterical epilepsy, the Oedipal wish for his father's death, his latent homosexuality.

In his two studies of artists—in the book on Leonardo (1910) and, with greater freedom, in the essay on Dostoevski (1928)—Freud does transpose meaning from the work of art to its creator. Yet he scarcely claims to have exhausted Leonardo's art by detailing the homosexual iconography in it; nor did he claim to have accounted for *The Brothers Karamazov,* "the most magnificent novel ever written," [54] by reconstructing how Dostoevski himself was haunted by feelings of parricidal guilt. At most Freud claimed that through the art work, as through the dream, an artist's preoccupations betray themselves. All art, even the most impersonal, is seen as a secondary mode of confession,[55] or psychic unburdening—though it is more than that as well.

To describe art as confession (rather than expression) betrays a strong rhetorical bias. But Freud's interpretative confidence extended not only to great paintings and novels; the process observed in art is no different from that in more private and unobtrusive symptoms. All slips of the tongue, amnesias, et cetera, give one away to the interpretative authority. In this Freud was as severe on himself (cf. his "Monaco" case in *The Psychopathology of Everyday Life* or the late essay, "On the Subtleties of a Parapraxis") as on his patients. As he was not content with discovering "alteration" in the dream but rather elected to use a hostile term, "distortion," so Freud did not think of the dream as "revealing" meaning but as "betraying" it.[56] At the same time he posited in all cases a certain amount of "resistance" against the detective work of the interpretative authority, even (and especially) when this authority was oneself.

V

Freud's interpretative method is astonishingly fertile and ingenious, above all in the way in which it raises "interpretation" to a necessity. This it does by postulating a generic source of meaning, the unconscious, from which all psychic productions flow. As the reservoir of psychic life in which contradictory attitudes and impulses coexist in mute turmoil, the unconscious has no way of speaking for itself. It can be approached only so far as it is represented, and at the same time "distorted," in dreams, art, and the acts of everyday life.

Here a comparison with constitutional psychology is useful to understand the decisive role which Freud assigns to interpretation in its most general sense, as psychological "explanation" or "understanding."

The constitutional psychologist begins with taxonomic description; he takes a standardized medical photograph of the body and "then he proceeds to the study of other manifestations of personality which are less objectively presented." The body is viewed as "an objective record" of ancestral habit and individual modifications, honest and unconcealing—although its objectivity is not "easily translated into the words of formal speech."

Nothing could be more unlike the linguistically oriented strategies of Freudian interpretation. Indeed so perfect is the opposition that the distinguished constitutional psychologist William Sheldon, from whom I borrow the description above, has discovered an inverse agreement. He notes that the method of psychoanalysis is also to cut through the "compensating camouflage" of "conscious language habits." Therefore, he argues, by the "unconscious" psychoanalysts really mean—though they don't know it—the body. Psychoanalysis starts with what is most subjective, talk; the constitutional psychologist starts with what is most objective, the body record. Although psychoanalysis aims "for the South Pole by swimming north," the final aim of the two psychologies, Sheldon concludes, is the same.

Sheldon's argument is ingenious, but it rests on a misunderstanding of Freud's position. No psychoanalysts would deny that the body has its own language. (Ferenczi thought he could interpret conclusively from the patient's posture and body type at the first meeting.) But the body is an objective record only in a most limited sense; what is important about an individual lies in the historical dimension—in memory, whose complexity there is little likelihood the body can record. Moreover, the purpose of the years of talking and listening which comprise the psychoanalytic therapy is not "cutting through" talk and thus, in Sheldon's words, "at last coming down to the bedrock of the characteristic structure of the biological organism." The purpose is the interpretation of talk itself. In contrast to the constitutional psychologist, who thinks of behavior as "resulting" from the body, in "logical cause-effect thinking," the far more adequate psychoanalytic view does not see the body as the cause of anything, unmediated. In radical opposition to constitutional psychology, Freud puts language before body. This is the principled indirection (the constitutional psychologist calls it "subjectivity") in Freudian theory and therapy that raises the art of interpretation to the highest relevance.

While providing the necessity of interpretation, the idea of the fathomless unconscious at the same time limits and, to an extent, deforms the interpretative method depending on it. With the unconscious as background, the Freudian method tends to demote any psychic text under scrutiny to a rank of meaning in which the individual and particular, if not wholly irrelevant, nevertheless are drastically revalued at a much lower causal significance. It may seem odd that a method of interpretation which has restored the importance of detail itself—one of the greatest achievements of psychoanalysis—should yet provide the best arguments against uniqueness in psychic texts. But the bewildering variety of parts are put together in order to show the sameness of wholes.

In theory, "the dream is not a faithful translation or a point-for-point projection of the dream-thoughts, but a highly incomplete and fragmentary version of them." [57] And as the dream incompletely reproduces the dream-thoughts, so the dream recounted is incomplete with relation to what was dreamed. Hence Freud assumed that nothing in the dream is likely to have an unmediated meaning, interpretable at its face value. He offered a method encumbered by a principled indirectness. The dictum of the nineteenth-century English critic William Hazlitt (who anticipated many of Freud's principles of aesthetic insight) that "poetry represents forms chiefly as they suggest other forms, feelings as they suggest other feelings," [58] holds for the dream or any psychic text in the Freudian aesthetics. Assuming a dream never means what it says, that it is always a substitute for something else which cannot be said and leads to further associations which are in themselves substitutes,[59] Freud may compliment a dream so far as to call it an "exceptionally clever dream-production." [60] But this is the compliment paid by a gracious antagonist; Freud treated the dream as an opponent in the work of interpretation, trying by its cleverness to outwit the interpreter.

Freud's conviction that the dreamer does not know the meaning of his dream—that all psychic texts lie out of conscious reach of the mind that produces them—is supported by the view that the dream is only a substitute. Indeed, the dream itself is an interpretation or elaboration of a text.[61] And this provides the possibility of analytic re-interpretation. Freud assumes that the recollection of a dream—however inadequate—gives evidence as relevant as the dream itself; such a recollection is, if distorted, merely a further distortion. The dream may itself reflect the analytic situation.* In a sense he does away with the dream; what matters is what the patient now recalls, or says, about it. And in cases outside the special circumstances of therapy—or within therapy when the symbolic method is applied—the interpreter can dispense with the person altogether. The dream can tell us nothing about the symbol. Rather, Freud insists, only the symbols can tell us about the dream; and "their translation has to be provided by the analyst." [62]

So far as a psychic text—the dream, to continue the model instance —*is* treated in itself, its discursive structure is considerably devalued.

---

* Cf. the woman patient ("the cleverest of all my dreamers") who dreamed *without* wish-fulfillment in order, Freud says, to fulfill the wish that he be shown wrong in his theory that every dream can be explained as a wish-fulfillment (*The Interpretation of Dreams*, SE IV, 151).

For the dream becomes intelligible only as the result of what Freud called "secondary elaboration." The psychic text may be viewed as stringing out in time mutually contradictory but coexistent motives, as in a play; or, as in a painting, it may be read as condensing and presenting statically a basically temporal or sequential complex of motives. Either way, part of the work of interpretation is disintegrative: its purpose is to dissolve a psychic text back into its contradictions.

One of the most brilliant forms of the Freudian method is as a mode of narrative dissolution. It goes unerringly to those moments in which some kind of reversal or exchange of motive takes place: this is how Freud unriddled the acquired virginity of Ibsen's Rebecca and the delayed remorse of Lady Macbeth. In its extreme form, the psychoanalytic tendency to level a text appears as a tendency to bypass "plot" in favor of verbal analysis. This, I believe, is what Freud means when he says we must decode the dream, applying the solvent of interpretation not to "the dream as a whole but to each portion of the dream's content independently, as though the dream were a geological conglomerate in which each fragment of rock requires a special assessment." [63] Repeatedly throughout *The Interpretation of Dreams* Freud dismisses what is said or heard in dreams as being superficial in contrast to what is seen. Dreams are expressed predominantly in visual images, and only secondarily make use of material from other senses such as the auditory.[64] Yet this is somewhat misleading. Actually, Freud's method disparages the necessarily visual aspect of dreams; visual content is entirely filtered through the patient's oral report and the piecemeal analysis of it. Proceeding synthetically from parts to the whole, from events to total meaning, Freud finds his major clues in the words (not, however, *all* the words) of the dream or other symptomatic text, rather than in its structure.

Subscribing as he does to the modern premium on spontaneity as a criterion of aesthetic and psychological good, the Freudian interpreter tends to view plot with suspicion. The unformulated preference is for verbal analysis because, however abstract, a single word or image is still less intellectual, less planned, than the relation between characters or events. In plot, or narrative, one can contrive; but in the depths of one's imagery,* the psychologist supposes, one cannot lie. Such a preference can become the norm for literary and moral analysis only in an age of psychology. Linguistic analysis is certainly indispensable to motivational insight, because language is common property. But the Freudian stress on verbal analysis nevertheless seems to me more significant as one of the many ways in which the dream, or work of art, is deprived of its unique qualities.

Without reference to a specific action-and-character situation, the Freudian critic is liable to awkward blunders. There is the danger of irrelevance: he may permit too many meanings to enter a discussion. (With his habit of introducing a maximum number of ambiguities, the critic William Empson often exhibits this fault.) But all dictionary meanings of a word do not inhere in the pre-conscious levels of mind; not all are relevant to the examination of a particular text. And there are the graver dangers of therapeutic injustice and downright intellectual absurdity. The interpreter may understand too narrowly or crudely, taking words in their literal etymological sense without regard to the changes of voltage that occur with changes of context. This is a perennial risk in the use of the free-association method. Trapped within his own set of therapeutic expectations, the analyst may fail to sift the patient's verbal clichés from genuinely expressive phrasings. Without historical sensitivity, the psychologically trained ear cannot cope with the fact that, whatever their original force, words do wane; images become superficial. Freud's remarks on Dostoevski, for example, suffer from a facile identification of the novelist's attitude toward the "Little Father, the Czar" and his attitude toward his own father. Freud argues that Dostoevski chose to accept undeserved punishment from the Czar "as a substitute for the punishment he deserved for his sin against his real father." [65] This is no less strained than the conclusion drawn by the French writer Taine that in England there was a remarkable recognition of the authority belonging to the head of the family because sons spoke to their fathers as "the governor."

---

* Kenneth Burke's phrase.

Taking words as things in themselves, instead of in context, mars the Freudian interpretative method. To this extent there is justice in the charge that psychoanalysis plays with words.[66]

To follow our analogy between art and dream: even when Freudians attend the context and derive meaning not just from words, which are properly accessory, but from plot and character, nevertheless Freudian methods of interpretation tend to de-individualize the text. Psychoanalysis is characteristically insensitive to the subtle surface at which much of art and life exist. It has its case book of basic plots expressive of the "family romance"; these are discoverable in every story, refracted in every symptomatic event.

In this respect, psychoanalytic preoccupations commingle with those of other anti-historical sciences of man. Nothing more clearly overrides the autonomy of the aesthetic imagination than Freud's attempt to rationalize it. It is typical of rationalist science—an intellectual equivalent of the industrial process—that it finds a uniform production of symbols, myths, and works of the imagination; these are then classified and identified with one another. As the Deist and rationalist students of comparative religion simplified Christian dogma until they discovered in it the same ultimate truths as, say, in Zoroastrianism, so the psychoanalytic rationalist simplifies the variety of emotive expression to find universal meanings beneath. Separate and often irreconcilable details of myth, religion, dream, and art are arranged together in the same basic assortment of plots and symbols.* An interest in the shared motives of men offers little basis for distinguishing among works of the imagination. The modern quest for basic themes of the imagination—call them "psychological" or "mythical" —has the effect of cataloguing literature and life in static juxtapositions. Here is the Oedipus theme, there the castrating women. Like all conventions of analysis, just those small alterations of sensibility that have been, historically, productive of significant change may be overlooked. The Freudian themes are at once useful and dangerous.

---

* Hence to Freud the occurrence in dreams of material from fairy tales and myths and the occurrence in fairy tales and myths of material from dreams becomes equally relevant. Freud's account slights the religious origins of communal art: he derives myth from private, family tensions of which religion is one possible "projection." His notion of myth is thus basically anti-historical.

Freud saw the uniqueness of a work of art as merely the artistic trappings * around a stereotyped psychological expressiveness. Emphasizing unconscious "intention" [67] rather than calculated effect, he tends to slight the variant forms in which contemporary material is linked with a gallery of prototypes in the dreamer's past. The interpreter's ceaseless activity of thematic juxtaposition blunts a regard for every development of character except those which are inevitable. Surely Freud is right in saying that the dream, like art, recreates the past. But like art, the dream also says something contemporary, even unique.

VI

Psychoanalysis cannot account for the aesthetic effect itself.[68] Yet there are standards of art implied by Freud—just as there is such a thing as a good dream, an expert dreamer.

It is surprising that, among the standards implied, Freud omits the criterion of verisimilitude. Because the therapist appraises action by its adequacy to reality, we might expect some transfer to art of criteria, such as fidelity of reproduction and adherence to probability, that would link Freudian norms to the literary norms of realism. Actually, Freud's writings bear anti-realistic implications. The clinical naturalism with which he treated art—separating it sharply from reality—saved him from realism. Art was judged not by the reality principle but by the pleasure principle, as conation rather than recognition. The Benthamite idea of an art requiring no interpretation, of art grown to the clarity of science, did not interest Freud. Art, for him, did not copy the apparent order of the outer world but instead testified to the grandeur and insufficiencies of the inner. Though it may feed a scientific psychology with its most fruitful clues, art remains an autonomous way of thought. Thus the private thought-art of the Freudian patient

---

* Freud's appreciation of the novel was entirely dramatic. Nothing in his long essay on the obscure *Gradiva*, or the fragment of analysis of *The Brothers Karamazov*, leads the reader to think of these in their artistic individuality, as novels. Freud treats them as he would a play or any other psychic text—for the revelation of character and motive. (Thus *The Brothers Karamazov* is linked with *Oedipus* and *Hamlet* as the third great artistic representation of the problem of parricide.)

is of a distinctly modern style; it depicts, like symbolism and surrealism, the subjective overtones of objects, not their literal use. Oddities of perspective, memory images, word connections are all assembled together, not by the tests of everyday experience, but presumably because they all share, for the artist-patient, the same emotional overtones. Therefore, although Freud can be read as sponsoring an aesthetic with realist implications, his influence has not been for realism —except on the arts of everyday life. So far as Freud's ideas have been assumed by painters and writers, they have encouraged familiarity with the unfamiliar, and unremitting meditation on unapparent worlds. Though the errant and arbitrary forms of thought which Freudianism encourages the artist to exploit are illusions in the practical sense, it nevertheless legitimates these as a valuable clue to the reading of inner reality.

Correspondence to reality is never, for Freud, an aesthetic criterion, but only an intellectual one. And because he viewed all language as ambivalent, and all thinking as essentially dichotomous, the criterion of consistency could have no real meaning, in the realms of either character or art.

In place of these two criteria, verisimilitude and consistency, Freud erected the aesthetic category of complication. Were it not for this criterion, the same basic plot structure and symbolic components could serve to comprehend all emotive statement. In terms of motive, works of art may be very similar indeed; at least Freud's concentration on those motives basic to human nature—rather than on their individual characteristics—tends to draw the works together. With the criterion of complication implicit, however, the Freudian interpreter retains the option of going beyond a simple analysis of a work's motivational structure, which does not differentiate among works of the psychological, folk, and poetic imaginations. The analytic standard of complication permitted Freud to refine his aesthetic distinctions.

Take, as a problem in comparison for Freudian aesthetics, two plays of Shakespeare, one conventionally considered his greatest and the other his worst. How, by Freudian standards, shall *Titus Andronicus* be judged any differently from *King Lear,* since in both the same character problem is discoverable? Freud himself discussed *King Lear* in an essay called "The Theme of the Three Caskets" (1913), in which he isolated, in a number of instances drawn from art, myth, and fairy tale, the connection between the number three and the symbolism of death as dumbness.* In the essay, he incidentally summarizes the situation of the aged Lear in this way: "He should have recognized the unassuming, speechless love of the third [daughter] and rewarded it, but he misinterprets it, banishes Cordelia, and divides the kingdom between the other two, to his own and the general ruin." [69] Now a Freudian critic might justly point out that *Titus Andronicus* has a remarkably similar plot. Its central figure is also a haughty old man who makes a drastic error of judgment. Lear chooses as heirs his two bad daughters instead of the good Cordelia; Titus sponsors Saturnius for the Roman succession, instead of the good Bassanius who (like Cordelia) refuses to flatter him. Further, each play has a victim-figure in the shape of a mute, dutiful virgin: the meek and suffering "Cordelia figure" in *Titus Andronicus* is Titus's only daughter, Lavinia. *Titus Andronicus* has all the basic plot components which Freud found fascinating in *King Lear*. If, then, *Titus Andronicus* has as dignified

---

* Freud connects the third, silent daughter of Lear with the third, leaden casket of Portia in *The Merchant of Venice,* a story (Freud tells us) which is borrowed from the *Gesta Romanorum* and occurs also in an Estonian folk-epic. He then moves to connect the Shakespeare plots with parts of the Trojan myth, where the third goddess (Aphrodite) is judged by Paris the fairest; with the fairy tale *Cinderella,* where the prince prefers the youngest and fairest of three sisters—and finally with the three Fates, the third of whom is Death. In Cordelia, as in all these versions, Freud argues, the representation of this loveliest, most desirable, and virtuous of women is a façade. Just in "the reversal of the wish," in that very meek and unassuming speechlessness which is a sign of her helplessness, is still betrayed "the all-powerful goddess of Death" (*Collected Papers* IV, 256).

Freud's analysis of *King Lear,* however, goes beyond the finally unassimilable point of a "triad" of women. The interpretation of Cordelia as death rests first upon the symbolic portent of her speechlessness, and only secondarily—and, I think, gratuitously—upon her position as *third* in a group of women. (In many versions of the myth, three *men* [often they are brothers] appear and, after a competition, the third and youngest wins.) It seems legitimate, therefore, to transfer the interpretation to other instances where "three" is not involved, as Freud does not hesitate to do when instancing the heroine of Grimm's fairy tale "The Twelve Brothers" as another death-figure because she remains mute for seven years. So, in *Titus Andronicus,* there are no triads. But the only daughter of Titus, meek and literally dumb, bears unmistakable resemblances to Lear's third daughter, Cordelia.

a set of motives as *King Lear,* on what basis might a Freudian critic judge it an inferior play?

One basis that I think might be acceptable to the Freudian scheme is the excessive literality which characterizes *Titus Andronicus.* Note, for instance, the difference between the dumbness of the ambiguous virgin-victim in *King Lear,* which is feigned, and the literal dumbness (Lavinia has her tongue torn out) of the corresponding character in *Titus Andronicus.* True, *King Lear* has the gruesome on-stage blinding of Gloucester. But this is picayune as compared with the cavalcade of amputations, slaughters, cannibalism, and other atrocities on and off stage in *Titus Andronicus.* The Freudian critic might also object that the images of bodily torture around which *King Lear* is organized are more resonant, capable of bearing more complication than the dog imagery which unifies *Titus Andronicus.** But since this is a more refined point and harder to prove, let me restrict myself to the minimal accusation, with respect to plot: *Titus Andronicus* fails to provide sufficient altering and complicating of the violent motives underneath its plot to be aesthetically successful. "Complication" I take as the aesthetic parallel of the psychological category of "distortion," which Freud finds the distinctive characteristic of dreaming.†

Nevertheless, the value of the aesthetic criterion of complication is partly canceled out by the fact that, for Freud, complication does not entail variety. Historically and logically, the imputation of variety has

---

* See Caroline Spurgeon, *Shakespeare's Imagery* (New York: 1935).

† No doubt partly under the aegis of Freudian psychology, the criterion of complexity today dominates Anglo-American literary criticism. I refer not only to the opinion of I. A. Richards and William Empson (both avowedly influenced by Freud) that poetry is good to the degree that it is complicated—or, as their critics would say, simply hard to construe. A like view also appears more covertly, in that many modern critics, including those who disagree with the techniques of poetic analysis developed by Richards (the ambiguities of the reader's mind) and Empson (the ambiguities of the text), deplore the traditionlessness of modern society, *vis-à-vis* its usability for poetry. The relation of the poet to the moral and social disorder of our era is regularly spoken of much as the Freudian interpreter might describe the relation of dreamer to the unconscious. The critical commonplace about the poet struggling to find an idiom adequate to the complexities of modern life reminds one of the problem of the sleeper in finding a dream-idiom adequate to the complexities of his dream-thoughts. In both cases the aesthetic criterion of complication is clearly implied.

been connected with that of optimism. Thus theologians have held that God's creation is good and beautiful at least partly because it is variegated; there was a derivative idea, widely maintained in eighteenth-century criticism, that the beauty of a poem or a painting is dependent on variety. A good part of the pessimist case made by *The Interpretation of Dreams* and *The Psychopathology of Everyday Life* stems, I think, from Freud's implicit denial that the complexity of meanings discoverable in the inner life indicates the presence of genuine variety and contrast. The ingenuity found in the psychic text being examined is not at all the same thing as variety. Even while focused upon the cluttered detail in the symptomatic text, the Freudian argument seeks an invariant—even stereotyped—meaning beneath. Whatever is idiosyncratic in the dream may be noted and then dismissed as part of the "manifest" disguise, an effort of the dream's "work" to conceal a standard wish. With his assumption that, sooner or later, he will ferret out the plain egoism beneath the fancy dream work, Freud may have laid down too short a trail through the contrast and variety of manifest contents, considering them as aspects of an essential sameness, not as genuine psychic trends in themselves. It is this assumption which narrows the psychoanalytic portrait of mind and leads Freud to an unwarranted pessimism.

At least penultimately, however, Freud sees a good chance for a varied psychic product. Psychoanalysis is never an immediate science but always one of implications, a science of expressions not of instincts. It is not instinct which the Freudian science examines as the root problem, but the instinctual or natural imagination. Freud found what he thought to be a hypocritical culture producing dissonant personalities who in turn expressed themselves in ambiguous psychic products. It is significant that he inaugurated his science with the task of interpreting these psychic products (dreams), rather than with the task of interpreting character. His science is truly a psychology in the sense that it studies the body though the language of the mind. (For this reason interpretation has a central place in Freudian psychology.) But this recourse to the mental does not, as I have said, guarantee a genuinely individuating psychology. Indeed, in his very presumption of a uniform kind of mental activity to be disclosed by dreams, Freud asserts the uniformity of mind. All ideas and objects, values and attitudes are viewed as implications of imaginative functions excited by the instincts—and these imaginative functions are conceived as minimal. As a science of the natural imagination and its cultural distortions, Freudianism attributes all ingenuity to the attempt to conceal the plain figure of the dream. The interpreter may be adept at unraveling the dream's ingenious subterfuges, but his final task is to cut through this ingenuity to the bedrock of instinctual need.

This simplifying need especially dominates Freud's work in later editions of *The Interpretation of Dreams,* where the symbolic method of interpretation became (reportedly under the influence of Stekel) increasingly important. One never knows, in the interpretation of any element of a dream, wrote Freud,

    (a) whether it is to be taken in a positive or negative sense . . .
    (b) whether it is to be interpreted historically (as a recollection)
        . . .
    (c) whether it is to be interpreted symbolically, or
    (d) whether its interpretation is to depend on its wording.
    Yet, in spite of all this ambiguity, it is fair to say that the productions of the dream-work . . . present no greater difficulties to their translators than do the ancient hieroglyphic scripts to those who seek to read them.[70]

Unfortunately Freud did not give equal weight to these four interpretative strategies. One key to the hieroglyphs of the mind—symbolism—tends, in practice, to engulf the other three listed above. Without assuming the projective busyness of the mind as hardened into symbols, Freud was unable to complete his therapeutic understanding. The hypothesis that all associations are completely "determined" by some meaning lying behind them was a capital device but not complete enough; for in the dream life—Freud spoke frankly—there are always cases "where association fails altogether or, if something is finally extorted, it is not what we need." [71] What was needed was a more uniform, less empirical interpretative key, a "new principle" to provide those "constant translations for a series of dream-elements" [72] which would integrate the fluctuant interpretations to be gained by the method of free association.

If free association indicates that we are never free, Freud's theory of symbolism diminishes freedom even more. Symbolism indicates that language is a prison, and traces all modes of perception back to stereotyped desires. The Freudian interpretation reduces all thought to objectifications, and all objects to symbols of the minimum self. If the subjects treated in dreams are "few in number"—sex organs and activities, death, the relations to parents, siblings, spouse—each of these few subjects "can be expressed by many symbols practically equivalent." [73] The task of the Freudian science remains a kind of literary criticism, the discovery of equivalences of symbols and actions through perceptual analogies. Symbols are the natural forms of imagination, and even everyday actions—such as running, digging, walking —can be only the symbols made animate, peculiarly impersonal and beyond conscious control. The body becomes a collection of bodily images; and the images of the mind (exhibiting all the organs of the body) become the only way to approach the root reality, the inaccessible instincts.

The entire set of Freud's interpretative distinctions—between what is manifest and what is latent, conscious and unconscious, distorted and authentic—enforces this presumption: that all mental acts are stratified, and that one must proceed deviously in interpreting them. But it does not follow from the conscientious indirection of Freud's interpretative method that what is beneath the manifest, the conscious, the distorted is always repressed sexuality. Nothing inheres in his method as such to lead him to insist on sexuality as the root motive, and all others as derivative, "standing for" the disposition of libidinal impulse. To explain Freud's specific interpretative recourse to sexuality,* we must look beyond the interior logic of his interpretative method—which need not imply base meanings at all, though it must imply concealed ones—to the ethical imperative which guides it. This

---

* Freud's instinct theory is explicitly dual: there are both sexuality and aggression. Yet the analysis of the other instinct, aggression, despite its nominal equality with sex, was not developed (e.g., into a theory of character stages). Cf. *An Outline of Psychoanalysis,* p. 7, where Freud says there is no energy which stands in relation to the aggressive instinct (it could not have been called "mortido") as libido stands in relation to the sexual instinct.

imperative is the day-to-day therapeutic chastisement of ethical aspiration. Ultimately Freud's interpretative method is aimed against, and therefore distorted by, the belief that we all live self-deceived on the seemly consoling surface of manifest meanings. As he once declared, "Mankind has always known that there is spirituality. I had to show that there are also instincts." [74]

No doubt Freud overestimated the originality of his attack. In one sense he is in an ancient tradition which we may call, without pejorative intent, ethical naturalism. The sentiment for limited ethical objectives has been a major theme at least since Montaigne. Freud is scarcely unique in his reaction against what he conceived to be the prevailing overvaluation of our reason and our moral aptitudes. It is a commonplace of intellectual polemic that during recent centuries—the blame is sometimes fixed on the Enlightenment, sometimes on the nineteenth century—reason has been assigned too high a place too easily. Hence it becomes the duty of alert minds to show that we are really natural beings, irrational, capricious, limited. But, as the historian of ideas A. O. Lovejoy has shown, the rationalist eighteenth century is a myth made popular by romantics in the succeeding period: such apostles of rationalism as Pope and Hume declared explicitly that the motive and guide of human life is—and should be—not reason but the passions. The nineteenth century is no more consistent a candidate: the age of rationalism and prudery was also the age of Darwin, Schopenhauer, and Zola. The survival of the fittest in no way indicated the survival of the most rational. It was left to the most romantic of philosophers, Hegel, to make a new divinity of Reason—as History. Surely the romantic and now permanent revolution against the ancient regime of reason is against a regime largely invented by the revolutionaries themselves.

Neither his fervor against the overestimation of reason, nor his impulse to deflate human self-esteem through the revelation of repressed motives makes anything distinctive in Freud's thought. What is distinctive arises, first, from the powerful polemical breadth which he gained by his interpretative techniques: the quality of humiliation in his interpretative method is designed not merely to lower what was once elevated, but, more subtly, to elevate what was once lowered—

the ordinary, half-base motives and acts of which we are more comfortably conscious, perhaps, than Freud believed we could be in our everyday life. Second, what is relatively novel (though there are precedents, in the work of de Sade, for instance) in Freud is the particular avenue along which he made his attack: his singular concentration upon sexuality among the several destructive passions by which mere reason has been dethroned. Freud expanded the idea of sexuality to fill the category of natural impulse, rather than, as his critics often have it, contracting natural impulse to the narrow meaning of sexuality. His interpretations not only issue from an aesthetic method but also serve a certain polemical intent. To give his aesthetics a specific sexual meaning points toward the imagined antagonist, sexuality itself.

CHAPTER FIVE

SEXUALITY AND
DOMINATION

*It is said, it was because Adam ate the apple that he was
lost, or fell. I say, it was because of his claiming something
for his own, and because of his I, Mine, Me, and the like.*
—THEOL. GERMANICA

WHEN sexuality is summoned to testify against spurious pieties,
the mode of reproach has rarely been dispassionate. Farce is
one rhetorical weapon against high civilization. But after the straightforward goatish farce of pagan writers like Aristophanes and Pe-
tronius—that is, since the introduction of Christian ideas—it has often
soured into loathing and disgust; think of *Troilus and Cressida,* of
Swift, and Aldous Huxley. Irony is the other common weapon. But
irony readily transposes itself into a new earnestness; de Sade displays
this, Lawrence too, and, in a limited way, Freud. For the latter, sexuality was important not least rhetorically, as a "humiliation of the
highest possessions of civilization." [1]

I

As a critic of sexual customs, and as the authority for a new ease
in enunciating the sexual fact, Freud is always earnest, even didactic.
His clinical materials may be interpreted as an argument in definition
—more accurately, as a remonstrant confronting of definitions: the
prurient (enforced by "culture" or "civilization") versus the natural
(revealed by "science"). The misunderstanding of sexuality is no
intellectual error, nor an accidental ignorance, but one way in which

culture conspires to obtain "the mental energy it needs by subtracting it from sexuality." [2] In the first of his *Three Essays on Sexuality* (1905), Freud reacted to the conspiracy with a daring sensual relativism. Without the "authoritative prohibition by society," he argued, we would see that a so-called perversion "answers fully to the sexual inclinations of no small number of people." [3] By discovering a universal disposition to bisexuality and a childhood diffuseness of sexual aim, Freud assaulted prevailing prejudices by showing "normality" in its accepted meaning to be another name for the conventional. No healthy person, he declared, "can fail to make some addition that might be called perverse to the normal sexual aim." [4] The implication of such a statement is greater tolerance for those who aim perversely. As it turns out, the perverted, for Freud, are being childish, persisting in earlier stages of sexual gesture. As children we are all normally "polymorphous perverse." To preserve its moral doctrine of the free and adult man, society has created a sentimental doctrine of the free and asexual child. It was Freud's insight that the complex urges of sexuality are not born in the adult but are already present in childhood; in fact, the character of the adult is shaped by the specific erotic development of the child, just as, Freud believed, the character of modern culture derives from those open possibilities permitted in "primitive states of society and early periods of history." [5] This formulates a plea for tolerance of the child, for an end of maiming threats, for a new sympathy and indulgence.

Though he hoped for some reform of attitudes toward sexuality, Freud was no naïve advocate of the body's pleasures. The Freudian message in its main outlines embodies a program of reform familiar enough from having been repeated in one form or another in much of the literature of the nineteenth century—a lifting of the ascetic barrier, a relaxation of the moral fervor that created more hypocrites than saints, more sick minds than healthy souls. But, transforming the old emancipative polemic into a new therapeutic science, Freud's writings make a pedantic, even equivocal, climax to the great literature calling for a rehabilitation of the flesh. Not accidentally do the *Three Essays on Sexuality* comprise the driest book Freud ever wrote. The *Essays* succeed in deflating the sexual fact as well as championing its expression. Indeed in just the precise, bald style of the *Three Essays,* Freud's ideas take on a most equivocal cast. His recourse to mechanical concepts (tension, discharge, excitation), his allusions to the straightforward clamor of instinct, suggest scientific detachment. (That most of the changes made in subsequent editions of the *Three Essays* were not in the book's psychological argument, but in its extra-psychological supports from neurology, chemistry, and the like, indicates how much Freud valued the quantitative horizon of his theory of sexuality.)* But the look of quantification in Freud's idea of sexuality is purely terminological. The language of "tension-states" in the *Three Essays* contains a moral judgment far more powerful than any quantitative index the terms might suggest.

The quantifications which Freud offers in the *Three Essays* compose a vast ethical metaphor. If we inspect its vocabulary, his analysis appears to point in two directions: On the one hand, the quantitative language bears an oblique "scientific" plea for greater sexual latitude. It is a way of scoring points against the repressive order, the largest being that "normal" and "inverted" sexuality are innately and basically related,[6] despite the attempt of culture to maintain their distinction. This Freud states as: "The differences in the end-products," sexual activities, "may be of a qualitative nature, but analysis shows that the differences between their determinants are only quantitative." [7] On the other hand, with his rhetoric of sexual quantities, his mapping of the body into "zones" of sexuality, indeed with the first significant distinction made in the *Three Essays*—that between the sexual "object" and the sexual "aim" [8]—Freud goes far toward depersonalizing the sexual life. The meaning of the intimate in human relations becomes accessible to science as a quantitative, if not a quantifiable, process. Without ever treating sex statistically (as such later sex reformers as Kinsey were to do) Freud does, for rhetorical purposes at least, presume that its pleasures and pains all issue from the mechanical demands of genital and other organ sensations.

---

* Freud took the trouble to keep "up to date" only two of his writings—the *Three Essays on Sexuality* and *The Interpretation of Dreams*—thus testifying to the importance these two books had for him. The *Three Essays* went through four editions: it appeared in 1905, and then, newly revised, in 1910, in 1915, in 1920.

Certainly Freud intended "sex" to mean more than genitality. Nevertheless, to avoid "faintheartedness," [9] he insisted on using the word. It was the shock therapy of honesty: Freud would say "sexual" even where he might more accurately have said "erotic." In his earliest papers he kept his meaning narrow. He first ascribed neurosis not merely to sexual causes but in particular to the effects of excessive masturbation,[10] echoing the established pre-Freudian stigma of the neurotic as a degenerate. Then for a time his surmise—far from unfounded, given the backstairs condition of master-servant relations in respectable homes for centuries—was that premature sexual experiences, usually with the servant classes, were "at the bottom of every case of hysteria." [11] But these specifics were soon discarded. By the second decade of his psychoanalytic observation, Freud ceased to advert to masturbation as a causal factor, and even before 1900 he had discovered that the tales commonly furnished by his patients of infantile seduction by nurse or governess could claim the psychological truth of fantasy. From then on, the meaning of sexuality enlarged for Freud, till it covered the entire range of his interests. He used it to label concrete sensual acts as well as the feeling of parent for child ("parental narcissism"), and child for parent (incest wishes), and even the bond between leader and follower ("identification"), teacher and student (the analytic "transference").

Though Freud has been accused of having reduced everything to the narrowly sexual, actually he used the term "sexuality" very widely. He himself claimed to use it "in the same comprehensive sense" as ordinary language uses the word "love." [12] * But at the same time, by continually stressing how much that is problematic and repellent—how much else besides tenderness and loyalty—infuses sexuality,

---

* Freud preferred to speak, he said in 1910, of "psychosexuality" rather than sexuality alone—using the word "in the same comprehensive sense as that in which the German language uses the word *lieben.*" Cf., also, in *Group Psychology:* "Even in its caprices the usage of language remains true to some kind of reality. Thus it gives the name of 'love' to a great many kinds of emotional relationships which we too group together theoretically as love; but then again it feels a doubt whether this love is real, true, actual love, and so hints at a whole scale of possibilities within the range of the phenomena of love" (SE XVIII, 111). Again, on another page: language has "carried on an entirely justified piece of unification in creating the word 'love' with its various uses" (ibid., 91).

Freud proposes an essential tension between sexuality and love. To reprove the naïveté of love by unearthing the sexual daemon beneath is an intention he carries out repeatedly and effectively. This is the polemical advantage his wide use of the word "sexuality" gained for him. Without praising it, Freud concentrated in the attributes of sexuality every variety of emotion. Sympathy and attachment, respect and contempt, parental love and filial piety, friendship and enmity, bodily victories and symbolic defeats, aesthetic pleasures and an interest in the ugly—all are assimilated to this unifying source.[13] But subterranean exchanges of meaning occur when a salient conception acquires such scope. The reader discovers Freud protesting that he doesn't know what all the fuss is about: his use of the term "sexuality" is not at all "sexual" in the simple, literal sense. "What psychoanalysis called sexuality was by no means identical with the impulsion towards a union of the two sexes or towards producing a pleasurable sensation in the genitals." [14] But at the same time he pulls the reader up short, insisting that when he says "sex" he means sex—genitalia and their direct expression, not the secondary tracery of civilized sublimations. Here, in the shifting relation between primary and secondary sexuality, is a vital ambiguity in the Freudian argument, one scarcely to be eliminated, because with it would go some of Freud's basic constructions: for example, the role of sexual relations as paradigmatic of social relations.

In the light of this progressively enlarged and constricted conception of sexuality, there is scant justification for Freud's having invoked for his conception of love the most ancient and respectable lineage. To declare amiably that "when the apostle Paul . . . praises love above all else, he certainly understands it in the same 'wider' sense" [15] as the psychoanalyst, does not help reconcile the Freudian meaning to the Pauline. In the relevant Pauline text, I Corinthians 13, love (translated in the King James version as "charity") has an authoritative, compelling quality which is in Freud's conception as well. But the Christian compulsion of love is different in both origin and effect. *Agape* is a sentiment that limits the self to a respectful relation with the not-self; it projects a spontaneous and unmotivated regard for others which excludes the Freudian connection of love and the aggrandizement of the self. In the Christian sense, too, love is authoritarian; but the two senses of authority differ. Freud traced love back to the parental fact of domination. Power is the father of love, and in love one follows the paternal example of power, in a relation that must include a superior and a subordinate. Christian theology refers love forward, to the ever-present example of Jesus, who, in a series of unique demonstrations, taught the figure of divine love. Jesus revealed the authority of love. Examining ostensibly the same emotion, Freud discovered the love of authority. Neither is Freud much closer to the other great authority on love whom he invoked more frequently —Plato, with whose idea of *Eros,* he maintained, his own definition of sexuality "coincides exactly." [16] The similarities are attractive. For both, sublime love, friendship, social unity are transformations of an original fund of sexuality. Yet the psychoanalytic Eros is basically unlike the Platonic. Indeed Freud's idea of sexuality serves as a critique of the Platonic idea, in which the emotion takes on the merit of its object, so that "higher" love (i.e., love for "higher" objects) is, according to the *Symposium,* more valuable than the "lower." In Freud's view, however generously he invested Eros with meaning, there remains a bankruptcy clause; his doctrine amounts to an unremitting chastisement of the "sacred" on behalf of the "profane (or animal) love." [17] Thus his earliest, dualistic construction of Eros was concerned to sift what is genuinely sexual from the sublimated versions of it, those in which culture tames sexual energy and diverts it to its own purposes. Of course sexuality can be attached to the most noble objects. But these are the guises of a Caliban, molded into a thousand acceptable shapes by a succession of Prosperos. Unfortunately Caliban remains Caliban—underneath; in Freud's conception, sexuality remains bound by its original instinctual character.

Not only did Freud employ sexuality to deflate the pride of civilized man, he further defined it pejoratively by those qualities which make the sexual instinct intractable to a civilized sensibility. To discount the extraordinary malleability of the instincts as a truism encouraging to a new doctrine of sweetness and light, he stressed, instead, the enduring models of affection and related bodily aptitudes which sexuality cannot transcend. While in one sense he reclaimed the varieties of sexual expression—most notably in the first of the *Three Essays,* on the "sexual aberrations"—as a great leveler of the instinct, Freud overstated the monotony of such expression, erasing the delicacies and differences at its very core. Whatever the variety in object, he contended, "the fundamental processes which promote erotic excitation remain always the same." The ancients understood this correctly, Freud believed, and therefore glorified the *instinct* as such rather than its object. Thus "excremental things are all too intimately and inseparably bound up with sexual things; the position of the genital organs—'inter urinas et faeces'—remains the decisive and unchangeable factor." As "the genitals themselves have not undergone the development of the rest of the human form in the direction of beauty" but "have retained their animal cast," so "even today love, too, is in essence as animal as it ever was." [18]

Muffled by the impersonal, scientific tone, Freud communicates to us a mixed aversion and respect no less ambivalent than that of other observers of the sexual fact as it appeared in the nineteenth century —of Maupassant, for instance, with his stunning discussion-story on the sexual instinct, "Vain Beauty." Freud was no celebrant of the senses; there is no trace of the lyrical in his analysis of the sexual instinct and its satisfactions. He hardly claimed or—from what we know of his life—himself desired to be rid of the civilizing aversions. While urging, for the sake of our mental health, that we dispense with such childish fantasies of purity as are epitomized in the belief that Mother (or Father) was too nice to have done those nasty things, Freud at the same time comes to the tacit understanding that sex really is nasty, an ignoble slavery to nature.

A sense of the ineradicable harshness of sexual life especially colors Freud's child psychology. The essay "On the Sexual Theories of Children" (1908) contains a grim catalogue of the ways in which children become sexually knowledgeable: a boy's "horror" (Freud's word) upon discovering that women lack a penis; a little girl's shame and envy upon making the same comparison; the child's attempts to grasp the enigma of reproduction and birth by grotesque (yet stereotyped) conjectures, like "the cloacal theory"; and, above all, the violence which children are said to impute to the sight or sounds of their parents' intercourse. "Whatever detail it may be that comes under their observation" or fantasy, Freud insisted, "in all cases they arrive at . . . what we may call the *sadistic conception of coitus,* seeing in it something that the stronger person inflicts on the weaker by force." [19] Projecting backward into the child's intuition his own understanding of the element of rape in every sexual encounter, Freud assigned the child, precisely in his ignorance, the power of a seer. Every child "in part . . . divines the essence of the sexual act and the 'antagonism of the sexes' which precedes it." [20] That the child cannot conceive of a tender sexuality, that all sexuality must look alike to the child—these are not demonstrated facts. But the power of any myth does not depend on its demonstrability as fact, but rather on the persuasiveness of the attitude it embodies, the further attributes it engenders, and the actions it encourages. Freud's myth of the child as the ignorant observer of the sexual antagonisms tells us less about the child than about Freud's conception of the sexual relation. Here is no antinomian celebration of sexuality. Pleasure is defined, after the manner of Schopenhauer, as a negative phenomenon, the struggle to release oneself from unpleasure, or tension. As a great English wit put the case against sex, "The pleasure is momentary, the posture is ridiculous, and the expense is damnable."

In the third of the *Three Essays,* Freud stresses that sexual excitement, because it is a form of tension, must be "counted as an unpleasurable feeling." [21] Only the act of discharge is acknowledged as a genuine pleasure; the mutual caresses, however pleasant, which precede orgasm are purely anticipatory, the "fore-pleasure" essentially unpleasant unless quickly surpassed. To consider sexuality as "detensioning" renders ironical the idea of pleasure in union, for the erotic longing is abolished at the moment of fulfillment.

To understand pleasure as its own abrogation is scarcely a form of hedonism; such a conception serves better as a critique of it. The quest for pleasure becomes a self-defense against the increment of tension; defined in this way, as a kind of treadmill, pleasure loses any ecstatic implication of spontaneity. It becomes a matter of saving and spending, an account that needs to be kept in balance. Whether dammed up by social repressions or allowed, in a permissive society, more scope, the capacities of the individual for pleasure remain limited. What Freud termed his "economic point of view" makes of sexuality not only a limited quantity but one which is always expended in a miserly way.* A hedonist psychology would project a harmonious image of mutual gratification, an idea of one ego's sensual happiness furnishing at once the happiness of the other. Freud's conception of sexuality as an exchange suggests a bargain of fools each of whom is bound to find out that he has invested far more libido than the "object" was really worth. Objects disappoint, instincts are stupid, love cheats when it does not delude.

Such bitter and economic strictures underlie much of the argument in the *Three Essays*. Freud indicates little sympathy for the forms of psychic dalliance. The preliminaries to the sexual act are a necessary hazard, but there is a danger

> if at any point in the preparatory sexual processes the fore-pleasure turns out to be too great and the element of tension too small. The motive for proceeding further with the sexual process then disappears, the whole path is cut short, and the preparatory act in question takes the place of the normal sexual aim.[22]

Too much investment in preliminaries contradicts their ends. Normally, forepleasure does no more than act as an "incentive bonus," [23] making possible the attainment of a greater resultant pleasure. What remains is to get down to the serious business at hand, in order to gain a slight margin of emotional profit.

A similar disapproval of lingering informs Freud's definition of the perversions. They are, so to speak, the forepleasures of one's entire sexual development. While tolerable as a stage, in a maturing sex life the perversions should be traversed "rapidly on the path towards the final sexual aim." [24] Alike "in childhood, in primitive states of society and early periods of history," Freud assumed there is "freedom to range equally over male and female objects." But this freedom

---

* The point that Freud's conception of pleasure is a psychological analogue of scarcity economics has been made brilliantly by David Riesman. Cf. his essay, "The Themes of Work and Play in the Structure of Freud's Thought," *Psychiatry*, XIII, 1 (1950), 1–16.

is irrecoverable; it was "the original basis from which, as a result of restriction in one direction or the other, both the normal and the inverted types develop." [25] Sexual indeterminacy in adult life is "regressive." Maturity involves the restriction and definition of sexual aim, including a general suppression of earlier erotic zones (especially the coprophilic) so that the genital zone has predominance.

Freud is strictly evolutionist in his conception of sexual normality: the genitals are understood as "the *latest* of these erotogenic zones." [26] But he was far from sanguine about the psychological adequacy of final—or normal—eroticism, culturally necessary as it is. There is something to be deplored in this suppression of all but the genital aim of sexuality. Monogamous marriage, as he remarks dryly in the course of analyzing some marriage jokes in *Jokes and Their Relation to the Unconscious,* "is not an arrangement calculated to satisfy a man's sexuality." [27] Freud also advocated, as if in opposition to his evolutionist view of sexuality, a lifting of sexual repressions so as to free sexuality, in part, from the service of monogamic reproduction. Its emancipation from reproduction would remove the moral horror that now attaches to the perversions—that is, to modes of sexuality other than those necessary to the preparation and execution of genital intercourse. In the quantitative formulae of the *Three Essays,* sexuality becomes something more than one appetite among others. Tracing the sources of infantile sexuality (in the second essay), Freud advances a notion of sexuality as a generalized surplus energy arising from "internal processes" whose "intensity" has exceeded "certain quantitative limits." "Indeed," he concludes, "perhaps nothing very important takes place within the organism without contributing a component to the excitation of the sexual instinct." [28] Freud's idea of mechanical detensioning is thus translated into a conception of sexual energy existing not only as desires directed toward individual objects but as a general vitality of the self.[29]

Yet Freud's conception of sex has a constrictive implication, as well as the liberating one adumbrated above. Libido is directed originally not toward others but toward the self. "Narcissism" is our first erotic disposition. This bodily self we first explore and like, before we know what it is to like other bodies, gives a starting point from which the

individual attains the duality of mine and thine—the opposing claims
which, striving for reunion, characterize all eroticism.[30] Thus Freud's
ideas of sexuality as a general energy of the self may be given another
interpretation: that satisfaction from an object is but a devious means
of self-love.

Loving, the body is loved, and thus any object is absorbed into the
subject; even adult loves retain their autistic and self-regarding character. That love must serve the self or the self will shrink from it, that
the self may chase love round an object back to itself again—this is
Freud's brilliant and true insight, reminiscent of La Rochefoucauld's
keen detection of the ego behind the curtain. To care is the polite
form of desire; the man who desires nothing cares for nothing. All
loves are unmasked as self-satisfactions: from the love of the child for
the parent-provider, to the love of spouses which reincarnates these
parent-images, to the parent's "narcissistic" love for his own children.
The duplicity of erotic sentiment is Freud's theme.

II

These dualities of attitude toward the sexual describe Freud's
central insight into the duality of *love*. He divided love into two
components: sensuality narrowly considered, on the one hand, and
feelings of respect and affection, on the other.

How does this division occur? As with most questions, Freud found
an answer in the life of the child. For the "affectionate current is the
older of the two." Affection or tenderness is not a sublimation of
sexuality, as Freud himself sometimes supposed and as his interpreters have invariably presumed; affection, deriving from the infant's
gratitude to its all-protecting parents, is the primary form of love, prior
to sensual feeling.[31] Of course "from the very beginning," "contributions" from the sexual instinct are carried along with the tender re-
spectfulness for and gratitude to authority. In this earliest form of
love the "first sexual satisfactions are experienced in attachment to
the bodily functions necessary for the preservation of life." That,
throughout childhood, figures of authority monopolize our sexual
interest sets the dilemma of our emotional lives: our tendency to

fixate upon the first relation to authority. The tie with authority remains, even when finally, in puberty, there supervenes "the powerful 'sensual' current which no longer mistakes its aims"; the child then tries to "pass on from these objects which are unsuitable in reality"— the parents—"to other extraneous objects with which a real sexual life may be carried on." [32] The drama of love consists in the degree to which sensuality can be infused with tenderness. If in time the new sexual objects can "attract to themselves the affection that was tied to the earlier ones," the authority figures,[33] one will reach adult sexuality with a minimal risk of neurosis.

For a "normal" love, the two currents, affection and sensuality, have to fuse. Freud emphasized that humane and enduring relations, upon which civilization depends, presuppose a sexuality merged with affection. Such amalgams, to be stable, are the result of a long and delicate process of domestication. Nature and culture both conspire against the merger. Culture does so by its notorious tendency to repress sexual pleasure. But Freud rightly viewed this as a less serious threat to normal sexuality than the one offered by nature.

Freud's view has been simplified on this point. He is generally understood to have accounted for the difficulties of domesticating sexuality by the unruly nature of the instinct itself: sexuality refuses to be tamed, its component perverse aptitudes resist suppression for the sake of lasting monogamic relations. In this view, the fusion of sexuality and tenderness mainly involves the difficult task of sublimation imposed by culture on obstreperous sexuality. This account has a place in the psychoanalytic canon. But Freud had a more profound view of love—expressed, characteristically enough, in his genetic analysis. There the opposition is not between sexuality and its sublimations but between sexuality and the response to authority. Tenderness and respect, in Freud's construction, arise from the relation to authority; because these more civil sentiments precede sensuality, they cannot be merely its sublimations. By "nature" (that is, originally) love is authoritarian; sexuality—like liberty—is a later achievement, always in danger of being overwhelmed by our deeper inclinations toward submissiveness and domination. Indeed, sensuality becomes a mode of liberation and Freud may be seen, in this

sense, as its champion. Tender love is a compliant and grateful response to parental dominance, and mature sexuality, which follows,
signifies a freeing from the parents.

Yet the domination persists, as Freud testified by making the
Oedipus Complex the nucleus of all neurotic problems. Stated briefly,
the components of the Oedipus Complex are, first, the sensual current
(incestuous love for the mother), contradicted by, second, the relation
to paternal authority; deference to that authority defines every successful resolution of the Oedipus Complex. The child's sensual current is
inhibited by such deference and thus it becomes a precondition of
culture. This, if I read Freud correctly, answers the objections of
anthropologists such as Malinowski that what Freud called "natural"
(e.g., the Oedipus Complex) was only "the natural byproduct of the
coming into existence of culture." [34] Freud's subtler point is that in
"nature" there exist already the two essential elements of culture. The
Oedipus Complex, which expresses the tension between sexual assertion and submission to the parents, is not a pre-cultural formation
but carries within it the dualistic form of culture. It is this erotic
dualism which accounts for the characteristic tension between order
and rebelliousness present in every culture. By showing that the tie to
authority arises prior to relations of desire, Freud ingeniously accounted for social compliance and the formation of moral ideals as
well.

A later distinction, in his *Group Psychology* (1922), between
sexual and social emotions—what he called "object-love" in contrast
to "identification love"—rests on the same notion of the priority of
the relation to authority. Again, *two* types of love are distinguished,
one being of "what one would like to have" (object-love), while the
other, originally that of a child for its parents, is of "what one would
like to be" (identification). Preceding sexual feeling, "identification
is the earliest and original form of emotional tie." [35] Like his earlier
term, "tender feeling," identification derives originally from the model
submission to the parents. It is, too, the mechanism of all implicit
authority, as contrasted with explicit authority. Whatever its explicit
content, the authority of teachers, friends, leaders, depends upon the
implicit and doctrineless power of command that inheres in the

mechanism of identification. Freud made the connection between love and authority by suggesting that it is the "so-called identifications," not the "object cathexes," which explain social cohesion. The political leader exercises his authority by "putting himself in the place of the subject's parents," [36] thus evoking the earliest, even pre-sexual, form of love.

As Freud's sense of the compelling social nature of love grew upon him, he became more aware of sexuality—the secret act of the private individual—as a safeguard to the de-individualizing functions of love as authority. A similar intuition led George Orwell in *1984* to portray the "proles" as retaining within the totalitarian society a degree of mindless freedom based upon their hypersexuality, while the ideologically engaged are forbidden the dangerous exercise of sexuality. We can measure the speed and distance of the modern retreat from a political doctrine of freedom by this touting of whatever appears refractory in human nature, as if freedom were thereby being proclaimed as inherent in the life-giving act itself.

In deriving the higher love (tenderness, altruism, etc.) from the relation to authority, Freud made a rather unconventional accusation. The problem becomes one of taming the higher feelings rather than the lower; it is, on the whole, the tender, respectful pre-sexual feelings which, by withholding their cooperation as long as they do from the developing sexual feelings, produce the neurotic alternatives: sensuality without affection, or affection without sensuality. For there exists a strong tendency for the two currents, affection and sensuality, to become "divided." [37] This dualism in the capacity to love is characteristic of most neuroses. The most "perverse sexual aims" can develop in "people in whom there has not been a proper confluence of the affectionate and the sensual currents." [38] When this dualism is in the ascendant in a religion, it takes on either an ascetic or orgiastic aspect. An example of the latter is to be found in some of the gnostic heresies which arose within early Christianity; these simply accented a different part of the orthodox dualism, positively valuing the demands of the flesh as identical with those of the spirit.

Freud recognized as one medium of neurosis the hypersensuality of the "masses," in whom sensual pleasure occurs without the accompaniment of tender feelings. But he was more interested in the complementary type, "in people of culture" who have an excess of tender feeling, and who, out of too much respect for one another, perform the sexual act without special pleasure. Ours is a culture, Freud declared, of "anaesthetic men" and "frigid women." [39] His idea of *psychic* impotence is designed to include compulsive promiscuity and even sexual brutality. But he attends mainly to instances of sexual deficiency, such as the model case of the civilized man, so respectful of his even more prudishly reared wife that he "only develops full potency when he is with a debased sexual object," one which fulfills "the condition of debasement." [40] The cultured man chooses his wife after the model of his mother and sisters, women of his own class who, he has been taught, are above sexual desire, and who indeed cannot give themselves up "wholeheartedly to enjoyment." Yet, though precisely with this type his sensuality is blocked, "all the tenderness in him belongs to one of a higher type." This duality of love is institutionalized in the prostitute, or in "the tendency so often observed in men of the highest classes of society to choose a woman of a lower class as a permanent mistress or even as a wife." [41] Thus Freud made the standard triangle of many nineteenth-century French novels—frigid wife, sensual mistress, husband torn between passion and respect—a paradigm of sexual ineptitude among the civilized classes.

What first strikes us about the foregoing quotations is their period flavor. It did not require the researches of Kinsey to tell us that in some times and places the classes may be no more repressed than the masses. The late eighteenth and early nineteenth centuries bred a type of sexual virtuoso among the western European aristocracies that has not yet been surpassed, in quality or in quantity, in our democratic age. Don Juan cannot be a child of the streets, and at best the child of democracy can only grow up to contribute his share to the Don Juanism of his peer group. Once it was poverty and grinding toil that kept the lower-class man of Freud's imagination from playing either Don Juan or Caliban; now it is prosperity and the installment plan. But despite his nostalgia for the sexual freedom of the lower classes,

Freud was never drawn simply to exhort the civilized to be sexually more expressive. Early in his work, he did tend to ascribe neurosis to failures of sexual outlet. As late as 1912 he wrote:

> The most immediate, most easily discerned, and most comprehensible exciting cause of the onset of neurotic illness lies in that external factor which may generally be described as *frustration*. The person was healthy as long as his erotic need was satisfied by an actual object in the outer world; he became neurotic as soon as he is deprived of this object and no substitute is forthcoming.[42]

The "frustration" theory was never abandoned. Nevertheless, Freud recognized that the problem of neurosis was not one of optimal sexual expressiveness. His examples may be dated, but his ethical point remains challenging and thoroughly confutes the reputation of Freud as a libertine reformer. Adultery may well be a neurotic phenomenon, representing the dissociation of the two necessary components of mature sexuality. Freud considered sensuality without affection a degrading state of affairs, and set forth his conception of "a completely normal attitude" [43] in love and marriage as a fusion of tenderness with sensuality.

Even with examples less extreme than the psychic impotence of the civilized classes, Freud's analysis runs along these same lines. How difficult an achievement he makes satisfaction in love: it is scarcely the animal and easy state described in our conventional moralizing literature, but rather the ideal and therefore most elusive condition of man. Freud's own concept of sexuality is remarkably moral. Not sexuality as such but contradictory attitudes toward it are the object of his science. Because of these competing attitudes (which make every present affect best understood as a substitute or "surrogate") love becomes a problem, indeed the greatest problem, and therefore the one most needing to be brought under rational control.

It was Freud's genius to see that sexuality begins not in adulthood but in the life of a child. I do not mean simply what his contemporaries found so shocking, his discovery that children posses sexual feelings. More valuable is his idea that in childhood *love as a problem* is set: contrary to the popular view of childhood as the happiest time, Freud pictures childhood as invariably unhappy. Bacon recommended as an expedient of health the frequent recollection of our early years, because they are a period of life which we seldom look back upon without pleasure. Freud recommended as therapy the systematic recollection of our early years, because they are a period of life which we can never in honesty look back upon without pain. This pain is caused by something beyond the vagaries of parental understanding or the accident of being a lonely child rather than one of a small herd. Beyond the wounds of the child and the scars of the man, there is something in the heart of love itself that makes love pathetic.

The history of the sexual impulse, as Freud related it in his *Three Essays on Sexuality,* is one of dissatisfaction. Love begins in self-love (narcissism); it is fundamentally centripetal and self-deluded. Then, as love grows out of the egoistic pleasures of infancy into childhood, dissatisfaction grows along a parallel course. There are the inevitably frustrated incest impulses of the child, the competitions for parental love, the consequent enmity between siblings. Finally there is the disappointment lurking in all adult love. Freud revived the romantic issue of reality versus love, giving a new sense to the old saw that love is blind. From a discussion of deviations in sexual aim conventionally considered repugnant, he moved with significant abruptness to warn against the psychological "over-valuation" characteristic of love in general. In love "the subject becomes, as it were, intellectually infatuated (that is, his powers of judgment are weakened) by the mental achievements and perfections of the sexual object and he submits to the latter's judgments with credulity." [44]

No world appears less triumphantly passional than Freud's. Throughout his work he underscored the perils and illusions of sexuality, "the most unruly of all the instincts." [45] In the discussion of inversion (the first of the *Three Essays on Sexuality*) especially, Freud seems to be arguing against any notion of a normatively harmonious sexuality. His dictum that a neurosis can always be traced to a disturbed sexual life hardly indicates a joyful interpretation of sexuality. As he declared that sexuality "remains the weak spot" in the process of *"cultural* development," [46] we may infer that it is also an individual's weakness. Freud argued far more strongly that sexuality is vulnerability than he did that it constitutes strength—the major source of prized qualities such as tenderness, ebullience, creative energy.

Frustration is the obverse side of the problem of sexuality, the principal side presented to the reader by Freud. He presented the other side as well, perhaps the more complex and interesting one—of sexuality as a problem in the mechanics of satisfaction. Not frustration but something in the nature of sexuality itself determines that there shall be, ever, a "mental absence of satisfaction." [47] While it is true generally that instinctual desires become more imperative when frustrated, only of sexuality is the converse also true: that the value the mind attaches to the instinct invariably sinks when it is gratified. Alcoholics (Freud's counter-example) do not need to vary their brand to maintain their pleasure, nor to emigrate to "dry" countries in order to stimulate their dwindling pleasure by new obstacles. Something of this sort does in fact characterize the "relation of the lover to his sexual object." [48] Throughout history, "wherever natural barriers in the way of satisfaction have not sufficed, mankind has created conventional ones to enjoy love." * Freud's sensitivity to the transitoriness of sensual fulfillment deserves comparison with that of the novelists of Romantic introspection: with Benjamin Constant, in *Adolphe,* whose "heart grows weary of all that it has and sighs for all that it has not"; and Proust, who describes in *La Prisonnière* how "every person we love and, to some degree everyone, is for us a Janus who offers us his pleasing face if the person leaves us, but his dreary face if we know he remains always at our disposal." That this problem of satisfaction is a discovery of Romantic literature, from Rousseau's *Confessions* to confessional novels like those of Constant and Proust, documents again the consonance of psychoanalytic and Romantic motifs. Psychoanalysis is itself an *erotic* psychology, a playing out of the Eros myth as science. Freud did indeed analyze Eros, but he took its operations too much for granted as somehow in the nature of

---

* Thus, during the licentious era at the waning of classical civilization, "love became worthless" and "life empty." When Christianity entered, its ascetic demands "created psychical values for love which pagan antiquity was never able to confer on it" (SE XI, 188). Freud does not add that Christianity also moralized love, and linked it to everyday conduct, in a way pagan antiquity could never conceive.

things, without seeing that Eros operates first of all as a major world religion which has but lately put into service biological and psychological rhetorics.

Freud did more than notice, with the Romantic novelists, that "something in the nature of the sexual instinct itself is unfavorable to the achievement of absolute gratification." He offered an answer: this "something" in the nature of the instinct that is unfavorable is its early attachment to the parents. The reason that "the value the mind sets on erotic need instantly sinks as soon as satisfaction becomes readily attainable" is that later loves are only surrogates for the original one. Though the child's desires for the parents are frustrated by the incest taboo, the sexual instinct remains related to its first object. The force of these original passions explains for Freud the individual's restiveness within monogamy, as it also accounts for the fatigue of promiscuity, whereby "the original object" is "represented by an endless series of substitutive objects none of which, however, brings full satisfaction." [49] Far from being a champion of unbridled sensuality, Freud acutely understood the intimate connection between libertine and ascetic behavior. Both are excesses, deriving from an imperfect emancipation from childhood's insatiable love of authority-figures. Both a Saint Augustine and a de Sade may be understood as fixated on the fantasies formed during childhood "which have later after all found a way out into real life." [50] If from Freud we may infer that monogamy is not a very satisfactory arrangement, the results of his science may also be taken to show that man is a naturally faithful creature: the most inconstant sexual athlete is in motivation still a toddler, searching for the original maternal object.

Romantic love, the "over-valuation" which is the characteristic erotic idea of Western culture, was similarly explained by the unique relation to the parents. For the delusion that "the loved one" is

unique . . . irreplaceable, can be seen to fall just as naturally into the context of the child's experience, for no one possesses more than one mother, and the relation to her is based on an event that is not open to any doubt and cannot be repeated.[51]

So men and women live trapped in a series of erotic illusions. Freud sought not to strengthen these illusions, but to break them. Any notion that his is a doctrine of sexual expressiveness only, undervalues his fresh arguments against Romantic love. Sexuality is the wayward, transient force of life—to be exercised but not praised.*

Freud's three important essays on "The Psychology of Love" (1910, 1912, 1918), from which I took the preceding observations on degraded love objects, are really a critique of romantic love. Unlike his negative point, that the erotic relation to parents governs our later affections and fills them with discontent, the positive critique is ambivalent. On the one hand, he seems simply to be urging a more realistic attitude toward erotic relations. On the other hand, there is a subtle psycho-political judgment involved: the primal form of love —that of child for parent—is the model instance of an authority relation, and Freud advanced an ideal of love purged of parental influences, an exchange of equals. It is the therapeutic goal of psycho-analysis to abrogate the power of the prototype, to cut the umbilical cord of authority—so that love may be truly between persons, not between imagoes. Thus Freud's ethical intention reverses his conceptual meaning. He rarely took sexuality to be simply a compartment of life, an objective desire, one appetite among others that clamor to be satisfied. Sexuality is *prefigurative,* the clue to the meaning of later conduct and appetite; if a patient manifests some moral or gestural abnormality the analyst assumes he will find a premonition of it in the early sexual life during the course of treatment.[52]

Yet, as far as his ethical intention is concerned, it is clear that Freud wished to check the prefigurative jurisdiction of sexuality. More pre-

---

* His admonition to his fiancée that marriage survives on respect, not love, is allied to the point made publicly, in a number of essays, that a woman must expect to lose her lover the day she takes him for a husband. Mixed with personal possessiveness and a Victorian sentimentalism about women, so far as his own wife was concerned at least, there is an admonitory note in Freud's letters that anticipates his great critique of the romantic ideal of love.

See also his remarks on John Stuart Mill's famous essay, "The Subjection of Women" (which Freud translated for the German collected edition of Mill's works), in another letter to his fiancée; there he writes: "Nature has determined women's destiny through beauty, charm, and sweetness" (quoted by Jones, op. cit., I, 176).

cisely, by advocating that sexuality be freed from domination (i.e., that the sexual aptitudes be detached from the parental models), psychoanalysis would change the prefigurative effect of our erotic behavior. In a reformed character, sexuality would be acknowledged as an objective need, demanding expression whatever the subjective complications. Allowing sexuality a greater objectivity, Freud implied, would reduce the momentous and prefigurative implications of erotic acts, thus leaving us free to make sexual decisions on a more conscious level, with much less at stake. Far from advocating pan-sexualism, Freud's aim was to put sexuality in its proper place.

III

To achieve psychological freedom through some form of regression is a contradiction in terms. In Freud's matured conception of psychoanalytic treatment, retrospection replaces regression. And retrospection is focused, more than upon any other point in the patient's past, on the Oedipus Complex, that nuclear configuration of sexual desire, repression, and identification with a parent-figure which all persons experience. Psychoanalytic therapy concentrates on getting the patient to review particularly the relation to his parents so as to effect a *modus vivendi* with it. Authority is Freud's basic problem, neurosis the occasion for examining its vicissitudes; his therapy attempts to erode the childhood laws by which authority operates. But in proposing a re-education which would unmask the erotic illusion by which obedience is maintained, Freud exhibits his essentially ironic view of human freedom: the emancipation from erotic authority must come though a replica of erotic authority—the "transference."

This is not to deny that the therapy, as discussed in Chapter III, is an intellectual exercise. But it is also a struggle, in which the analyst must use his authority to penetrate the defenses of the patient and to transmute past loyalties into present energies. Although Freud complained of his early patients' recalcitrance—Dora did not develop a transference; neither did the young subject of the paper on female homosexuality—one surmises from these case histories that Freud began by being fairly tolerant of his patients' questions and arguments. By the time the papers on technique were written, in 1912–1915, however, he apparently had become less permissive intellectually. The gauntlet of objections through which a therapist had to run ought to be shortened, the proving-ground of the transference more swiftly reached. Now, Freud asserted, the first aim of the treatment consisted in attaching the patient "to the treatment and to the person of the physician." [53] Intellectual assent could come later, when it was less hedged round by resistances. Of course, "intellect is a power too . . . one that is all the more certain in the end." Without it, transformed into faith by the mechanism of the transference, the "physician and his arguments would never even be listened to." [54] But despite the intellectualist leanings of his therapy of self-consciousness, Freud came to rely far more on the power of love. "Love is the great educator," he proclaimed,[55] even though it is also the great problem.

Freud's reasons for magnifying the role of the transference in therapy include the familiar one that, after all, "logical arguments are impotent against affective interests." [56] Yet it is *not* simply that the physician needs an assent deeper than the intellectual, or that he hopes more easily to intimidate the patient with the keen edge of erotic attachment. Were these the only reasons, the transference would be a mere adjunct, useful because it governs that recognition of authority without which the physician cannot proceed with the cure.[57] Freud used the transference in a more central way: it becomes itself the cure. Analysis aims not only at doctrinal assent, attained through the passions of the transference. It aims at a transformation of the passions, chiefly the passion of dependence itself. By the First World War, Freud's therapeutic beliefs had enlarged beyond the power of reason to dispel emotional fixations, to include a subtler version of Breuer's procedure: the emancipative power of a repetition of passion's decisive form. Self-consciousness, to emancipate, needs another self, a sympathetic audience before which the unacted part of life can at last be acted out. "The main instrument . . . for curbing the patient's compulsion to repeat" the same unhappy emotional patterns is the device of according this compulsion "the right to assert itself" once more—in the patient's attachment to the analyst. The analyst renders harmless the compulsion to repeat by admitting

> it into the transference as to a playground, in which it is allowed to let itself go in almost complete freedom and is required to display before us all the pathogenic impulses hidden in the depths of the patient's mind.

Transference reproduces the larger conflict exactly; it is the play-within-the-play in the psychoanalytic drama.

> . . . We can regularly succeed in giving all the symptoms of the neurosis a new transference-colouring, and in replacing his whole ordinary neurosis by a "transference-neurosis" of which he can be cured by the therapeutic work. The transference thus forms a kind of intermediary realm between illness and real life, through which the journey from the one to the other must be made. The new state of mind has absorbed all the features of the illness; it represents, however, an artificial illness which is at every point accessible to our intervention.[58]

Because the transference unavoidably repeats the patient's life struggle with authority, at this point a liberating reconciliation with authority has to take place. Itself a repetition of the authority-love, the patient's transference—carefully commented upon by the physician *—is to be used to break the prematurely fixed hold of parents and other authority-figures. Freud urged that the dominational Eros, absorbed into the analytic context, be used against itself. In the therapeutic parody of authority, the pliability of Eros can be brought home to the patient. He must be convinced that his feelings are unrelated to the analyst's person (even if this is not entirely the case), but arise because "anyone whose need for love is not being satisfactorily gratified" will be roused "by each new person coming upon the scene." [59] By thus stressing the formal pattern of authority, the patient will be freed to alter the form of his or her capacity to love.

---

* Cf. Otto Fenichel, *The Psychoanalytic Theory of Neurosis* (New York: 1945), p. 571: "Any psychotherapeutic method makes use of transference, but only in psychoanalysis does this consist in *interpretation* of the transference, that is, in making it conscious."

The analyst, too, must keep in mind the formal character of Eros. In his esoteric papers * Freud took special care to instruct psychoanalysts that theirs was an office *charisma,* not a personal one. The analyst "must recognize that the patient's falling in love is induced by the analytic situation and is not to be ascribed to the charms of his person." [60] If we view the psychoanalyst historically, as the descendant of earlier moral physicians, this routinization of *charisma* in the transference marks a conspicuous development. *Charisma* (at least theoretically) is no longer a personal gift, as in the religious healers, but a technical function; it is the power of the dominational Eros that is transferred. At the same time, of course, Freud insisted that the patient's feelings must not *appear* inevitable. The patient is not supposed to know what lies ahead: the transference must not be robbed "of the element of spontaneity which is so convincing" [61]— an almost impossible demand in this era of popular psychoanalytic sophistication.

What considerations, then, require the analyst to restrain his own erotic response? Freud dismissed "moral decree" and appealed to "the requirements of analytic technique." [62] To become erotically involved with the patient would bring the physician "down to the level of a lover." [63] From the pedagogic point of view, the patient's "passionate demands for love" [64] are devices of resistance, attempts to undermine the analyst's authority by drawing him into the world of accessible love-objects.† In the outbreak of psychotherapeutic healing stimulated by the success of the psychoanalytic movement, the lifting of Freud's ban on the erotic response of the therapist was bound to occur. For this neither Freud nor his movement can be held responsible. Yet among his very first disciples the theoretic justification of a therapeutic "love-transference" was advanced. During one period of his career, Ferenczi in particular maintained that the prime force in the analysis is the permissive explicit approval given patients

---

* The seven so-called "papers on technique" (1912–1915) which were written "not for patients, but for physicians" (*Coll. Papers* II, 382).

† The patients, at first denying the sexual roots of their neurosis, "later on disclose the over-estimation of sexual life which has them in thrall," and try to take the analyst "captive in the net of their socially ungovernable passions" (*Collected Papers* II, 390).

by the analyst. Possibly Freud's demand that the analyst suppress his own feelings, and remain cool and aloof toward the patient, misstates the analyst's task. Freud demands an impartiality and intellectual dispassionateness that he does not seem to have preserved with his own patients; surely, too, it is desirable that the analyst not bully the patient, or claim infallibility for himself or his science. On the other hand, any claim that physician and patient can meet as equals in treatment makes nonsense of Freud's therapeutic doctrine. His insight seems to me the true one that the "love" which the therapist might bestow upon the patient cannot be disentangled from the relation of "a superior and a subordinate" [65] which analysis presupposes in every erotic relation.

More important, Freud based his demand that the physician suppress his own erotic feelings on an appeal to the goal of the treatment, a liberation of the patient's sexuality. The patient's emotions toward the analyst prove therapeutically useful. To break the dominational pattern and emancipate sexuality from mere service to authority, an authority-figure is needed. But precisely because the analyst was a *therapeutic* authority-figure he must not reciprocate the patient's love. Such counter-transference would only strengthen the images of parental authority which the analysis aims to depose. For purposes of confronting Eros, the erotic authority of the analyst must be intellectualized, essentially parodied. The psychoanalytic pedagogy is a mock warfare of loves, a "new edition of the old disease." [66] Our capacity for love "is disabled by infantile fixations." [67] By detaching it from inaccessible objects of the past and projecting it onto the figure of the analyst, the transference reactivates this disabled capacity for love. Thereby infantile fixations are dispelled—rather, reconstructed —and a new beginning in sociability can be made. The therapist must follow an intricate course: between maintaining in himself the surrogate of erotic authority and exposing its form to the patient's understanding. At the same time the patient's sexuality cannot be permitted a futile expression; the therapeutic situation is, after all, not life but only a re-education for life.

To aim at making libido "accessible to consciousness and at last serviceable to reality" [68] thus constitutes the first paradox of psychoanalytic treatment: it is authoritarian—to cure the love which has remained attached to childhood figures of authority, or at least to render the burden of authority tolerable. Further, the second apparent paradox, it is ascetic—to cure asceticism. For, to cure the particular asceticism that afflicts the patient, to liberate sexuality, the treatment "must be carried through in a state of abstinence." [69] The patient, "incapable of true satisfaction," must be deprived of any "discharge by surrogates" until true satisfaction becomes possible.[70] According to the secular counter-discipline which Freud outlined, the analytic couch posture can be viewed not merely as an aid to undistracted mental activity, but as an ascetic measure. Patients do "not wish to be deprived of a view of the physician," [71] but during the analytic hour it is necessary that they be so deprived. Such therapeutic asceticisms help fix the patient's "desire and longing" upon the "work" of treatment.[72] More germane, it seems to me, is the negative gain. These measures protect patients "to some extent from the many hostile influences seeking to detach them from the analysis." [73] In order that the patient be fully attached to the analyst he must be detached, at least temporarily, from competing relations, friends, and lovers. But this may be felt less as a deprivation than as a profound liberation. Supported by the promise to the physician "to form no important decisions affecting his life during the course of the treatment, for instance, choice of a profession or of a permanent love-object," [74] the patient has a rare opportunity to disengage himself temporarily from living's endless chain of crisis and commitment. Therapy not only allows a willing suspension of belief but allows the moral life itself to become suspended.

IV

By insisting that the emotions generated in an analysis are part of the analytic *situation,* and arise without regard to the individual personalities of either patient or physician, Freud seems to say that it does not matter who is involved: certain characteristic erotic responses will occur. Yet it made a great difference to Freud, as therapist, who was being analyzed—whether male or female. Not so much in his case histories as in his theoretical remarks, Freud shows condescension toward his female patients. The mental evolution which he traces through childhood is invariably predicated of the boy-child; he usually adds that the same mechanism (with the appropriate reversal of parental objects) applies to the little girl—in simpler and less assertive form.[75]

Not only does Freud aver that girls *feel* biologically at a disadvantage, inferior, because they do not possess a penis; he affirms that they *are* in the grossest sense something less than boys.[76] In the chapter entitled "The Psychology of Women" in the *New Introductory Lectures* (1933) he makes explicit some deprecations of women that are implicit elsewhere in his work. Here Freud appeals both to the bio-psychological *de*scription of women as intellectually less able and the psycho-moral *pre*scription, that they had best leave the things of the mind alone, since these interfere with the exercise of their sexual function. Freud faced the great problem created by the emancipation of women: "intellectual training" may cause them "to depreciate the feminine role for which [they are] intended." The romantic in Freud saw a happy destiny for the sexually relaxed "caretaker's daughter": she "will find a lover; perhaps bear a child . . . perhaps become a popular actress and end as an aristocrat." Meanwhile, the poor little upper-class girl, too well brought up, is destined to become the more neurotic half of a wretched marriage.[77] In thus charging that sexual and intellectual are incompatible in women, Freud exhibits again his belief that the two qualities are basically opposed. This opposition between sex and intellect remained an unquestioned part of Freud's doctrine of human nature.

That sensuality is connected with incomplete individuation, that it is on the whole regressive, incompatible with the rational and progressive temperament which Freud acknowledges as "masculine," is equally unquestioned. Assuming that somehow the sexual development of women proves specially limiting, he remarks that "the difficult development which leads to femininity" seems to exhaust "all the possibilities of the individual";[78] his concession that "an individual woman may be a human being apart from this" (her sexual function)[79] speaks for itself. There is a premature arrestment in the life cycle of each woman; "psychological rigidity" sets in long before it does in men. In contrast with that of a man of thirty, still youthful and incompletely developed, the libido of a woman of about the same age "has taken up its final positions, and . . . there are no paths open to her for further development." [80] The task of resolving a woman's neurosis may be viewed as quite different from that of a man's. Arguing in his great essay, "Analysis Terminable and Interminable" (1937), that no individual analysis can be permanently terminated if it aims at a thorough cure of neurotic disorder, Freud also concludes that the analysis of women is even more superficial in aim than that of men.* He contrasts the job of psychoanalysis with male patients—to *develop* their capacities, sexual and otherwise —with the more limited aim, in the case of women patients, of *resigning* them to their sexuality.[81] Analysis cannot encourage in women new energies for success and achievement, but only, finally, teach them the lesson of a rational resignation to the demands of their natures. Freud sees sexuality as woman's problem in a special sense, beyond the general sense in which it is a problem for all persons, male or female.

Freud's special attitude toward women is evident as early as *The Interpretation of Dreams,* in the theory of dream symbolism. Here are some of the definitions—by now well known—with which Freud marked out a symbolic dictionary in *The Interpretation of Dreams,* and (seventeen years later) in Lecture 10 of the *Introductory Lectures.* A landscape, like a house, a church, a town, a citadel, "on account of its property of enclosing within it the human being" is

---

* This ideological point does not cancel the historical one: psychoanalysis began as a therapy for women (though more of the case histories are of men), and the classical problem of psychoanalysis is hysteria, at first thought to be exclusively a women's disorder.

It is also apparent that the therapy is really constructed, whatever the neutrality of role professed, in the image of the masterful and male analyst and the docile, cooperative female patient. When Freud described the phenomena of transference, he plainly had in mind the object-sensuality of the female patient. Freud did not long consider why—he mentions it once, without comment—the phenomenon of "negative transference" (strong hostile feelings against the analyst) appears more commonly among his male patients (*Collected Papers* V, 316–57).

female.[82] Anything round or liquid is female, while hard, pointed, or complexly shaped objects are male. Being upright and elongated, persons are male symbols—regardless of sex or age; [83] so are birds, airplanes, Zeppelins, kites, balloons, because they fly.[84] The female genitals are "organs," the male a "mechanism," an "apparatus." [85] Male symbols are activities, tools and implements and machinery, created things, forming things; female symbols are receptacles, materials (such as wood and paper), natural objects.

In sum, Freud assigned sexual meanings to the most elementary attributes of "thing"—extension, solidity, protrusion—and those of "void," dividing nature itself between the sexes. His symbolism is a table of the basic aesthetic images available to the mind, but of a special sort: it is a symbolism of power and passivity. *Most* symbols refer to the male organ, Freud declared.[86] All elongations—extension emphasizing length rather than width—symbolize the penis; [87] purposiveness and intention itself are masculine; all direction is erection. The model of all Freud's symbols for the female genitals is the space which provides the room for extension, or, less pejoratively, the space without which extension is unimaginable. By this symbolism Freud projected his own prejudices about women into the fixed substrate of the mind. Nietzsche, another great misogynist, prefaced all his deprecations of women with the admission that one's attitude to women is a matter of personal temperament, "my" truth but not necessarily "yours." Freud, however, has in his symbolic asserted a misogyny native to all persons, including women themselves. Balancing the idiosyncratic *over*estimation of any love object, Freud detected a shared *under*estimation of women, a "repudiation of femininity" [88] rooted in biology itself, but which—more significantly, from a psychologist's point of view—inheres plastically in the natural imagination below all cultural or individual variety.

Freud's symbolism is too generalized to be convincing. All objects are either containers or contained. All objects fall somewhere between the two extreme possibilities of object-shape: the most diffuse and the most angular. All three-dimensional objects are relatively convex or concave, up or down, high or low. What Freud did, in making every seeable thing at least potentially available as a genital symbol, was to assign sexual analogues to the very nature of perception.* Spatial relations provide a stock of analogical criteria so inexhaustible as to make the criteria lose value.

The same objection holds when we turn, in the psychoanalytic dictionary, from the nouns we have been so far discussing to the only other part of speech the unconscious knows, apparently—the infinitive verb. Freud explained all climactic processes (e.g., climbing stairs, running) as the rising to consummation and falling away of coitus.[89] But the Freudian symbolic allows no reasonable discrimination among processes. Resolution or climax characterizes any ordered activity, effort, or event; efficiency as well as pleasure depends on events having such a form. For Freud to assign sexual intercourse as a sub-sense to work, play, and art is an arbitrary concretion of the aesthetics of form. One could with equal plausibility propose any other elemental activity as the prime analogate, and indeed others have been proposed, the best-known theory, after Freud's, being Otto Rank's that all neurotic crises contain an ultimate reference to the traumatic experience of birth.†

A second main defect of the Freudian symbolic is that, based as it is upon such extremely formal criteria, it passes over all sorts of lacunae and discrepancies with, at best, slight notice. Functional, relational, and plastic criteria for interpreting symbols are employed indiscriminately, even when one analogical criterion contradicts or, more generously, supplements another. Sometimes an object is interpreted on the basis of its shape: thus pointed objects are male symbols, round objects female. Other times the Freudian interpreter may ignore shape in favor of relational criteria. In such cases, the feminine still has the same criterion (concave shape), but the male object can assume any shape so long as it is enclosed within the concave female symbol: a foot in a shoe, a hand in a glove, bread in an oven, a person in a room all symbolize the position of male and female genitals. Any two objects in the relation of up-and-down or top-and-bottom (e.g., a horse and rider) are sexual symbols,

---

* Cf. *The Interpretation of Dreams,* SE V, 372: "It is fair to say that there is no group of ideas that is incapable of representing sexual facts and wishes."
† Cf. Otto Rank, *The Trauma of Birth* (New York: 1929).

whatever their shape, in virtue of the relational analogy to the commonest position in coitus. Again, Freud based an alternative and sometimes contradictory set of symbolic interpretations on the analogy to biological functions. The analogue of menstrual periodicity transforms a time-piece (e.g., a wrist watch, a wall clock), whatever its shape, into a feminine symbol.[90] Again, the concave shape of jars, vases, boxes, and suitcases invariably made them female symbols. But the criterion of shape can be superseded by function, as when Freud listed vessels containing liquid (for example, watering cans) as invariably male. Trees, to take another example, have had an exceptionally versatile career in the psychoanalytic symbolic. Being tall and erect (the criterion of individual shape), the tree Freud interpreted as a male sexual symbol.[91] But an eminent disciple of his, Karl Abraham, used a functional analogy, the fact that a tree bears fruit, as a basis for making it a female symbol.[92] Again, Rank and Sachs think wood "male," because of its hardness and because it comes from a tree (the "tree phallus").[93] But Freud, using an equally plausible functional analogue, could assert that wood is always a female symbol, being a material (from *mater* = mother) out of which things are made.[94]

Like all quests for hidden meaning, the psychoanalytic quest for universal symbols in our ordinary behavior lends itself to arbitrariness and contradiction. Yet, at the price of numerous internal contradictions, Freud's symbolic does remain consistent with his covert ethical theory of the war between the sexes, which was so overt a theme in nineteenth- and twentieth-century literature. Freud's symbolic dictionary announces that—like children and primitives—women are closer to "nature," while men are closer to "things." The male principle is active, the female principle is passive, fructifying, the unformed material of things. Ultimately the tension between male and female is, in the Freudian symbolic, that between unconscious and conscious. To women Freud paid the always handsome tribute of a throwing up of hands before the mystery of femininity, as was regularly paid during the Romantic era to the unconscious, to will, to nature herself. "Throughout the ages," he declares in the *New Intro-*

ductory Lectures, the "problem" of women "has puzzled people of every kind." [95]

Two images of female character recur in Freud's writings. One is the image of the seductress. Freud found it psychologically justified that men have a certain fear or dread of women:

> The man is afraid of being weakened by the woman, infected with her femininity and of then showing himself incapable. The effect which coitus has of discharging tensions and causing flaccidity may be the prototype of what the man fears; and realization of the influence which the woman gains over him through sexual intercourse, the consideration she thereby forces from him, may justify the extension of this fear.[96]

This romantic image of the adult heterosexual encounter is repeated in Freud's view that fear of the female is normal to the psychology of the male during early childhood, and that "castration fear" is always felt at the sight of the female genitals. (The figure of the deadly Medusa, the sight of whom turns men into stone, is interpreted by Freud as a mythological representation of the castrated and castrating woman.) [97] But there is another image that illustrates the seductive role of women: that of the mother—as passive and the source of unqualified affection. This is the point of Freud's statement that the one unambivalent emotional relation is the feeling of a mother for her son.[98] Again, it dictates his interpretation of the childhood of Leonardo da Vinci. The plight of Leonardo's mother, Caterina, is cast in familiar melodramatic terms. She is the passive and maternal woman, cast aside by her lover as soon as she has satisfied his selfish sexual demand.*

The dual image of woman—as mother, as temptress—governs the oversubtle interpretation Freud makes of one of his own dreams. In the dream scene three women are standing in a kitchen; after recalling a childhood scene of his own mother standing in the kitchen kneading dough, Freud associates the three figures, one of whom is "the mother who gives life," with the three Fates.[99] And the three

---

* That Leonardo's mother was condemned by society to lasting censure for having borne a bastard—a crucial assumption in Freud's reconstruction of the artist's childhood—seems factually dubious. Standards of sexual propriety in the Italy of the fifteenth century were less strict than those of Freud's time.

Fates are, in another context, interpreted as the "three inevitable relations man has with women": with the "mother who bears him, with the companion of his bed and board, and with the destroyer." [100] No doubt Freud's images of femininity owe far more to romantic fiction than to his own mental history. For the beloved as mother, recall Goethe's treatment of Werther's first view of Lotte, distributing bread to a crowd of children about her knees. The beloved as *femme fatale* becomes more prominent in the fiction of the latter half of the century: Mérimée's Carmen, Gautier's Cleopatra, Nastasya Filippovna in *The Idiot,* and in the work of Swinburne, Pater, Wilde, D'Annunzio. In *Peer Gynt* both types of female images appear, each dignified to mythic proportions. Released by his mother's death, the life of Ibsen's Everyman is divided between the maternal woman who waits for him (Solveig) and the sensual woman (Anitra) of his wanderings' encounters. After experiencing pleasure, power, riches, fame, Peer returns as an old man to Solveig, who rocks him on her breast, singing a lullaby, as the play ends. The trajectory of feminine mystery and power behind Ibsen's myth-play is just that invoked by Freud in interpreting *King Lear* and other tales which involve three women. Freud interprets the triad of sisters as a projection of the three Fates, and the Fates as a mythological representation of the "different forms taken on by the figure of the mother." First there is "the mother herself"; then "the beloved who is chosen after her pattern"; and finally "the Mother Earth." The "old man" (Freud means Lear, but what he says perfectly applies to Peer Gynt) "yearns after the love of woman as once he had it from his mother" but in vain, for instead—recall the last, fatal embrace of the mother-beloved Solveig, and of Cordelia—"the silent goddess of Death will take him into her arms." [101]

In an age which thought itself deficient in emotion, Freud acceded to the belief which made of woman the principle of vitality, the ground of creation and death. Falling victim to one of the varieties of mother symbolism,* Freud never broke off his unacknowledged romance with the Dark Lady. Even a potboiler like Rider Haggard's

---

* Jung has given the original and unsurpassed account of mother symbolism in *Symbols of Transformation,* Collected Works, V (New York: 1956).

She came in for Freud's approbation: he read the "hidden meaning" of Rider Haggard's "strange book" as the equivalence of the "immortality of our emotions [to] the eternal feminine." [102]

V

It is not surprising that Freud's suspicion of the feminine character has evoked strenuous rebuttal, led by his one-time colleague, Alfred Adler. What Freud called "penis envy," Adler called "masculine protest"—a term as distinctly critical of male hegemony as Freud's was of women. Adler finds the phenomenon a historical product rather than a physiological necessity, thus encouraging us to try to outgrow or escape this psychological limitation imposed by our culture. The Adlerian (and later "neo-Freudian") critique of Freud's anti-feminist psychology seems to me correct, at least in its large outlines. Freud did allow that the intellectual inferiority characteristic of most women might be attributed to the extraordinary mental repressions under which they mature in our culture.[103] * Yet in the final analysis his personal intuitions mastered him, and cultural causes were slighted in favor of the biological differential and an "innate" inferiority.†

A denial of the Freudian psychology of women cannot depend on historical reductions of Freud's own psychology. It is not enough to say that Freud himself reproduced the "masculine protest" [104] characteristic of his time and place. His misogyny, like that of his predecessors, is more than prejudice; it has a vital intellectual function in his system. In the nineteenth century strong links, the forging of

---

* Indeed, he was often more daringly sociological in his explanations than we now appreciate. Whether a certain type of sexual behavior is called perverse is a matter of cultural definition; without "the authoritative inhibition of society" we would see that homosexuality, for instance, fully corresponds "to the sexual inclinations of no small numbers of people" (SE VII, p. 229). See also Freud's remarks on slaves in ancient times, on nobility, etc. (ibid., p. 230). But on the other hand, notice Freud's blindness to the sociological determinants of feminine character.

† The fullest extrapolation of Freud's views on women is to be found in Helene Deutsch's influential two volumes titled *The Psychology of Women, A Psychoanalytic Interpretation* (New York: 1947). For a statement of the neo-Freudian critique of Freud's views, see Karen Horney's book, *New Ways in Psychoanalysis* (New York: 1939).

which have not yet been closely studied, existed between irrationalist philosophy and misogyny. Freud's views echo those of Schopenhauer (in the essay "On Women") and Nietzsche. And just as sympathetic expositors of Schopenhauer and Nietzsche want to dismiss these philosophers' views on women as idiosyncratic and philosophically irrelevant,[105] so the neo-Freudians (led by eminent women analysts like Karen Horney) would like to omit that part of Freud's work as mere culture-prejudice, maintaining that much of the remaining doctrine can be realigned without damage. But actually the pejorative image of woman serves as a measure of the general critical component in Western philosophies. That the great critical figures in modern philosophy, literature, psychology—Nietzsche, Lawrence, Freud— were misogynists is a fact the significance of which has not yet been properly assessed.

I have overstated the consistency of Freud's deprecation of women; by liberating women (as he did children) from sentimentality and prudery, Freud put women on an eye-level of equality with men. But this line of argument does not release him from the implications of his misogyny. True, Freud would take women down from the Victorian pedestal of chastity and pure feeling; thereby he dispels one respectable form of masculine condescension. But what he substitutes for it is an even less disguised hostility. Within the nineteenth-century panorama of moral attitudes there were always viable *two* forms of misogyny. One was the Victorian form in which Americans were once schooled, which idealized women as natively innocent and above sex. The other was the view still in the ascendant, partly because of Freud's influence, in which women are conceived (by both women and men) as naturally more sensual.

It is possible to classify by national traditions these two types of misogyny. In the nineteenth century French writers as diverse as Michelet * and Comte exalted women as the conservers of high ethical standards and of traditional and pacific culture; the same view is to be found in English novels and polite essays. German writers— poets, philosophers, politicians—took a patronizing view of women as fundamentally anti-intellectual and of a lower ethical ambition

---

* Freud mentions Michelet's book *Woman*.

and cultural caliber than men; a similar view is to be found among the great Russian novelists. In the Franco-British version, women perform the role of cultural conservation; in the Russo-German version, the domestic role of women is seen as anti-cultural. The first misogynistic attitude is based on the *sexual* deficiency of women (the Victorian image): women are considered more delicate emotionally and more cultivated, in contrast with the crude, earthy energies of the male. The second misogynistic attitude is based on the *intellectual* deficiency of women: the child-bearing female represents the natural heritage of humanity, while the male carries on in spite of her enticements the burden of government and rational thought.

In both styles of disparagement a division of the sensual from the intellectual capacities is presumed.* Freud's view is plainly of the Russo-German school: women are erotic hoarders in the male economy of culture. In the strife between sensuality and culture, women represent the senses. Women represent "the interests of family and sexual life," men "the claims of culture," [106] Freud writes. Women express what is primal and static as contrasted with masculine dynamism. Because symbols of origins and arrestment are feminine, the element of misogyny in Freud's doctrine may be linked directly to his idea of nature as developmental. Any arrestment of natural development is Freud's basic definition of illness. In his conception masculinity is active and proper to the virtues of a person, while the feminine is passive and proper to the constraints a person may suffer through the persistence of certain primal forms.

Toward the idea of "the upward development of mankind" Freud showed an intellectual ambivalence familiar to students of moral letters in the nineteenth century. There is not only the head but also the heart to consider; for a hundred and fifty years the head has argued against itself. The "culture lag" theory, for example, is but one among many arguments advanced by intellectuals that man has developed intellect at the expense of emotion, thus upsetting the

---

* Cf. Helene Deutsch, *The Psychology of Women*, I, p. 290: "Women's intellectuality is to a large extent paid for by the loss of valuable feminine qualities: it feeds on the sap of the affective life and results in impoverishment of this life either as a whole or in specific emotional qualities."

balance upon which the good life and a genuinely high culture depend. Men will educate themselves into demonic creatures, Burckhardt prophesied. In his own private vision of the end of history, he saw the now-familiar figure of secular mythology, the intellectual cripple—crippled by his overdeveloped intellect. The evolutionist vision of rational development drove Nietzsche to his deepest nightmare, of the last man, the mass man, whose posture is reclining, whose feeling is ennui, bored in a world in which intelligence has made of passion a routine. Similarly Freud accepted as an article of faith that culture "originates mainly at the cost of the sexual component instincts, and that these must be suppressed, restrained, transformed." [107] But this process may in time spell the end of the race, for as "the world of the senses becomes gradually mastered by spirituality," [108] the sexual pleasures enjoyed by our ancestors may become indifferent or even intolerable to ourselves.

Freud was not wholly a late Romantic. Despite the apprehensions he voiced about the loss of civilized sexual vitality, and despite his romanticizing of the sexuality of the lower classes, he remained a rationalist. In order to complete his rationalist creed, he needed to incarnate the irrational, without which his rationalism lacked purpose.

How significant that Freud combined his rationalist creed with a Romantic mythology of women. To the same degree as he respected intellect, he made the ordinary *Hausfrau* whom he had elevated into a mystery, a "problem," the scapegoat of his rationalism. It is in his Romantic typology of the sexes that Freud's rationalist inclination most clearly emerges. In explaining how "women have but little sense of justice," how "their social interests are weaker than those of men," how "their capacity for the sublimation of their instincts is less," [109] Freud places a strong positive accent upon the sense of justice, upon social interests, upon the capacity for instinctual sublimation. In his polite and profound misogyny, the rationalist Freud is confirmed: men must come to terms with the sexual and overcome it. His special theory of female sexuality is equivalent to the general message that sexuality must be neither denied nor thwarted, but mastered.* A

---

* Cf. his negative image of the artist as sensualist—like women and other "weak" characters (*Collected Papers*, IV, 470).

sense of apprehension appears to underlie Freud's treatment of the subject.* Women live dangerously close to "the archaic heritage." [110] Hence the ascription to them of the deficiencies already catalogued: greater vanity, less sense of justice, less intelligence and weaker social interests, and that propensity to early "psychological rigidity" which Freud describes in his essay on the feminine character [111] in the *New Introductory Lectures*. There is a very German comparison of women with the compliant "masses" in *Group Psychology and the Analysis of the Ego:* as it is a woman's deepest desire to be mastered, he says, it is the deepest desire of a people to be ruled.[112] Freud's misogyny, we shall see later, bisects the most conservative elements of his political psychology.

In the light of a misogyny that supports his rationalism, Freud's insistence on "an original bi-sexuality in every individual" [113] assumes the status of an ethical judgment. His idea of bisexuality presumes an *original* unity of male and female characteristics and sexual inclinations. But this does not alter the pejorative import of the differentiation which Freud sees as proceeding from the period of infantile sexuality. If the antithetic qualities of male and female are in actuality blended in each person, so that "pure masculinity . . . is not to be found either in a biological or psychological sense," [114] rationality (male) will always be hedged in by the emotions (female).† The highest and healthiest freedom is, then, not to deny the emotions, the unconscious life, but—knowingly—to enact their demands. Freedom is not emotional but rational, not a passion but a strategy, not feminine but masculine, not static but evolutionary: it is the capacity to follow the developments nature proposes instead of repeating the past in a series of disparate presents.

---

* Although a Jew, and therefore one for whom, as son, the relation to the mother must have been specially fraught with meaning, Freud achieved a notable repression of it in his own self-analysis—a repression which Ernest Jones accepts without question in his life of Freud.

† This doctrine of psychological bisexuality also makes possible another anti-feminist implication: women who display high intellectual or ethical achievement can be judged, psychoanalytically, more male than female. See Freud's remarks upon "women analysts" in the *New Introductory Lectures,* pp. 149–50.

CHAPTER SIX

THE AUTHORITY OF
THE PAST

The terrible original text homo natura *must again be recognized. In effect to translate man back again into nature; to master the many vain and visionary interpretations and subordinate meanings which have hitherto been scratched and daubed over the eternal original text,* homo natura: *to bring it about that man shall henceforth stand before man as he now, hardened by the discipline of science, stands before the* other *forms of nature, with fearless Oedipus-eyes, and stopped Ulysses-ears, deaf to the enticements of old metaphysical bird-catchers, who have piped him far too long: "Thou art more! thou art higher! thou hast a different origin! . . ."*

—NIETZSCHE

FOR THE rationalist Freud, even sexuality is an achievement. To be achieved, it must be cut off from its profoundest complicity with the irrational, its relation to the past. Not that Freud underestimates the irrational. By his instinct theory, which posits the existence of an unresolvable warfare between erotic and aggressive instincts, Freud plainly states that the irrational component cannot be eliminated. The most that can be hoped for—and this is the aim of his therapy—is to take from irrationality the oppressive advantage it derives from its relation with the archaic, the atavistic. A healthy sexuality is one which is freed of its history.

For the Romantic Freud, sexuality when achieved means this freedom. Freud wears the face of an emancipator, physician to sick individuality in search of its abrogation in the instinctual life. Neurotics "try to make the past itself non-existent." [1] Therefore, psycho-analysis turns its patients to examine the past, to recall them to the erotic essentials of their natures. A healthy sexuality is one which can *reclaim* its history.

Freud shares the retrospective impulse of Romanticism, without, however, sharing its nostalgia; the past, for him, is condemned as permanency, burden, neurosis. His standing as a rationalist equally depends on this hatred of the past. If the Enlightenment sages left one sense sharpened, it was the sense of the past as a burden to be re-examined; whether the burden should be dropped becomes the problem of civilization set for Freud by his rationalist ancestors. Progressive rationalism, however, is not the stopping point for Freud. The past is not simply dead weight to be cast off by enlightened minds, but active and engaged, threatening to master the present.

The most energetic mutation of Enlightenment rationalism in the natural sciences, the theory of evolution, shares this antagonism toward the past. But as a counterpoise of the official optimist version of evolutionist reasoning, which hinged on the interpretation of time as an undirectional progress from the primitive to the mature, there was an evolutionist pessimism which stressed the limits of development and the staying power of our original condition. Freudian ideas represent a climax, rather than a new departure, in a remarkable chain of reasoning about the relation between sickness and the past. Early in the nineteenth century, Carl-Gustav Carus, a lonely figure working between the then sealed borders of physiology and psychology, argued that the sickly part of the soul is really a repetition of the lowliest stuff of organic nature. During his Croonian lectures (1884) Hughlings Jackson, a great English neurologist whom Freud admired, spoke of psychoses as the dissolution of the complex system of functions and the reconstitution of the simplest and lowest elements of the nervous system. About the same time in France the psychologist T. A. Ribot used the word "regressions" to explain how memory, through some injury, might revert backward from the contemporaneous to the ancient; this he illustrated by such eruptions of spontaneity in the civilized character as automatic writing. Contemporary with Freud, Pierre Janet described a hierarchy of steps in mental functioning through which the mind could descend as well as ascend to any level. Moritz Lazarus, leader of the German school of *Völkerpsychologie,* construed mental illness as a sinking into the fantasy world of the "natural man." Freud summed up an entire movement of poetic and scientific thought when he identified the abnormal with the primitive.[2]

I

All these connections between sickness and the past depend on the idea of parallelism. Perhaps no scientific idea has found easier acceptance in both the trained and popular mind than the "phylogenetic law": that embryonic development recapitulates racial development, that ontogeny is a short, rapid summary of phylogeny. In Viennese intellectual circles around 1900, the works of Darwin's German apostle Ernst Haeckel, especially his *The Riddle of the Universe,* were extravagantly praised. At some point in the 1870s the University of Vienna intended to have Haeckel join the faculty. When he declined, the university appointed the zoologist Carl Claus to the vacant chair, and it was under Claus, an ardent evolutionist, that the student Freud did his first serious biological research. Though Freud nowhere uses Haeckel, he was familiar with and accepted as indisputable scientific truth the phylogenetic law as it was popularized by Haeckel.

Yet Freud did not much employ this biological version of the analogy between individual and racial development; and he made scarcely more use of the psychological form of the recapitulation idea —according to which the maturing individual mind repeats the development of *mind* through the evolutionary series—than he did of the biological version. A more nearly sociological version, familiar through the variety of uses to which it was put by Herder, Herbart, Comte, and Spencer, is the one he most often employed. This idea— that the individual mind presents in its development a résumé of the stages of human *history*—reached Freud especially by way of anthropological literature. Because he was interested less in the end of the recapitulatory series than in its beginnings, he followed with special care contemporary writing on the psychology of primitives.

The first locus of the primitive which Freud found in individual mental life was the dream. Although he rightly insisted that the connection had not been scientifically developed, it was scarcely unknown. In *The Birth of Tragedy* Nietzsche remarked on how the dream, by returning us to the dark origins out of which human culture has developed, offers modern man the means of continually revising his high estimate of himself. Freud quotes Nietzsche's statement that in dreams "some primeval relic of humanity is at work which we can scarcely reach any longer by a direct path." Dreaming, in Freud's view, is an example of regression, a revival of the instinctual impulses which dominated childhood and of the methods of satisfaction which were then available to the child. Behind every childhood is revealed "a picture of a phylogenetic childhood—a picture of the development of the human race." Dream-interpretation becomes a form of archaeology in which the analyst has the task of recovering "mental antiquities." The analysis of dreams, Freud expected, would lead to a "knowledge of man's archaic heritage, of what is psychically innate in him." [3]

The second locus in which Freud found the primitive in present life was even more familiar. All the anthropological studies on which he depended—Frazer's *Totemism and Exogamy* most heavily, books by Atkinson, Lubbock, Tylor, Robertson Smith, Crawley, Marett, Lang—made free use of the analogy between the primitive and the child. It was more customary to construe the primitive era of civilization as the "childhood of the race" (cf. Rousseau, Herder) than to invert the image, making of childhood the primitive era of the individual. Nevertheless Freud was repeating a theoretical commonplace when he asserted that in the few years of childhood, "we have to traverse the immense evolutionary distance from the Stone Age to participation in modern civilization." [4] He exploited both parts of his analogy, attributing to "primeval people the same feelings and emotions that we have elucidated in the primitives of our own times, our children," [5] and attributing to "the psychic life of present-day children, the same archaic moments . . . which generally prevailed at the time of primitive civilization." [6] Thus materials on the irrational ways of primitives—Freud's point of departure in *Totem and Taboo* (1913) —were readily applied, by analogy, to the behavior of children and neurotics.

Freud did not fix wholly on the beginnings of recapitulatory development. He was especially drawn to schemes of growth on the evolutionist model. In his individual psychology there is the sexual-characterological sequence of "oral," "urethral," "anal," "phallic," and "genital" phases. Further, there is his implicit acceptance of the positivist theory of history, according to which mind evolves from animism through religion to science; this scheme not only underlies Freud's explicitly social essays, from *Totem and Taboo* to *Moses and Monotheism* (1937–1939), but was also adapted to his individual psychology. Presumably following anthropologists such as E. B. Tylor, who had been influenced by the English Comtists, Freud saw "the evolution of human views of the universe" in the inevitable three stages.[7] Psychoanalysis turned the Comtist triad to interpretative account by translating the intellectual into "the *libidinous* development of the individual." Freud asserted in *Totem and Taboo* that

> the *animistic* phase would correspond to narcissism both chronologically and in its content; the *religious* phase would correspond to the stage of object-choice of which the characteristic is a child's attachment to his parents; while the *scientific* phase would have an exact counterpart in the stage at which an individual has reached maturity, has renounced the pleasure principle, adjusted himself to reality and turned to the external world for the object of his desires.[8]

Now intellectual history is full of scientific myths, to which psychologists have contributed more than their share. The Swiss psychologist Jean Piaget internalized the liberal myth of the transformation of society from primitive collectivist tyranny to modern individualist democracy, by making of it a psychology of character development from "heteronomy" to "autonomy." Thus Freud psychologized the liberal myth of growing human rationality into the theory that the individual evolves from narcissism to mature libidinal sociality. These hopes are suggestive, yet they were not the ones on which Freud elaborated. For nothing was more foreign to his mind than the optimistic temper in which the three-stage positivist theory was regularly set forth.

To be sure, it was the evolutionist faith in a more rational future which inspired Freud's late polemic on religion, *The Future of an Illusion* (1928). But his hopes for progress and reason were balanced by anxieties, fairly conventional with civilized minds of his era, about the high cost of civilization in terms of sexual vitality and the feasibility of permanent progress. His warnings in *Moses and Monotheism* against the trend whereby "the world of the senses becomes gradually mastered by spirituality" [9] echo this typically modern anxiety as to the price of civilization—the anxiety typical of psychological man. Freud feared that "the evolution of culture . . . may perhaps be leading to the extinction of the human race." [10] As a late Romantic in a world sick of romance (reality had become so much stranger), he saw the utopian possibility as the end of possibility. Hence he returned to an analysis of origins.* If the plant appears twisted, if life begins to wither away, the condition of the root becomes the inevitable question.

II

It was in *Totem and Taboo* (1913) that Freud linked his psychology to the study of the primitive in history. The anthropological material in the book is culled from field anecdotes cited by senior authorities—Codrington, Spencer and Gillen, Frazer, Lang, Tylor. For some time Freud had been defining neurosis in terms of arrestments of psychic life—treating childhood as a literally "primitive" beginning of life, and dreams and other neurotic formations as residues of the primitive. Now, no longer content to call neurotics

---

* G. Stanley Hall, theologian turned psychologist, who first invited Freud to America, expressed in his autobiography the aim of a psychology respectful of origins: "to conceive the whole world, material and spiritual, as an organic unity, to eliminate all breaks and supernaturalism, and to realize that everything within and without was hoary with age, so that in most experiences we were dealing with only the topmost twigs of vast but deeply buried trees." [11]

primitive, he drew from a growing literature on the irrationalities of primitives to illuminate the behavior of neurotics.

To confront the author of *Three Essays on Sexuality* with *Totem and Taboo* may seem unfair. The practicing clinician ought not to be embarrassed by the armchair anthropologist. It appears, at first reading, that in *Totem and Taboo* Freud merely ornamented his science with exotic anecdote and bizarre speculation. Yet, whether right or wrong, these speculations convey the soaring and plunging quality of Freud's mind more accurately than his apparently aseptic clinical studies.* Through anthropology, Freud's psychology was able to make its first clear breakthrough to overtly social concerns— although these had always been covertly operative. Contemporary anthropology supplied Freud with a vast array of what we might call cultural symptoms. Such an ambitious (and now professionally neglected) work as Frazer's *The Golden Bough* (1890), from which Freud borrowed more than from any other, is a mine of data. With their enormous catalogues of observations, the anthropologists were the first behaviorists of the cultural sciences. Just as he used his clinical researches to gather individual symptoms, Freud used the data of anthropology as a source book for studying the irrational. The prehistoric crises of the race illuminate, for him, the meaning of neurotic crises among historical men. At the same time, the neurotic crises of historical men reveal the original prehistoric crises.

Once upon a time, we read in *Totem and Taboo*, "psychic reality, concerning whose structure there is no doubt, . . . coincided with

---

* While serviceable in expanding to the social the scope of his psychology, Freud's anthropological codifications of children's behavior seem to me otherwise to limit his perspective. Here Freud's Darwinian models certainly played his clinical intuition false. Anyone who has read the case of the precocious "little Hans" (1905) will agree that Freud does not do his masterly analysis justice by later finding in it proof of the "same archaic elements . . . which dominated human culture in primitive times" (*The Question of Lay Analysis*, p. 34). In his anthropology, indeed, we find deposited just the questionable elements in Freud's attitude toward children. He had little feeling for the autonomy of childhood. Yet his attitude shows the essential constructive ambivalence he has helped to stabilize among parents. At the same time that he deepens the parents' sense of authority, he renders more subtle and difficult to discharge the parental sense of obligation to children.

actual reality." It was Freud's propensity to defer to acts of violence as the original repressed substrata of all social action. Compound the recapitulation theory with this belief, add his understanding of the basic wishes of children as egoistic and murderous, and you have Freud's reasoning that later neurotic *wishes* coincide with the *deeds* of primitive men. In the beginning, thinking and doing were identical: "Men actually *did*" what now, according to clinical testimony, they only wish to do.[12] The incapacity of psychotics to distinguish between thought and reality supplied Freud with another clue to what primitive life was normally like: "There is not only *method* in madness . . . but also a fragment of historic truth." [13]

The historic truth which Freud reconstructed was based mainly on Darwin's view that "the primitive form of human society was that of a horde ruled over despotically by a powerful male." [14] To this conjecture of Darwin, Freud added the theory of the Scottish anthropologist and student of comparative religion William Robertson Smith: that sacrifice at the altar is the essential element in every primitive cult, and that such a sacrifice goes back to a killing and eating by the clan of its totem animal, which was regarded as of kin with the clan and its god, and whose killing at ordinary times was therefore strictly forbidden. Thus Freud was drawing on a modern version of euhemerism, the ancient theory that the gods were deified men, deified because they had lived heroically here on earth and were worthy to mount the heavens. But though Freud's theory of myth was euhemerist, rather than rationalizing, as in modern social science, the historical figures themselves were bound to psychological prototypes; the historical actions he inferred from neurotic fantasies were necessary—granted the nature of man.

Animated by an older and perhaps more naïve concern for the nature that drives history, Freud never ceased inquiring into prehistorical causes of events. His ante-historical research ended in a neat harmony of instinct and primordial event. Linking up his own judgment of the murderous nature of man * with the desire to kill

---

* From "Thoughts for the Times on War and Death," SE XIV, 292, and "Why War?" *Coll. Papers* V, 274: While man has no business to exclude himself from the animal kingdom, "that instinct which is said to restrain the

the father which he detected in adult neurotics, in children, and in the evidence of dreams, Freud supposed that primitive man really did kill his. Men have always known, he concluded in *Moses and Monotheism*, "that once upon a time they had a primeval father and killed him." [15]

Freud did not apply this conjecture only to the violence of individual psychic impulses. Individual violence, in real life and in fantasy, points back to historical violence. Once accepted, the idea of the horde was enlarged upon by Freud as the historical model for all subsequent modes of community, and as exemplifying the tendency of all regimes today.[16] Assuming that there existed, under the original leadership of the primal father, nothing but "group feelings," it followed, for Freud, that the first act of individuality had to be rebellion, specifically the killing of the primal father by his sons. Thus individuality gains meaning in Freudian theory as an act of libidinal alienation, of anti-sociality.

The sons desired to kill the father, but afterward they never ceased to regret it. As they gained their freedom they missed their thralldom. Political-religious history is a record of man's irrational attempts to reinstate the primal father. The will, once free, found itself wanting also to renounce its freedom, not just from prudence—what Freud, echoing Hobbes, called "the struggle of all against all" [17]—but also from remorse and craving for authority. As children must love their parents, so did the first citizens love their ruler; his reinstatement, at least in symbolic form, as God, was as natural as his deposition.

In Freud's own origins myth all history is divided, by the act of parricide, into two stages. With this act, the political stage—submission characterized by guilt—was laid over the primal one. The primal murder signaled not merely the beginning of political society but also the beginning of all ritual. Politics and religion, understood by Freud as originally ways of reuniting the many under a single authority, came into existence together, as the profoundest expressions of the ambivalence of human will.

The surest of hands is at work sorting the rich mythic evidence,

---

other animals from killing and devouring their own species we need not attribute to him."

connecting, through psychoanalytic ideas, social and life history. Yet the very consistency of his selection of data exposes the weakness in Freud's reconstruction of social origins. His identification of the prototypical event with the primal *father* murder excludes other possibilities that ought not to be left unconsidered. The murder of the father is but one theme in the myth literature extant; the fratricide motif occurs quite as significantly as that of parricide. If the exemplars of the parricide motif—Oedipus and the other regicide characters that stride across the universal stage—are moving, so, to the post-mythic mind equally, are the exemplars of the fratricide theme—the sons of Oedipus, Joseph and his brothers, Cain and Abel, Arthur and his knights, the Trojan peers, the *Nibelungen,* the daughters of Lear—indeed, all the brothers and sisters who have been so fatal to one another.

A third myth complicates the Freudian selection: the Abraham myth (cf. Kierkegaard, *Fear and Trembling*). Unless dismissed as "manifest" content, in the Abraham myth it is the father who would kill the son, not the son who would kill the father. Propitiatory sacrifice of a prophet (Moses, Christ) or a tragic hero (Oedipus, Hamlet), on behalf of his sinful people, is as much a son-killing as a father-killing. The fact that the death of Christ, the Son of Man, at the hands of his own brothers, the masses, is sanctioned by a more primary Father, God, may be interpreted as a sublimated solution of the fratricidal scapegoat mechanism.

The great murder myth of the Old Testament is the killing of primal brother by primal brother. The first moral question, expressed in the story of Cain and Abel, was not, as Freud implies, "Am I my father's son?" Rather, the primal question was, "Am I my brother's keeper?" *Hamlet* can be read, psychoanalytically, in a way neither Freud nor Ernest Jones * considered. After all, it is the killing of the brother that is the demiurge of the plot. Claudius instructs Hamlet, in their first scene, that nature's most "common theme is death of fathers . . . from the first corpse till he that died today." But the

---

* Cf. *The Interpretation of Dreams*, SE IV, 265–66; Ernest Jones, *Hamlet and Oedipus* (London: 1949; an amplified version of a paper of 1910, "The Oedipus Complex as an Explanation of Hamlet's Mystery").

first corpse was a brother. The primal curse is the usurpation of the throne by fratricide. Hamlet sees the horror of brother against brother. What the ghost—the dead father who is also the dead brother—reveals is a fratricide; and later Hamlet kills his prospective brother-in-law, Laertes. Fratricide is what makes life rotten in the state of Denmark.* Freud seems to have been deaf to the importance in myth of both sororicide and fratricide, although it fairly shouted at him in his analysis of *King Lear* and of the ninth of Grimm's Fairy Tales, "The Twelve Brothers," in his essay "The Theme of the Three Caskets." Instead, he writes as he rarely does, belaboring the obvious: the symbolism of death as dumbness in myth literature.

The theme of fraternal rivalry does play a decisive, if secondary, role in Freud's social theory. The civil war of the brothers, as distinct from their revolt against the tyranny of the father, is, psychologically, the original condition of political society. Freud was led to assert, finally, a "sort of social contract" theory.[18] After the rebellion of the sons, and the collective killing and devouring of the father, there followed a brief matriarchal interregnum characterized by the free disposition of erotic goods. But the "fatherless society" proved impossible in the long run. With the dissolution of the father's monopoly over the women of the horde, each of the guilty sons desired instinctual sovereignty; each envied the power of all the others. New forms of inhibition were necessary to forestall a chaos of suicidal and murderous pleasure-seeking. Failing to acquire the absolute rights possessed by the original father, each covenanted with all to submit themselves to sexual restrictions and to new patriarchal surrogates. First, then, the contract of the brothers arose out of a Malthusian calculation of the value of scarce resources and the necessity of restraint—in this case, the value of the female commodity in a scarcity situation. But even the hard light of Freud's economic sex-calculus cannot spoil the grandeur of his critical account of social origins. In the contract of the brothers there came into being "the essential element of civilization": [19] the renunciation of instinctual gratification. Equal in their renunciation as they were once equal

---

* The King first casually speaks the truth when he ascribes to Fortinbras his own guilty thought that "by our late dear brother's death our state [is] disjoint and out of frame." (*Hamlet*, I, 2)

in submission to the father, the brother-clan is able to tolerate new coercions.

All social relations, in Freud's view, are coercive. The difference between the confinements of civilization and the tyranny of nature lies in whether coercion is exercised from within or without. Now, from one point of view, we may read Freud's myth of primal origins as a parable on the futility of rebellion. For after the democratic interval of matriarchal permissiveness, the revolt against the patriarchal authority is promptly succeeded by new bondages, new sacrifices. But there is a difference. These are sacrifices self-imposed, which makes rebellion not altogether futile. Owing to a novel psychological ingredient, namely the *guilt* which the brothers feel over their supreme crime of parricide, this succeeding reign of authority is not simply a renewal of primal despotism but an advance beyond it—to civilization. Civilization begins when the paternal taboos are self-imposed, when repressions are implemented in the interest of the group. The private sexual expenditure of creative energy must be dammed up and redirected toward gaining knowledge and building artifacts useful to all. Freud derived each "great cultural victory" from separate feats of instinctual renunciation. The use of tools was a mimicry of the gratifying exertion of sexual intercourse, and therefore a substitute for it; fire was secured when primitive man first denied his urge to put it out with a stream of urine (urethral eroticism); dwellings were "a substitute for the mother's womb, that first abode, in which [man] was safe and felt so content, for which he probably yearns ever after." [20] However fanciful these conjectural prototypes of work and first cultural possessions appear, Freud's basic point remains a valid one: that human culture is established through a series of renunciations. The sacrifice of self is the beginning of personality.

The act of renunciation is at once the establishment of fellowship in society and of the Father as God. The war of the generations ends in the deification of the dead father and in the socializing guilt of the brothers. Men stand, as a band of brothers, at the genesis of society when they renounce their aspirations to become, each above all, the supreme Father, and instead worship the father they have murdered (e.g., the primal father, then Moses, Christ, *et al.*) as God in heaven. God, according to Freud, is the positive projection of the act of renunciation.

Although Freud's "scientific myth" remains more myth than science, its merits lie in the judgments of value that it conceals. *Totem and Taboo, Group Psychology, Moses and Monotheism,* and allied works of Freud can no more be dismissed because the anthropology upon which they drew is now outmoded than that great polemic on the emancipation of women, *The Origin of the Family,* is refuted by citing the discredited conjectures on matriarchy and group marriage by Lewis Morgan which stimulated Engels to write his book. As illustrated propositions of value, Freud's social essays stand, even after their anthropological shorings have buckled beneath them. The evolutionist argument habitually shrank from saying a thing *is* something, and instead preferred to report that it *began* in a certain way. Freud's idea of primal history—added to his psychological Lamarckianism—gives another example of the frequently tortuous attempts in nineteenth-century evolutionary ethics to escape saying that man has a nature and that it is torn between the desire to please and the desire to be pleased. Society *begins* with a crime. Man *begins* as a killer, Freud argued. Yet not merely a killer, but a *remorseful* killer. And the primal crime is the crime to end all crimes.

If we look to the manner in which evolutionists disclose the origin of a thing in order to detect their attitude toward it, then Freud's elaborate description of the origin of society in a "primal crime" discloses his basic attitude toward the history of society as a murder mystery, and toward the main problem of humanity as that of aggression. Freud thus combined the critical aims of psychology and anthropology. His psychology sought to deflate our sentimentalizing on civilized human nature, as anthropology sought, by its revelations of the primitive, to shake our complacent sense of the progress of modern social institutions and familial customs. In anthropology Freud recognized a great polemical discipline subjoining his own, equally intent on questioning the pride of civilization. Every part of

Freud's theory, from his child psychology to his political psychology, is affected by the attitude veiled in this romance of origins. The doctor living quietly in Vienna proposed a myth of human existence as terrifying as any of those he loved to read in world literature. If he was wrong, his error was a great error. Better great errors than small truths; and, perhaps, to borrow Freud's own borrowing fom Polonius, his bait of falsehood snared a carp of truth.[21]

III

In Freud's parable of origins, the victories through renunciation that man has been able to achieve in the development of culture all presuppose the guilt feelings which originally followed upon the primal crime. So important an experience was the primal crime that it "must have left some permanent trace in the human soul." [22] This trace, he argues, contributed an "archaic heritage" to our psychic lives that "corresponds to the instincts of animals," but differs from animal instinct so far as it includes "not only dispositions, but also . . . traces of the experiences of earlier generations." [23] That difference makes it, however, no less permanent. And the question remains for Freud: How are the experiences of the past transmitted? In what form does the prototypal event live on in the life of the group? To say that the primal crime must have left "something comparable to a tradition" [24] begs the question. How is tradition possible?

Of course, there is literature, and culture. But Freud rejected the conscious transmission of culture for what he considered a more profound continuity. The deepest instinctual secrets are not rationally preserved and disseminated by parents and teachers; they are remembered. Freud was Lamarckian: "What was acquired by our ancestors," he thought, "is certainly an important part of what we inherit." [25] He could not imagine social or biological science without Lamarckian hypotheses. He was of course on a well-traveled road. Nietzsche announced that the crucial inheritance was that of character, and Samuel Butler had certified instinct as "inherited memory." [26] The primitive survives in memory, the representative of the past among the faculties. Against the overconfidence of reason, representing the future, Freud asserted the ancient claim of memory to a greater power than reason had allowed. The connection between psychoanalysis and Lamarckianism cannot be overemphasized. Not only Freud, but Ferenczi, Jung, Adler, Reich—major disciples and schismatics—require the Lamarckian hypothesis. As Lamarckians, however, none presume a simple linear transmission of attitudes. Rather, the primal act must be denied, forgotten, in order to persist in the unconscious.

Finally, thus, the problem of tradition was solved. Tradition was defined as the prototypal content of the mass unconscious. Like the individual, the group, Freud boldly asserts, may "retain an impression of the past in unconscious memory traces." Jung, Freud warned, solved nothing by introducing the idea of the collective unconscious.* The "content of the unconscious is collective anyhow." [27]

Without the hypothesis of the mass psyche, Freud found the dynamic as well as the achievements of tradition incomprehensible. Tradition is "equivalent to repressed material in the mental life of the individual." On the conscious surface of a culture, the repressed content of the past is something "vanished and overcome in the life of a people." [28] But this is just what defines the impact of memory:

---

* Jung's parting with Freud is over the problem of the past, rather than over the "collective unconscious." For Jung, the source of neurotic conflict is not the repression of desires but the exhaustion of the historical appropriateness of some responses to the neglect of others. This makes him, even more than Freud, an equilibrium theorist, viewing character as a response to the historical situation and that situation constantly in jeopardy of becoming obsolete—or, in Jungian terms, one-sided. In this way Jung has clarified Freud's historicist psychology by cutting away its biologistic underbrush and directing its critical animus toward the present rather than the past. For Jung, neurosis is not, as for Freud, a failure of presentness, but rather a loss of plasticity, of potential responses which, through neglect, have been allowed to slip into unconsciousness. In the unconscious (not in reason) there is a reservoir of strength from which man ought to draw to meet the demands of the day. He must learn to see that what once was true may be true again, that what was once needful may be needful in the here and now again, that nothing old in the world of ideas is incapable of becoming novel. Jung favors therapeutic renascences as an antidote to the banalization of ruling ideas. Freud is for therapeutic reformations, which will abolish the tyranny of nostalgia that calls up renascences and gives to them a symptomatic appropriateness.

one's reaction to it, against it. Prototypal events—the primal crime and its repetitions, like the murder of Moses or the murder of Christ —take on the weight of tradition when they are repressed, and the reaction to them is, of course, unconscious. History, as the trail of the prototype, became for Freud a process of the "return of the repressed," [29] distorting extensively yet eternally recapitulatory.

Freud's scientific myth of the primal father serves other, more surprising, purposes when the historical argument is consigned to a proper irrelevance and the evaluative function is exhibited alone. *Totem and Taboo,* where the collective prototype is first broached, contains much on the origins of religion. Freud's myth of the primal father discloses his own left-handed admiration for monotheistic religion and offers Jewish monotheism the most pervasive of modern legitimations, that of psychological truth. (This' was a subject daringly amplified in his last completed major work, *Moses and Monotheism.*) If the first father was God, then other Gods are later, and corruptions.

Freud was thus at odds with the commonly held view according to which religion begins in polytheism—the worship of vague, plural, local spirits with limited powers—and only after a long process of ethical mastery and intellection attains to the concept of a single deity. By beginning with the purest worship (of one father), from which humans regularly fall away, Freud departed from the evolutionary optimism of both modern science and modernist religion.*

---

* A minority of scholars has, however, supported the notion of a primitive monotheistic belief antedating the Jewish or Babylonian or any recorded peoples. Trying to salvage the supremacy and priority of the monotheistic idea, the Christian anthropology of Ratzel and his pupil Frobenius discovered the towering figure of one god everywhere on the "culture horizons" of the most archaic peoples. A similar notion of a primordial monotheism, from the secular anthropological point of view, was put forward by Andrew Lang in his *Magic and Religion,* published in 1901. (Freud cites Lang's *The Secret of the Totem* [1905] frequently in *Totem and Taboo.*) And the Jesuit scholar Father Schmidt, in his massive *Origins of the Idea of God* (whose first volume was issued the same year as *Totem and Taboo*), also supports the theory of an originally pure idea of one God which, as the result of some primeval experience of guilt, had been forgotten, degenerating into the farrago of magico-authoritarian beliefs that we now understand as primitive religion.

Totem and Taboo is a thoroughly evolutionist treatise, but Freud's evolutionism was uniquely and pessimistically focused on the permanent limits of development.

Even his Lamarckianism reflects this pessimism. While Adler favored Lamarck over Darwin because the former's teleology supported his own evolutionist optimism,* Freud's version had a consistently gloomy cast. What appealed to Freud was not its teleological verve but the near-fatalism of the theory which supposes, in William James's famous definition, "the same emotions, the same habits, the same *instincts* [to be] perpetuated without variation from one generation to another." [30] Lamarck (and Darwin too) offered "serviceability" as an explanation for the persistence of certain emotional forms and accidentally produced tendencies to action. For Freud, archaic and individual memories are neither efficient nor serviceable. Once acquired, they persist in the individual (and through the generations) as the final cause of neurotic misery.

The entire evolutionist concern with "vestiges" has a pejorative implication: they are maladaptive. The thesis, stated biologically, may be found in Darwin's *Expression of the Emotions in Man and Animals,* where he argues that the movements we call expressive were once parts of practical activities—for example, baring the teeth in anger is an abbreviated expression of a formerly more complete reaction of attack. Such movements have now become "survivals," technically purposeless, useless by-products valuable as a sign of emotion, not as the preparation for an act. In the same way, except psychologically, not biologically, Freud showed that neurotics are beset by vestiges of their individual past. And, following out the phylogenetic analogy between the race and the individual, Freud described the individual as burdened also by psychological vestiges of the collective past. In *Moses and Monotheism* he wrote:

---

* Cf. Adler in his *Social Interest* (London: 1938), p. 270: "Lamarck's view, which is more akin to our own [than that of Darwinism] gives up proofs of the creative energy that is inherent in every form of life. The universal fact of the creative evolution of all living things can teach us that a goal is appointed for the line of development in every species—the goal of perfection, of active adaptation to the cosmic demands."

In the history of the human species something happened similar to the events in the life of the individual. That is to say, mankind as a whole also passed through conflicts of a sexual-aggressive nature, which left permanent traces, but which were for the most part warded off and forgotten; later, after a long period of latency, they came to life again and created phenomena similar in structure and tendency to neurotic symptoms.[31]

The language here is big, and vague; and Freud did not become much more specific in describing the parallels. It is clear that he was interested not so much in our evolution from the past, individual and collective, as in the hazards of our reversion to it. If there are original traumas in group history as well as in the life of the individual, evolution supplies no safe distance from them. Thus Freud transformed the usually optimistic analogy of children and primitives into a grim disclosure of the power of the primitive in history and of childishness in the individual adult.

Because he understood the past as the direction of faith, it seemed to Freud that faith was a quality of one's relation to the past; or rather, of one's bondage to it. Yet, in his own way, he saw the necessity—and inevitability—of faith. Without faith—the "positive sign" of the transference—no cure is possible. The transference "clothes the physician with authority, transforms itself into faith in his findings and in his views." Neither "intellectual insight" nor "arguments" decide the outcome of the therapeutic struggle; faith is the decisive factor. And "faith repeats the history of its own origin; it is a derivative of love and at first it needed no arguments." [32] This says nothing for the historic religious faiths. On the contrary, pitting the basic mechanism of faith against the contents of the old faiths, Freud deplored the sense of dependence most people feel in regard to some higher being, as if they were still children living in a childish age. He found it "humiliating . . . to discover what a large number of those alive today, who must see that this religion is not tenable . . . try to defend it inch by inch, as if with a series of pitiful rearguard actions." [33]

Freud was not only concerned to describe the power of the past; he also hoped to prescribe a means of emancipation from it. Through his scientific myth of origins he hoped to be able to "specify the point in the mental development of mankind at which the advance from group psychology to individual psychology was achieved also by the individual members of the group." [34] Scientific myths, in contrast to religious myths, are designed to free individuals from their psychological thralldom to primal forms. Freud may have been alluding to Frazer's definition of myth as the earliest mode of scientific cognition, when somewhat facetiously he offered the scientific myth as a substitute for the prototype. "Does not every science," he asked Albert Einstein in 1932, "come in the end to a kind of mythology?" [35] But the mythology of science is radically different from other sorts. Modern scientific myths are not myths of transcendence but myths of revolt against transcendence. In Freud this revolt took curious form, as a critique of those archaic and instinctual images—the prototypes— around which our roles and perceptions of roles are organized.

IV

This heady conjectural account of social origins, these analogical encompassments of the great human leap forward into culture, turn our analysis back to the genesis of the prototypal method itself, and to some assumptions of the anthropology to which Freud was indebted.

One illuminating connection * is with Goethe. In the decade or so before 1800 Goethe was engrossed in the botanical studies out of which he formulated his theory of the metamorphosis of plants. Goethe posited a so-called ancestral plant (*Urpflanze*) which evolved into the multiformity of plants as now existing. This botanical conception, translated into psychology, describes Freud's conception of the prototype.† In Goethe's words: "With this pattern, and the key thereto, one can still discover plants *ad infinitum* which must be consistent

---

* As Ludwig Binswanger, Fritz Wittels, and others have pointed out. See L. Binswanger, *Ausgewählte Vorträge und Aufsätze* (Bern: 1947).

† Goethe absorbed the general idea of the prototype from Diderot and Ribonet. It is worth stressing how many of the notions of Romanticism, and laterally of anthropology, originated in the French Enlightenment: not only the notion of the prototype but also the understanding of the world-view of primitives as animistic. Cf. Ernst Cassirer, *The Philosophy of the Enlightenment* (Boston: 1955).

with the pattern; that is to say, they might exist even though they do not, and hence they are not merely poetic shadows and apparitions but have intrinsic truth and necessity. The same law is capable of application to all other living things." [36]

Goethe did not object when Schiller pointed out that such conceptions belong to the realm of ideas rather than of facts. The ancestral form does not appear to the sense, he replied, but to the mind. Here Goethe's theory of evolution contradicts both that of Lamarck and of Darwin. Goethe's is an idealistic morphology. No matter that there never was a first and unique instance of the plant, which then begot all other plants in all their varieties. The transformation by virtue of which the various parts of a plant—its sepals, petals, stamens, and so on—are differentiated from one primal organ, the leaf, is an ideal, not a real genesis.

As little as Goethe's *Urpflanze* was a real plant was the Freudian *Urmensch* a real person. The *Urmensch* was not a factual beginning; it is an expedient of scientific reflection and reduction. Criticism by anthropologists of Freud's ahistoric conception has been excessive, expressing, as it does, indignation at an idealism that anthropology itself has not completely abandoned, though it is hidden now behind all kinds of prefatory disclaimers. A more pertinent difficulty with psychoanalytic anthropology is that, unlike Goethe, who was less aggressive toward his imagination, Freud found the ideality of his constructs a handicap. In one place he does agree to call his account of primal events a "just-so story," intended "to lighten the darkness of prehistoric times." [37] But Darwin had professed those events as a factual beginning, and Freud could not resist the temptation to have it both ways. Elsewhere, in *Totem and Taboo,* he claimed that the murder of the primal father was a literal historical event.

This deficiency in facts is one that Freud shared with the whole of evolutionary social science, but particularly with nineteenth-century anthropology, which regularly substituted for historical documentation a logical history backward along the parallel lines or diffusional routes of cultural invention. We can better appreciate the dilemma of anthropological method by recalling that the science of man is not young, nor is cultural diversity—its central problem—such a recently stated one. To go back no farther than the eighteenth century, anthropology was already flourishing then, under the significantly different name of "cosmography." In the eighteenth century cultural diversity was examined on a world-wide and history-wide scale. But in the nineteenth century, when the departmentalization of the social sciences came into being, the scope was radically curtailed. Cosmography became anthropology, withdrawing from the problem of total diversity to inspect more closely surviving primitive cultures.

This congruence of past with present feelings and social bonds allows the recovery of the non-literate past by observing our contemporary primitives in jungle and nursery. Pre-literate and embryonically literate peoples, while offering a valuable perspective on humanity as a whole, are dangerous samples for the understanding of historic civilization. It was their history-less condition that frequently provoked anthropologists to a programmatic overvaluation of savage simplicities, and to the use of what Freud, exemplifying the practice in *Group Psychology*, called "scientific myths" [38] of the primal form of human relations. Thereby a set of events, regarded as unique and non-recurrent, may be withdrawn from rational verification, and all subsequent (dated) history treated as repetitions of the conjectured prototype.

The appeal to conjectural history is older than Goethe and modern anthropology. In the study of language, for example, there have been particularly tenacious endeavors to discover an "original form" or "linguistic root" in the primordial past or, as in Leibniz's concept of a *lingua adamica,* in an ideal future language whose objectivity our cognition must progressively approach. But the error is particularly exposed in the social developmentalisms that flourished in the nineteenth century—the theory of descent from a common ancestry, which Freud borrowed from Darwin, being one of many instances. A method that may succeed in the natural sciences—though even one of these, geology, is said to be in historical difficulties—does not warrant confidence in the linear identities of past and present when appropriated by psychoanalysis.

Freud's appeal to a doctrine of uniformism accounts for a good part of his intellectual resistance to accelerations of historical change. Any object, event, or sequence of events can be fixed with a psychoanalytic center of gravity. The prototype or trauma may "cathect" with little regard for the context, because the object itself will stand for something else. But Freud's stress on the power of the past, while it does amount to a denial of social and historical changes in their own right, shows equally an extraordinary sensitivity on his part to the presence of prototypical motives, often in a vestigial and distorted form, in the artifacts of culture and the private art of dreams.

To detail Freud's affinities with nineteenth-century social science is not within the compass of this book. But at least one other giant of the period, Bachofen, deserves mention. What joins Freud's method to Bachofen's is their use of indirect sources in constructing conjectural history. Bachofen's notion of patriarchy as emerging from a prior matriarchal rule—which Freud rejected—is founded on a study of Aeschylus' *Oresteia,* especially the third play of the trilogy, the *Eumenides. King Lear* and *Faust,* Bachofen noted, show a similar "Aeschylus structure." One thinks immediately of Freud's penchant for finding the "Sophocles structure" in Ibsen, Dostoevski, Shakespeare, and practically every literary work he examined after he first translated *Oedipus Rex* as a Gymnasium student.

Bachofen's method of raiding archaeology, mythology, and poetry to discover "prehistory" has been essential to psychoanalysis in both its individual and its cultural applications. It is in myth and art that prototypes are extolled, and there Freud (like Bachofen) mined lodes that were rich in examples. By thus assimilating literary analysis to a theory of origins, Bachofen prepared the way for the elaborate and literary Freudian origins mythology.

V

Freud has no theory of gradual evolution from primal events. The earliest events stand isolated in the prehistory of individual and group, persisting unchanged alongside the latest.* Yet scarcely anything that

---

* See *Civilization and Its Discontents,* pp. 14–15: "In the realm of mind . . . the primitive type is so commonly preserved alongside the transformations which have developed out of it that it is superfluous to give instances

Freud discovered in the constitution of individual minds requires
the Lamarckian hypothesis. For example, the existence of a dream
symbolism uniform throughout different cultures is, as already noted
in Chapter Two, no reason for assuming that these symbols are "a
fragment of extremely ancient inherited mental equipment." [39] First,
dream symbols may not be as invariant as Freud supposed. Freud
held that "the relation between a symbol and the idea symbolized is
an invariable one," [40] but his own discussions provide many examples
where the same symbol—for this dream, that dreamer—means different things. Second, while it is true, as Freud notes, that symbolism
occurs "quite independently of direct communication and of the
influence of education by example," symbols need not have been
hereditarily transmitted. Freud claimed that the "ultimate meaning
of the symbolic relation . . . is of a genetic character." This genetic link between sexuality and symbolism he found in a "former
identity" of which the symbolism is a "relic and a mark." [41] Here
Freud seems to have been following the example of Darwin. Darwin
had reasoned (against the objections of Spencer) that language arose
as an adjunct of sexuality, specifically from the activity of calling the
mate. Freud supported the view that "all primal words referred to
sexual things" [42] and only subsequently lost their exclusively sexual
significance. But we need not accept these conjectures to understand
the facts of sexual symbolism. We can just as well suppose that the
symbols testify to the presence of a general prerational, or unconscious, method of apprehending the peculiarity and connection of
things—a method which each of us has at his command, though
it is overlaid by the knowledge achieved by rational culture.*

---

in proof of it." Here a difference from Goethe should be noted. In Goethe's
theory of the metamorphosis of plants, the ancestral leaf permutates as blos-
soms, filaments, and pistils, as calyx, seed, and fruit, the leaf disappearing
except as a "form idea." In contrast, Freud saw in all psychological metamorphosis the reappearance of the basic form of the instincts themselves, always present as the indestructible factors in events.

* Georg Groddeck in his *Book of the It* (1922) early summarized the "naturalness" of symbols without historical surmise: "Symbols are not invented,
they are there, and belong to the inalienable estate of man; indeed, one might
say that all conscious thought and action are the unavoidable consequence of

If Freud's recourse to the convention of a prehistoric past may be considered a flaw in his individual psychology, it is equally so in his collective psychology. His chief contribution to the study of myth is his description of a *psychological* process out of which myth develops.* Yet Freud clings to a euhemerist explanation as well—the idea that all myths record historic events or figures (e.g., Moses, Jesus) that can eventually be traced back to an actual proto-mythic person, the primal father, and a literal proto-mythic event, his murder by the sons. The same dual motif appears in his religious anthropology, where he holds both the psychological and euhemerist positions—that is, he maintains that monotheism was both original and historical. In *Moses and Monotheism* he tells us that the Aton religion is "the first case in the history of mankind, and perhaps the purest, of a monotheistic religion." But he also says that "when Moses gave to his people the conception of an Only God it was not an altogether new idea, for it meant the reanimation of a primeval experience in the human family that had long ago faded from the conscious memory of mankind." [43] All mankind lives in the shadow of the same primeval trauma. In consequence, there are specialized historical traumas—such as the murder of Moses.

A similar dualism emerges in Freud's reconstruction of the Moses story. From behind the historical Moses of the Jews, Freud draws the image of the personal Moses of his own private religion; the greatest Jew becomes marginal even to Jewry, having been born an Egyptian nobleman. The historical Moses emerges as a variation on the prototype of all founding fathers. An important source of Freud's reconstruction was the myth of infant exposure † as it appeared in the life stories of Moses, Cyrus, Romulus, Oedipus, Perseus, Hercules, and Christ. Because of its aptness for the myth, Freud's conjecture is that

---

unconscious symbolization, that mankind is animated by the symbol" (pp. 43–44).

* Thus his account of the dream work as analogous to the folk work in myth, including such operations as "splitting," "multiplication," and "displacement."

† Cf. Otto Rank, *The Myth of the Birth of the Hero* (New York: 1952).

Moses did not die naturally but was killed by his adopted people, the Jews. Such reasonings on the basis of "psychological necessity" underlie his historical argument. This experiment in psychohistory remains novel and daring, but has accomplished little except to ruffle historians and offend some of Freud's fellow Jews.

VI

With Nietzsche, Freud proclaimed the master science of the future to be not history but psychology. History becomes *mass* psychology. For the historical phenomena of religion, "the only really satisfactory analogy," Freud thought, was to be found "in psychopathology, in the genesis of human neurosis; that is to say, in a discipline belonging to individual psychology, whereas religious phenomena must of course be regarded as a part of mass psychology." [44] Freud looked to find such an analogy to any historical phenomenon—any manifestations of mass psychology—in the mental life of an individual. The parallel relation between individual and group was "rather in the nature of an axiom." [45]

Freud applied the axiom to every kind of historical and individual experience. For example, anthropology was of use to him because he saw an analogy between the taboo customs of primitive groups and the compulsion neurosis of modern individuals. This analogy was supported by such parallels as that in both taboo and obsessional symptoms "the prohibitions lack any assignable motive," that both are "maintained by an internal necessity," that they are both "easily displaceable," and that they both "give rise to injunctions for the performance of ceremonial acts" which emancipate from the forbidden.[46]

A more subtle analogy is advanced in Freud's interpretation of the history of Judaism and Christianity. Between "the problem of the traumatic neurosis [the psychological event] and that of Jewish monotheism [the historical event]" he saw a complete series of correspondences. As individual neurosis is precipitated by a trauma, so Jewish monotheism begins with the traumatic event of the killing of Moses. Further, there is in common between traumatic neurosis and Jewish monotheism the feature Freud termed "latency." For the trauma is made dynamic by the latency period it must serve.* The repression of Mosaic doctrine at the time of the killing of Moses (the traumatic crime that formed the Jewish character) is understood as "the latency period in the history of Jewish religion." [47] But collective repression does not, any less than individual repression, "disappear without leaving any trace." It lives on as a potential in the inherited biological structure of man, as "dormant tradition," [48] later coming to the surface again and creating the historical character of the Jews.

Freud's analogy between individual psychology and social history received its most famous development, however, in his theory of religion and obsessional neurosis. After *Totem and Taboo* (1912) Freud never doubted that the correct model for understanding religious experience was the neurotic symptoms of the individual. Obsessional neurosis is private religion, and religion is mass obsessional neurosis. The pious are the neurotics of another culture epoch. Penance is analogized to obsessional acts. Freud reports that his insights into the "origin of neurotic ceremonial" and into "the psychological

---

* Freud referred to a supposititious disjunction in primitive biological continuity, in order to explain the intervention of what he called a period of "latency" between childhood sexuality and the onset of mature sexuality at puberty. While Hall gave for this period the ages of eight to twelve, Freud included the years from five to twelve. (See, for example, *Moses and Monotheism*, p. 118, where he discusses "the beginning twice over of sexual life," and *The Ego and the Id*, p. 46.)

Hall interpreted most of the non-volitional movements of infancy as rudimentary impulses to perform acts which must have been of importance in some prehuman stage of life. He understood children as rehearsing in adumbrated ways the social life of their ancestors—a conception which, although no longer directly influential, still finds echoes in the child psychology of Piaget, where even in play forms the evolution from primitive magical obedience to democratic consensus is supposed to be repeated. Accelerations and retardations in the rate of growth of individual children were read by Hall as traces of ancient fluctuations in the development of the race. Adolescence recapitulates some prehistoric period of storm and stress, while the characteristics of children from the ages of eight to twelve, Hall conjectures, represent the culmination of one stage of life—probably maturity—in some remote and perhaps pigmoid stage of racial evolution. For the most part, however, such biological and historical correspondences are ignored in Freud's writings. He preferred to state the analogy between primitive and child—and, further, between the sexual evolution of the mind and the evolution of culture—in more psychological terms. Cf. G. Stanley Hall, *Adolescence* (New York: 1905), I, viii–x, xiii, 48, 160, 202, 215–16, 264, 356, 366; II, 70 ff., 192–94, 212–19.

processes" of religious ceremonial depend entirely upon the inferences his analogical method has emboldened him to draw about the latter from its resemblances to the former.[49] He required no other evidence, certainly not the study of cult or ritual in terms meaningful to the religious. Take, as an example, two actions: a nun tells her rosary, a neurotic counts the buttons on his shirt. Although the conscious intention and social contexts of course differ, the underlying psychological mechanism might be judged the same. Viewed in terms of their unconscious motivations, both nun and neurotic are engaged in compulsive or obsessional actions. While in older moral psychologies it is the act that transforms the compulsion, from the psychoanalytic view it is the compulsion that transforms the act. The manifest purpose of the nun's action is dismissed as superficial. Freud's method of analogy allows the observer to understand the psychological mechanism informing the nun's and the neurotic's action as identical. Thus piety is translated, all too easily, into neurosis.

Freud's analogical method often led him to an arbitrary selection of criteria, and to hidden shifts from one criterion (the psychological) to another (the historical). However, it is important to notice not only the construction of the basic Freudian analogy but also the evaluative position that underlay that construction.

By this enticing analogy between individual neurotic behavior and that of whole social groups, and by the related reading of "primitive" motives into present actions, Freud suggests a way out of the inconclusiveness of historical study. History was conflated into symptom, its bewildering clutter arranged into grand sequences of progress and regress. Finally, the Freudian analysis permits an arbitrary devaluation of the social contexts within which given psychological processes operate. Events may be sifted into two layers: behind the ostensible variety of social acts (the manifest content) lies the more profound variety of latent psychological motive. What is definitive for the public and the social is the private and the pathological. All psychologistic social theories are dependent on such a translation of the public into the private.

Hegel announced just the opposite relation between the latent psychological and the manifest historical. If Freud hinged meanings on the private psychological motive, Hegel hinged them on the public historical context. Public contexts are autonomous and supreme as systems of social causation. Hegel decided that the world spirit has its own immanent purposes, to which private psychological constellations are secondary. The world spirit uses Napoleon's personality; Napoleon's personality does not use the world spirit. His own mode of considering personality, Hegel concluded, "excludes the so-called psychological view." [50]

Marx followed Hegel in his anti-psychological orientation. Capitalism elicits certain personality types; personality types do not first elicit capitalism. It is impossible, in Marxist terms, to discover capitalist personality types in primitive society. The capitalist personality is "personified capital." Marx would never have said capital was a "personification" of a certain character type, as Freudians view the parsimonious businessman as an elaboration of the "anal character." For Marx, "except as personified capital, the capitalist [as a personality] has no historical value, and no right to . . . historical existence." [51] As the stages of capitalist development evolve, so will the personality types evolve within that historical process. Thus an ascetic character structure is the psychological referent at one point, when abstinence is required by the objective process of capital accumulation. In later stages, "a conventional degree of prodigality" may be the historical demand placed upon the psychological material.

For both Hegel and Marx, psychological direction can be meaningful only when understood as a response elicited by the action-demand implicit in a given period of historical evolution. For both, in contrast to Freud, "nature" is merely a variable of the historical process, and therefore irrelevant as a motivational explanation of historical processes. Freud, however, has regular recourse to "nature" as the constant of social analysis. Historical processes, according to Marx, are characterized by change. But for Freud, the more things change the more they remain the same. Society, as a psychological process, is what it has always been. Freud the social theorist, so far as he was identical with Freud the natural scientist, showed the traditional positivist eagerness to eliminate the challenge of history by finding lawfulness in nature. As a positivist, Freud managed to reduce time to a developmental sequence in which man, by virtue of his rational adaptability, can always be what he ought to be—his appropriate self. Individual history recapitulates racial history, and each historic stage is proper to man's developmental situation.

The popularity of psychoanalysis, in an age suffering vertigo from the acceleration of historical events, may be partly ascribed to Freud's rehabilitation of the constant nature underlying history. Among the educated, and more especially the educated adolescents, now so thoroughly persuaded of the naturalness of their needs, the rejection of both Christianity and Marxism testifies to the general disappointment with all constructions subordinating nature to history. It is in this sense that the sociologist Karl Mannheim understood both Christianity and Marxism as utopian doctrines. Indeed, Mannheim awarded Marxism the honor of having been the last utopianism of Western culture,* before the socio-genetic analysis of sociology and psychoanalysis together closed off the future to all illusions.

VII

History, to the late nineteenth century, was the specter that haunted European culture, the spirit in which all things had to be explained. Twentieth-century psychological ethics has seen through the camouflage of historical argument. For Freud, psychological knowledge was the only necessary data; history was not evidence but exemplification, as in theological argument. Indeed, Freudianism's interpretative habits are similar to those of religious historiography, with its one tremendous period of which all else that is good or bad are exemplifications, and this is perhaps an element of its appeal to those in quest of a religiosity that will at the same time debunk all revelations. However different, Jacobins and Communists are both radicals, and radicals can be considered as "radical personality types" before they are considered as Frenchmen or Germans, ancients or moderns, of this party or that. The situations studied by the Freudian natural historian are thus recurrent. That the repetitions are not exact but proximate— Hitler is, after all, not Christ, though both share the common psy-

---

* Cf. *Ideology and Utopia* (New York: 1936).

chological function of being "father-images"—is due to disguises put on by nature to cover the identity of its repetitions. But the psychological functions remain the same.*

Freud did not distinguish human purpose from natural development. History did not begin with civilization, with self-consciousness; prehistory was by far the most significant part of any historical process, Freud implied in *Totem and Taboo*. Every case history was really a prehistory, from the point of view of the consciousness of the patient.

For the very reason that Hegel thought Africa no proper subject for the historian, Freud would consider it most proper. The eruption of Vesuvius was as natural to Freud as the eruption of the unconscious in a political revolution. A historical event was at the same time a natural one, a challenge to which the personality, like any organism, tried to offer the response of conformity. What was given in time past became thereafter pregnant with future. Every pathogenic experience implied an earlier one, the later one "endowed" with the earlier's pathogenic qualities, however inappropriate these qualities were to the present. For Marx, the past is pregnant with the future, with the proletariat as the midwife of history. For Freud, the future is pregnant with the past, a burden of which only the physician, and luck, can deliver us.

Thus, in Freud, change becomes constancy, history nature, development repetition. It is not simply that psychoanalysis can explain nothing current without referring to something past. All theories of

---

* As another example of the repetition of psychological roles in widely different historical and ethical circumstances, see Freud's analysis, in a letter to Thomas Mann (November 29, 1936), of Napoleon as a figure modeled after the biblical Joseph. Napoleon had an elder brother named Joseph whom the young Napoleon hated intensely. He later identified himself with Joseph and this hatred changed into an intense love, his hostility toward other innocent persons being simultaneously displaced. Napoleon also loved his mother very much and tried to take the place of his father in caring for the siblings. He married a young widow named "Josephine" and was never able to turn against her even though she treated him badly. The Egyptian expedition may have expressed a desire for the realization of the Joseph fantasy which was later fulfilled in Europe: "He takes care of the brothers by raising them to princes and kings. The good-for-nothing Jerome is perhaps his Benjamin" (*Int. Zeitschrift für Psychoanalyse und Imago*, XXVI, 1941, pp. 217–20).

organic causation agree to so much. Psychoanalysis adds that not all the incidents of the past, whether of individuals or groups, persist; not all past events are equivalent. For Freud, the past that lives, that is so difficult to expunge, is that which is farthest from the present. It is the "remoteness of time" that is the "really decisive factor." [52] A certain event, or events, necessarily in remote rather than recent history—indeed, at the beginning—becomes determinative of all that follows. The sickness of the present lies in the determination of origins to reassert themselves. But the persistence of the past in the present also gives the present its multiple levels of meaning, and psychology its depth.

Freud took development for granted. That children become adults, that the lower becomes higher, the simple complex, the unknown known—such optimistic commonplaces he shunned. His desire was always to find, in emergence, sameness; in the dynamic, the static; in the present, latent pasts. The analogy between individual and society was one way of stabilizing the evolutionary scheme, by viewing it structurally. Through the conception of the prototype he read the same permanence into temporal relations. Given Freud's disrespect for history, the therapist is granted a vast interpretative latitude. Although the material of therapy appears successively (as the patient relates it in the analytic sessions), and can be plotted along the lines of the patient's own life-history, Freud's concern is to develop modes of transposing events and attitudes, to make them conform with his essential fiction of the timeless unconscious. The unlimited harvest of memories, associations, and symbols are to be collated *thematically,* independent of their time sequence. Freud practices the same liberty in his social analysis. For instance, as we have seen, he linked religious phenomena not merely to unique historical events but, analogically, to perennial family emotions—like the Oedipus Complex—whose form persists even through changes of social context.

Of course, Freud's attitude is not all of a piece. By pointing out in both individual and society the immutable strife of the instincts and the ineffaceable influence of past events, he proclaimed the repetitiveness of human life and the constancy of nature-history. On the other hand, by analogizing society to the individual, who plainly does mature and change, Freud presumed the evolution of society. In one attitude, implemented by the method of analogy, time is a unilinear, unidirectional line of progress. In the other, exemplified by the conception of the prototype, time is unchanging. The symbolic relation of feminine to masculine, the images of the circle and the ascending line, the moods of pessimism and optimism—these express Freud's basic attitudes and embody his rich contradictions.

If any one of these attitudes prevailed over any other, it was pessimism. Through psychiatric treatment an individual can mature and acquire a permanent overlay of rationality; but it remains doubtful that society as a whole progresses or, if it does, that the achievements of progress can be maintained. Freud's primary image is horizontal and conservative. He saw equally at work in nature "two kinds of processes . . . operating in contrary directions, one constructive or assimilatory and the other destructive or dissimilatory." [53] But he found no consolation in this "oscillating rhythm," this eternal recurrence. As there was no progress in nature, there could be nothing new in history— humans are still killers, and war is part of the circular movement of social development. Analogously, "the experiences of the first five years of childhood exert a decisive influence on our life [and] resist all efforts of more mature years to modify them." [54]

Even the one hope, the primacy of intellect, was intimately derived from the "death instinct"; here the positivist evolutionist coincided with the Romantic conservative. The straight line of evolution, if drawn far enough, ends in the same place as the circle of origins. Freud's evolutionary history is as unfree as his idea of nature-history. Ethically the two aspects of the Freudian method (analogy and prototype) end in identity: both constructs are doctrines of fatalism. I have said that Freud was a Romantic conservative; perhaps the essential fact that united Romantic conservatives across the eighteenth century and into the nineteenth was that they did not fancy revolutions. Revolution could only repeat the prototypal rebellion against the father, and in every case, like it, be doomed to failure.

This is not to say that Freud venerated the past. A certain type of past, however, did attract him—not the ages of order so much as the ages of heroes; Greeks, not Latins or Catholics; Semites, not Jews. In collaboration with William C. Bullitt, Freud wrote a psychography of Woodrow Wilson, but his interest was not in contemporaries, heroic or not. More often he uses heroic figures of the antique past (such as Moses and Hannibal) to illustrate his values and doctrine. Indeed, for Freud, to view the present as autonomous would be an illusion. It would be to "experience the present naïvely, so to speak, without being able to estimate its content."[55]

Freud's well-known pessimism as a social theorist must be seen in terms of his conception of time as repetition. No future is open, no past closed. Anticipating the failure of the future to be anything except a past yet to reassert itself, Freud shares in the great gibe of all anti-utopians: not "I told you so!" but, more quietly, "I could have told you so." All observable presents point to the past. Memory is a temptation, offering greater delights than the present. There is no permanent relief either in succumbing to the temptation or in subduing it. Catharsis can only be transitory. The lot of rational humans is to face up to the comfortless world as it was, is, and will be.

This is not, of course, to disavow the prophetic element in Freud's teaching. Rather, the prophet compounded the Stoic. Both prophet and Stoic have as their chief duty the maintenance of self-identity in the face of permanent crisis. The Stoic function of Freud's crisis psychology is the day-to-day maintenance of self-identity. This maintenance function of depth psychology takes on special moral import in a culture where man is considered an actor of roles rather than an enactor of either soul or instinct.

Freud's orientation was in another way close to the prophetic. The function of a crisis psychology, as of prophets, is to heighten the sense of threat and fear in the face of losses of self-identity, and to offer a control: hope, as the psychic state supplied by adhering to tradition, with the prophet as instructor. Freud, in this sense, was on the side of tradition. For him the past constituted the most dynamic part of the present. Tradition was never remote, but continually in the process of reasserting itself. He sought to remind people of it, and of its importance.

But Freud's prophetic temper must not be labored too far. To be a prophet is to assert that there is no way out of tradition, not to try systematically to circumvent it. Freud's end, processionally and valuationally, was to outwit tradition for the sake of a personality type unknown to history thus far, the psychological man—man emancipated by rational analysis from commitments to the prototypal past. Because tradition and the repressions have failed him, psychological man must now admit that he can be all things to himself, as well as to all other men. His identity is for him to choose; none can choose him, as in the days of living gods and imposing fathers.

CHAPTER SEVEN

POLITICS AND THE
INDIVIDUAL

The First Law of Politics is that a body politic is divided
into a ruling class and a ruled class. *Human beings are born
babies. . . . They can survive only in nurseries which they
cannot rule. . . . Every body politic, whatever else it contains, contains at least a nursery, that is, a ruled class . . .
and a ruling class.*

—R. G. COLLINGWOOD

FOR ROUGHLY a century—if we take the years from Fourier and
Bentham to the triumph of Freud—the study of politics concerned
itself mainly with institutions. Fourier, in designing his utopia, took
individuals just as they were, expecting by the perfection of living and
working arrangements to turn individual vice into social virtue.
Bentham also bypassed the unbounded problem of the individual; this
he delegated to religion. Instead, he concentrated on the permanent
reform of institutions; the greatest happiness of the greatest number
was never the aim of an individual psychology, although since 1832
Bentham's formula has grown ironically appropriate; the individual
in a mass society has become, characteristically, something even he
himself can view quantitatively—he wants more, he gets less.

The reform of institutions by which the liberal and radical mind
(Marx's psychology is no more individual than Bentham's) hoped to
achieve a true and lasting transformation of human society did not
appear to bear up under the test of events. Of all the positions to which
liberalism has retreated in the face of recalcitrant events, psychoanalysis is not only the most influential but also the most easily learned.

With Freud the units of political analysis resume their archaic dichotomous form—the irreducible One and his equally irreducible opposite number, the Many. Applied to society, the Freudian analysis follows a pattern familiar, even traditional, among political theories: it seeks to find some free space between these irreducible, and therefore irreconcilable, units. Here lies the attraction of Freud, and perhaps one explanation of his influence. Instead of breaking away from the ancient dualisms which political theory has never tired of ranging under new names, Freud rehabilitates them. In the old-style political theory that gains new life through his moral psychology, Freud appears once again as the closer of an era, the parodist of our habitual style of moralizing, rather than as the inventor of a new style.

I

When it came to extending his individual psychology to the study of groups, Freud exhibited the same contradictions and ambivalences —the same libertarian as well as repressive sympathies—we have observed in earlier chapters. His psychology appears at first as a naturalist's straightforward account of a human nature "below," though not necessarily ennobled by, the environing culture. But in a psychology whose defining insight is into the tensions between social "height" and natural "depth," the decisive ethical approbation may go either way. On the whole Freud stands with Hobbes, as opposed to Rousseau; not that man is good and society corrupts him, but that man is anarchic and society restrains him. But this is too undialectical a formulation to be final. Freud's social psychology—like Darwin's biology—requires more than a Hobbesian reading.

For Hobbes, membership in any community is a temporary and limited commitment, altering in no essential way the solitary and private character of individuals who have "no pleasure, but on the contrary a great deale of griefe in keeping company where there is no power to overawe them all." Freud also recognized the permanently unsocial natural man. Far more subtly, I think, than most naturalistic accounts of human motives, psychoanalysis is able to explain how the anti-social individual is enseamed within the social fabric. *Homo homini lupus:* the Hobbesian words echo through Freud's social psychology. The natural man is rapacious and self-centered. But Freud recognizes as well the natural sociability of man, his permanent emotional need for community. The natural man is instinctually libidinal, a creature born into a hierarchy of love—which goes a long way toward modifying the Hobbesian view. To use Freud's family metaphor, there is not only a sibling rivalry, the model of social divisiveness; there is also a natural love and dependence on the parents. Man is from the beginning a thrall to society, being born into the society of the family. Although so far as Freud stresses the basic component of human aggressiveness he apparently agrees with Hobbes, he complicates the Hobbesian contention that the law of cunning and force is all that obtains in nature. There are force and freedom, Freud agrees. But there are also love and authority. And superior to all is the law of "primal ambivalence," which provides every strong hate with a counterpart of love, and hobbles every act of aggression with a subsequent burden of guilt.

Neither Hobbes nor Freud was content with supposing that social life is instituted by sheer power. Both imagined the state to be founded on a more permanent basis—on consent, "a sort of social contract." [1] But note the difference. The purpose of social-contract theories as used—however diversely—by Hobbes, Locke, and Rousseau was to explicate not the historical origin but the original *legitimacy* of society. The latter-day anthropological fiction of a social contract which Freud set forth in his myth of origins serves, however, a different function. The problem of legitimacy does not concern him; he is not a political philosopher. As a psychologist, however, he is concerned to unveil the sources of social order. For Hobbes, the motive for the social compact is prudence, a species of fear. A prudent calculation of the dangers of anarchy leads to the considered handing over of rights by all to one, who is then charged with the responsibility of protecting all against each. Freud constructs a social contract theory from different inferences about human nature, crediting the natural man with a considerably less rational character. He treats political society not as an artifact designed out of fear and prudence for the purpose of limiting universal egotism, but as the expression of man's irrational longing for the return of authority. The primal father having been murdered, the situation created by his removal induces in the course of time "an enormous increase" in "longing for the father." [2]

Government, therefore, does not *originate* in a social contract. In Freud's version, the social contract appears as a counter-revolutionary response to the overthrow of patriarchal government. It does not implement the prudence of the group; only in a carefully defined sense does it represent the majority will of the citizen-brothers. Social-contract myths may be reinterpreted psychoanalytically as a reassertion of the will of the father against the rebellious impulses of a chastened sonship. The law of primal ambivalence is conveniently at work, matching rebellion with guilt, aggression with submissiveness. So far as the social contract symbolizes the advance of society into historic political organization, it does so not as the victory of the many but as their first and model defeat. Now, by new restrictions on sexual conquests (the decrees of totemistic exogamy), "no one could or might ever again attain the father's supreme power, even though that was what all of them had striven for." [3] The wish of each brother to rule had to remain unfulfilled, except to some extent in the individual family.

To restrict freedom of action appeared to Freud the aim of authority in all its forms—as horde, as family, as government. Restriction of freedom is the defining characteristic of the group. Rational criticism or irrational impulse may change or qualify the restrictions; but human beings are not often rationally critical, and their outbreaks of impulse are safely conventional. At best, one set of restrictions can be substituted for another. Restriction in principle remains, and freedom is limited to the possibility of changing masters. Individual freedom has never been the aim of any society. This assumption of Freud's is common, whether spoken or unspoken, to political theory from Plato to Marx, and beyond to the soundest contemporary social thought. When historians speak of the decline of an institution, such as the medieval Church, they mean, first of all, a crumbling of its power to coerce. The decline of one institution signals the rise of another—in this historical instance, the state. Or, to take a more recent instance of declining institutional authority: the sociological picture of the modern family in decline shows initially the diminishing of its powers to restrict the liberties and prescribe the moral tastes of its younger members, this decline of parental authority being coupled with a rise in the authority of peer-groups outside the home. But Freud went beyond the general assumption of historians and sociologists about the interaction between social institutions. The connection he drew, on the basis of the then current anthropology, between politics and the primitive is fundamental to his view that all social relations, whatever their variety, are mechanisms of authority.

Freud took exceptional care to emphasize the repressive character of primitive society, for in it he found a model for the repressive character of all societies. A large part of *Totem and Taboo* is devoted to charting the severities of primitive social order. In this book more than anywhere else Freud made explicit his characterization of society as repressive. Its picture of the rigidity and scarce pleasures of primitive culture was adapted from what Freud had read of contemporary anthropologists. But in his effort to show primitive inhibitions as the prototypes for modern neuroses, Freud outdid even the anthropologists in his grim reading of the primitive's social world. At the same time, *Totem and Taboo* permits an audacious two-way traffic in ideas of regression and persistence. The way opens from primitive constraints not only to modern neuroses but beyond, to the "moral and conventional prohibitions by which we ourselves are governed."[4] The avoidances or taboos which the anthropologists discovered as the earliest mode of social discipline, Freud viewed as the model of all social discipline; all repression is of natural impulse.

Here Freud may be compared with Émile Durkheim, who also used materials from primitive culture to advance a thesis about social discipline. Durkheim stressed the ways in which primitive society purged the nascent individual of all but social needs and activities; Freud emphasized the prohibitive and restrictive bent of primitive law. But there is an important difference. Durkheim assumes among primitives a collective consciousness; subsequent history, for him, is the history of its individuation. In contrast, Freud assumes that below all forms of consciousness there lurks the instinctual individual, upon whom society makes, more successfully, the same kinds of encroach-ments it makes today.* The primitive examined in *Totem and Taboo* is little different from modern man except that he does not have the misfortune of harboring a modern inside him, while that most modern of character types, the neurotic, suffers the uneasy existence within himself of an unacknowledged primitive. Traces of the primitive inhabit all moderns, and in this sense all moderns are latent neurotics.

Totem and Taboo is really an allegory on the present, its lesson being the necessity of authority. Freud did not detect in the severities of primitive law evidence of an original concern of each for all. Rather, the existence of taboo indicated to him an ineradicable human inclination to anarchy. Because individuals continue to be rebellious, society must be suppressive. Here Freud followed Frazer, quoting from *The Magic Art and the Evolution of Kings:*

> The law only forbids men to do what their instincts incline them to do; what nature itself prohibits and punishes, it would be super-fluous for the law to prohibit and punish. Accordingly we may always safely assume that crimes forbidden by law are crimes which many men have a natural propensity to commit.[5]

The law testifies to the power of hidden and unabated desires, "to an inner need into which conscious insight is lacking." For this Freud in-fers that desire itself testifies to the necessity of law. The unconscious-ness of wishes justified the elaborate prohibitions of primitive society, and presumably of our own.

One prohibition, above all, became germinal to Freud's concept of the instinctual individual: the incest taboo.

> Instead of assuming . . . from the legal prohibition of incest that there is a natural aversion to incest, we ought rather to assume that there is a natural instinct in favour of it, and that if the law re-presses it, as it represses other natural instincts, it does so because

---

* Another difference between Freud and Durkheim: Durkheim, as a sociol-ogist, tried mainly to discriminate among the historical forms of law. He was interested in precisely the evolution from *droit repressif* (the penal law which prevails in primitive society) to *droit restitutif* (modern, contractual law in a society characterized by the division of labor). Freud's genetic reasoning, however, led him, if not to deny the difference between primitive and modern law, at least, in his predilection for inner similarities, to discount it.

civilized men have come to the conclusion that the satisfaction of these natural instincts is detrimental to the general interests of society.[6]

The literal universality of the compulsion, brought over from primitive strivings into modern fantasy—the maze of amorous feelings for the mother and envy of the father which culminates in the Oedipus Complex—may be questioned. But it is hard not to concur in Freud's refusal to take aversions, either social or personal, at face value.

Freud's contribution to the negative interpretation of law, which he took originally from Frazer, consists chiefly in his matching of instances of neurotic with primitive ceremonial. He transforms law into a negative expression of instinctual individuality. Yet Freud does not describe the individual as wholly anarchic. While the desire to violate the law—the desire of the child to kill its father and sleep with its mother, the classic Oedipal fantasy—continues in the unconscious, obedience, too, is a positive desire. In likening the self-imposed prohibitions by which neurotics legislate against forbidden impulses to the elaborate rituals by which primitives ward off moral disorder, Freud sets up a dialectic whereby the self craves its own restriction. Antinomian feelings automatically give rise to compensating self-reproaches, and these in turn to that "renunciation of a possession or a liberty" psychologically experienced as repression and publicly objectified as taboo or law.* Unless one understands human nature under the most universal of Freud's rubrics, ambivalence, taboo (read "law" or "repression") appears unmotivated and enigmatic. But, granting ambivalence, the dialectic between repression and rebellion which Freud sees as constituting cultural history is unbreakable. Every new permissiveness will be countered by fresh repression.[7] In the struggle between law and impulse, there can be neither victory nor defeat. Only the ego, with its arbiter's stake in the psychic life, may resolve the stalemate, assigning inner need and internalized constraint their just expression in a rational compromise. But this hope of reason remains on the horizon of Freud's analysis, which for the most part firmly controls a

---

* Freud's entire discussion of primitive taboo in *Totem and Taboo* is important as a historical prototype of his all-important psychological category, repression.

vision of human nature in which, at least in *Totem and Taboo,* constraint and rebellion are shown to be equally inevitable.

By psychologizing social revolt and coercion Freud weights his scale against impulse and in favor of law. Society is repressive; rebellion is not justified. For the freedom that humans seek is still the freedom to become master. The "conscious impulses" of rebellion have their unconscious sources in envy. The desire for power is "contagious." Anybody is liable to catch it; nobody is immune; "everyone, perhaps, would like to be a king." [8] Envy is the characteristic passion of the weak, only the strong are not "burning" with it. Even in the elaborate courtesies shown to leaders, Freud characteristically finds evidence of envy. Respect, deference, rules of etiquette are derived from the primitive's "dread of contact" with persons—rulers, the dead, the newly born—toward whom he is, unconsciously, hostile. Because all gestures of submission are ambivalent, respect and affection for the powerful must conceal unconscious hostility.

This fresh and subtle casting of doubt upon the motives of opposition to authority exhibits only part of the Freudian psychology of politics; there are also fugitive notes of sympathy with rebels and both sorts of rebellion—repressive and instinctual. Breaking the law may be not simply a futile gesture arising out of personal maladjustment but a justified sundering of the bonds of cultural repression. As he revered heroic lawmakers like Moses, considering them the creators of cultures, Freud nevertheless sympathized with the heroic lawbreakers who mock at their culture and liberate the instincts. Even so unlikable a figure as Shakespeare's Richard III receives a brief measure of sympathy. In the person of the deformed king, Freud saw exemplified the dormant claim of all "to be an exception, to disregard the scruples by which others let themselves be held back." His remarks on Richard III are very Adlerian. Power, and the desire for power, becomes a condonable response to early injuries. Every play needs an appropriate response from its audience. Thus Freud explained the effectiveness of Shakespeare's portrait of an evil king: all of us, having suffered injury, will "clearly perceive the fellow-feeling which compels our sympathy even with a villain like him." [9]

II

Of all Freud's books, none has been so unanimously rejected as *Totem and Taboo*. It has become ritual fare for the anthropologists and other social scientists, an occasion for the methodological slaying of the great father. *Totem and Taboo* was fiction, illustrating nothing except Freud's own gloomy prejudices. It applied, if at all, to simple groups like the family, but hardly to the complex articulation of society, either primitive or civilized. A decade after its publication, as if to answer his critics, Freud left the cover of conjectural prehistory. *Massenpsychologie und Ich-Analyze* (1921) contains an implicit rebuttal of the charges against *Totem and Taboo*. Freud proposed to deal this time not with "a relatively simple group formation . . . but . . . with highly organized, lasting and artificial groups." [10] Although he thus dropped the evolutionist fascination with origins for a more contemporary analysis, *Group Psychology* is marked by an even more significant prepossession, manifest in the very title. The English rendering "Group" misses the immediate political sense of the German *Massen,* a word charged with reactionary connotations within a genre of political psychology—mainly French and Italian—which was widely read at the turn of the century.

Taine's *Origins of Contemporary France* (1868) is perhaps the earliest example of this school of thought, and reveals its deepest animus: against the French Revolution and all its consequences. The bourgeois revolutions of the nineteenth century appeared to conservative observers to unleash a new force: the emotion of the masses, stronger by far than historical institutions or political ideas. (Revealingly, the Italian pioneers of the school, such as Lombroso in the 1880s, subsumed the psychology of the masses under a new science they called "criminal anthropology," the study of crowd life from the criminological point of view.) Elite sentiments were hardly peculiar to nineteenth-century social theory; more significantly, these sentiments now took the form of a scientific social *psychology*. The accent of the new psychology was unlike that of earlier modes of conservatism, and certainly an advance over the fossilized legalism that characterized political theory of that time. The difference between a legalist and a psychological political theory is in the feeling that institutions—churches, armies, parties—really count for less in politics than the emotions of conflicting culture-classes. It is this psychological approach to politics which connects Freud with minds of a most special and often reactionary bent—Taine, Bagehot, Lombroso, Sighele, Le Bon, Bernheim. However they may disagree among themselves, all share with Freud a concern for what we may call the "politics of culture." *

In his political psychology Freud was no innovator. The mixed suspicion and sympathy with which he described the masses echoes both the best and worst political writing of the late nineteenth century. Suspicion bulks larger than sympathy. After 1848, and again after the Commune, disillusion with democracy set in even among those intellectuals who had made, or at least supported, the revolutions. The disappointment then centered on the experience of democracy in France, as today a conventional pessimism takes its precedent from the outcome of the Russian Revolution. Temperate expressions of disappointment came in Freud's time from English critics such as Walter Bagehot (in his perceptive "Amicus" letters) and from Lord Bryce (see his great essay on "Obedience"), but these conventional complaints about the instability of democracy took a much darker polemical turn in the imagination of Continental writers. Perhaps this is because, for the English, their own Glorious Revolution had settled matters. On the Continent, after all, the liberal revolutions had failed; the emerging alternatives were more extreme.

A fair sample of the kind of cliché about the revolutionary character that prevailed on the Continent may be culled from one of Freud's letters, written during the winter of 1885–1886, which he spent as a medical student in Paris. Writing to his future wife, Freud describes his impressions.

---

* It is as a result of this insight that, for example, anti-Semitism has been recognized in recent years both within and without the Freudian perspective, not as a peripheral problem but as fundamental to the study of modern political life.

The town and the people are uncanny; they seem to be of another species from us. I believe they are all possessed of a thousand demons. Instead of *"Monsieur"* and *"Voilà l'Echo de Paris,"* I hear them screaming *"A la lanterne"* or *"A bas dieser und jener."* They are the people of psychical epidemics, of historical mass convulsions.[11] *

Between this youthful rhetoric and the later scientific psychology, Freud translated two of Bernheim's volumes on suggestion and read academic social psychologists such as William McDougall. Indeed, he attributed to McDougall's book *The Group Mind* (1920) the stimulus which led him back to collective psychology. Perhaps supported by these intervening influences, Freud's *Massenpsychologie* of 1921 does not entirely leave behind his youthful fantasies of Paris as still the city of the Revolution and the Commune. So little did Freud consider his own disdain of the masses to be distinguished from that of his sources that in *Group Psychology* he copied out whole passages from the most profoundly anti-democratic of these polemics raised to the level of social psychology—Le Bon's *The Crowd* (1895). Though Freud's debt to this notorious racist and intellectual servitor of the French military class reflects no secret admiration for authority beneath his critique of the repressive society, still his work is tinged—not altogether harmlessly—with the authoritarian colors of his predecessors.

Everything Freud took from earlier books on *Massenpsychologie* he reworked to make one invidious main point. All his derogatory observations on the group—its resemblance to children, savages, and neurotics—are sharpened for comparison of it with the individual. The group is defined as what the individual, ideally, is not. A group is characterized by the eruption of unconscious desires and by "intense emotional ties" which deprive individual members of "independence and initiative." In a group,

all their individual inhibitions fall away and all the cruel, brutal and destructive instincts, which lie dormant in individuals as relics of a primitive epoch, are stirred up to find free gratification.[12]

---

* For another hint of Freud's conventional romance of the French Revolution, see his remarks on Maury's dream of being guillotined (*The Interpretation of Dreams*, SE V, 496–97).

The difference between this and earlier versions of the same point is that Freud, while concentrating on the primitive irrationality of the crowd, omits to blame history—a consolation Le Bon did offer. Le Bon and the others were shocked by democratic politics, not by all politics. Unaware of such ancient refinements in the theory of democracy as between "people" and "mass" or "citizens" and "mob," Freud detected the upthrust of barbarism in collective life as such. The independent intelligent citizen, cherished by Rousseau, is given no more credence, psychoanalytically, than the increasingly rational proletarian of Marxist utopianism. Interested in the emotional currents surging beneath the surface of ideology and institution, Freud found no reason to regard the group mind as specially created by industrial urban society. The mob, which loomed to some, such as Burckhardt and Nietzsche, as a fresh threat to European culture and of which the Marxist proletariat was a defiantly positive version—was for Freud the common denominator of all politics.

This difference between the *Group Psychology* and the position held by Le Bon is worth noting, since it was only by discounting the historical emergence of masses that Freud absorbed the specifically anti-democratic anxieties of the earlier writers into his own anti-political animus. In Freud's view the task of psychology lay not in justifying conservative apprehensions nor in condemning radical hope (with which he had an ambiguous sympathy) but in an appraisal of how the rational individual sinks into barbarism under the compulsions of group life. From the perspective of his individualist psychology, Freud asks how and why individuals *en masse* feel, think, and act so unlike their separate selves.

Le Bon supposed that in the crowd unconscious feelings supervene, which meant to him (as to Freud) a regression to certain primitive states of mind. But this idea of the upthrust of the unconscious did not solve but merely restated the problem of the transformation of personality. Therefore Freud rejected it. Further, he rejected the persuasive thesis that in a crowd there comes into being a new and single mind differing from the minds of the individuals composing it. Though he agreed that certain contents in the unconscious were indeed collective, Freud never resorted to the notion of a trans-individual psyche that Jung was to revive.* In accounting for the double metamorphosis of each person in a crowd—"the intensification of the affects and the inhibition of the intellect"—[13] Freud refused to go beyond the duplication and coincidence of individual psychic processes. He explains collective psychology on the basis of individual acts of identification with a leader or leader-principle; the sharing of a common emotional situation is a secondary matter.

Nor was Freud willing to explain group life by the term "suggestion," which renders gratuitous the competing supposition of a group mind. In this account, the barbaric propensities of the crowd derive from the literally hypnotic stimulus of the emotional environment, with its protective anonymity, upon the uncritical ("suggestible") part of each individual mind. Bagehot and Tarde had called this tendency "imitation," or "unconscious imitation." But once hypnotism had been admitted, through the differing efforts of Charcot and Bernheim in the early 1880s, to a place near the sciences, the daemonic image of the hypnotist became a staple of conservative polemics. Something was "suggested" to the weak-minded persons who made up a crowd; and the crowd, as if hypnotized, became of one strong mind.† Freud himself saw no qualitative difference between the hypnotic relation in the clinic and the emotional organization of society. "The hypnotic relation is (if the suggestion is permissible) a group formation with two members." [14] Literal and manifest differences—such as the fact that the hypnotic subject usually forgets what occurs during his trance, while the crowd remembers—are passed over in favor of similarities more profound.

---

* This idea has an honorable ancestry in German intellectual life, beginning with the "folk-soul" of Herder; versions of it have been upheld in recent times by Wundt, Durkheim, and McDougall as well as by Jung.

† According to the description of Bernheim: "Among all peoples, suggestion was practiced consciously or unconsciously by priests, charlatans, and magicians. Seen from the most general point of view, suggestion has dominated the entire history of humanity. Since the original sin was suggested to Eve by the serpent and to Adam by Eve, until the great wars engendered by religious and political fanaticism, until the bloody horrors of the Revolution and the Commune, suggestion has played a role." Bernheim, in effect, provided a new key to the understanding of politics—in particular to those historic moments when the "suggestibility" of the masses is turned against the old priests, charlatans, and magicians by the new.

In the group, as in the hypnotic relation, Freud found "the same humble subjection, the same compliance, the same absence of criticism . . . the same sapping of the subject's own initiative." [15]

Nevertheless, an instinctual capacity for hypnotic suggestibility explains politics no better than an instinct for "submission" (McDougall) or "obedience" (Lord Bryce), the satisfaction of which alone makes men happy. Unattracted by such special-instinct hypotheses, Freud moved in another direction—toward a deeper identification of our social with our natural affections. The transformation of the individual into a cipher of the group did not come under the heading of an "irreducible primitive phenomenon" [16] of suggestibility, as Bernheim proposed, but under that of the far more manipulable and concrete power of love. If unity expresses the essential mystery of political society, and "a group is clearly held together by a power of some kind," to what power can this mysterious unity "be better ascribed than to Eros, which holds together everything in the world"? [17] Of course Freud knew of other, powerful answers to this question, the most persistent being that of Thrasymachus: community of interest as such is the basis of social unity. But to argue solely from expediency and mutual advantage is to treat the matter in "far too rational a manner," and implies what is plainly untrue, that social cohesion does not outlast "the immediate advantage gained from the other people's collaborations." [18] Whether his solution—that "libidinal ties are what characterize a group" [19]—is correct or not, there is no doubt that he grasped the inadequacy of established explanations of social unity as founded on economic interest and political expediency; his psychological solution has been singularly influential upon post-Marxian social science.

If libidinal bonds are stronger than expediency, they also chafe the more. Libido may supply to society the means toward its unity but no criteria by which this togetherness can be judged. Having established the primacy of the libidinal bond, Freud made of unity an end in itself. All the associations to which people belong, from the first family to the world state, were united by love. The love relation was Freud's vice of the universal, and he proceeded to apply it not only to individuals in their private capacity but "in the firm expectation of finding in them conditions which can be transferred to the ties that exist in groups." [20] In this transferred sense, the condition of obedience is erotic. If everywhere we are born free, it is because we are, according to Freud, born perfect egoists; if everywhere man puts himself in chains "perhaps after all he does it *'ihnen zu Liebe.'* " [21]

We can discern Freud's apprehension about politics in the very duality of his image of love. To find libidinal dependence at the heart of sociability is, at least until made specific, to arrive at a most ambiguous formula. Freud's idea of the libido as uniting society is to be taken in a broad sense; such libidinal bonds include directly sexual feelings as well as others which are diverted from the sexual aim or prevented from reaching it, such as the tie of male comradeship. Thus conceived, love may seem not so sinister a power in politics. We might even project into Freud's theory a meaning like that of Fourier, who posited a Utopia of social cooperation through the mass manipulation of libidinal energies and the harnessing of pleasure to social work.* Freud did in fact admit the notion of a "desexualized Eros." His comment that "the erotic instincts appear to be altogether more plastic, more readily diverted and displaced than the destructive instincts," [22] further supports this interpretation. But, as I have suggested, such positive versions of political eroticism remain undeveloped. From Freud's individual psychology, his image of love takes on a darker coloring than can be conveyed by comfortable terms like "sociability" or "affection" or, for that matter, "love." Eros is either greedy and sadistic or abjectly submissive. It is this second, masochistic possibility that Freud ascribes to the feelings of the crowd. The love through which we become sociable signifies a willful self-defeat: the "I" submerges itself in the group. By this connection it is not so much politics that becomes an elaboration of love, as love itself that becomes political—the power which effects compliance. There is only a short step, psychologically speaking, between being in love and being hypnotized. Indeed, Freud thought it

---

* Such a utopian socialist interpretation of Freud has been set forth by Herbert Marcuse in *Eros and Civilization* (Boston: 1955).

more plausible "to explain being in love by means of hypnosis than the other way round." [23]

The explanations of social cohesion given by Freud and by his predecessors in social psychology all fail in the same way: they profoundly overestimate the community of groups. Freud's explanation has one notable advantage over the others in the emphasis he puts on the implicitness of the coercion that defines the political relation as such—between leaders and led. Freud's belief that politics is founded in the group's erotic relation with authority is made concrete by his claim that authority is always *personified*. Political societies are characterized by the ability to concentrate authority. As the horde presupposes a chief, as to be hypnotized requires a hypnotist, as love presupposes an "object"—in the same way the group presupposes a leader.* The mutual ties among members of a group disappear, Freud asserted, "at the same time as the tie with their leader." [24]

Freud's image of the leader first appears in *Totem and Taboo,* in the figure of the persecuting father of the horde. The first ruler was a perfect egoist who loved no one but himself. Only under "the idea of a paramount and dangerous personality, towards whom only a passive-masochistic attitude is possible, to whom one's will has to be surrendered," could Freud picture "the relation of the individual member of the primal horde to the primal father." [25] Even when he drew upon constructions other than the Darwinian horde-myth, transforming primal father into hypnotist, the figure remains the same. Freud drew the lesson that leadership is a hazardous concession for any people to make. The first qualification of the true leader, as Freud construes him, is that he remain uninvolved with those he

---

* In the valuable comparison between mass action and the compulsive acts of a hypnotized subject, Freud accused Le Bon and others of this school of ignoring the central feature of the comparison, "namely the person who is to replace the hypnotist in the case of the group" (*Group Psychology,* SE XVIII, pp. 76–77). For the same reason Freud rejected Wilfred Trotter's thesis (in *Instincts of the Herd in Peace and War,* 1916) that man is a "herd animal" because Trotter left "no room for the leader." Man is rather a "horde animal, an individual creature in a horde led by a chief" (*Group Psychology,* pp. 119, 121).

leads, and at the same time destroy his followers' wills to remain separate.

Such a pejorative definition of the leader in certain respects finds grim confirmations in recent political reality. The function, if not of every leader, at least of both modern dictators and modern monarchs, supports the Freudian contention. Whether or not a monarch or a mass leader has great executive ability or power, modern politics suggests that his primary function may well be psychological; he acts as a center around which otherwise disturbed lives can be organized. Freud explicitly argues the negative side of his case: that relaxation of the libidinal ties which bind the members of a group to a leader and therefore to each other, leaving the constituent individuals feeling isolated and insecure, is what causes groups to dissolve in panic. Conversely, we suggest, isolates may react to their loss of membership by reconstituting a group, complete with hieratic roles, in order to restore their self-identity. The histories of juvenile street gangs in America, as of totalitarian political movements in Europe, illustrates the process of national panic and the achievement of irrecusably new identities. A crisis of identity has set in all over the Western world, the result of that very crisis of authority mirrored in every therapeutic encounter.

In the established sociological conception the charismatic father-leader is inevitably displaced by bureaucratic organization. In contrast, Freud asserted that the father-leader is never replaced permanently by the follower-"sons." To be effective, organization must in some sense incarnate the founding father. Nowadays this view is gaining in credibility. It is possible that the liberal interregnum has ended and another age has begun: the age of the hypnotic persecuting father, a figure not at all incompatible with a mammoth bureaucracy which operates simply as an extension of his ego. Both fascism and Stalinism showed some of this quality. According to George Orwell's powerful mythography of the future, by 1984 we shall have seen a complete reincarnation of our hypnotic persecuting father in the political system. "I love Big Brother" is the perfected slogan of erotic submission. It can be matched, on the other side, by the final degrading command—"Kiss me"—which Cipolla gives to the mass-man Mario in Thomas Mann's ornate Freudian allegory of modern politics, *Mario and the Magician*. If Freud seems to discern in all politics a certain quality of madness, it is appropriate to recall that he considered the state of being in love not only like being hypnotized but as "the normal prototype of the psychoses." [26] The *Führer* is as easily understood in this romantic psychology as the *Verführer;* indeed Kierkegaard's image of the seducer as the purest sort of lover is in the same spirit as Freud's insight into love as the basis of the state. "The credulity of love" becomes, in Freud's extreme and hostile view, "the most fundamental source of *authority*." [27]

To arraign politics thus, almost wholly in what we now recognize as the totalitarian image, overdraws the immediacy of authority. Politics is not a permanent mass meeting, with an erotically fascinated crowd responsive to a demagogue's command. Freud's polarizing mind grasps only mass politics, the politics of love and hate. Therefore he yields to the despair of all political psychologists, including socialists like Silone in *The School for Dictators,* at the childishness of the masses, and at their blind credulousness in the face of the most primitive appeals. Certain psychological qualities appear in all situations where the crowd becomes a spectator and politics their entertainment, no matter what the discursive content of what they witness. It is this tyrannical democracy of emotion that Freud takes as the model of politics.

Certainly, all of politics shows something of this dangerous emotion in the aggregate, though the concept has far more relevance to parades than to town meetings. But, by the very fact of its adequacy to a certain kind of modern politics, Freud's psychology becomes inadequate to others. It does not illuminate the emotions behind hard bargaining and counterbargaining; administration and executive order may be still more important, as a model of political behavior, than the mass meeting. Committee psychology may be more to the point than mass psychology. Behind every demonstration of personal magnetism by the star performer, there are smaller meetings at which the less enthusiastic but more significant decisions are reached. Freud imputes a fatality to political life that is rarely present and indeed belied by the uncertain outcome of political infighting among leaderships. Even the sort of politics where the audience lies fascinated under the spell of a magician has its hucksters, its ballyhoo, its technicians switching on haloes of light around the main attraction of the evening. In a technological mass society Freud's erotic leader requires a build-up. The participating audiences at the modern theatricals of power require more and more door prizes before they will accept the enthusiasms constantly being manufactured for them. Freud missed the function of apathy, which might be construed as the positive side of "panic-dread," in the psychology of the bit actors on the political stage. He acknowledges no neutralist emotions in either public or private life.

III

Freud's magnifications of the power of leaders, in *Totem and Taboo* and *Group Psychology,* caricature political authority. As he says, of the primal father:

> He, at the very beginning of the history of mankind, was the "superman" whom Nietzsche only expected from the future. Even today the members of a group stand in need of the illusion that they are equally and justly loved by their leader; but the leader himself need love no one else, he may be of a masterful nature, absolutely narcissistic, self-confident and independent.[28]

Freud invariably imagines the leader, whether persecuting (the primal father, God) or persecuted (the primal brother, Moses or Christ), as a man who is self-confident, who has "few libidinal ties," whose will, in contrast to the weak intellects and collectivized wills of his followers, needs "no reinforcement from others." [29] Beyond these points, Freud does not concern himself with the psychology of leaders. Having set out to study the unity of the group, Freud takes for granted the creative glamour of leadership. But, quite circularly, in his effort to get at this unity he subsumes all political life, without differentiating it in kind, under the spell of authority.

This abstract, overformal approach tends to reinforce the claim of permanence around all specifications of authority. The conservative implications of Freudian psychology are clear: nothing qualitatively different happens in history. With the leader forced to play father-imago because his followers are children, politics becomes an un-changing strife between the generations. On the psychological pendulum of ambivalence, social changes become recurrences; social relations are seen through to the permanent psychological needs they satisfy. Social protest takes on a dubious value as another manifesta-tion of the ambivalence of all emotions. Respect and affection for privileged persons, Freud holds, are opposed in the unconscious by intensely hostile feelings. Equally, the "distrust" commonly felt toward rulers by the ruled is not motivated, primarily, by a rational assessment of the rulers' failures and misjudgments; it is another "expression of the same unconscious hostility." There is even the implication that no ruler is genuinely powerful, except through the illusory ascriptions of his followers. Justice and rectitude are absorbed into the pathology of submission. As in paranoia so in politics: "the importance of one particular person is immensely exaggerated and his absolute power is magnified to the most improbable degree." [30] By his psychology of libidinal participation Freud has founded a genetics of power.

In another respect, however, he does not legitimate authority. Au-thoritarian doctrines generally sanctify the social process; Freud questions it. His social psychology is also a critique of authority, partly because he saw politics in such an ineluctably authoritarian guise. The exposure of the authoritarian prototypes, in all their power, becomes the aim of psychoanalysis.

Freud's monumental image of the father as the prototype of au-thority is directly connected with his idea that authority of all sorts is undergoing a crisis in our society. He deplored the psychological malaise which occurs when strong leaders are no longer respected.[31] Yet Freud himself contributed to this crisis, as he contributed to the alarm about it. Psychoanalytic thought brackets the father as a problem, however basic; it favors taking a detached if not antago-nistic attitude toward authority, thus supplying the crisis of authority with a new language and rationalization. Along with the great de-bunking by contemporary social science of legitimacy and the "inter-ests" behind social institutions and office, the whole concept of legitimacy has taken on a transparent quality, to which Freud added a psychological polish.

The energies behind Freud's debunking science derive mainly from his use of family and genetic models. All emotions, Freud supposed, begin privately and are rationalized outward.* Politics can be traced back along a chain of projections to the individual. The veneration and exaggerated esteem which rulers attract is but the last of a developmental series beginning in "the relation of the child to its father." [32] By subjecting politics not merely to psychology but even more specifically to (in Spencer's phrase) the psychology of domestic institutions, Freud reveals his anti-political bias.

His analogue between parents and rulers may seem to do no more than repeat a comparison made since antiquity. Bentham described the child as born "into a state of perfect political society with respect to his parent," and from thence "successively into a number of different states of political society more or less perfect, by passing into different societies." This would seem identical with Freud's understanding of the ruler-figure as a "father-image." But, unlike Bentham's, Freud's intent is not descriptive; it is critical. Freud does not concentrate on the father-figure as such, but rather on the manner in which parental models persist and continue to influence public conduct. Any modification of the social order becomes in this way assimilable within the natural mode of government, the family. Thus the sentiment of patriotism may be exposed as a resolution of sibling rivalry, the aims of revolution parodied as regressive disobedience.

Nothing could have a greater appeal to educated classes in the West, tired as they are of the taxing sincerities involved in political

---

* Freud's idea that the stuff of public emotions is really private affects "transmuted," instead of having a logic of its own, occurs as early as 1896, in his paper "The Defence Neuro-Psychoses." Cf. *Collected Papers,* I, 165: "The affect of reproach can with the aid of some psychical reinforcement transmute itself into any other unpleasant affect; when this has happened there is nothing to hinder the substituted affect any longer from becoming conscious. Thus self-reproach (for having performed a sexual deed in childhood) can easily transform itself into *shame* (lest another person should come to hear about it), into *hypochondriacal anxiety* (lest some bodily injury should result from the action which evoked the self-reproach), into *dread of the community* (fear of punishment by the world at large for the lapse), into *religious anxiety*. . . ." (Freud's italics.)

engagement. Analogues with the personal such as Freud drew serve to debunk all public pieties. To the ruled, Freud applied the familiar equation between the masses and children; political sentiments thus derive from the model of filial piety. As for rulers, the political personality in Freud's view is one agitated by ungratified cravings for affection (or deference), which have been both accentuated and unsatisfied in personal relations. The political personality becomes an escape artist. His cravings are merely "displaced" upon the body politic.

No politics can be very ardent once the psychological man discovers how symptomatically he is acting. A follower can never be as ardent after he recognizes his leader as a father-image. A believer cannot remain quite as true to his belief after discovering how much displaced feeling there is in it. "Displaced" differs by only one small letter from "misplaced." A Freudian should be interested in the similarity. Freud harbored a formidable rationalist suspicion of enthusiasm, and his psychology shows his anti-radical animus by discounting all enthusiasms alike.

Whether concerned with the pathology of leaders or followers, psychoanalysis has fed the contemporary suspicion of politics. One idea popular in early Freudian studies is that the man of power himself is neurotic.* But the search for power need not be a reaction to powerlessness; it may indicate a healthy identification with power. The political career of a younger Taft or Roosevelt may well include a "working through" or "acting out" of an early "identification" or "fixation" on his father. Even were father-identification an original motive, normally such a motive would mature and become detached from infantile sources. Once we qualify Freud's assertion that the criterion of a motive's importance is how deeply it is buried in the past, we obviate almost all those geneticist suspicions of political leadership that inform the contemporary literature of political psychology.†

---

* A classic instance of this is the case of Shakespeare's Richard III, mentioned earlier. For another instance, see Hanns Sachs's *Caligula* (1924).

† See, for example, the work of Harold Lasswell, not only in an early book, *Psychopathology and Politics* (1930), but also in a later one, *Power and Personality* (1948).

Nothing of even marginal value will be lost from this department of applied psychoanalysis if it ceases to concentrate on the neurotic aspect of leadership. A conception which recurs more significantly, both in direct statement and by therapeutic implication, has to do not with the political leader as a sick person but with the pathological condition of his followers. Not Hitler but the German people, not Mussolini but the Italian people, would be the objects of psycho-political analysis. The pessimism of this kind of analysis is evident in such Freudian studies as *The Authoritarian Personality*. Depth psychology has demolished the optimistic faith of democrats in the rationality of a free citizenry, by discovering that the average citizen (in or out of a crowd) is not rational. But this is no reason to despair. There remains what is for Freud perhaps the highest rationality: knowledge of the irrational, a knowledge which may be used homeo-pathically, so to speak, to arrive at rational decisions essential to democracy. Ideally a democratic electorate "in a free society, chooses leaders and physicians," for "the problem of democratic leadership . . . is equivalent to the development of social health rather than disease." [33] The medicinal taste of modern liberalism is unmistakable in this quotation from Harold Lasswell.

A solution to the problem of democratic leadership cannot be so easily prescribed. By resorting to a technocracy of social psychiatrists who will use cartoons, movies, television, and even, when necessary, "narco- and hypnoanalytic aids to the general reduction of tension in the community," [34] democratic culture might relax itself into a condition of submissiveness to power from which it could not re-cover. Liberalism, based on a notion of rational educability, supplied an essential ingredient to the Freudian compound. But there is no reason why a state-bound psychiatric cadre should have to serve democratic ends. Lasswell's assertion that "today we are . . . aware that too much emphasis has been given to dialectic, and that other ways of talking and thinking are needed to supplement it" [35] glosses over the fact that these other ways are intractably irrational, and in a mass society more susceptible to manipulation than ever before. Citizen-patients can now be convinced that their resentments con-cerning the regime are grounded in purely private difficulties. If the soldier at the front refuses to kill, the psychiatrist can—and does—explain to him that his reluctance can have nothing to do with the objective circumstances of war, which most of his fellow soldiers are quite capable of enduring. To the extent that the citizen-patient is convinced that his anxiety has subjective roots, he may be prevented from asking embarrassing questions about the objective political situation. Success, a place of honor in the social order, has come to the moral physicians. We read many accounts of their social utility: of their success, by means of brief, energetic explanations, in preventing soldiers from cracking up on the front lines. But the image of the protesting soldier and the exhorting state psychiatrist suggests that psychological insight is by no means compelled to serve a Reason higher than reasons of state. When social action is conceived as the precipitate of personal emotions, protest against society can be explained away as a neurotic symptom. It is here that psychiatry may play a significant role in an authoritarian ideology: by viewing an admittedly sick society in terms of that subtlest of all authoritarian images, the hospital.

Psychology is hardly alone in contributing to the spreading sense of political disengagement. Such clinically induced apathies express a wider revulsion against the naïve division of social conduct into right or wrong. Conflicts of right have been rediagnosed as disturbances of value. Truth becomes mere theory, the manifest rationale for a practical response that arises out of deeper sources.

The prophet of disengagement here resembles the prophet of the final engagement: both Freud and Marx trace defects' in the social order to something beyond it—Marx to the economic order, Freud to the psychological.* For both, the political becomes a secondary type of phenomenon, subject to a relatively easy terminal analysis. But here, as elsewhere, psychoanalysis runs a grave danger of being overformal. Seeking the basic motive of war, psychology turns up

---

* Take, for example, the explanations of race prejudice. Marxists explain race prejudice as a rationale for economic exploitation; Freudians explain it as a projection of unacceptable inner strivings onto a minority group; both proceed by looking behind the phenomenon, and in a sense explaining it away.

varieties of aggression; but these scarcely cover diplomatic history or strategic interests. Yet Freud wholly scrapped "interest" as a unit of analysis, preferring "motive." Exploring the functions of institutional authority, psychology revives the classic analogue of state and family; but this scarcely distinguishes among creeds and aspirations—all of these lose shape in the powerful solvent of motivational analysis.

Certainly Freudianism has contributed a new dimension to the revolt of social science against questions of truth and error. Marx would have said that people change their political adherence not because they change their minds and see their views are in error, but because of their involuntary stake in their class positions. Freud would have said that political preferences are created not out of rational insight but because of an attachment to a political father—a Lenin, a Roosevelt, a Hitler. The father-image puts the stamp of his moral character on his followers, as Moses (Freud's favorite example) created the Jewish character or Lenin formed the Bolshevik character.* There can be no differences over principles but only among competing personal identifications. From Lasswell's political science to Koestler's vulgarization of Freudian theory in his anti-political novel *Arrival and Departure,* public issues have become dramatized private issues.

The most persuasive example of this Freudian reduction of the political has been its treatment of revolutionary enthusiasms as belonging to a neurotic character structure. Psychoanalysis has been received most congenially in America since the discrediting of political radicalism, for psychoanalysis sees the revolutionary simply as a special type of neurotic who displaces his aggressions onto the public level. Freud offers a brilliant formula with which to shrink the revolutionary character—as basically in revolt against his father.† Revolutionary ideologies—left and right—may be treated as rationales for Oedipal conflicts. Take, for example, Lasswell's equation for the study of politics: $p \left\{ d \left\{ r = P \right. \right.$. Political man (P) expresses a "dis-

---

* A thesis advanced by the Freudian political psychologist Nathan Leites. See his *A Study of Bolshevism* (Glencoe, Ill.: Free Press, 1953).

† See Freud's remarks on Dostoevski in the essay "Dostoevski and Parricide" (1928).

placement" (d) and "rationalization" (r) of private motives (p).[36] What is definitive for the social is the psychological. The public and social is only the "manifest content." The "latent content" is the psychological mechanism which is masked by the manifest content. Socio-psychological theory is explicitly dependent upon such a translation of the public into the private. Viewed psychoanalytically, neither Saint Paul nor Leonardo da Vinci—nor Hitler, for that matter—is fully accessible as prophet, artist, politician. This is at once the attraction and the ambiguity of the penetration of social science by psychoanalysis. Modern man is attracted by the possibility of avoiding the public reference; in response to the harshness and ubiquity of public life, he has sought out those doctrines that are the intellectual modalities of the most private interest. Freudianism represents a movement towards a new sort of inwardness, and away from a social world that Freud always saw in shades of gray.

IV

As physician and confidant of man in his egoistic wish-dreams, Freud implicitly condones the repressiveness of society. While he suggests a more conciliatory attitude on the part of society to the instincts, he assumes that the interests of the individual and society will remain opposed. The acquisition of rights by powerful leaders he supposes justified by the anarchical tendencies, the weakness, passivity, and credulity of the masses. The final point in his indictment refers to the "laziness" of the masses. Freud makes notably few direct references to the medicinal necessity of work—though it is negatively urged by his regular disparagements of public and private fantasy, whether in dreams, neurotic withdrawnness, or ethical utopianism. In his most openly polemical essay, *The Future of an Illusion,* however, the theme is overt. Men must work. Freud makes the old scourge a test of maturity and independence. Take the fact that "men are not naturally fond of work," add to it that "arguments are of no avail against their passions"—and you have the "two widely diffused human characteristics"[37] which make a coercive society inevitable.

The messianic strain in Freud led him to admire resolute and ruthless minorities. In the *New Introductory Lectures* he imagined a group of "men of action, unshakable in their convictions, impervious to doubt, and insensitive to the sufferings of anyone who stands between them and their goal." [38] Writing to Einstein, Freud imagined a Platonic Republic whose rulers are a "community of men" who have achieved second nature and thus "subordinated their instinctual life to the dictatorship of reason." [39] If the masses are naturally ungrateful to their betters, their recalcitrance makes the attempt to govern in their name take an even more ruthless form, as in Soviet Russia. Freud expressed ironic admiration for the Bolshevik minority, the iron men who were making "the tremendous attempt to institute a new order of society." [40] But he was certain (writing in 1927) that the Bolsheviks, like all other pre-psychological revolutionaries, would fail.

Not that Freud dismissed lightly the hope of a free and leisured society. He was impressed by the notions of the socialist Josef Popper-Lynkeus, a fellow Viennese. The attempt to bring about a free society appealed to him, particularly (he saw a just realism in the paradox) where the attempt itself was coercive, as with the reforms then going on in Russia. Utopian hopes might be shored up with this much psychological confirmation: man is equipped, after all, with the most varied instinctual predispositions. Is it not possible, then, if human nature is malleable, to remold it? Freud thought not. Experiments (such as socialism) in the overcoming of political oppressions meant the supersession of one form of public authority by another, and Freud held a near-tautological conviction that the group was irrational in all pursuits.

Admittedly, the group may be capable of far nobler achievement than isolated individuals "in the shape of abnegation, unselfishness, and devotion to an ideal." [41] But the group is not thereby redeemed, in Freud's eyes: its moral achievement is made possible by the fact that the rational powers are, by the very warmth of membership, correspondingly suppressed. Rationality, from the perspective of this social psychology, is disintegrative of group life. Given his presumption of an irrationality rooted in group life, Freud's deference to a private ideal of rationality is the more easily understood.

If society is held together by its irrational regard for and dependence upon a leader, then society, so far as it is stable, is always, in the broad sense, authoritarian. Defined as the bond of unequals, a society of true equals—of individuals—is to Freud unimaginable. Freud's criticism of equalitarian ideals seems more firm and original than his old-fashioned fear of the indolent, childish masses. He advanced beyond nineteenth-century liberalism by psychologizing its conventional laissez-faire critique of a society of planned equality. The predicted inability of equalitarian creeds and orders to furnish adequate economic motives for exertion was translated by Freud into the absence of a sufficiently strong *libidinal* motive. Exertion, here too, is commended—as if Freud feared a satiety of the emotions, both political and private, once the impulsions of scarcity were removed. He implies that without erotic inequality, erotic scarcity, and consequent erotic competition—sublimated in part, of course, to social advantage —we would lack those antagonisms and attractions that sustain community. It is a familiar argument, transferred to exotic ground. Substitute economic for emotional reward, and Freud's psychology appears as the last transfiguration of classical economics into a moral doctrine.

For all his sympathy with the necessity for authority and inequality, Freud's is a liberal mind. He opposed the meliorist view of society according to which coercion is itself only the result of defective cultural organization through which men have become embittered and revengeful. Resignation to the necessity of some form of social or cultural coercion is very much within the liberal canon. Equally liberal is Freud's discounting of Marxism or any other ideal of social perfection; it was an accommodation to social authority which he envisaged, not its abolition. His recognition of the necessity of social coercion—in psychoanalytic currency, repression—hardly makes him an advocate of this or that repressive system. Indeed, in his anatomy of the familial models of power and of the inner compulsion that draws together the members of chance crowds, of churches, of states;

in his evocations of the parricidal guilt from which obedience springs —in all these ideas, the ethical tenor of Freud's science appears skeptical, remaining unstirred by the large possibilities of altering the political order.

In yet another sense, Freud's familial models militate against authority. In likening citizens to children, and leaders to fathers, he tarnishes whatever halo may remain around political authority. His analogy between the state and the family—and, potentially, his therapy of emancipation from family bondages—directly challenges the basis of social respect. "From the time of puberty onward," Freud writes,

> the human individual must devote himself to the great task of *freeing himself from the parents*. . . . For a son, the task consists in releasing his libidinal desires from his mother, in order to employ them in the quest of an external love-object in reality; and in reconciling himself with his father if he has ,remained antagonistic to him, or in freeing himself from his domination if, in the reaction to the infantile revolt, he has lapsed into subservience to him. These tasks are laid down for every man; it is noteworthy how seldom they are carried through ideally, that is, how seldom they are solved in a manner psychologically as well as socially satisfactory.[42]

True, it is ostensibly in order to become "a member of the social community" [43] that the individual must free himself from his parents. But the wider analogy holds. If government needs the funded capital of filial piety, and if outgrowing paternal authority measures individual health, is Freud not giving social rebellion a place in the normal course of human affairs?

So far as Freud distinguished the state and the family, the implications are equally prejudicial to the state. The rise of political society, as set forth in *Totem and Taboo,* occurs in two stages. First there is horde government, the rule of the primal father; then, family government. The state is not simply modeled on the family, Freud explained. The family itself is really a chastened reconstruction of the primal horde.[44] Thus Freud saw in politics a revival of the horde sentiment, reserving to the erotic claims of the family a certain humane tension with the grosser, more primitive and absolute claims of the state. His view, for instance, that directly sexual love, "the love for women," has no place among the social emotions * illustrates his conservatism and his misogyny, but it also illustrates a view of the family as being not only the very model of political affiliation but also exerting a limit upon it: a competing loyalty and repository of erotic capital.

Freud reproduced much of the hostile folklore of liberalism against the state. His images of war are especially expressive of liberal apprehensions. Since collective behavior invariably stems from the unconscious, politics acts as a catharsis for groups—much as art does for individuals. Wars and revolutions are outbreaks of archaic attitudes. War "strips us of the later accretions of civilization, and lays bare the primal man in each of us." [45] Politics is not the instrument of rational interest that Marxists would have it be. In Freudian usage, which discounts the idealistic rhetoric of governments even more heavily than does Marxism, "interests" serve nations "at most, as *rationalizations* for their passions; they put forward their interests in order to be able to give reasons for satisfying their passions." [46] The same reasoning is applied, in *Totem and Taboo*, to the sources of primitive law. Freud dismissed as superficial the notion that law is "imposed by chiefs and priests for the protection of their own prop-

---

* *Group Psychology*, SE XVIII, pp. 140–41. See the following passages, especially. "Directly sexual impulses are unfavorable to the formation of groups. In the history of the development of the family there have also, it is true, been group relations of sexual love (group marriages); but the more important sexual love became for the ego, and the more it developed the characteristics of being in love, the more urgently it required to be limited to two people—*una cum uno*—as is prescribed by the nature of the genital aim. . . . Two people coming together for the purpose of sexual satisfaction, in so far as they seek for solitude, are making a demonstration against the herd instinct, the group feeling" (p. 140).
And later: "In the great artificial groups, the church and the army, there is no room for woman as a sexual object. The love relation between men and women remains outside these organizations. . . . Even in a person who has in other respects become absorbed in a group, the directly sexual impulses preserve a little of his individual activity. If they become too strong they disintegrate every group formation. The Catholic Church had the best of motives for recommending its followers to remain unmarried and for imposing celibacy upon its priests; but falling in love has often driven even priests to leave the Church. In the same way love for women breaks through the group ties of race, of national divisions, and of the social class system, and it thus produces important effects as a factor in civilization" (p. 141).

erty and privileges." [47] The mass of evidence collected by anthropologists on the ambivalent treatment of rulers supplied Freud with ample proof that those who administer the law are themselves exposed to it in a way that indicates it does not, primarily, reflect their interest. Even tribal or national interest is too individualized, too rational a motive for collective action. Self-interest is at best the consequence of deeper motives characteristic of all societies.

Collective action is for Freud the major expression of man's barbarism: the state permits itself misdeeds and violence which "would disgrace the individual." [48] Compared with the course of individual development, the morality of nations remains at a relatively primitive level. Freud dismissed the Wilsonian illusion that wars may have some ethical goal. They represent, rather, a revulsion from all ethical goals, a brutal shock therapy for a civilization that has overextended itself. Most heroic actions are not decisions in favor of "certain abstract and general goods" but simply a response to pressure from the unconscious.[49] Sacrifice for one's father- or motherland is not noble; psychoanalysts explain it by the "death-wish" and other sadistic formulas.

With Freud's revulsion from political violence and collective idealisms, many readers will sympathize. However, when he tries to penetrate the psychology of the soldier he goes astray. For the quiet Jewish doctor, living throughout World War I as a civilian in Vienna, "the secret of heroism" was a kind of madness. The soldier is a berserker; he is possessed by that instinctive heroism, rather, rashness, which knows no moral motivation and foolishly "flouts danger in the spirit of . . . 'Nothing can happen to *me*.' " [50] The man of violence is not an individual but a carrier of archaic, sub-individual impulses. He is merely another version of the mass-man, all too ready to cast off the controls of his super-ego. Surely Freud simplifies the matter. By presuming that the super-ego counts for little in war, he misses the more terrifying fact that mass murder often presupposes a strong super-ego and positive identification with national ideals.*

---

* Thus it is commonly said that the reason the Italians compare unfavorably as soldiers with, say, the English or the Germans, is that they have weaker super-ego controls.

The savage, as Freud himself points out, at least performed penance after murder to allay his sense of guilt.[51] But the modern civilized killer does not share this sense of guilt with his savage predecessor— not because he has shed all moral scruples, but because his public morality is too sharply divided from his private. With persuasive simplicity, Freud has the soldier draw on the resources of the id in order to fight, and the state that makes war is less the incorporation of moral ideals than the vessel of brutal archaic aspirations.*

Freud's fear of the state appears to contradict his authoritarian commendation of strong leaders. Actually, this seeming contradiction can be synthesized by reference to a more inclusive attitude—toward the individual. Freud's Janus-faced conjectures on group life all serve his defense of the individual. When the state is attacked, as in the essay "Thoughts for the Times on War and Death" (1915), it is because Freud assimilates the state to the masses, seeing it as a Jugger-

---

* I have discussed here Freud's explicit psychology of the soldier, and its lack of realism. Indirectly, however, Freud contributed much that is subtle and true to our understanding of the fundamental importance of morale, rather than morality, as the real need of the soldier. His notion of the mutual "identification" of the members of a group has been a singularly fruitful insight in the study of war neurosis, the behavior of troops under pressure, and so forth. (The notion of "identification" is a useful refinement of the older notion of "sympathy" with which social psychology really begins.) Freudian students of social militancy have stressed the factor of mutual identification among followers, rather than direct identification with a leader. For certainly the influence of a Napoleon, a Wallenstein, even a General Patton does not explain the unity of the many sub-groups which comprise an army. Identification means not only hero-worship but also the demand for justice and equality —a concern that all followers be accorded the same treatment, due to envy that may arise at the possibility of one of them being specially favored. Thus it is cross-identification which is important. Feeling different, either inferior or superior, means, in Freudian terms, an incomplete identification and a consequent reluctance to fight. Thus, for example, in the case of the Jew in the army—Freud relates one of the many jokes on this theme in *Wit and Its Relation to the Unconscious*—it may mean an unwillingness to be killed. The Jew's sense of his cultural separateness may make him a poor soldier; it is, if we may coin it so, the Shylock complex. The same sense of exemption characterizes all individuals with low identifications with the group, like the Negro soldier who steals or refuses to fight in battle. Thus, psychologically, we can understand the new concern of armies with the elimination of segregation and the nationalization of cross-cultural loyalties. Of course, in certain cases, the desire for exemption can proceed from a confluence of motives hampering identification—both feelings of superiority (as of culturally superior persons) and of inadequacy (due to physical weakness).

naut rolling over the solitary conscience. But when, as in other writings, the repressiveness of the political society is condoned, it is because the state has been assimilated to the individual (i.e., the culture hero, the moral teacher) and posed against the rabble needing government. This accent on the individual underlies Freud's diverging prejudices and is a key to the unity characteristic of his beliefs as a whole.

V

Freud never articulated a truly social psychology. Against the main drift of contemporary social science, his concern remains the individual and his instincts. Politics is first of all something that goes on in the mind, analogically subjectible to the same analysis as individual order and disorder. Freud did say that his was a psychology both individual and social, that individual and social psychology were the same.[52] But the parts of his analogy are not equivalent; the reference is always from society back to the individual, from the manifest public (act) to the latent private (emotion). His interest in the social consistently mirrors his concern with the individual. It is because he is first of all a student of the individual that Freud could entertain the notion of individual and society in active and prolonged conflict with each other, in a theory that supports at different analytical points the claims of both. Notice that he asks not only how the individual endures the social order, but how the social order endures the individual. In our time the first question is imperative; but for the second question many of us have lost sympathy. It is common to hear that the individual is merely an ideological invention of Western culture, apparently outdated by technology and disproved by sociology. The contest between individual and society, if acknowledged, seems unequal and the result in every case a foregone conclusion.*

---

* It is common to deny that there is such a necessary conflict at all. Such diverse challengers as Marxists and neo-Freudians have discounted Freud's portrait of asocial competitive human "nature" versus repressive "society" as mirroring only the pathologies of modern capitalist society, holding that in fact the interests of individual and society are not genuinely opposed. Cf. Francis H. Bartlett, *Sigmund Freud: A Marxian Essay* (London: 1938); Erich Fromm, *The Sane Society* (New York: 1955), pp. 74–77.

So far as social psychology is characterized by its assumption that the individual is the thrall of society, Freud is not a social psychologist. On the whole, modern social psychology inclines to an organicist position, and therefore stands outside the liberal defense of the individual within which, historically, the Freudian psychology belongs.

Of course Freud acknowledges as necessary the civilizing labors of society, its efforts to tame the unsocial individual. Nevertheless, his summing up of social demands as "renunciation" qualifies the sanction he grants to civilization. His psychology controverts the organicist idea that individuals realize their personal value through the *polis*, the church or holy community, or the state. Organicist sentiment had declined throughout the late nineteenth century. Freud's own sentiments were formed by an ascendant doctrine of individuality, according to which "society" meant the sacrifice of individuality, not, as in earlier notions of organic community, its fulfillment. This championing of the individual as alien from the great community is a vaunting element in the psychologizing philosophies of Nietzsche and Stirner. It reappears in Freud as the therapeutic attempt to separate the private affections from their neurotic displacement onto public authority. Only Bentham, among the great moral psychologists of the nineteenth century, was able to identify the individual with the social good. The utopianism of Bentham—and in the liberal doctrines adopting the Benthamite good of the greatest happiness for the greatest number—lay in this identification. Freud, however, saw the relation as an antagonism. By the largely romantic coupling of renunciation with good conduct, he perceived a permanent antithesis of individual and society. It is the cost of sacrificing individual happiness to the moral tyranny of society that provides the subject of Freud's psychology. Society's ideas of the good become an object for the psychiatrist's examination.

Here is a startling inversion of the traditional concern: moral ideas are named as the *problem* of life rather than as the basis for a solution to the problem. The Freudian dislike of social idealism, as a way of symbolizing and masking power, emerges in a powerful suspicion of self-sacrifice as sickness. Placing satisfaction even before achievement, Freudian doctrine questions all achievements by asking first of all what sort of satisfactions they permit. Some compromise, if not with achievement then with simple efficiency in continuing one's appointed tasks, must be reached. The problem of the quality and value of this compromise supplies the material of psychoanalysis both as doctrine and as therapy. Freudianism exhibits high culture at last taking inventory, checking on its own costliness.

Defending the individual against inevitable subjugations, without much confidence in his client, Freud expresses his intense ambivalence toward the political community. The power of the modern community to cripple the individual may be curtailed by analysis of the origins of communal power in a period when its legitimacy is no longer taken for granted. In this sense the Freudian doctrine is liberalism finally developed to the stage where it acts as a medicine for itself, mediating the antagonism of social influence and private desire. Social life is analyzed at the moments when it fails to respect the right of the individual to satisfaction.

From his therapeutic concern for the individual we can evaluate Freud's pejorative analysis of the state, of the mass, of the crowd, of the antheap of culture measured against the lonely private intelligence. This concern for the individual, as opposed to his commitments to culture, he inherited from a *Zeitgeist* thoroughly saturated with Schopenhauer and Nietzsche. In this sense it is true that Freud harbors an elitist theory. The cultivated persons who have achieved their individuality and reconciled themselves to their instinctual nature are the subjects of his medicine; for this cultivated individuality is an achievement of maturity and not given naturally at the beginning of our lives. Freud shows us not the rebel individual of our democratic affections, feeling his erotic unity with all mankind and yet his splendid isolation, but the self-conscious prudent man whose mind has freed itself inwardly from authority, and who therefore no longer pays the price of conflict and neurosis.

I do not mean to say that Freud advocates what psychoanalysis has become in some recent versions—an ethic of social adjustment. However, the prudence which he recommends comes very close to being a restatement of that ethic: in the psychoanalytically educated character, there may well be submission to social demands, not from enthusiasm but from a prior calculation of personal need. Psychoanalysis sponsors a rational alienation from public enthusiasm. Such a rationally alienated person learns how to guard against social overinvestments, and how to make them when necessary. Freud's social message is rational and manipulative. However much Freudianism may itself function as an ideology, it inculcates—as I have tried to show—skepticism about all ideologies except those of the private life.

Psychoanalysis is the doctrine of the private man defending himself against public encroachment. He cultivates the private life and its pleasures, and if he does take part in public affairs it is for consciously private motives. "How far is this favorable to the moral development of man?" the historian Burckhardt asks, delineating the Renaissance ideal of the private man. "He wins as private individual, as citizen he sinks." * Freud bears the same message. It is fair to accuse him of a medical egoism, allied to that of other nineteenth-century defenders of the individual against society—Nietzsche and Stirner, for example. Individual health, not the perfection of society, is the psychological measure. As nature, in Freud's conception, is separate from the conscious purposes of man, so Freud assigned to man a nature apart from the purposes and meaning of society. Upon the scientific doctrine of cold nature, indifferent to value and for itself alone, Freud superimposed the doctrine of man for himself. The individual struggle for self-mastery becomes the condition of more outward masteries. It is in this psychological form that the toughness of Darwinian ethics perpetuated its influence beyond the laissez-faire age into the age of mass society, past the decline of the ruthless capitalist spirit to which Darwinism had given ideological support.

Even in an atmosphere of conformity, inner freedom is possible. Freedom is no more than a metaphor, for Freud, when applied to any form of society; it can be properly said to exist only within the person, when there is a right balance among parts of the psyche. The quest for

---

* This rise of psychological man parallels the rise of the modern state, which has centralized all power. Thus Hobbes, the first absolutist political philosopher, is also the first philosopher of the private man.

social freedom is superficial, indeed, a contradiction in terms. Rather Freud understands freedom and tyranny as states of mind. Informing all political tyranny is a basic "psychic tyranny." The American psychoanalyst Lawrence Kubie defines such tyranny as the "dominance of unconscious compulsions and fears." The nature of conformity is not to be grasped by analysis of the social structure or of the interests of the powerful, for it "occurs in the rich and in the poor, in the intelligent and in the unintelligent, in the citizens of a free community and in the citizens of a totalitarian state, among believers and non-believers." [53] Psychoanalysis exposes the triviality of much contemporary agonizing over the conditions of social organization that encourage conformity. It undercuts the whole problem of the freedom of the individual in any society, emphasizing instead the theme of the anti-political individual seeking his self-perfection in a context as far from the communal as possible. All politics are corrupt, in the democratic community as well as in the totalitarian state. Since freedom is a psychic condition (residing essentially in the individual, not in him as a member of a group), the possibility of freedom exists in all societies. Psychoanalytically speaking, there were free slaves in Athens, as there are enslaved citizens in New York. This view of freedom lies behind the indifference to politics of many educated Americans of liberal political persuasion who have been instructed by Freudianism. Psychoanalysis, by its turn to the inner life, puts fundamentally into question the received criteria for discriminating one regime from another, let alone for determining the best regime. Thus Freud undermined the ancient concern of political philosophy and substituted for it the inquiry of a political psychology, asking in what manner and degree must the individual be constrained within his social relations.

CHAPTER EIGHT

THE RELIGION OF
THE FATHERS

Why atheism nowadays? "The father" in God is thoroughly refuted; equally so "the judge," "the rewarder."
—NIETZSCHE

I
T IS on the subject of religion that the judicious clinician grows vehement and disputatious. Against no other strongpoint of repressive culture are the reductive weapons of psychoanalysis deployed in such open hostility. Freud's customary detachment fails him here. Confronting religion, psychoanalysis shows itself for what it is: the last great formulation of nineteenth-century secularism, complete with substitute doctrine and cult—capacious, all-embracing, similar in range to the social calculus of the utilitarians, the universal sociolatry of Comte, the dialectical historicism of Marx, the indefinitely expandable agnosticism of Spencer. What first impresses the student of Freud's psychology of religion is its polemical edge. Here, and here alone, the grand Freudian animus, otherwise concealed behind the immediacies of case histories and the emergencies of practical therapeutics, breaks out.

I

There was no reason why Freud should have been so engaged by the problem of religion—at least no obvious, psychoanalyzable reason. He had never gone through a phase of faith; no family pieties had stifled him, so that he had to speak out. His free-thinking father, emancipated from the provincial ghetto life of Galicia, raised his children in a secular atmosphere. After a childhood devoid of religious impulse and schooling, Freud was easily converted to the Darwinian gospel and a lifelong faith in science. In such a background there is nothing that promises erudition in religious questions, let alone sympathy for them; but neither is there an incentive to react strongly against the old articles or new moods of faith. Yet the animus is there.

We can gauge its extent by noting Freud's claim to encompass impartially, as a psychologist, the entire historical variety of religion. What appears in *The Future of an Illusion,* in the essay on "Obsessionalism and Religious Practices," and in other writings as a generalized critique of religion is of course not impartial; nor is it evenly distributed. Aiming at religion in general, Freud's critique hits Christianity most accurately; and by Christianity he had in mind mainly the Roman Catholic Church, as he saw it in the fiercely anti-Semitic Vienna of his day.

To balance this strong animus toward Catholic Christianity, Freud's feelings about his own religious origins were tolerably hospitable. Freud viewed himself as as "little an adherent of the Jewish religion as of any other." [1] Toward a Judaism that entailed beliefs theologically distinct from Christianity, he had no attitude at all. Yet, despite his irreligion, Freud felt intensely Jewish and lived his life in largely Jewish society. His is the familiar history of the European Jewish intellectual. His friends were all Jews, his patients mostly so; his private culture—jokes and family sentiment—exemplify a Jewishness more binding than religious orthodoxy. Even some of the neurotic traits in Freud's character point to his origins in Eastern European Jewry; for example, that obsessive anxiety for the health of wife and children which is a common by-product of the Jewish son's close and persistent bond with his mother. (Until a year before his marriage, at twenty-seven, Freud lived at home, and later, as husband and father, apparently transferred to his own family a good deal of his maternal anxiety.) [2] However little nostalgia he harbored for Jewish ceremonies or custom, Freud did acknowledge himself as a psychological Jew— and indeed he had many of the rigidities of that curious and heroic type in late European history.

It is easy to dismiss Freud's Jewishness as a residual attachment, or as a reflex against the anti-Semitism of the majority culture around him. But it deserves more serious consideration; for here concealed are a number of connections between his personal psychology and his psychology of religion. In considering himself a psychological Jew, Freud meant to define "Jew" more fundamentally, in terms of a certain kind of character rather than by adherence to a specific creed.

Freud found in the perennial Jewish character, rather than in any belief, the source of his personal integrity, his moral courage, his braininess—and, above all, his defensive attitude toward the world. As he linked the insights of his admired contemporary, Josef Popper-Lynkeus, into the "hollowness of the ideals of our present-day civilization" with the fact that Popper was Jewish,[3] so Freud claimed for his own moral stamina the same source. Such ethnic pride projects his desire for that unhampered critical utterance which is the religion not of the Jew integrated into his own community but of the "infidel Jew," [4] standing on the edge of an alien culture and perpetually arrayed against it. In one respect, then, I take Freud's Jewishness as a rationale for his critical pugnacity. His minority-group loyalty reinforced his image of an embattled psychoanalytic minority.*

From an early age, Freud in his critical sentiments had been erecting a mystique of the Jews. Even when his admiration became fixed on a figure not actually Jewish, it served his Jewish moralism. As a boy, when he finally came to realize the consequence of belonging "to an alien race," and was forced by the anti-Semitic feeling among his classmates "to take up a definite position," he invoked "the figure of the Semitic commander" Hannibal. "To my youthful mind Hannibal and Rome symbolized the conflict between the tenacity of Jewry and the organization of the Catholic church." [5] That the schoolboy Freud should have chosen Hannibal as his "favorite hero" is no more surprising than that the aged scientist should at last write of Moses.

---

* Cf. the essay "Resistances to Psychoanalysis," *Coll. Papers* V, 174: "Nor is it perhaps entirely a matter of chance that the first advocate of psychoanalysis was a Jew. To profess belief in this new theory called for a certain degree of readiness to accept a position of solitary opposition—a position with which no one is more familiar than a Jew." In his image, the minority shrinks at times to a group of one—a Moses, himself—the solitary opponent of organized error.

A similar feeling infuses his admiration for Oliver Cromwell, for whom he went so far as to name a son; [6] the Puritan commander, with his intellectual soldierliness and sense of certainty, appealed to the unbeliever Freud, psychologically, as a Jew. The affinity for militant puritanism, not uncommon among secular Jewish intellectuals, indicates a certain preferred character type, starched with independence and cerebral rectitude rather than with a particular belief or doctrine. The figure of the minority radical was especially compelling for Freud. During his long life he saw psychoanalysis move from its position as a minority movement, censuring what it took to be the dominant beliefs of the culture, to a point at which many of its tenets were accepted and partly incorporated into the dominant beliefs. Nevertheless, it is part of the logic of a critical theory that it can only acknowledge with reluctance its successes; so far as it is still critical, it continues to understand itself as on the defensive. It is not accidental, I think, that Freud's defiant interest in religion grew upon him late in his writing life. As he saw the critical impact of his therapeutic ideas weakened by success, he turned to the most resonant image of estrangement he could find—his Jewishness. Being a Jew helped Freud to maintain, throughout his career, his self-image as a lonely fighter.* Hannibal had almost brought down mighty Rome. Despite his later eminence, Freud's object remained to bring down the mighty Romes of our ascetic civilization, now so corrupt and, even worse, ineffectual. Freud always kept his "desire to go to Rome." But he wanted to go as a Hannibal of the mind, as Lord Protector of its dark dominions.

A motif to which Freud recurs in analyzing his own dreams is ambition. Sometimes it is prosaic and career-harried, as in the dream whose underlying wish, he discovered, was his desire to become a professor; [7] at other times it is a more noble ambition which he evokes, as with the recital of this memorable childhood incident:

---

* "To deny a people the man whom it praises as the greatest of its sons," was another stroke of genius in Freud's lifelong intellectual act of estrangement. Thus to intuit that Moses, creator of the Jews, was himself an Egyptian transformed the greatest son into the greatest stranger, a lonely fighter even against his own armies. (See *Moses and Monotheism*, p. 3.)

I may have been ten or twelve years old, when my father began to take me with him on his walks and reveal to me in his talk his views upon things in the world we live in. Thus it was, on one such occasion, that he told me a story to show me how much better things were now than they had been in his days. "When I was a young man," he said, "I went for a walk one Saturday in the streets of your birthplace; I was well dressed, and had a new fur cap on my head. A Christian came up to me and with a single blow knocked off my cap into the mud and shouted: 'Jew! get off the pavement!' " "And what did you do?" I asked. "I went into the roadway and picked up my cap," was his quiet reply. This struck me as unheroic conduct on the part of the big, strong man who was holding the little boy by the hand. I contrasted this situation with another which fitted my feelings better: the scene in which Hannibal's father, Hamilcar Barca, made his boy swear before the household altar to take vengeance on the Romans. Ever since that time Hannibal had had a place in my phantasies.[8]

Freud would have preferred a heroic father to such a prudent one; he once dreamed of him as a Garibaldi, a national emancipator.[9] To argue, as Freud was to do, that our image of God derives from the experience of the father does not preclude understanding that there are many fathers. One of his charges against Christianity is that its father-image is not sufficiently strict and demanding. Perhaps with the Roman theology in mind, Freud valued unyielding spiritual pride, such as that with which he credits the Jews. He questions the "kindness" of the Christian God, who "must lay a restraining hand upon his justice. One sinned, and then one made oblation or did penance, and then one was free to sin anew." [10] The creator of the Jews—Moses—was neither kindly nor indulgent, as Freud depicts him; soldierly and uncompromising rebels like Hannibal, Cromwell, or Garibaldi symbolized to him the moral tenacity of the Jews.*

---

* Freud's feeling for the persistent character of the Jews was shared, in the Victorian and Edwardian periods, not only by marginal Jews (Disraeli's proud defensive mystique immediately comes to mind) and by Jewish self-haters like Otto Weininger, but also by friendly rationalists and liberals. Freud's remark that the Jews must have "behaved in Hellenistic times as they do today" reminds me of E. M. Forster's description, in a story with a Hellenistic setting called "Philo's Little Trip" (in *Pharos and Pharillon*), of "six Hebrew gentlemen of position and intelligence, such as may be seen in these days filling a

Freud attributed his intellectuality, as he did his moral courage, to his Jewishness. "For various reasons the Jews have undergone a one-sided development and admire brains more than bodies." The Greek balance between intellectual and physical cultivation "is certainly preferable . . . but if I had to choose between the two I should also put the intellect first," Freud once said to Ernest Jones.[11] "For two thousand years," he declares in *Moses and Monotheism,* the Jews have exercised their "preference" for intellectual and "spiritual endeavour."[12] It is a sentiment that Jewish intellectuals who have repudiated orthodoxy but are still covertly attached to their sacred history have frequently expressed in an effort to preserve the old élan of being divinely chosen. I need not point out how self-deceptive this superiority complex, cultivated by an able and insecure European post-religious Jewish intelligentsia, has become. The setting of Jewish aspiration has shifted from the learned Germany of Freud's era to athletic and nervous America. In the American environment, Jewry has altered its inherited preference for intellect. Several generations and suburbs away from the dismantling of orthodoxy, many Jews have become too comfortably aware of their purely psychological —or, for that matter, sociological—Jewishness to remain Jews or become intellectuals. According to the Freudian assumption, to become self-conscious about a prototype helps dissolve it. Among educated Jews in Europe and now in America, from whom it has chiefly drawn its partisans, Freudianism may be seen as breaking the last painful strands of religious identification. Under psychoanalytic tutelage, the felt ambiguity of being a Jew without religion can be understood as part of a neurotic submission to an exhausted authority, and dispelled. Freud himself retained more loyalty to his Jewishness than his doctrine permits.

II

That doctrine has proved the least answerable of recent adversaries to both Judaism and Christianity, just because it takes so seriously the

---

first-class carriage in the . . . express on their way up to interview the government." Freud's partisanship is of course Hebrew, while Forster sides with the Greeks. Both take for granted a persistent Jewish character.

inner dynamics of the old faiths. The articles of faith matter not at all. Freud's own Jewish attitudes illuminate, better than any atheist posture, the entirely anti-intellectual approach of the psychologist to religion. In *The Future of an Illusion,* Freud's major essay on religion, where he appears in such a sharp polemical mood, his greatest contempt is reserved for the philosophers of religion—those who try to make religion intellectually, as well as emotionally, attractive. In view of the strategy of peeling off manifest contents that is generally characteristic of his therapeutic method, it is not surprising that Freud decried the subtleties of the philosophers of religion. He accuses them of stretching "the meaning of words until they retain scarcely anything of their original sense." Philosophers of religion may call "some vague abstraction which they have created for themselves" God, and "pose as deists, as believers." But the "higher and purer idea of God" which they "pride themselves on having attained . . . is nothing but an insubstantial shadow and no longer the mighty personality of religious doctrine." [13]

Freud has little to say of religious inquiry. His argument never confronts theology, for which he cares nothing, but is based strictly on a view of religion as a certain emotional set. The rational theology of Saint Thomas, Calvin's cutting logic, the entire inquisitive and speculative bent of Western religion remain unacknowledged. This intellectual superstructure Freud saw as merely a disguise or rationalization for the deeper emotions, which were as much political or moral as religious. Like Schopenhauer and Nietzsche before him, and like D. H. Lawrence and others after, Freud interprets the cognitive pith of religion as a displacement of the emotion toward authority.

Rejecting the religion of the intellectuals, Freud went about his main business, the attack on the religion of the naïve. Yet his rejection of the intellectual content of religion, his charge that religious intellectuals were trying to fill the expanding silence of God with their own voices, accords with the main defense of religion in the last century as well as with the main attack. For a growing number of the thoughtful, from Pascal to Harnack, no bridge seemed long enough to reach from the God of Aristotle and Saint Thomas to the God of Abraham, Isaac, and Jacob. Freud found the crossing easy—and irrelevant. The conceptual God was simply a pale abstraction of the living God. The bridge led nowhere; it was only the cleverest way of leaving the scene of the old God's death. Yet all this cleverness had little to do with religion. White peacock and bull father, totems marched out before tribal brothers, sovereign kings of families covenanted together, communion rites and fertility images—these are religion. Not even the God of Abraham and Isaac would do as the authentic deity. The God of Freud's polemic is still less cognizable. Behind the One God of Judaism, as he explained in *Moses and Monotheism,* stands the remote figure of a bloody mountain deity; and behind that deity looms the awesome figure of the primal father, the missing link between anarchy and culture.* Freud conceived of no God not originally mortal, none that did not incarnate the human craving for authority—just as in the social sphere he could conceive of no political unity based on anything other than erotic attachment to a personal leader.

What Freud contributed to the discussion of religion was not a critique of orthodoxy. To disparage theology as merely intellectual sums up the genius of that liberal and sentimental piety—the evasive religion of the heart—which, in the nineteenth century, had succeeded large segments of Protestant orthodoxy. When in mid-century, after many premature announcements, the old fatherly God did really die, he was replaced by a model man, compounded of the highest moral sentiments and sweet reason. In order to avoid the finality of death, the mighty anthropomorphic personality was dismissed respectfully as a poetic but not exclusively valid representation of God—for the many. Thus Matthew Arnold, one of the most thoughtful representatives of liberal religion, wrote:

> It is undeniable that the old anthropomorphic and miraculous religion . . . no longer reaches and rules as it once did. . . . [But] it is not to be imputed merely to the inadequacy of the old materializing religion, and to be remedied by giving to this religion a form still materializing, but more acceptable. It is to be imputed, in at least an equal degree, to the grossness of perception and materializing habits of the popular mind, which unfit it for any religion not lending

---

* As I have noted in Chapter Six, pp. 188–99, Freud based his view upon the origins fiction proposed by Darwin and Atkinson.

itself, like the old popular religion, to those habits; while yet, from other causes, that old religion cannot maintain its sway. And it is to be remedied by a gradual transformation of the popular mind, by slowly curing it of its grossness of perception and of its materializing habits, not by keeping religion materialistic that it may correspond to them.[14]

Arnold's polite faith, which he hoped could somehow be spread from the cultured few to the uncultured many, is precisely the solution to the religious problem with which Freud began. Assuming that such a dematerialized God cannot, as Arnold hoped, attract the naïve and uneducated, Freud taunts us with the old personal God, the true God of the naïve. For the Freudian psychologist, with his unquestioned assumption that individuals are motivated only through an appeal to the emotions, God can hardly be a first principle or an abstract composite of moral enthusiasms. In Freud's view, religion excluded any cognitive function; it was as purely associated with feeling as science was with reason. By this application of his psychology, Freud accepted a major trend of nineteenth-century belief and interpretation of belief, rejecting the theology of the mind for the religion of the heart—in order to move on from this to the rejection of religion altogether.

Such a tactic characterizes all modern attempts at a psychology of religion, even that made in a work as complex and persuasive as William James's *The Varieties of Religious Experience* (1903). James was aware of the reductive import of the psychological approach to religion; by distinguishing *varieties* of religious experience he tried to mitigate this reductionism, as Freud did not. But James, too, for all his analytical delicacy, was still a psychologist, with a psychologist's one-eyed interest in religion. Like Freud, later, he found the emotions of the naïvely religious more interesting, more fundamental, than the intellectualized responses of those who have experienced faith more subtly, though no less powerfully.* Freud was, however, more polemical than James, and he was less impressed by the therapeutic value and moral authority of religious belief.

---

* Studying the phenomenon of conversion, for example, James passed over evidence of the conversion experiences of intellectuals, or conversions based on doctrinal grounds, in favor of the experiences of untutored and disturbed minds swayed by revivalist fervor.

Further, Freud's analytic apparatus is less complex than is James's; it consists largely of connecting religion with the emotional need for authority. His geneticism lies behind this connection. Through religion, the needs of the past revive. Adults feel their helplessness in the world at large, as if still children. In "the child's defensive reaction to his helplessness" Freud found what he thought a perfectly adequate model for the adult religious experience of "unknown and mighty powers." [15] * Religion is linked with the weakness of childhood and contrasted with the heroism of true maturity. "There is no question that religion derives from the need for help and the anxiety of the child and mankind in its early infancy." Freud's point is that adults are only a little less helpless today, but that at least they need not convert helplessness into a fantasy of some beneficent relation to power. To the rejoinder that man *is* weak, Freud would reply that religion does not overstate the weakness of the human condition but expresses too much pride in it. Religion corresponds to the childhood of the human mind and is suitable to ages of intellectual weakness; the evolutionist moral of Freud's description is that we must grow up, develop beyond religion.

The rhetoric of Freud's analysis depends almost entirely upon evocations of "childishness." By religion he appears to have in mind the famous feeling of dependence, with God conceived as the sovereign father of the extensive human family. Even less generalized religious feelings, those not attached to apprehension of a personal deity (the image of the father enlarged), are reduced to childishness. Take, for instance, the well-known passage in *Civilization and Its Discontents,* where Freud summarizes a correspondence with the novelist Romain Rolland.[16] Rolland had inquired whether Freud would admit the sense of an all-embracing, indefinite consciousness, an "oceanic feel-

---

* One may compare Freud's idea of religion as deriving from the timid propitiation of the "all-powerful Father" with Spencer's theory that all forms of religious worship are derived from the propitiation of deceased ancestors, and that our idea of the deity derives from our fear of ghosts (*Principles of Sociology,* 1897). Both Freud's father-theory and Spencer's ghost-theory are ways of discounting religion as a form of "projection"—a type of analysis which received its classic statement in the writings of Ludwig Feuerbach, especially *The Essence of Christianity* (1841) and *The Essence of Religion* (1854).

ing," as a genuine variety of mystic experience. Freud answered no; and, as we would expect from his unfailing recourse to origins as a therapeutic (and at the same time scientific) mode of explanation, he played on the positivist affront of childishness. He called Rolland's religious feeling primitive; this sense "of belonging inseparably to the external world as a whole" is nothing but a survival of the primitive ego-feeling which is normal to infancy. Here, as elsewhere, Freud shows how far he is from sharing that sentiment for childhood which unites Christian orthodoxy with modern Romanticism, old faith with new sensibility. Christian and Romantic alike refuse to regard a child-like simplicity of vision simply as a mode of immaturity, holding that children may know something—of morals, of beauty—which adults with their complex and limited experience have forgotten.

What Freud disparages as infantile feeling could plausibly be treated as a saving inclination of the self to assay some simple reconciliation with the world. Surely reconciliation is a universal motive. Freud had self-consciously echoed [17] the mythological notion asserted by Plato, that even the orgiastic impulse was an attempt to overcome the duality of the sexes and restore their original unity. But he treats the interior movement toward reunion as regressive. The mystic's cherished break through the sense of individuality is treated by Freud as a regression, a flagging of the ego in its irresolvable struggle with the alien world. Every such reconciliation merely evades the permanent conflict between self and not-self. The permanence of conflict is Freud's leading theme, and part of his hostility to religion stems from an awareness that religion somewhere assumes a fixed point—in Christianity, the figure of Christ—at which conflict is resolved. In contrast, Freud maintains an intractable dualism; self and world remain antagonists, and every form of reconciliation must fail.[18] Indeed, nothing so well represents Freud's own irreligion as his feeling for the irreconcilable. It also explains how he could make an exception, in his anti-religious critique, for the Jews, whom he so admired for their tough, uncompromising monotheism and their "usual stiff-necked obduracy" [19] in the face of persecution and reproach.

To his disparaging view of religion as derived from the dependent sentiments of childhood, Freud subjoined another charge, that religion is basically a "feminine" preoccupation. He was not referring by this last to any institutional fact, such as the female monopoly on lay devoutness which is an important feature of the history of Christianity, at least of Catholic Christianity, in the West. He intended, rather, a psychological judgment beyond all the facts of religious history—a further caricature of religion as being beneath the masculine dignity of reason. Freud is concerned to show the pathos of the religious *man* who is, like a woman, "forced to obey unconditionally." [20] To be religious, as Freud sees it, is to be passive, compliant, dependent—essentially feminine traits. This is the main point he saw illustrated by the paranoiac seizure of an eminent Dresden jurist, Dr. Paul Schreber, on whose memoirs Freud commented in a lengthy essay (1915). One feature of the intricate messianic delusion to which Schreber fell prey, while confined in a mental hospital, was the belief that he had changed his sex. Schreber's desire to be a woman submitting to the masculine God, Freud took as an exemplary case of the submissiveness which defined the religious attitude. Again, in his own case, the "Wolf Man," Freud explained his patient's childhood streak of piety as a projection of the boy's feminine attitude toward his own father. Not only is a spontaneous religiosity inconceivable to Freud, he even gave religion a sexual character in order to convey the power of religious thralldom.

These genetic disparagements of the religious spirit are, I should say, the least viable part of Freud's psychology of religion. Resembling all too closely the "nothing but" argument by which animus is sanctified as science, Freud's reasoning is actually tautological: he will admit as religious only feelings of submission and dependence; others are dismissed as intellectual dilutions or displacements of the primary infantile sentiment. (A like objection applies to the analogy he drew between religious acts and the obsessional ceremonies of neurotics.) [21] What is chiefly interesting in Freud's critique is not its blunter tactic of scientist name-calling—religion as childish, feminine, obsessional—but the general implications of a *psychology* of religion, as a cultural symptom as well as a mode of diagnosis. I have noted earlier that Freud largely rejected as irrelevant the philosophic and historical study of religion which flourished among the post-orthodox minds of the nineteenth century. But notice the source, and the power, of that rejection. In the Freudian rhetoric of faith as childishness, and of religion as a political device representing the oppressive claim of the community over the individual, we may detect a revival of the great tradition of Enlightenment criticism. It is this animus of the Enlightenment which has gained, under the aegis of Freud's intellectual authority, a new precedence among the educated but religiously illiterate of our time. The basis of Freud's critique of religion is now old enough to have been forgotten; through his writings the superseded standards of the Enlightenment take on a new freshness.

The fact that Freud was confronting not religious orthodoxy but a defense of Christianity (and today in America, of Judaism) which had already receded and merged with a vague defense of religious feeling as such gives his critique an aptness and novelty which a close look at its actual texture does not sustain. This apologetics—the repudiation of dogma for experience, of creed for feeling—seems virtually to invite a final, psychological reduction. Further, it seems likely that the rapidly accumulating data of anthropology lent new sense to the Enlightenment quest for an original, or "natural," form of religion, behind all variety and complication. Freud's lack of respect for the historicity of religions is comprehensible only if we see behind it his acceptance without question of the value of this quest.

This reduction of the liturgy and doctrines of historical religion to representations of universal "natural" (i.e., psychological) motives was first proposed in the eighteenth century by deists and rationalists. In the nineteenth century, when comparative religion emerged as a mature discipline, it was carried on chiefly by missionaries and other church-affiliated researchers. One of the earliest was the German pastor-scholar Ghillany, who in 1842 published a book in which he derived the Passover from a rite of human sacrifice, and portrayed the Christian Eucharist as a modified Jewish sacrament of god-eating (theophagy).[22] The post-religious implications of such study became evident only slowly, so that these church-affiliated scholars could study religion comparatively and yet insist that creed and faith remain untouched.* When the study of comparative religion was taken over by secular scholars and absorbed into the rising and more inclusive discipline of anthropology, conclusions overtly hostile to religion were drawn. Belief in a variously represented God was succeeded by an interest in various beliefs about God. It was at this point that Freud put forth his own contribution. Accepting the reduction broached in the Enlightenment and documented by the sciences of comparative religion and anthropology, he added to it the category of projection. Both the doctrinal essence and the ritual manifestation of religion were interpreted by Freud as projecting the revolt against, and subsequent acceptance of, the father. To the "identity," established by the anthropologists, "of the totem feast, the animal sacrifice, the theanthropic human sacrifice and the Christian Eucharist," he adds a unifying motive: that each rite is "at bottom" nothing but "a new setting aside of the father, a repetition of the crime that must be expiated." †

The challenge of Freud's critique, by which the differences of history are bleached into a sameness of motive, is more thoroughgoing than that posed previously by generations of erudites in search of the common faith underlying the complex historical varieties of religion. By tracing parallel occurrences of the myth of the dying Savior, out-

---

* Their disclaimers were, however, not always convincing. Robertson Smith was tried by the elders of the Scottish Church for advancing a thesis much like Ghillany's.

† *Totem and Taboo,* SE XIII, 154–55. The original commemorative rite of parricide, "the ancient totem meal," is "revived again" in the Christian communion, a new totem feast "in which the company of brothers consumed the flesh and blood of the son—no longer the father—obtained sanctity thereby and identified themselves with them" (ibid., 154). "The memory of the first great act of sacrifice thus proved indestructible, in spite of every effort to forget it. . . ." The prototype of rebellion persists deeply in the memory of its defeat, when "at the very point at which men sought to be at the farthest distance from the [parricidal] motives that led to it, its undistorted reproduction emerged in the form of the sacrifice of the god" (ibid., 151–52). In this way, Freud sought to encompass what his predecessors, such as Robertson Smith, had already established sociologically as the priority of "cultus" to "doctrine"—a psychological version of the religious ritual as (in all its variations) expressive of the original alienation from authority. Ritual commemorated the original crystallization of the dual impulses of human nature into the character of culture as such. "We can recognize in all these solemn occasions the effect of the crime by which men were so deeply weighed down but of which they must none the less feel so proud" (ibid., pp. 154–55).

side Christianity, in Greek mystery cults and Mithraism; by exposing the patchwork of biblical texts; by showing how liturgy was shaped by ecclesiastical politics—in these ways the historical method shook Christianity. But, outside the enclaves of biblical literalism, the shocks could be absorbed. Liberal Christianity could let go of the historical Christ and keep only the personal Jesus. Indeed, liberal Christianity absorbed the historical method into its own canon of argument, taking its stand on a universal and inherently spiritual "need," of which dogma was one plausible if limited historical expression. Not just the intellectual justification for tolerance in a variety of liberal denominations, but also the great nineteenth-century, largely middle-class Protestant religion of culture developed out of Enlightened, comparisoned, and scienced Christianity. Indeed, that Christ should have emerged as "Christ, Scientist," as in one remarkable upgrading of his professional title, marks the bathetic climax of Enlightenment therapeutics in America.

The style of attack which reached its climax in Freud was more damaging than historicism, more damaging than Christianity as mind cure. A psychology of religion cannot be fended off in quite the same way, by partial incorporation. Embracing the findings of the comparative—that is, historical—study of religion and adapting as well the liberal refutation, psychology can reject the universality of the "religious need" in human nature by dissolving that specific need into emotions characteristic of more than religion. There is no distinctively religious need—only psychological need. The psychologist still has the option, however, of being friendly or hostile. If friendly, he will argue that religion is "psychologically" valuable; this is the position of Jung. If hostile, he will counter that the need can be satisfied by something better, more mature, than religion; this is Freud's view. That "something better" is rational science, in the service of a less wasteful development of human satisfaction.

III

Freud is a popularizer of the religious problem, speaking in the authoritative voice of science, to an audience on the whole post-religious * and unfamiliar with the lines of self-criticism laid down by the theologians themselves. Upon many brought up within a weak or defensive religious environment, his arguments for atheism have had a great emancipating impact, giving them reasons for a break already in process.

On religious minds, however, he has a different effect—one of those reversals to which the psychoanalytic method is liable. Given the intellectual poverty and lame spirit of organized religion today, it is ironic but not surprising that Freud should be understood by a number of influential clerical spokesmen as contributing new authority to their side of the old argument between the rationale of faith and faith in reason. One of the more curious turns in the history of Freud's reception is that by which his atheist psychology, despite the indignation with which it was first greeted by professional guardians of morality, has been taken up by a number of eminent religious minds as if it were a prop and not an assault. Whatever is serious in the current revival of religion is evocatively, if not substantively, Augustinian in temper; it proclaims the wretchedness of the human condition and rather muffles the voice of God. For this sort of religiosity Freud performs a delicate service. His atheism being dismissed as a personal aberration, Freud's psychology has been pressed into service, mainly as independent testimony to the religious "depth" for those no longer persuaded of its existence by theological rhetorics. Again, Freudianism may buoy up those who recoil from the optimism of liberal religion. Chastened by decades of failure to convince themselves that every day in every way they are getting better—under Christ and/or the prophets—liberal Christians and reformed Jews now flock to a moral psychology which, in Freud's own ironic words, confirms "the habitual pronouncement of the pious: we are all miserable sinners." [23] It is stressed that Freud did acknowledge a native moral evil (in the instincts). He did assume a universal sense of guilt. His view of nature

---

* By "post-religious," I mean an attitude so far removed from ultimate concern that neither piety nor atheism can appeal to it. "Religion" is accepted, like any other service, as another good to be consumed by those who have a taste for it.

was pessimistic. These things are taken as evidence of the affinities between the religious and psychological view.*

Freud merits respectful treatment by the theologians; they can use him more than they can any other thinker who has ever been fundamentally hostile or indifferent to them. Today a Christian anthropology that does not incorporate large quantities of Freudianism cannot serve Christianity. Nevertheless, the theologian who subjoins psychoanalytic to theological conceptions is foolhardy. The irrationalities to which Freud drew our attention are to be mastered through rational self-control; he does not enjoin faith. He detected neither accident nor mystery in the world. Even its "depths" conform perfectly to the laws of nature, those laws which it is the business of science to extend. To be sure, Freud was not sanguine about the average man's powers of reason. But he never wavered in his attachment to the public fellowship of science and its powers of explanation. In contrast to Jung's, nothing in Freud's theory supports the claim of any intuitive system of explanation or response.

It is just those Freudian terms with a religious resonance—such words as "guilt," "anxiety," "conscience"—that reproach the corresponding religious notions. Take, as a case, Freud's treatment of conscience. While not denying the natural development of a moral sense, he offers little support to the religious conception of it. In Freud's usage conscience is an instrument of parental dominance, the accretion of ordinances by which, as the sociologists say, a child is "socialized" and its resentments "internalized." It is precisely the religious view of conscience as intelligent and reflective as well as passionate

---

* I speak here only of the theoretic appeal of psychology for religion, and vice versa. There is also a less obtrusive trend of rapprochement going on—and, to my mind, a more dangerous one, since it stakes its claim below the level of theological argument and psychological theory. I refer to the affinities which have been discovered between the pastoral techniques of religion and the therapeutic techniques of psychiatry. Here, both sides have contributed to the new amity: ministers and theologians attempting to repair the encroachments which psychiatrists have made on their professional preserve as the authority who is consulted when people are in emotional and moral straits; psychiatrists anxious to repudiate the unavoidable doctrinal implications of their clinical practice by a new generosity toward the successes of the religious "cure of souls."

that here comes under attack, for Freud argues that conscience is furnished by social authority and remains, unreflectively, at authority's disposal. This refusal to acknowledge that conscience may be at odds with its social sources surely simplifies the moral process. Because he views society reductively, as the family-in-large, Freud overestimates the degree of consistency in the ethical injunctions to which people are exposed. (This error mars his therapeutic writings, as well as his general consideration of the super-ego.) He assumes that parents, as well as "teachers, authorities, [or] self-chosen models and heroes venerated by society," [24] all preach the same line; he underestimates the cynicism and cleverness of the young and exaggerates their naïve impressionability. For Freud, however, freedom of conscience is a contradiction in terms; there are only alternative submissions.

In place of such freedom there is the empirical capacity for aggression—a capacity without which Freud cannot explain the moral order and the individual's need for religion. For him the instinct of aggression plays the same role, formally, that Christian psychology assigns to free will. Thus aggression is the psychological potency that enables man to rebel against authority, in the person of the primal father (as, in the religious account, free will allows us to rebel against God), and at the same time it supplies the means by which men can end their rebellion. Freud's idea of the "introjection" of aggression formally resembles the religious idea of the free act of faith; it reconciles the subject to authority. He did not hold the comforting view that aggression is a secondary emotion, a consequence of the frustration of love. On the contrary, as he saw it, aggression is as original as sin. Again, this meta-instinctual strain in Freudianism, these dark expectancies concerning the permanence of aggression, have appealed to those for whom psychology is religion touched with science. But Freud's view does not invite this response, for what the religious think of as moral evil—these aggressive feelings and the reaction to them—he discusses as entirely natural. His remedy, too, is far from a religiously acceptable one. To reduce human aggressiveness he recommends that we reduce our overextended moral aspirations, since aggression is, in part at least, a reaction against too fervent a desire for personal virtue.

The gulf between psychoanalytic and Christian psychologies appears even more sharply in the related idea of guilt. Though Freud saw guilt as in some degree inevitable and objective—as the religious do—any further likeness to the religious prepossession is deceptive. Guilt may be innate, original, natural, a feeling prior to action. But this Freudian conception of guilt is cast strictly within the critical language of pathology. First of all, in Freud's account, repression forces a backward flow of the destructive instincts upon the self. And apart from the externally imposed restraints exercised by civilization (the repressions), everyone inherently suffers from a residue of the "death instinct," so that hostilities which are not directed outward upon others turn back upon the self in the form of "an intensified masochism" and feelings of guilt.[25] * Its origins having been explained thus naturalistically, the sense of guilt can hardly be considered a reliable index of real felony and warrantable remorse. Since no distinction is drawn in the Freudian scheme between natural and moral evil, no room is left for guilt as distinct from ignorance. The overscrupulous and conscience-ridden person is in the grip of certain prepossessions of which he is unaware; and the presumption is that his guilt will dissolve in the rational self-consciousness fostered by therapy. Guilt indicates lack of self-understanding, a failure of tolerance toward himself on the part of the natural man.

However, as Karen Horney has pointed out, even after analysis (after the patient "knows"), patients may still have feelings of guilt. She is mistaken, though, when she accuses Freud of seeing guilt as merely private and missing the all-pervasive weight of ideology. That this is not his view Freud makes clear in *Totem and Taboo* and thereafter. He supposed guilt the normal attitude of an individual toward authority, social as well as individual. One of his favorite theses is that human beings have an ineradicable social heritage of guilt. The great religions are attempts to solve the problem of guilt; they are all

* When the positive redirection of the death instinct outward takes place, Freud wrote, "it is then called the instinct of destruction, of mastery, the will to power" (*Coll. Papers* II, 260).

"reactions to the same great event," the murder of the primal father, "with which civilization began and which, since it occurred, has not allowed mankind a moment's rest." [26] Religion attempts to appease the sense of guilt; at the same time, only by perpetuating it (by such commemorative repetitions of the parricidal act as the Christian communion) does the authority of faith continue. Morality too stands under the sign of guilt. The best behavior of which we are capable is "at bottom" an attempt "to conciliate the injured father through subsequent obedience." The social and religious meaning of guilt is summed up by Freud in the following formula: society was "based on complicity in the common crime; religion was based on the sense of guilt and remorse attached to it; while morality was based partly on the exigencies of this society and partly on the penance demanded by the sense of guilt." [27] The sense of guilt is thus the pivot for Freud's conception of morality and religion. Religion, he says elsewhere, proceeds by "fomenting an ever-increasing sense of guilt." [28]

The Christian theologians—especially liberal Protestants—who have expressed a certain fondness for Freud's affirmation of the saving sense of guilt are mistaken to see any support in this for their own position. Freud held that religious sentiment is a phase resulting from certain historical processes of repression (and subject to historical fluctuations); for him the sense of guilt is a flexible instrument, and "it is possible that cultural developments lie before us, in which yet other wish-gratifications, which are today entirely permissible, will appear just as disagreeable as those of cannibalism do now." [29] Aldous Huxley makes Freud's point effectively when he shows the horror with which the inhabitants of *Brave New World* regard us, their ancestors, for our obscene practice of bearing children alive, like mammals, instead of in a civilized fashion, out of test-tubes. The strength of Christian culture has depended on the use it has made of the funded potential of human guilt feelings, and Freud argues that, whatever its value in the past, the "creative sense of guilt" [30] has now increased beyond all use. Religion itself has become the sort of collective neurosis by which we can no longer save ourselves from a personal one.

Man is a remorseful killer, and religion is the history of his guilt. But why "guilt" at all? The animals feel none. Guilt is incurred by the infraction of a law or principle. And how powerful must that *Schuldgefuehl* have been, if the whole complicated, infinitely anguished story of religion grew out of that feeling. But Freud refused to go the one step further, to admit the universal objectivity of guilt. So, too, Otto Rank held that without the repression of the incest urge, civilization was unthinkable. But it did not occur to him to ask why man should have repressed the incest urge. Whatever so evidently tore man out of the context of nature was itself repressed.

"When an instinctual trend undergoes repression," reads one formula in *Civilization and Its Discontents,* "its libidinal elements are transformed into symptoms and its aggressive components into a sense of guilt." [31] That guilt about which Freud writes is above all the *sense* of guilt, a psychological not a moral fact. In the Freudian rhetoric repression has a very special meaning, both individual and social; indeed, it is the conception at which psychoanalysis meets Christianity back to back, so to speak. In the Christian psychology what is supposed to have been repressed, causing bad conscience, is one's higher nature—the moral sense. In the Freudian psychology what was repressed, causing a sense of guilt, is one's lower nature—the instinctual desires. Thus, in Christianity the sense of guilt is characteristically a sign of augmented moral delicacy; in Freudian psychology the sense of guilt is a source of private illness. In a culture undergoing the final reversals in religious meaning and value, the psychoanalytic inversion of Christianity's saving sense of guilt has had a curious appeal. Freud's meaning and that of Christianity are indeed close but completely at odds.

Having so redefined guilt as the repression of one's lower nature, Freud could demonstrate how treacherous was the floor under conventional piety. The sense of guilt as defined by Christian culture seemed to Freud a sandy foundation for morality. Indeed, he noted, it was possible precisely out of a "conscience phobia" to commit the most horrible crimes. Freud was aware of the morality, so highly praised in modern fiction, of the holy sinner. As a reader of Dostoevski, he noticed "in so many Russian character types" a special odor of sanctity around sin. "Russian mysticism has come to the sublime

conclusion that sin is indispensable for the full enjoyment of the bless-
ings of divine grace, and therefore, fundamentally, it is pleasing to
God." [32] Of course, even though he mildly caricatured this theological
fancy, Freud respected the necessity in a repressive culture of incorporating sin into the larger doctrine of grace. Moral dualism could be
a conscious expedient of cultural coercion. "The priests could only
keep the masses submissive to religion by making these great concessions to human instincts." [33]

Holy sinning, Freud recognized, is not simply a religiously permitted outlet for natural impulses, sponsored chiefly by certain historical forms of Christian (Catholic and gnostic) belief. The phenomenon of holy sinning might occur in any individual whose masochism, the cumulative backwash of the death instinct, "creates a
temptation to 'sinful acts' which must then be expiated by the reproaches of the sadistic conscience or by the chastisement from the
great parental authority of Fate." Since, guilt is really pathological, a
guilty conscience may not necessarily imply a turn to the good. Certain unmotivated crimes may be explained as a kind of suicide of
conscience.

> An individual may, it is true, preserve the whole or a certain amount
> of his morality alongside his masochism, but, on the other hand, a
> good part of his conscience may become swallowed up by his mas-
> ochism.[34]

The "pale criminal" [35] whom Freud had in mind commits his crimes
in order "to provoke punishment" from authority. His acts are attempts to justify a pre-existing sense of guilt. Convinced that he has
committed some crime (the nature of which is left uncertain), he feels
he "must do something inexpedient, act against his own interest, ruin
the prospects which the real world offers him, and possibly destroy
his own existence in the world of reality." [36]

Such an interlocking of weakness, rebellion, and obedience has
been examined with extraordinary intensity in the modern novel.
Raskolnikov (*Crime and Punishment*) and Stavrogin (*The Possessed*) are both ethical criminals, holy sinners. The type not only
has fascinated the great Russian novelists and introspective Roman
Catholics such as Bernanos, Mauriac, and Graham Greene, but has

also summoned Existentialist ideologues to a strenuous defense of writers with personal histories of criminal offense. The Existentialist characterization of writer-criminals—de Sade, Rimbaud, Jean Genet —as inverted men of faith draws upon the idea that crime can be an ethical act, more admirable than merely conforming to the proprieties. I doubt if Freud would have agreed with the Existentialists that such crimes may be freely and coolly chosen, without compulsive residue —as an *acte gratuite*.* But a similar admiration for the antinomian character—the figure of the instinctual hero who is guilty of "presumptuousness and rebelliousness against a great authority" [37]—is a basic theme of Freud's work.

To resist the demands of conscience may be an act of maturity, since conscience may be a source of crime as well as of piety. The aim of Freudian psychiatry is, however, not the triumph of instinct over moral feelings but the reconciliation of instinct and intelligence. The intellect is set to helping the instincts develop, tolerantly, like a prudent teacher.[38] Conscience, however, directs us to repress the instincts. The conscience-stricken thus do not appear by Freudian standards to be very intelligent. By viewing conscience as in opposition to intelligence, Freud exhibits a prejudice against virtue fairly common among secular intellectuals—the idea that the merely good person is not likely to be either very clever or very strong.† "Morality," the sadism of the super-ego, appears as a stupid alternative to "the will to power," the sadism of the ego.[39] (Recall that Dostoevski, really a very secular intellectual, did not make the saintly Alyosha the cleverest of the brothers Karamazov.) Subscribing to the weakling

---

* See Sartre, *Saint Genet* (1952), and the studies of Simone de Beauvoir and Maurice Blanchot on de Sade. I should argue that the capacity for gratuitous crime does not necessarily testify to inner liberty. One might find, for instance, in the very surrealistic repetitiveness of the atrocities (and the interminable speeches justifying them) in de Sade's novels an index of the irrational and compulsive. The ethical criminals of de Sade and the Existentialists seem no less compulsively motivated than the wretched Stavrogin.

† The snobbishness in Freud's attitude toward the conscience-stricken is also suggested in his little essay, "A Religious Experience" (1928). Freud had received an evangelistic letter from a young American medical student who reported how his realization that God must exist came to him one day while watching a "sweet-faced dear old lady" being wheeled into the cadaver room. Freud replied tartly that if he wanted to be a first-rate doctor he ought to get rid of his mother-image (*Coll. Papers* V, 243–46).

theory of conscience so popular in nineteenth-century literature, Freud shows once again in his conception of the guilt feelings how entirely opposed to Christian religious psychology is his psychology of religion.

IV

There is one curious exception to the general negative in Freud's psychology of religion; it is to be found in his underrated study *Moses and Monotheism*. Despite his prevailing idea of religious experience as the training ground of suppliant personalities, in this profound little book on the origins of monotheism Freud allowed for revolution from above as well as for instinctual resurgence from below.

He fixed on the Cromwellian aspects of the eleven-year reign of the young Egyptian Pharaoh Amenhotep IV (1375 B.C.). The Pharaoh's conversion to the monotheistic cult of Aton (in whose honor he changed his name to Ikhnaton) set off an unsuccessful attempt by a high-minded minority at a drastic imposition of new ideals upon both people and priesthood. Ikhnaton's lieutenant, Moses—for so Freud identifies him—continued the revolutionary effort. Freud conjectures that, in despair after Ikhnaton's death, the Egyptian Moses turned to an alien Semitic community which had immigrated to Egypt several generations before. He left Egypt with them, accompanied by his immediate followers, hallowed them by the Egyptian custom of circumcision, gave them laws, and introduced them to the Aton religion— in an even more exacting version than that taught by his master Ikhnaton, for Moses relinquished the connection of Aton with the sun-god of On. As Freud reconstructs the story, Moses was repudiated by his adopted people, the Jews. Yet precisely on the ostensible failure of the moral hero depends the success of his doctrine. On this point Freud's entire reconstruction of Hebraic monotheism, and (in less detail) the origins of Christianity, turns: a deposition of the moral hero and the subsequent remorse. For at one time, Freud boldly conjectures, the Jews must have killed Moses,* throwing off

---

* In the Old Testament narrative, of course, Moses dies a natural death, but in several non-canonical accounts, among them that of Origen, he is murdered.

the puritan faith as the Egyptians had done before them. If monotheism may be seen as a repressive revolution conducted by Moses from above, the murder of Moses represents a counter-revolution, a popular reassertion of the instincts in old cultic forms. After the death of Moses—Freud continues his conjecture—the Jews relaxed into the religious habits of their neighbors, taking up the debased worship practiced by the Midianites. But still an obscure memory of the Mosaic religion lingered. Remorse for the killing of Moses continued to work underground, until in time the Midianite tribal deity, Jahve, was divested of his original warlike attributes, becoming more like the old pacific God of Moses, Aton.* Thus the suppressed puritanism eventually reasserted itself. At least, in *Moses and Monotheism,* Freud acknowledged that civilization can be moved by spiritual as well as instinctual discontents.

Freud's conception of the relation between Moses and the mob assigns to discontent a different value from the one we get in *Civilization and Its Discontents,* a book that deals with consciousness in its painful transition from the religious to the scientific stage. In the prophet, the seer, the moral genius, discontent can still be spiritual, at odds with the libidinal discontents of the mob. By the time the psychologist appears, discontent must be libidinal, at odds with the over-extensions of civilization. The discontent of Moses and the prophets was of another time. To Freud the issue is different now and discon-

---

Freud says he found this suggestion, that Moses was actually murdered, in the writings of the great biblicist Ernst Sellin.

* Although *Moses and Monotheism* has been much derided by professional historians, some of Freud's purely imaginative reconstructions have received independent support from recent biblical scholarship, particularly the Swedish. The way in which Freud's reconstruction justifies the disagreeable paradoxes of the Old Testament idea of divinity seems, if a bit overformal, quite convincing. There were, originally, two different Gods: one the God of the Egyptian Moses, "as all-loving as he was all-powerful, who, averse to all ceremonial and magic, set humanity as its highest aim a life of truth and justice," the other a "rude, narrow-minded . . . violent and blood-thirsty" invention of the Midian priest whom the Bible also calls Moses (pp. 74–75, 78). All the canonic writings of Jewish religious history can be reinterpreted, in the Freudian view, according to the manner in which they go about concealing the gap between the Mosaic law-giving and later Jewish religion, the gap that was filled by the worship of Jahve—the manner in which they not only conceal but also carefully cover over the duality.

tent has another object—the spirit, not the flesh. Freud's praise of spiritual discontent as once being a critical force can hardly flatter religions strong chiefly in their prophetic and critical resources and not in their priestly overlay. The sentiments of bitter and personal opposition to the world, which give an innominate tension even to orthodox religious expression, pass unnoticed by Freud. It is a major omission. Freud took the traditional religious posture of obedience to the divine at face value, at the same time failing to grasp the emancipated potential in that posture. No more rugged individualist has ever existed in Western culture than the religious virtuoso. Had Freud applied his presuppositions consistently to religion, he would have noticed the other side of religious experience, the achievement of unyielding individualism in opposition to current social sanctions. Prophetic denunciation of society counts for something in the Western tradition—for as much, in fact, as the persistent civic submissions that Freud prefers to consider.

Mythologizing on the origins of monotheism, Freud does admit the possibility of a rebellion against moral conformity on behalf of an even more stringent ideal. On the whole, however, he assumed religion to be conformist; the idea of it as subversive of the established tyrannies of compromise is one which Freud never entertained except in *Moses and Monotheism*. Even there, he was giving vent to the aristocratic bias which supplied what little was sympathetic in his attitude toward religion. The only defense he could entertain for religion was that, in virtue of its social function, religion is a force for order. And religious leaders like Moses are for Freud sympathetic figures so far as they elevate the moral standards of the rabble. Far from admiring instinctual revolt, Freud's own identification is with the benevolent culture-despots of the pre-scientific ages who raised the level of popular aspiration and occasionally succeeded in transforming their own super-egos into law.* When a culture ceases to venerate its great men,

---

* The drama of the teaching struggle, death, and posthumous triumph of Moses had a special significance in Freud's inner life. The teacher is, for Freud, the universal martyr image—characterized by his *charisma* and wisdom, suffering the resentment of his students and public, who are his children. There is no doubt that Freud, as a great teacher, identified himself with Moses. He writes that Michelangelo's "Moses," in the Church of San Pietro in

Freud feared the onset of that *misère psychologique* which conservative critics of the nineteenth century found to be endangering our civilization.[40] But Freud's faith in the moral genius as the founder of the culture went further than most. As he sought the Moses at the heart of all going systems and creeds, he hypostatized the founder of founders—the primal father—and assumed a natural moral system based on the story of this figure's death-sacrifice to the resurgent masses.

The life of the race is, I should say, much slower and more secular than Freud imagined. Each case of progressive despotism can be matched by scores in which the benevolence of despots rots culture and misdirects progress. Refinement is rarely a matter of sudden personal impulsions or emancipations by clever dedicated chiefs. Among high cultures, the Greek was conspicuously lacking in moral geniuses. The Olympian gods were all-too-human, and even the euhemeristic myths supporting them were discredited by the Periclean age. Only in that meanest of all Greek nations, Sparta, did a Moses figure arise: Lycurgus, the law-giver. Freud's own Moses is altogether too statuesque. Little that is recognizably Old Testament in feeling gets into *Moses and Monotheism*. It is a study of the moral hero putting a higher civilization over on the rabble with the burning-bush trick and the tactic of the mountain retreat. Moses is the only rugged individualist Freud ever described, stronger and more successful than Nietzsche's Zarathustra, who also came down from a mountain retreat to elevate the popular Vedic polytheism into a high-minded ethical dualism. While Nietzsche's great man fails, Freud's great man even in his death succeeds: though the Jews rebel against the tenacity and intellectual fierceness of Moses' character, and abandon the religion he has taught

---

Vincoli in Rome, attracts him irresistibly. ". . . No piece of statuary has ever made a stronger impression on me than this. How often have I mounted the steep steps of the unlovely Corso Cavour to the lonely place where the deserted church stands, and have essayed to support the angry scorn of the hero's glance! Sometimes I have crept cautiously out of the half-gloom of the interior as though I myself belonged to the mob upon whom his eye is turned—the mob which can hold fast no conviction, which has neither faith nor patience and which rejoices when it has regained its illusory idols" (*Coll. Papers* IV, 259–60). Perhaps this is the most intimate self-image the new Moses ever committed to paper, addressing it to the unconvinced, impatient, illusion-ridden, idolatrous mob that is the public.

them, after his death they are bound to it all the more. Compared with the realism, in Nietzsche's book, of Zarathustra's ultimate philosophic failure, Freud's *Moses and Monotheism* is a triumph of psychological romance.

Freud insists that it was the Egyptian Moses who chose the Jews, not the Jews who chose Moses. Moses stamped the Jewish people with its special character. He is to Freud the greatest of moral geniuses, the culture-savior, the "tremendous father-imago" of the Jews. The Jewish masses, who are "his dear children," live under his authority, if they live as Jews.[41] Before Moses they were like all others —that is, not Jews. Freud strangely ignores Father Abraham and his Covenant: "It was one man, the man Moses, who created the Jews." What the Jews came to understand as their chosenness by God reflected the fact that Moses had stooped to the Jews; they were his "chosen people." [42] To Moses, finally, the Jews owe their character— their tenacity, their moralism. Moses first and thereafter definitely fixed the Jewish type.[43]

Compare Freud's reverential treatment of Moses with his remarks on Christianity in *The Future of an Illusion*. While the Jews remained in his imagination what Moses had made of them, he never allowed to Christianity the revolutionary emblem of the character of Jesus. Christianity meant always the Church,* a repressive social institution engaged in a highly ambivalent ritual preservation of an imago which the participants have never really trusted. He discounts the martyrdom of Jesus by calling it a "repetition of the Mosaic prototype." Jesus is "the resurrected Moses" and of course "the returned primal father." [44] Because the killing of Christ post-dates, and (psychologically) reproduces, the killing of Moses, Freud concludes that Christianity operates less imperatively than Judaism—a form of genetic

---

* Freud always saw religion in an authoritative (i.e., political) mode, and the Roman Church, with its highly bureaucratized militancy, was the nearest fit to his theory. When he turned to an analysis of political institutions, he considered that we might "with advantage take the Catholic Church as a type." In the Roman Church, as in an army, what is important is that "the same illusion holds good of there being a head—in the Catholic Church Christ, in an army its Commander-in-Chief." Though churches and armies may differ "in other respects," they share the same psychology of militancy and unity around the person of a leader (*Group Psychology*, SE XVIII, 93–94).

discounting in reverse. Surely Christ was no mere epigonal repetition of the Mosaic prototype. Nothing of the singular and exemplary power of Christ attaches to the image of Moses. Yet Christianity, for Freud, is a "Son religion," Judaism is a "Father religion." In its inner meaning Christianity is the institutionally organized remembrance and recapitulation of the deposing of the father by the son. Freud sides with the father. In his view, Judaism stands for the true father, against the spurious assumption by the Christians of the son. The Christian tradition, however, does something more than again projecting the filial revolt. Freud's doctrine of the psychic trinity—Father, Son, and People—has Christ as an ambivalent figure in the mythos of history. In one sense, Christ is the incarnate God, himself father of the rebellious sons (the mob—who must kill him), thus recapitulating the primal crime. In another sense, equally true, Christ is the Son of Man, defying the Father God. Here the father of the people becomes as well the son, dying by the wish of the father. This is the double role of all tragic heroes, Oedipus and Hamlet as well as Moses and Christ: to die the representative deaths of both son and father.

To conceive Christianity as a rebellion against, as well as a repetition of, Judaism, also shows psychoanalytically how Christianity itself prefigures that endemic form of resentment in our culture, anti-Semitism. The Jews, Freud observed, refuse to acknowledge their relation to a newer authority. "The poor Jewish people, who with their usual stiff-necked obduracy continued to deny the murder of their 'father,' has dearly expiated this in the course of centuries." Envy of such freedom from guilt becomes a reproach against it. "Over and over again" the Jews "heard the reproach: 'You killed our God.' " Freud concludes: "And this reproach is true, if rightly interpreted. It says, in reference to the history of religion: 'You won't admit that you murdered God,' " [45] as if any person can be free of parricidal guilt in the civil wars of the mind.

V

Although he never considered the truth of either Jewish or Christian faith to be viable—except as the truth of any psychological record—

Freud did not underestimate the social function of religion. Against this social function, indeed, he posed his final devastating critique.

The Enlightenment critique, to which Freud owes much, ascribes a natural origin to religion.* From this basic idea Enlightenment polemicists drew the most varied conclusions. Voltaire, for instance, dismissed all historical religions as superstitious and mistaken, corrupt and dangerous; against them he set the "religion of reason," unconnected with any supernatural hopes or appeals. Others, like Leibniz in his *Theodicy,* Locke in the *Deus,* Lessing in the *Education of the Human Race,* took a more accommodating position—regarding Christianity as but one historic stage in the approach to a purified or absolute religion, still to be revealed. Freud combines these two strains, the hard and the soft Enlightenment attack. In the bitterness of his invective against the worn religious patina of authority, in his insensitivity to differences among historical religions, and specifically in his underestimation of the originality of Jesus as a religious leader,† Freud is quite Voltairean. On the other hand, in his respect for the civilizing achievements of religion we catch sight of a progressive Feuerbachian Freud, one for whom even Christianity might appear a step forward in the education of the human race. Of course, in both interpretations Christianity loses its uniqueness. As Leibniz asserts in the introduction to the *Theodicy,* Jesus had only finished what Moses started. Christianity expressed a natural feeling, one of several ways, the deist Locke declares, "of atoning the merciful Father." Deistical criticism was polite to Christianity, granting it a high place in the ascending line of progress. But the evolutionary principle could not accept Christianity as its final incarnation, and by Freud's time the Enlightenment temper was shorter and the treatment of religion less polite. In the course of development, Christianity had overstayed its time. For this reason Freud, in *The Future of an Illusion,* "singled

---

* Cf., for instance, Hume's *Natural History of Religion,* which Freud quotes in *Totem and Taboo,* p. 77.

† Psychologically, the redeemer is always the same figure, the tragic hero, "the chief rebel and leader" against the primal father. "If there was no such leader, then Christ was the heir of an unfulfilled wish-phantasy." If, on the other hand, there was such a historic event as the overthrow of the father by the son, then Christ was one of a number to take the role, the "successor" to it, the "reincarnation" of it (*Moses and Monotheism,* p. 137).

out one such phase of development, which more or less corresponds to the final form of our contemporary Christian culture in the west." [46]

Freud refers not to Christianity but to "Christian culture"; the difference, a most important one, is his view of Christianity as the chief instrument of coercion in the larger system of coercions defined as culture. To his readings in anthropology Freud probably owed his understanding of religion as an externalization of moral authority, thus transforming it into social control.* Earlier it had been decided by Kant that the "numinal" sphere is unapproachable rationally; only the moral sphere, the relevance of religion to society, is comprehensible. This notion was taken up and driven to one logical conclusion by the new science of anthropology: beginning with Feuerbach and including Durkheim and his epigone, it was accepted as axiomatic that the numinal serves significantly as an instrument of social control. This was not a conspiracy of priests but a universally self-imposed limitation on the freedom of man. Religion became, therefore, the representative constraint with which humanity had hobbled itself. Thus the anthropologist Salomon Reinach, at one time widely read, defined religion as "a body [ensemble] of scruples which puts obstacles to the free exercise of our faculties." With this notably one-sided view Freud, on the whole, agreed. The cultural value of religion, he insisted, has been purchased at too high a cost.

It was a distinction made by the anthropologists which gave Freud his most delicate instrument for assessing the exact cost of religion. Frazer, his chief mentor in anthropology, had advanced the following account of the difference between "magic" and "religion." In the earliest stage, argued Frazer, only magic existed. More exactly, magic and religion were identical; the functions of sorcerer and priest were combined or, at least, not yet differentiated from each other. But eventually, as society developed and religion with it, magic and reli-

---

* To externalize moral authority meant to weaken it, Freud thought. For the churches had to make "great concessions" to human instinct. Here Freud is attending only to the Catholic idea of the Church, and not, for example to the modern Protestant. (See pp. 66–69, The Future of an Illusion.) Given his sense of the parallels between structures of religion and power, Protestantism as such scarcely enters Freud's horizon. Because he saw religion always in a political way, the Roman Church adequately filled his need for example.

gion became distinct—indeed antagonistic—as religion attempted to monopolize magic and render it routine. (The Eucharist would be an example of this.) Frazer's argument thus implicitly distinguishes the professional magician who is also a priest (Moses as he appears in the Bible before the Exodus might serve as an example) from the free-lancing magician who later sets himself up in competition with the organized cult. Avoiding the Voltairean error of reducing religion to magic, Frazer emphasized the difference between public magic, which may be a part of but not identical with religion, and private magic, which operates in competition with priesthoods.[47]

Set in its proper context, the distinction between magic and religion, Freud's blending of neurosis and religion appears very Frazerian. Neurosis was to Freud an equivalent to the private magic of the sorcerer, a kind of irrationality which can compete or blend with the brands of magic incorporated into public practice. As Frazer thought that "in the evolution of thought, magic, as representing a lower intellectual stratum, has probably everywhere preceded religion," [48] so Freud puts neurosis, logically and emotionally, prior to religion. Religion offers one solution to neurosis. It may incorporate, stabilize, and resolve a neurosis, as it did for a patient of Freud's known as the "Wolf Man." In this case the child's homosexual regard for his father was appeased and alleviated by the sudden onset of religious piety in his eighth year. The fact that his birthday was on Christmas Day made it easy for him to identify God with his father. In this way he could love his father by loving God "with a fervour which had sought in vain to discharge itself so long as his father had been a mortal." He could bear witness to his extravagant love for his father in ways "laid down by religion," and these expressions "were not haunted by that sense of guilt from which his individual feelings of love could not set themselves free." [49] Thus religion, rather than fomenting guilt, may drain it off—in this case by transposing the child's sexual anxiety into higher, public terms.

Once understood as shared magic,* religion, in Freud's view, is

---

* Freud accepted the view that magic is prior to religion. Cf. *Totem and Taboo*, SE XIII, 91–92: "Whereas magic still reserves omnipotence solely for thoughts, animism hands some of it over to spirits and so prepares the way

shared neurosis. Yet for Freud religion is not simply reducible to neurosis. When large numbers of people share it, a delusion takes on a different meaning. As great a difference obtains between neurosis and religion as between the neurotic who indulges in wasteful, private reverie and the poet who manages to sell his daydreams on the market of culture. Of course Freud could not entirely resist the temptation to reduce religion to neurosis, as he tended so to reduce art. The individualism of his psychology led him to grant a very limited bill of health to any shared illusion. He inclined to treat a public emotion like religion or a socially approved activity like art simply as a multiple of private emotions—ignoring the fact that a belief or act is not simply enlarged but fundamentally altered by being shared. Yet Freud nowhere makes the identification of religion and neurosis facilely, as has been often charged against him. His understanding is to this extent historical: the neurotic contents which in former times flourished under religious auspices (cf. his analysis of a seventeenth-century neurosis of demoniacal possession) are today more commonly elaborated in isolation. While today "neuroses appear in a hypochondriacal guise, masked as organic diseases . . . the neurosis of olden times masquerad[ed] in demonological shape." [50]

Freud's interest in the transition in Western culture from publicly shareable fantasies—e.g., religion—to private hypochondrias is thus not so remote from his interest in so-called primitive religion. In both the anthropological and the Freudian view, when religious belief declines the old magical (or neurotic) energies hitherto stabilized will be dissolved and freed for anarchic re-enactment independent of public sanction. Frazer's theory was that religion is historically later and ethically "higher" than magic, and most of his contemporaries, though their interest in primitive belief was characteristically accompanied by personal atheism or agnosticism, conceded, as he did, that religion was an advance on magic. In a guarded sense, Freud shared this view of religion as higher than (in his terms) neurosis, for he judged neurosis negatively, as the crumbling of religious commitments. Like

for the construction of a religion." In the Freudian interpretation, religion, since it is shared, includes ceding part of one's personal power—includes, that is, an element of renunciation absent in magic.

other nineteenth-century critics of culture, he approved the familiar correlation between "the extraordinary increase in neuroses" and the waning of religious faith.[51] Religion is a way to keep from falling into a personal neurosis or may be a way beyond neurosis; or, as in the case of the "Wolf Man," where the child's sudden access of religious piety, however neurotic its roots,

> put a restraint on his sexual impulsions by affording them a sublimation and a safe mooring; it lowered the importance of his family relationships, and thus protected him from the threat of isolation by giving him access to the great community of mankind. The untamed and fear-ridden child became social, well-behaved, and amenable to education.[52]

That religion may still give men confidence, comfort, and a sense of security may seem justification enough for it; it is not enough for Freud. In his view, religion bestows the very fears and anxieties that it then appeases. Religion may have been the original cure; Freud reminds us that it was also the original disease. And the cure is doubtful. Appeasement feeds what needs to be fought. Were it not for religious encouragements of anxiety, the individual would feel less anxious; the effect of this palliative is to remind the patient that he is ill. "It seems very unlikely," writes Radcliffe-Brown, "that an Andaman Islander would think that it is dangerous to eat dugong or pork or turtle meat if it were not for the existence of a specific body of ritual the ostensible purpose of which is to protect him from those dangers." [53] Freud thought only reason could resolve this pull between social functions and disfunctions. The lingering effects of early human weakness, to which religion was a response, can, he maintained, be rationally understood and attended, and the ancient response thus rendered unnecessary.

In an earlier stage of human development religion gave what Freud called its "value." But Freud took it as demonstrated that the main religion of the West was no longer authoritative; it had nothing more of worth to give this culture. Christianity was now nothing more than a painful "historical residue" of those valuable "repression-like processes which took place in antiquity." [54] In its own creative time, Christianity had deflected the brutality and aggressiveness of late pagan culture; it had turned the energies of Western man inward and refined in a new way his pugnacious energies. Christianity did heal over, if only like a cicatrice, the open life-and-death struggles of antiquity. But, Freud believed, the scar only hides the wound in our nature. The elevating of moral aspiration had lasted too long; the wound had begun to fester. Christianity, the remedy, had become religion, the symptom—a set of "neurotic survivals."

It was Freud's belief that now, after two thousand years of Christian culture, we are entering a new, scientific, phase of development, in which the instinctual renunciation he considered indispensable for man's communal existence has a chance of being maintained by rational means. As the chief instrument of culture, religion was an irrational means. Thus, as the logical outcome of inevitable development struggling against unconditional demands, Freud saw Christianity under the sign of its exhaustion. There is no more ambitious theme in the entire Freudian text; it announces that Christian culture is played out. This particular incarnation of the prototypal relation to authority has lost its energy. Failing as a system of repressions, Christian culture continues to exist only as a problem. Freud viewed himself as treating specific cases of the mental suffering produced during the interregnum between the failure of one system of authority and the establishment of another. It is to a new system of moral authority that Freud looked forward and into which he foresaw that psychoanalysis would be integrated.

Freud had a shrewd feeling, never quite articulated, for the incompatibility of the modern sense of self with our historic religious legacy. Individuals could no longer, "by accepting the universal neurosis" of humanity, be "spared the task of forming a personal neurosis." [55] In a civilization dominated by religious authority, we all suffered from the same neurosis and thus were saved from the alienation of private sickness. But as religion declined, Freud noted, neuroses increased, until modern morality—having lost the coercive backing of religion—became itself the problem of neurosis. I must emphasize that Freud condemned the religious repressions for instrumental reasons—not so much in themselves but because they were failing. Because religion could no longer compel character but only distract it, Freud dared suggest, in the name of science, a new ethical straightforwardness. Neuroses bespeak the specifically post-religious condition of men, produced by the abdication of religiously grounded moral authority. Faith has become a form of anxiety. Despite his occasional protests about its neutrality and limited purposes, Freud hoped his own science would contribute in a major way to the working out of an alternative to the historical systems of anxiety. Hence his prediction that the therapeutic effectiveness of psychoanalysis would increase as the "authority" of science increased, and would include finally heavy doses of suggestion for those who could not be treated analytically.[56]

VI

The psychological foundation of religion at which Freud aimed his attack appears at first too familiar to bear reviewing. In brief, he refurbished the old fallacy that the genotype of belief repeats the phenotype of dependence, and the more general fallacy that the origin of a thing determines its end. But Freud's scorn of our repetitions seems strangely contradictory, for at the same time that he saw religious belief as the inevitable result of childhood dependence and fear of parental authority, he also thought that we could outgrow our origins. The part of Freud's analysis that seems to be worth repeating is its evolutionist conclusion that by the inexorable and natural law of development we are losing our historical religion as a child normally loses his childishness. While regressions have to be reckoned with, Freud held, they do not affect the normality of development but rather make clear the necessity of the individual's keeping pace to avoid falling ill. "Is it not the destiny of childishness to be overcome?" he asks, his voice carrying all the coldness of the early positivist evangel. "Man cannot remain a child forever." [57]

This preferring of movement to fixation evokes a familiar response, one Freud has helped to apply in new ways. The nineteenth-century faith in progress, discredited in its straightforward historical version, prospers none the less in the form of the prevailing psychology of development. In this form Freud put forth his analysis of religion; it is, like other parts of his analysis, a critique of arrestments in development. I say Freudian analysis is at the same time a critique, not only to indicate how far from late positivist notions of value-freedom Freud considered his science, but also to show again how every point in his analysis is premonitory of all; one can always get from description to judgment in a single short step. Indeed, because in his case histories Freud never *reported* the facts but *interpreted* them, what passes for description in the Freudian method is already judgment.

Because faith claims exemption from the law of development, Freud judged that it is inappropriate to the present and has become by virtue of its self-exemption the most grandiose case of neurosis. However, Freud admits that he is, perhaps without warrant, "optimistic enough to assume that mankind will overcome this neurotic phase." [58] Of course religion has served culture well, shepherding mankind through its infancy. But as the mind matures, it appeared to Freud, every religion must die of disenchantment. Freud shared the Comtist hope that theologies would die a natural death from old age and exhaustion. He knew that science cannot kill them; they must wither from within. Death does not come all at once but slowly, and in parts. The signs of life in contemporary theology are, in the scientific view, those parts of the religious organism not yet aware that death is the general condition within which it lives. It is the function of Freud's psychology of religion to emphasize the general dying within which each specific revival must run its short course.

After the euthanasia of religion,* only those unconsoling scientific myths Freud mentions near the end of *Group Psychology* will remain —deliberate intellectual constructions and conjectures. But how far down through the class levels of culture can scientific disenchantment safely be allowed to penetrate? Freud did not share unambiguously the confidence of progressive rationalists, from the French Encyclopedists to Marx, that the ethical advances of the old faiths could be preserved in a scientific era. His particular doubt arises from his own adherence to a notion insisted on by modern critics, from Matthew Arnold to Ortega y Gasset, that parallel and superior to the struggle between *economic* classes there is a struggle between *culture* classes.

---

* Schopenhauer's phrase.

In the case of the cultured, Freud argues, religious motives for decent behavior may safely be replaced with secular ones. But the masses, inherently hostile to culture and held in check only by the authoritarian mysteries of traditional beliefs, may accept the liberating conclusions of scientific enlightenment "without having effected in themselves the process of change which scientific thought induces in men." What authority will hold them in check? "Is there not a danger," Freud asks, expressing the standard alarm, that "if they are taught there is no Almighty and alljust God," the masses "will feel exempt from all obligation to follow the rules of culture?" Then "everybody will follow his asocial, egoistic instinct" and "will certainly kill without hesitation." [59]

How to save the achievements of culture from falling along with their non-rational sanctions? Involved in our spreading concern to preserve good conduct without mythic rationalization, Freud indicated a certain sympathy for the defense of religion as a necessary illusion. In *The Future of an Illusion,* he conducted a dialogue on the subject. Notice that for Freud no conversation with a true believer is possible. The only defense of religion he could take at all seriously is what we may call the sociological one; * he could have understood de Maistre but not Pascal. In the dialogue he has his interlocutor readily admit that religion has only a "practical" value—namely, that without the illusion of a divine order the social order would disintegrate into barbarism. "One should conceal the fact" that faith is a necessary

---

* For the most part the English anthropological critics of religion (Frazer, et al.) remained untempted by any explicit faith, or by the sociological defense of faith. A notable exception was Ernest Crawley, author of *The Mystic Rose* (1902), a study of primitive marriage to which Freud had recourse in *Totem and Taboo.* Crawley conceded that nothing in Christianity is historically new or dogmatically true—that it is in fact a patchwork of paganisms. Still, he argued in another work, *The Tree of Life* (1905), religion is all more or less productive of "vitality," and therefore precious, so that no critical analysis finally matters, except to a few scholars who are willing to bear the burden of disillusion. That the critical analysis of religious ideology nevertheless included an appreciation of its social functions and value is a paradox reached by a line of French positivists from Comte to Durkheim. In a tumid form, the interest of modern sociology (cf. Karl Mannheim at the end of his life) in creating a "faith" appropriate to our time continues this earlier positivist ambivalence toward religion.

hoax—"in the interests of the preservation of everybody" and "for the protection of culture." [60] Freud's imaginary interlocutor is a tertiary of the Grand Inquisitor's Order. He does not argue very well against Freud, for he is plainly a secular intellectual, making a defense not of this or that creed or church, but of religion in general.

A great modern example of such a conversation is Schopenhauer's *Dialogue on Religion.* I should guess that Freud had read it, so closely does his own dialogue in *The Future of an Illusion* follow it. The friendly disputants created by Schopenhauer raise exactly the problem Freud raised. Both take for granted the absurdity of religious belief for rational men. The issue is only whether belief is necessary to control the unenlightened many (this is the position of "Demopheles") or whether the value of religion, now declining anyway, has not been overestimated and is not actually a force obstructing the Enlightenment goals: reason, progress, the true betterment of mankind (the position of "Philalethes"). Schopenhauer has "Demopheles" argue, in much the same terms as Freud's interlocutor in *The Future of an Illusion:*

> "The first thing to do is to control the raw and evil dispositions of the masses, so as to keep them from . . . committing cruel, violent, and disgraceful acts. If you were to wait until they had recognized and grasped the truth, you would undoubtedly come too late; and truth, supposing that it had been found, would surpass their powers of comprehension. In any case an allegorical investiture of it, a parable or myth, is all that would be of any service to them. As Kant said, there must be a public standard of Right and Virtue; it must always flutter high overhead. It is a matter of indifference what heraldic figures are inscribed on it, so long as they signify what is meant." [61]

Later in the dialogue, the position held by Freud is thus defended by Schopenhauer's "Philalethes":

> Philalethes: ". . . We won't give up the hope that mankind will eventually reach a point of maturity and education at which it can on the one side produce, and on the other receive, the true philosophy."

Demopheles: "You've no notion how stupid most people are."
Philalethes: "I am only expressing a hope which I can't give up.
If it were fulfilled . . . the time would have come when religion
would have carried out her object and completed her course; the
race she had brought to years of discretion she could dismiss,
and herself depart in peace: that would be the *euthanasia* of
religion." [62]

The issue debated by Schopenhauer is reopened by Freud in terms
which remained unchanged between 1851, the year of Schopenhauer's
dialogue, and 1928, when *The Future of an Illusion* was published.
There is an important difference, however. In Schopenhauer's dialogue, "Demopheles," who claims that religious illusions must be
maintained for the sake of culture, has much the better of the argument. Freud, on the other hand, awards to the position weakly advanced by "Philalethes," that religion can and must be overcome, the
victory in the debate. The defense of religion as a priestly lie, which
Freud puts in the mouth of his imaginary opponent, is acknowledged
as compelling. Yet Freud is prevented from assenting to it—he says
—by his conviction that, however gravely the loss of religious belief
threatens culture, there is no halting an "inevitable transition," not
by all the half-measures and insincerities philosophers can devise.
According to Freud, "we are just now in the middle" of this "abandoning of religion [which] must take place with the fateful inexor-
ability of a process of growth." If finally Christianity can be defended
only as a necessary illusion, then the religious intellectual must "despair of everything, of culture, and of the future of mankind," for he
will then be defending a "lost cause." Those anxious over the fate of
culture need neither despair nor "oppose the new development."
More sensibly, they should seek "to further it and to temper the force
of its onset." With God the father killed for the last time by the
development of his youngest son, Science, Freud suggests to the cultured classes that the only way they can save themselves is by a
"fundamental revision of the relation between culture and religion,"
in which the Christian coercions would be replaced by the rational
obligations of science. The only alternative to such a revolutionary
pedagogic program would be "the most rigorous suppression of these

dangerous masses and the most careful exclusion of all opportunities for mental awakening." [63] *

The portrait of our culture which Freud sketches, showing the awkward distance between an educated class of atheists and a mass of faithful, is, surely, over-simple. Today both classes and masses are emancipated from official rhetorics of submission to the divine. Freud's prophecies are inadequate to the lessons of modern history. Matters have turned out more horribly: the classes have shown a capacity for fresh barbarisms, and the masses have proved no less docile in their unbelief than they ever were in their belief.

More important, however, is Freud's misunderstanding of religion itself as social. All sociology, and now psychology as well, has been repeating Kant's mistake in regarding religion as the apprehension of our moral duties as divine commands. Religion provides that "solemn air of sanctity" which has been the established way of pledging allegiance to the laws of culture.[64] It is on this original identity of religion and authority that Freud's rejection of religion is based.

But such a sweeping identification of religion with its social function ignores one of the strongest and most valuable of Christian distinctions—between faith and the institutions and attitudes by which it is transmitted at any given time. Just as the early Christians were boorishly suspicious of the material plenitude and alien aesthetic and philosophic culture of their own time, there have been Christians fully as suspicious of Christendom. Kierkegaard diagnosed the malaise of the nineteenth century as such a confusion between religion and culture; and he warned that Christianity cannot survive unless detached from the abuses and distortions of a social order living under the faded title of Christendom.† By taking the identity of the churches

---

* Much of the secondary literature of the psychoanalytic movement ranges itself around this conflict between the declining authority of religion and the rising anti-authority of science. For an influential compromise, see Erich Fromm's *Psychoanalysis and Religion* (New Haven: 1950). Freud's harsh rationalist exhortation that science replace religion is translated by Fromm into the ideal of a "humanistic religion" without authority.

† Kierkegaard's knife-edge distinction between Christianity and Christendom lives on in Paul Tillich's division between the "Protestant principle" and Protestant middle-class churches.

with Christianity at face value, Freud did something he would never have countenanced in the analytic situation, where he was always alert to the differences between manifest and latent contents.

Had Freud not entirely subordinated religion to culture, he would have avoided the related error that religion is always consolatory, the chief mode of escape from the hardness of reality. His somewhat opaque distinction in *The Future of an Illusion* between religion and what is taken to be the scientific ethic—"resignation"—springs from this error. There is no necessary polarity between consolation and resignation; certainly neither term takes into account the calculated defiance which religious temperaments have displayed in the face of powerful antagonists. Freud's favorite example of tenacity and moral courage, the Jews, ought to have suggested to him the limits of his own analysis. The prophets' announcement of doom for Israel could have been consolatory only in a very severe sense—even for the remnant. From any social point of view the prophetic denunciations were truly subversive. That these mavericks renewed the basis of community does not mean they assumed authoritarian functions in any sensible usage; the prophet, even as he renews the repressions, destroys conformism. Nor does the religious feeling of dependence on providence support Freud's easy genetic reduction of it to an original social deference. As among the Anabaptist and Puritan rebels, one dependency may be used to contradict the other. Consolation, if such it be, of the religious sort is frequently charged with the most critical social and ethical potentialities.

If to equate religion with "consolation" is an error, it is equally misleading to equate science with "resignation." Science is inseparable from the rationalist aims of Western culture, which are as utopian as any vision of heaven.* Freud's conclusion that religion is a narcotic,

---

* Thus, the widespread idea that we are inexorably moving forward to a time, perhaps a thousand years hence, when people will become truly rational and all social problems will be solved by scientific engineering.

Though he rejected the religion of the highbrow, Freud felt no compulsion to reject the science of the highbrow. Religion is always an illusion, science never (*The Future of an Illusion*, p. 98). But might one not argue that science is—no less than religion—in the class sense, a matter of feeling? The popular science of the day by which the utopian hope for a robot man is marched

and that they who learn the lesson of science will be "brought up soberly" does not stand much examination. Science has its own mysteries and enthusiasms; attached by an umbilical cord to technology, science can only drift with the drifts of power in society. At least the clerics have a tradition of hostility to the state behind them; the scientists have only just begun to learn that they must fight, and they are embarrassed by their own bursts of ethical enthusiasm. Sobriety—moderation in all things, including worship—used to be the appeal of respectable religion against the sectarian waste of emotion. Today it is the appeal of a conformist technology against the painfully held standards of critical enthusiasm in both religion and science. From its transcendental consolations (e.g., the idea that gospel is superior to law), religious sentiment had at least the possibility of criticizing the social order, while scientific energies, by the facile transformation of the objectivity necessary to science into "value-neutrality" or "value-freedom," are easily enlisted to the aims of society, whatever these may be.

The success of Freud's own doctrine is probably as good a refutation as any of his sharp separation between "religion" and "science." Psychological doctrine, filtered down into textbooks, daily newspaper columns, salesmanship manuals, and the mental-hygiene movement, overtly anti-religious and carrying all the pomposity of an immature science in its train, actually now teaches mostly the character virtues of resignation and adjustment. With their powers of "positive thinking," their ethics of "living on a twenty-four-hour basis," the psychological cults in which America currently abounds do not even aspire to the halfhearted criticism still occasionally to be found in the churches. The popular drift of psychological science aims at freeing the individual most of all from the burden of opposition. On the other hand, religion, with its symbols of remembrance, may be that very submission to the past that will preserve in us some capacity for a radical criticism of the present.

---

round the totem test-tube is as naïve as, and surely more reprehensible than, the yielding to God's will.

CHAPTER NINE

THE ETHIC OF HONESTY

Honesty, granting that it is the virtue from which we cannot rid ourselves, we free spirits—well, we will labor at it with all our perversity and love, and not tire of "perfecting" ourselves in our virtue, which alone remains. . . .

—NIETZSCHE

FROM the beginning, Freud enunciated his science as a therapy. The significance of this is immense: bereft of religion and betrayed by the spurious objectivity of so many sciences, the modern mind has found nothing so convincing as a science that is at the same time a casuistry of the intimate and everyday life. Freudianism restored to science its ethical verve. That it did so by putting ethics itself under the scrutiny of science, as part of the therapeutic purpose of the science, is all the more reason for its appeal. In this way Freud has given us a popular science of morals that also teaches a moral system.

Belief cannot be separated from theory, any more than theory is separable from its consequences. As the rationalized mythology of our culture, modern science has played a larger role in reformulating our moral sense than its defenders often care to admit. Scientific theories function as new and powerful modes of personal belief. Psychoanalysis cannot disclaim its influence on the day-to-day consciousness of our age by calling itself simply a science. All the issues which psychoanalysis treats—the health and sickness of the will, the emotions, the responsibilities of private living, the coercions of culture—belong to the moral life. As a pathologist of the moral sense, Freud could in fact capitalize on the authority gained by science as a cultural ideal. Science claims simply to work. It frees man to observe, to present the facts honestly and come to no conclusion—while at the same time it passes the most detailed judgments and patently takes moral effect. Freud's reticence as a moralist has made him the more influential. His moralizing is of the sort peculiar to our age, most effective when executed with a bad conscience. He set himself up as the amateur moralist, not in the pay of any system, a strict scientist in search of hard facts who, in passing, could not avoid throwing light on the dark corners out of which morality grows.

I

While sometimes claiming that analysis was "entirely non-tendentious," [1] Freud elsewhere recognized that his science was as much philosophy as medicine. Psychoanalysis stands, he said, in a "middle position between medicine and philosophy." [2] Freud was anxious that analysis make the best of both worlds. He himself had "never really been a doctor in the proper sense." With a fine mordant flourish, he boasted that he lacked "a genuine medical temperament," the "innate sadistic disposition." As a child, he had never liked to "play the 'doctor game.' " [3] His "original objective" was philosophy; the shift from neurology to psychology satisfied his longing for philosophical knowledge; "psychology was just a way of expressing this." [4] More interested in problems than in patients, he had become a doctor against his will. But, having made himself over into a new kind of doctor, Freud could claim all society as his patient. It is the ambition of his claim that separates Freud and the psychoanalysts from the medical doctor—at least from the modern doctor's image of himself as a body-mechanic. Freud's physician was to be a student of history, religion, and the arts. Subjects having no connection with medicine, and which never enter the physician's practice, such as "history of civilization, mythology, the psychology of religion, and literature," [5] were to be storehouses from which the psychoanalyst would borrow select pieces of truth in defining symptoms. The first and permanent Freudian task was not empirical research but interpretative rearrangement of the intricate jumble of data accumulated by the cultural sciences.

A good idea of Freud's professional ideal may be gathered from his defense of lay analysis (1926). During the late twenties and early thirties the psychoanalytic movement was split by the question of whether those without scientific ordination—the M.D.—were to be encouraged, or even permitted, to become analysts. In urging that the practice of psychoanalysis should not be limited to physicians, Freud differed with the majority of his followers.* At the time of the controversy, four-fifths of the practicing analysts were medical doctors. The psychoanalyst, in Freud's opinion, must not allow himself to become simply another specialist in the medical profession. In his relation to patients, the analyst cannot avoid taking over the charismatic capital of the religious healer; he becomes, if he is a good clinician, "a secular spiritual guide." [6] † There are, in Freud's papers, traces of his fantasy life as a messianic figure, momentary visions of an analytic priesthood. This, despite the simoniacal terms of the analytic pedagogy, and its growing respectability—but then Freud was certain that his secular guides would not be hurt by simony. In the world as he understood it, money made men talk seriously and respectfully [7] to those whom they paid to listen.

Freud's struggle against being "swallowed up by medicine" has been—at least in America, the country most receptive to Freudianism—little heeded. Although psychoanalysis has not, as he feared, been shelved in "textbooks on psychiatry in the chapter headed 'Therapy,' next to procedures such as hypnotic suggestion, auto-suggestion, and persuasion," [8] the American psychoanalytic movement has taken the cover granted by the medical profession. Freud had something different in mind—a movement which would obtain the approval of the community and yet remain somehow superior to financial or profes-

---

* See the *International Journal of Psychoanalysis* (April 1927); the entire issue is devoted to the lay-analysis controversy. One must not overestimate the reverence of the psychoanalytic movement for its founder, when after all Freud's dearest organizational wish, lay analysis, was denied him.

† "Indeed, these words, 'a secular spiritual guide,' might well serve as a general formula for describing the function which the analyst, whether he is a doctor or a layman, has to perform in his relation to the public." The analyst has a skill which everyone needs, as everyone needed religious counsel in the older therapies. (This is one of the implications of Freud's belief that we are all neurotic, more or less.) Otto Rank and Hanns Sachs proposed that every family should have its analyst, overseeing domestic decisions and combining the roles of physician and pastor (*The Development of Psychoanalysis,* pp. 64–65).

sional success. The present generation of analysts cannot be blamed for betraying Freud's ideal. They came into a movement that had already become a profession. Their energy and imagination as a group shows up creditably in relation to the larger profession with which they have identified themselves. Surely the analysts cannot be blamed for failing to accomplish what intellectuals in our society find increasingly difficult—to catch the public ear, and still not become hired critics, entertainers in the negative. Liberal culture has shown its power not so much in the marginal freedom it allows dissenters as in its capacity to absorb—without the slightest indigestion—and even canonize its critics. Witness the enduring vogue of that acerb master Freud himself. The currents of American unbelief shift to carry along every critic. The analysts did not make the moral revolution in America; in fact they have been called into being by that very revolution, which, if not world-wide, is at least epidemic in the West. Now the analysts must perform a conservative function: that of getting their patients safely past those crises of identity that follow upon the failure of identification with the old authorities, which have not succeeded in maintaining themselves. When there is only enough fight left in a belief to hurt the believer, analysts have no choice except to help their patients to a truce with their unbelief.

Freud himself foresaw the rapidity with which his doctrine would become acceptable, the cure thereby becoming part of the disease. This insight lies behind his acrimonious deprecations of America and of the potential popularity of psychoanalysis in this culture. His uneasiness was even better expressed by his rather shrill insistence that true adherents to analysis must not merely have given intellectual assent but have come to their therapeutic belief after overcoming strong resistance. Anyone who has been disturbed by the multiplication of therapeutic beliefs current in America will know the uneasiness out of which Freud made his demand for resistance.

The word "therapeutic" needs amplifying. Therapy implies an intention to convert, to criticize one way of life and to work toward another. Of course patients ought not to learn psychoanalysis but about themselves; nevertheless the patient comes away with an experience of the doctrine that underlies the therapeutic encounter. The profound subjectivity of the doctrinal experience, where successfully absorbed, makes Freudianism immune to the dialectic of its own criticisms. There are loyalty and faith here, as well as a point of view. Psychoanalytic criticism does not set itself up to be criticized, feeding yet another ambiguity into the crisis of identity. So far as it clears away the residual identities that make people ill, Freudianism does not thereby destroy its own capacity to forge a new identity, for it helps bring to life what is essentially a counter-identity. Once the patient is free of the last authority, the therapist, he has achieved the only possible and real freedom; he is himself alone—however diminished that self may be. Thus are disengagements masked as liberations, modest encouragements to life for its own sake proposed as an ideal of freedom.

Freud's recognition of therapy as a moral pedagogy was paralleled by a shift in the type of patient psychoanalysis attracted. In the beginning psychoanalysis was not so exclusively scientific homiletics. Though the patients Freud treated did disclose doubts about what to do with their lives (for instance, "Lucy R."), there were always tangible symptoms—a paralyzed leg, a hand-washing compulsion, impotence—by the resolution of which one could certify the cure. Yet the transition from the uninformed patient, suffering limited and objective symptoms, to the informed patient, perhaps symptomless except for his acute sense of suffering, is forecast in Freud's own writings. To find the humdrum behavior of everyday life psychopathological, as Freud did, is to move nearer that excitement of the wholly interesting life that characterizes the nineteenth-century Romantics' attempt to escape precisely the humdrum in experience. All experience is symptomatic now. People seek treatment because they sleep poorly, or have headaches, or feel apathetic toward loved ones, or because they are dissatisfied with their lives.* Patients complain of

---

* Freud gives some good examples of this typical modern patient in the *New Introductory Lectures* (1932). People come to be analyzed (1) because of life ineptitude: cf. p. 63, the man who enters therapy because he doesn't know how to get rid of his mistress; (2) because of festering repressions, which cause lassitude and loss of efficiency in work: cf. p. 62, the medical student who is unable to take his exams; it turns out that his depression comes from the frustration of incest wishes toward his sister, just married; (3) or from impotence: cf. p. 67, a man in late middle age (between forty and fifty) who

the boredom and vacuity of their inner freedom, and desire to learn how to fill it by means of strategies that guarantee more direct satisfaction. In response to the increasingly diffused complaints of patients, psychoanalysis has had to grow more openly didactic. Conversely, because of its increasingly ideological bent, psychoanalysis may be said to be partly manufacturing its own clientele. As the aristocratic Roman summoned his philosopher when he was ill, as the Christian went to his pastor, so the dispirited modern visits his analyst. But the psychoanalyst does not compete with older therapists; his is not a therapy of belief but one which instructs how to live without belief.

Freud developed his sense of the times and of the place psychoanalysis had in them from the crude positivist chronology. History had moved to the last of the three stages: from (1) cohesive societies of primitive man, a system of repression implemented by taboos, to (2) religious cohesions, a culture of repression upheld by theologies, to (3) modern culture, an era in which the old repressions are being loosened but not yet superseded. Freud's work would lose in coherence without the positivist estimate of a contemporary crisis of belief. The "extraordinary increase in the neuroses" could only be understood, he thought, as the accompaniment to the failure of normative authority; it was the inevitable price mankind pays during the transition between waning moralities and the healthy indifference of science, as such, to all moralities. A culture extricating itself from religious constraints is bound to carry habits of constraint into the new, wider world. Its condition is still post-religious, its freedom still negative. Religion can no longer save the individual from forming his private neurosis, for he has become his own religion: taking care of himself is his ritual now, and health is the ultimate dogma. With the end of religious community, the sects become countless, each with a

---

experiences difficulties in having promiscuous relations. His present impasse is with a poor "piquant" virgin.

Otto Fenichel has asserted that "the average nervous patient who comes to see the psychiatrist complains mostly of anxiety, of a state of depression, of headaches or of disturbances of sleep" ("Symposium on Neurotic Disturbances of Sleep," *International Journal of Psycho-Analysis*, Vol. XXIII, part 2, 1942, p. 49).

membership of one. Freud's conception of nervousness is intimately bound up with his critique of religion in its last phase, long after it has ceased to multiply our diseased individuality into collective health. Marking the "intensity of people's inner lack of resolution and craving for authority," [9] Freud thus interpreted Western religion in its waning phase.

Though the intent of therapy is ostensibly to show the patient how to live without belief, the ideological effect of psychiatric treatment, and of the wider therapy of Freudian doctrine, is surely to replace the moral irresoluteness fostered by the decline of religion with a new theoretic resolution. Indeed, no scientific theory about religion has ever been disinterested: the substitution of theory for belief is one of the highest achievements of secular scientific culture. It is in this sense that Marxist theory functions as a substitute for religion. While analyzing established modes of belief as ideologies, Marx advanced a counter-belief that is at the same time his critical scientific theory. Counter-beliefs may become the basis of new ideological communions, as, for example, those withdrawn sects which are organized in self-conscious opposition to the remainder of Christendom. The Communist movement shows this exclusivist sectarian character, with capitalism cast in the role once played by Christendom—except that the Communist movement, as the last capitalist sect, has developed the characteristics of a universal church. Psychoanalysis creates little communions of counter-belief; more accurately, Freud mixed belief with theory, to create therapeutic communities of two.

II

We see in his consciousness of the decline of belief how much of a social and historical theorist Freud was. It is important to appreciate his thought historically to this extent: no more detailed attack on the overcivilized has ever been mounted. It is with the peculiar effect of modern "civilized" morality (Freud indicates his irony by putting "civilized" in quotation marks) that psychoanalysis is concerned. The nervousness of modern man, he maintained, was unique among the kinds of nervousness induced by civilization. Though he had not heard of J. Alfred Prufrock and would scarcely have approved the poet's diagnosis, Freud was certainly aware of that patient's disorder. Prufrock was a neurasthenic. Modern "civilized" morality, being itself hollow, had hollowed him out. If, as Eliot depicts him, Prufrock could not react energetically to the great war, nor to the chatter of frigid ladies in the drawing rooms, it was a symptom of his moral uncertainty. The knowledge that all decisions are his to make had left Prufrock tired and cynical. One of Freud's earlier manifestoes on culture, the essay " 'Civilized' Sexual Morality and Modern Nervousness" (1908), is in fact an analysis of the whole class of irresolute Prufrocks who seemed to him the characteristic neurotic personality types of our time.

Entertaining, for the sake of argument, the long-familiar idea that neurosis issues from the clamor and competitiveness of "the modern civilized life," Freud even makes the stock point about stolid rural folk declining in the city. "Neurosis attacks precisely those whose forefathers, after living in simple, healthy, country conditions, offshoots of rude but vigorous stocks, came to the great cities" and reached a higher plane of "cultural attainment." * He quotes some familiar critiques which link our "exhausted nerves" to the unremitting strain of urban culture. "Our ears are excited and over-stimulated by large doses of insistent and noisy music. The theaters captivate all the senses with their exciting modes of presentation; the creative arts turn also by preference to the repellent, ugly, and suggestive." Echoing the indictment customarily offered by cultured Europeans, Freud asserts that the strident and materialist American civilization breeds an especially high proportion of neurasthenics.† But all this, he argues, however true, is "insufficient to explain in detail the manifestations of nervous disturbance." The "increasing nervousness" of the present

---

* Cf. the blasé attitudes Georg Simmel found characteristic of the urban character in his essay "The Metropolis and Mental Life."

† Actually, the thesis as to the nervous debility of American civilization is of American origin. It was first offered by George M. Beard, in a pioneering book, *American Nervousness* (1881). Beard, who is chiefly remembered for having coined the word "neurasthenia," argued that without civilization there can be no "nervousness," and that nervousness (read "neurasthenia" or "neurosis") increases in proportion to the degree of civilization. Freud cites the book in *Collected Papers* (I, 142–44).

day is due to more than external causes—the fact that modern life carries "excitement into far wider circles than formerly." [10] It is in this statement that Freud anticipated the more sociological psychoanalysis of the neo-Freudians: neurosis comes from the peculiar strains and complexity of modern civilization. But he had no sooner taken up this explanation than he rejected it. Freud explained neurosis with more direct polemical effect, as the expression of antagonism between individual and culture: not the result of a one-way impress of society upon the individual, but rather of the "opposition" between the individual constitution and "the demands of civilization."

A patient of his once summed up the matter: "We in our family have all become nervous because we wanted to be something better than what with our origin we were capable of being." [11] Neurosis is the penalty for ambition unprepared for sacrifice. It was not at our traditional ethical ideals as such that Freud launched his attack; to these he offered the highest tribute—his personal adherence. The important gap that he wanted closed was the one between declining traditional codes of behavior and rising demands by the individual for a greater share of happiness now, as quickly as he can learn how to get it. Their sensual energies drained off in endless moral rearmaments, modern "civilized" men have made themselves nervous from too many self-demands.

The morality that gave civilized nervousness its particular quality for Freud was what other culture-critics have named "middle-class." Freud aimed his critique not so much at "peoples" as a whole as at certain "classes." [12] The forensic attachment of psychoanalysis to the problems and anxieties of the cultivated middle classes, uneasy in their refinement, has from the beginning lent a certain bias to its insights into the nature of illness.

Their marriages seemed to Freud to expose the misery of the middle classes. Behind its monogamous façade, marriage among them is eroded by status constraints and social ambition, by a characteristic "anxiety for the consequences of sexual intercourse" which "first dissipates the physical tenderness of the married couples for each other," and turns the subsequent "mental affection between them" to bitter hostilities. Freud judged married love among the middle classes impossible. "Under the spiritual disappointment and physical deprivation which thus becomes the fate of most marriages, both partners find themselves reduced again to their pre-conjugal condition" —abstinence—"but poorer by the loss of an illusion." [13] Indeed, the illusions of purity on which middle-class children are nurtured, Freud argues, create that impotence of men and frigidity among women which he considered endemic in the love-life of the civilized. Freud closes his great essay on modern nervousness with an urgent appeal for the reform of the prevailing "civilized" morality.

This appeal for reform is nowhere made specific, being embedded in his analysis of sexual affection as such. By his anatomizing of the erotic process, Freud reinforced on a theoretic level the very process of disenchantment that had made love so quick and disappointing. The erotic life, like the economic, becomes under Freudian guidance an area for methodical self-examination and systematic improvement, until finally love itself is a field for reason to conquer. In this sense, although Freud is critical of middle-class moralism, he himself may be charged with being very middle-class in his moral attitudes. His emphasis is on the economics of emotion; from it proceeds his injunction that some hoarding of affect is necessary to health. The analyst may be seen as an investment broker of the emotions.

Criticisms of the overcivilized classes seem to me debatable so far as they depend on the period envy of lower-class vitality mentioned in Chapter Seven. It is fitting that Freud's earliest recorded musing on the pathos of the refined classes—it dates from 1885, when he was twenty-seven—occurred in Paris, during a performance of *Carmen*. In a letter to his fiancée, from whom he had been separated during a long engagement, Freud reports on how, watching the opera, he was reminded of the disposition of the civilized to deprive themselves. "The mob give vent to their impulses," they love and hate uninhibitedly, while

> we economize with our health, our capacity for enjoyment, our forces: we save up for something, not knowing ourselves for what. And this habit of constant suppression of natural instinct gives us the character of refinement. . . . Why do we not get drunk? Be-

cause the discomfort and shame of the hangover gives us more "unpleasure" than the pleasure of getting drunk gives us. Why don't we fall in love over again every month? Because with every parting something of our heart is torn away. . . . Thus our striving is more concerned with avoiding pain than with creating enjoyment.[14]

It is different, Freud assumes, with the "common people." Beset by direct social hardship, they cannot afford the luxury of such complex individual feelings:

Why should they feel their desires intensely when all the afflictions nature and society have in store is directed against those they love: why should they scorn a momentary pleasure when no other awaits them? The poor are too powerless, too exposed, to do as we do.[15]

Fear of too much sensibility has been a standard anxiety of the educated since Rousseau. Characteristically, it goes along with an ambivalent attitude toward the lower classes—part disdain for their being rude and unrefined,* and part envy for their not having to carry the burden of culture.

Personal sympathy for the lower orders was balanced by Freud's professional concern with the higher. Exhausted as they were by "restrictions on sexual activity" together with "an increase of anxiety concerning life and . . . fear of death," the civilized classes, he thought, were gradually excluding themselves "from participation in the future." Although Freud does note among the civilized a "diminished inclination to beget offspring," their fate is sealed for reasons other than Malthusian. They have reduced their "capacity for enjoyment," and correspondingly, have become timid to the point of being unwilling "to incur risk of death in whatever cause." [16] A fear of overcultivation far more desperate than Freud's drove Nietzsche to his deepest nightmare: of the "last man," whose posture is reclining, whose feeling is ennui. Freud's last man would be not so much bored as debilitated, exhausted by the struggle to live beyond his psychological means, suspicious of his own moralism. In a way that Freud has oddly abetted, the civilized have grown keenly aware of their repres-

---

* This side of Freud's attitude, his disdain of the masses, is best exhibited in *Group Psychology and the Analysis of the Ego,* discussed in Chapter Seven.

sions and spend much time coping with them. The sense of political defeat that prevails in the West arises in part from a more general feeling shared by figures as different as Freud and Ernst Troeltsch: that fresh social energies can come only from the bottom of the culture-class hierarchy.

Suppose the civilized were to become trained in the detection of their own repressions? It is, after all, on the ears of the civilized, always alert to the burdens of civilization, that arguments against repressive culture have fallen most persuasively; the masses never need persuading. To make delicacy of feeling, not the lack of it, the problem of our health discloses how near the Freudian psychology drifts to a sophisticated primitivism. The continuing celebration of Freudianism demonstrates how viable a primitivist ethics remains in America. For reasons of libidinal economy, some of the heavier investments in culture will have to be written off. Thus Freud shatters the humanist hope that high culture itself may succeed religion as a source of moral controls.

III

However much, as a man of culture, he personally loathed barbarism, Freud gave it a certain therapeutic sanction. Believing that there are "many more hypocrites than truly civilized persons," he shared an image widespread in the era succeeding the prudish—that phoenix image of a better culture rising out of the ruins left behind by a resurgent barbarism. Violence could be a useful cathartic, medicine to an over-refined society. This is the meaning, as I read it, of Freud's oracular "Thoughts for the Times on War and Death."

The holder of these "Thoughts" was a man of culture who has transcended his own delicacies and inhibitions momentarily, to remark on their naïveté. The tone is Olympian. Yet plainly World War I alerted Freud's imagination. "People really die . . . often tens of thousands in a single day." [17] Freud experienced the war as a painful chastisement of those "citizens of the civilized world" who had been confident that base patriotisms had been replaced by "enjoyment of this common civilization." [18] He tried to explain to the refined what generosity had enlarged their illusions; "In reality our fellow-citizens have not sunk so low as we feared, because they had never risen so high as we believed." [19] Freud accused Europe of developing, in the pre-1914 era, a timid "museum" culture,[20] caring only to preserve its façades intact. European culture, consisting too much of "please do not touch" signs placed discreetly around reality, discouraged passion and excitement. A trained incapacity to accept reality, in particular death, limited the insights and actions of the cultured. Civilized morality had tended to "put death on one side." When the "highest stake in the game of living, life itself, may not be risked," life becomes impoverished, uninteresting. Civilized life becomes—here Freud used one of his more tendentious metaphors— "as shallow and empty as . . . an American flirtation, in which it is understood from the first that nothing is to happen, as contrasted with a Continental love-affair in which both partners must constantly bear its serious consequences in mind." [21] A more studied appreciation of death could reinstruct us in the serious consequences of living, Freud believed. As an alternative to the supine figure representing the ennui of the civilized, he envisioned one fixed in a stoic posture, dressed in a German uniform. It is war, he said, which will "sweep away" this enervating "conventional treatment of death." War returns us to our sense of reality. "Death will no longer be denied; we are forced to believe in it." [22]

I do not mean to exaggerate this profound eccentricity among Freud's ideas. The notion of rebarbarization is nowhere near the center of his thought. The therapy of war is admittedly an apocryphal item in the Freudian canon, but the arraignment of culture, which excited such a remedy, is fundamental to his thought. Not only is culture unrealistic, so far as it removes us from death, but it is the cause of emotional fatigue, that characteristic form of neurosis among the civilized. Freud charges cultural aspiration and the neglect of instinctual realities with being themselves responsible for cultural regression. Moral inflation ultimately induces moral depression. The "resulting tension" of the "unceasing suppression of instinct . . . betrays itself in the most remarkable phenomena of reaction and compensation." [23] Thus it is civilized morality that breeds war. War became for Freud a massive balancing of the psychic budget, bringing ethically bankrupt humans back to living within their means. Though war may seem to the cultured a "regression," some regressions may be therapeutic. War drew away the superficies of culture; it "has the advantage of taking the truth more into account, and of making life more tolerable for us once again." [24] War and revolution (they amount to the same thing, for Freud, since both have the same regressive character) were natural therapies for the over-civilized, as psychoanalysis was an artificial one.

Respecting as he does the laws of cultural development, Freud does not neglect a more optimistic possibility: that of a drift toward permanent peace. His rhetorical question to Einstein in the famous letter "Why War?" (1932) intimates this other, more hopeful sort of development. "Why do you and I . . . rebel so violently against war?" Freud inquires. "After all, it seems quite a natural thing, no doubt it has a good biological basis and in practice it is scarcely avoidable." In Freud's answer there is promise of a new world led by a third Adam in whom the instincts have been entirely reshaped by rational tutelage. "The main reason why we rebel against war is that we cannot help doing so." The truly civilized, such as Freud and Einstein, develop a "constitutional intolerance of war."

Congenital pacifism, Freud thought, was not a serious possibility for any except a handful like himself. A rational nature was for him at best a "utopian expectation." [25] Some few truly civilized may have no need of therapeutic regressions: most people need the relief supplied by war "from the constant pressure of civilization." [26] Freud put his question squarely to the cultured, imperiled by mass barbarism and yet themselves suffering from the burdens of culture. For our health,

is it not we who should give in, who should adapt ourselves to war? Should we not confess that in our civilized attitude towards death we are once again living psychologically beyond our means, and should we not rather turn back and recognize the truth? Would it not be better . . . to give a little more prominence to the unconscious attitude towards death which we have hitherto so carefully suppressed? [27]

It was 1915 when Freud acknowledged the collective reassertion of the death-wish. But just because death threatened and the complacencies of peace were blasted, "life has, indeed, become interesting again; it has recovered its full content." [28]

That an intellectual whose maturity fell within the forty years of European peace between 1870 and 1914 should assign a certain positive value to war is not surprising. Even that war was not quite total, and the chief weapons not yet ultimate ones. Still, it is depressing how many intelligent minds have held a hope for culture that involves the notion of sweeping things clean. Such an idea has appealed most obviously to totalitarian intellectuals, but it also has given pleasure to a mind as clear as George Orwell's. After watching British soldiers board troop trains, Orwell hopefully wrote in his diary: "How much rubbish this war will sweep away. . . . War is simply a reversal of civilized life; its motto is 'Evil be thou my good,' and so much of the good of modern life is actually evil that it is questionable whether on balance war does harm." [29]

Freud's sanguine interpretation of a culture dying to liberate individual energy has, I think, repugnant implications. There have been such things as overdeveloped cultures, breeding exquisites among the few while living on the brutalized many. But it is a desperate optimism that believes culture can be improved by diminution. Freud adduces in support the analogy of neurotics freed from the burdens of their accumulated memories. Analogy is never enough. Culture, indeed, needs corrective devices. But destruction is not correction; war creates nothing, releases nothing. The therapy of barbarism is perhaps the most dangerous form of the long-standing resentment of the cultured against themselves.

IV

Despite his criticisms, Freud was not unsympathetic to the old moralities. As a man of culture, he could admire the repressions. But, as a man of science, he had learned from case after case that "what the world calls its code of morals demands more sacrifices than it is worth." Society is not sufficiently wealthy [or] well-organized to be able to compensate the individual for his expenditure in instinctual renunciation. It is consequently left to the individual to decide how he can obtain enough compensation for the sacrifice he has made to enable him to retain his mental balance. On the whole, however, he is obliged to live psychologically beyond his income, while the unsatisfied claims of his instincts make him feel the demands of civilization as a constant pressure upon him.[30]

The tension between instinctual candor and cultural hypocrisy, which is the most general cause of the present human illness, must be acknowledged; the act of doing so describes for Freud the beginning of new health. A suspicion of falsehood is, of course, the negative preparation for any conversion. Psychoanalysis, however, demands a special capacity for candor which not only distinguishes it as a healing movement but also connects it with the drive toward disenchantment characteristic of modern literature and of life among the intellectuals.

Freud found the essential lie upon which culture is built in its zealous but faltering repressions. His way of mitigating them was, first, through rational knowledge, and, second, through a prudent compromise with the instinctual depths out of which rational knowledge emerges. He proposes that

certain instinctual impulses, with whose suppression society has gone too far, should be permitted a certain amount of satisfaction; in the case of certain others *the inefficient method of suppressing them by means of repression should be replaced by a better and securer procedure*.[31]

To replace inefficient moral commitments, Freud offers as a better and securer standard what I call his "ethic of honesty." This honesty Freud would have us achieve by working through the layers of falsehood and fantasy within us to a superior accommodation to reality.

We first meet the ethic of honesty in characteristic Freudian guise —as a merely therapeutic rule. He tells us that, at the very beginning of therapy, the patient must promise "absolute honesty." All facts and feelings are to be laid bare. Not even names can be excepted from communication.* Honesty, we learn, is "the fundamental rule of the psychoanalytic technique." [32] But what appears as a rule of therapy is actually a general cultural recommendation.

It is a measure of the negativity of Freud's ethic that he illustrated it by a "just suppose" story, a parody of the reticent manners and morals of the cultivated classes of the nineteenth century. It is a kind of modern pendant to the story of Adam and Eve, pointing to a new garden where honesty has supplanted false innocence. Suppose, Freud writes,

> a number of ladies and gentlemen in good society have planned to have a picnic one day at an inn in the country. The ladies have arranged among themselves that if one of them wants to relieve a natural need she will announce that she is going to pick flowers. Some malicious person, however, has got wind of this secret and has printed on the programme which is sent round to the whole party: "Ladies who wish to retire are requested to announce that they are going to pick flowers."

Freud is that malicious person, with the clear negative spirituality of an unbeliever fascinated by the pathology of belief; the ladies represent culture, made dishonest by the process of repression. Of course (as the story goes), after this disclosure

> no lady will think of availing herself of this flowery pretext, and, in the same way, other similar formulas, which may be freshly agreed upon, will be seriously compromised. What will be the result? The ladies will admit their natural needs without shame and none of the men will object.[33]

Thus in a story Freud published his ethical intention. We must accept our "natural needs," in the face of a culture which has censored open declarations of natural need. In championing a refreshing openness, Freud disclosed the censoring of nature, thus to ease the strain that had told upon our cultural capacities.

What makes neurotics talk is "the pressure of a secret which is burning to be disclosed." Neurotics carry their secret concealed in

---

* I refer to a paper "On Beginning the Treatment" (1913); the enjoiner can be found throughout Freud's psychoanalytic writings, beginning with *The Interpretation of Dreams,* when he explains his techniques of free association.

their talk—"which, despite all temptation, they never reveal." [34] Freud set out to hear this talk, root out the secret from within man, and hold it up before him to inspect and acknowledge. Freudianism was to be indiscreet on principle. "Disclosure of the secret will have attacked, at its most sensitive point, the 'aetiological equation' from which neuroses arise." The new revelation "will have made the gain from the illness illusory; and consequently the final outcome of the changed situation brought about by the physician's indiscretion can only be that the production of the illness will be brought to a stop." [35] Thus Freud reversed, once again, the usual conception: man's chief moral deficiency appears to be not his indiscretions but his reticence.

> The psychoneuroses are substitutive satisfactions of some instinct the presence of which one is obliged to deny to oneself and others. Their capacity to exist depends on this distortion and lack of recognition. When the riddle they present is solved and the solution is accepted by the patients these diseases cease to be able to exist.[36]

Such treatment by mutual self-exposure Freud considered quite extraordinary: "There is hardly anything like this in medicine, though in fairy tales you hear of evil spirits whose power is broken as soon as you can tell them their name—the name which they have kept secret." [37] What is for Freud "repression," psychologically understood, is "secrecy," morally understood. Secrecy is the category of moral illness, for it provides a hiding place for false motives. It is our secrets, hidden from ourselves, that fester and infect action. Thus the entire therapeutic undertaking, based as it is on the promise of "absolute honesty," becomes "a lost labour if a single concession is made to secrecy." [38] For secrecy provides the self with, in Freud's appropriately religious image, a "right of sanctuary" for disreputable citizens of the mental underworld. There are to be no refugees from honesty in Freud's program. He "once treated a high official who was bound by oath not to communicate certain State secrets, and the analysis came to grief as a consequence of this restriction." [39] I have referred in this book to the tyranny of psychology. In a period of political repression, human concerns often turn inward upon the most private aspects of living. Freud has reinforced this turn toward privacy and the inner life. But he has also helped make inwardness a symptom instead of a salvation. The inquisitiveness of psychology is tyrannical —and shareable.

Freud himself and many others following him, both disciples and detractors, linked psychoanalysis to the religious confessional.[40] Actually, all groups have some mode of confession. But Freud's rule of honesty has a special condition. Psychoanalysis claims not merely to know all, but also—acting on a principle unlike any in the therapeutics of Christian culture—to tell all. It is essential to the Church, as Pius XII has declared, that the secrets of the confessional can on no account be divulged "even to a doctor, even in spite of grave personal inconvenience."[41] For Freud it is therapeutically desirable that the entire society learn the secrets of the analytic couch. The new psychological man would be able quickly to detect dishonesty (or fantasy) in others. This in itself would act premonitorily against withdrawal into illness. It would hasten the "change-over to a more realistic and creditable attitude on the part of society."[42] When relatives, friends, and strangers from whom neurotics

> wish to conceal their mental processes know the general meaning of such symptoms, and if they themselves know that in the manifestations of their illness they are producing nothing that other people cannot instantly interpret,[43]

the disease has lost its essential function as an escape mechanism. Neurotics are too private, too reticent. By proposing to eliminate secrecy, Freud curiously reasserted the hegemony of public morality over private. "Tolerance of society," Freud wrote, "is bound to ensue as a result of psychoanalytic enlightenment."[44] Yet despite the Freudian emphasis on tolerance, this unfolding of the inward life cannot help but mean an increase in the power of the community as well.

What recourse, Freud asks, will people have "if their flight into illness is barred by the indiscreet revelations of psychoanalysis"? His answer hints another kind of civilization, one that is not built on reticence or hypocrisy: they will have to "confess to the instincts that are at work in them, face the conflict, fight for what they want, or go without it."[45] No more forthright assertion of the nature of freedom has ever been made. Freud did not glove the fist that symbolizes freedom, nor mistake it, as liberals often do, for the helping hand.

The ethic of honesty arose early in the middle-class era, and has been characterized by the modesty of its moral demands. "When one wants to eulogize someone," a French preacher of the eighteenth century explained, "one says: he is an honest man. But one never says, one dares not say, he is a true Christian, as if being a Christian were something dishonorable." An *abbé* of the same period describes the ethic of the new class: "You say to us confidently that you are honest men, but that you are not devout. . . . There you have it, my brothers, the eternal refrain, the favorite maxim with which the pretended sages of our century believe they can respond to everything." [46] It is this refrain that Freud perfected. Psychoanalysis has put into fresh expression the hard ethic of honesty, long in process of displacing the religious ethic, which, even as it admitted the universality of sin, proclaimed the inevitability of redemption.

To become candid about his egoism, to defy the admonitions that had made him feel secretive and ashamed of his self-interest, the honest man has needed a science exhibiting the pathology of moral aspiration. This science, however, is based upon a tautological, instinctualist conception of "desiring" or "aiming." Morality derives its energies second-hand, from a process of reaction against desiring. Freud could not speak of the desire to be good in the same sense that he could speak of desiring what we have to renounce for the good. Surely this is one-sided. Aspiration may be as genuine as desire, and as original. Instinctual desire has even been understood as a displacement of frustrated moral aspiration—as it is for some of Dostoevski's demonic characters such as Stavrogin (*The Possessed*) and Velchaninov (*The Eternal Husband*). The English critic V. S. Pritchett has pointed out that George Eliot was perhaps the last great novelist to concentrate on the desire to be good. Since then the passion to be good has become embarrassing, something to which it is better not to admit. To will to be good is anyway a contradiction in terms: the will is never good. Freud can conceive of a person's feeling guilty not because he has been bad but because, as a result of his repressions, he is too moral. This is one source of his influence: his diagnosis that we are sick from our ideals and that the one practicable remedy lies in an infusion from below.

V

The Freudian ethic of honesty is to be preferred to the "sincerity" commended by other nineteenth-century minds perplexed with the problems of waning belief and energy—for instance, by Carlyle in *Heroes and Hero Worship,* Nietzsche in his *Use and Abuse of History,* Sorel in *Reflections on Violence.* Sincerity, in their view, connotes the wholehearted engagement of character. Cherished with equal sincerity, all beliefs become equally meritorious; while "sceptical dilettantism" is held to be the curse of our modern, critical culture. To Carlyle the most repugnant sight is of minds "no longer filled with their Fetish," but given over to mere intellectual conviction. "It is the final scene in all kinds of Worship and Symbolism," [47] Carlyle laments. Jung deplores a similar process in modern culture, in which there is an exhaustion of religious forms and a removal from the emotional depths that energize and justify belief.

For Freud, too, honesty brings one into touch with the emotional depths, where all beliefs are equivalent. But to be in touch with the unconscious is, for him, the supreme mode of heightening self-consciousness, and to accept the equivalence of all beliefs is to dare life without them. Romantic sincerity suspects conscious emotion as shallow, proscribes braggart talk, reverences the rude, inarticulate hero who is in touch with his depths and can draw upon their energies *in action.* And here is where Freud's ethic of honesty differs from Carlyle's or Nietzsche's: in its quasi-cerebral, less activist emphasis on talk, on verbal honesty instead of psychological sincerity. In place of reticence, Freud prescribes talk—thorough, ruthless talk. Honest talk fills the gap in ideals, creates the condition of a new personal integrity. This painful intellectual working-through of illusions contrasts sharply with the romantic conception of honesty as a leap beyond the paralyzing dialectic of illusion and disillusion—into decision.

From this difference between two kinds of honesty we can estimate the gap between the competing psychological ethics of Freud and

Jung. Jung is in search of new emotional vitality. His is a situational ethic, based upon increasing the flow of creative energy. Hence he fears too much consciousness as well as too little, and attends particularly to the categories which the unconscious imposes upon conscious expression and which it is the function of the psychologist to discern. Doctrine, myth, works of art all in their plenitude express the vital credulities necessary to the creative life. Hence Jung's interest in the welter of world religions, and his preference for religions that permit welter, as in Asia, to the neater but narrower expressions of Christianity.

Freud, on the other hand, cannot conceive of an excess of consciousness. In this respect, Jung is the more balanced of the two. Energy means to Freud not the capacity for belief but the capacity to reject the swarms of beliefs that return to nag at one—or rather, in the Freudian scheme, to which one returns. Freud's ethic of honesty demands only the negative capacity to achieve and retain unbelief. Of the two ethics, Freud's is the more straitly hostile to religion, although in his too there is a therapeutic simulacrum of faith.

Nevertheless, the Freudian ethic may be liable to an indictment more grave than the verdict of Faith, in the second degree, that has sometimes been read against Jung: the charge of nihilism. As a purely explanatory and scientific ideal, honesty has no content. Though the Freudian training involves intellectual judgment (it is, after all, psycho*analysis*), based on a calm and neutral appraisal of all the demanding elements of a life-situation, still, the freedom to choose must end in choice. Here, at the critical moment, the Freudian ethic of honesty ceases to be helpful.

Being honest, admitting one's nature, does not resolve specific issues of choice. The Freudian ethic emphasizes freedom at the expense of choice. To achieve greater balance within the psyche, to shift the relative weights of instinct and repression, installs no new substantive rules of decision.

In this final suspension, Freud's ethic resembles Sartre's existentialism, which offers a related criterion, authenticity, as a way of judging what is good in human action. André Gide offers lucid disillusionment as the distinguishing mark of humane conduct. But what guarantees that an authentic action, or one conceived in perfect lucidity, will be good or in conformity with human nature? Similarly, after a long process of self-recuperation through lucidity, the Freudian choice may be not more humane but rather more arbitrary. One need not be self-deceived in order to act maliciously. Freud gives no reason why unblinking honesty with oneself should inhibit unblinking evil. Lucidity may render us exquisitely articulate and unapologetic about our aggressions. If, as Freud himself implies, the dangerous energy of the self is guided inward only to prevent a fiercer war without, perhaps the repressed character is still preferable to the honest man. Openness of character may well elicit more, not less, brutality. Unaided by the old transcendental ethics of guilt, or by the rationalist ethics of a future harmony through knowledge, the Freudian lucidity may pierce the deepest shadows of the self without dispelling one degree of gloom.

There is a risk in the ethic of honesty of which Freud is aware. Some lives are so pent-up that a neurosis may be "the least of the evils possible in the circumstances." Some of those "who now take flight into illness" would find the inner conflict exposed by candor insupportable, and "would rapidly succumb or would cause a mischief greater than their own neurotic illness." [48] Honesty is not an ethic for weaklings; it will save no one. Neither will it necessarily render our natures more beneficent. Psychoanalysis prudently refrains from urging men to become what they really are; the new ethic fears the honest criminal lurking behind the pious neurotic. Still, he argued, with all these dangers, his therapy of honesty came modestly priced in a culture where all prices are too high.

Freud's greatness seldom elevates. This was not his purpose. He was a digger, not a builder, an archaeologist of the psyche. Digging at the foundations was the moral mission left to the psychologist after philosophy and religion had raised man too high. According to the Freudian counsel, man must not strain too far the limitations of his instinctual nature. Therefore, knowing, becoming conscious of these limits, is itself a primary ethical act. Consciousness, self-knowledge, interpretative revelation and decision, candor, talking things through —all presume a necessary reduction of ethical aspiration. Without this imperative, Freud's conception of therapy is meaningless. "A little more truthfulness," [49] Freud recommends, instead of the painful old passion for goodness. Psychoanalysis shares the paths of truthfulness common to rationalist doctrines. People ought to be forthright. If they express their true natures, goodness will take care of itself. The ethic of honesty does no more than establish the capacity to break the moral habits into which decisions, once made, tend to form themselves. Freud's is a penultimate ethic tooled to the criticism of ultimates. It regards the disposition of human potentiality as a matter beyond prescription.

As a negative and penultimate ethic, Freud's is dependent on that which it criticizes—ethics that are positive and ultimate. The ethic of honesty presupposes the existence of repressive authority. This psychoanalytic assumption that the traditional moral values of our culture have been inhibitory depends in turn on a more fundamental assumption, now widely accepted in the social sciences: of civilizations as systems of restraint. As I have shown in Chapter Eight, Freud considered the structure of convictions upon which Western civilization has been operating to be renunciatory in character. Therefore strategies of unbelief, of disclosure, of negation are themselves positive—effecting a studied release of energies heretofore inhibited by the ascetic character of the Western moral system. Honesty is enough only if one assumes, as Freud did, that our real natures have been too much inhibited.

This does not mean that Freud desired an unconditional release of human energies. He is, as I have said, ambivalent toward repressive culture: its major critic and yet defender of its necessity. Given the inability of most minds to be both as critical and as cautious as his own, Freud considered it at least

> a debatable point whether a certain degree of cultural hypocrisy is not indispensable for the maintenance of civilization, because the susceptibility to culture which has hitherto been organized in the minds of present-day men would perhaps not prove sufficient for the task.[50]

Ultimately Freud took the position that the hypocrisies of civilization, being the cause of neurosis, themselves frustrate the purpose of civilization. The neuroses actually represent those socially inimical forces which have been suppressed. Nothing, therefore, is gained by suppression. No advantage is purchased by the sacrifice of mental health. Civilization has a treacherous ally in the neuroses, one that periodically turns against it. Fortunately, from the psychoanalytic point of view, Western culture appears to have lost its capacity to breed charismatic founding fathers, around whose example or teaching new doctrines of compliance may be composed. Of the voices arguing subtly against all possible fathers and the sacrifices they command, Freud's is now the dominant one—antagonist not of this father or that but of the troubling, uniquely human impulse to find a father. His regard for health, at the expense of culture, has been incorporated into the standing American protest against everything past, although he himself protested against the complementary American illusion of a better future. Being a very intelligent protest, Freud's is hidden beneath a science whose very nature as a moral science it denies; for the illness it proposes to treat scientifically is precisely our inherited morality, and therefore it is, in its own terms, both a natural and a moral science.

VI

If Freud takes sides against culture, it is only for therapeutic purposes. He believed no more in instinct than in culture; for his day and age he sought only to correct the imbalance between these two main categories of the moral life. He is the architect of a great revolt against pleasure, not for it. He wrote no briefs for the pleasure principle. Rather he exhibited its futility. It is toward the reality principle that Freud turns us, toward the sober business of living and with no nonsense about its goodness or ease.

Of course the pleasure principle does have an important place in the Freudian scheme, which has led to a false comparison of Freud with the English utilitarians. The resemblance has a certain plausibility. Every action, for Freud as for Bentham, may be tested by the criterion of pleasure, and all actions, being performed, must have been pleasurable enough to be performed.* Oral eroticism and mathematics, sodomy and social welfare, low interests and high—all are pleasures. Even suicide pleases the suicide; sadism pleases at least the sadist. Pleasure is, for Freud, identical with motivation in general; there can be no other motive. The "compulsion to repeat," the motive he emphasized after his World War I studies of battle neuroses, appeared to qualify the pleasure principle. Actually, it turned out to be merely another, subtler form of pleasure. The war neurotic repeats his trauma, and if the repetition does not seem to us very pleasurable that is nothing to the neurotic. The pleasure principle is a very subjective one. Further, Freud had a notion of the scarcity of pleasure which seems utilitarian. Each case history detailed the limits of pleasure, its manufacture at home, its expenditure and exchange in the market-place. But emotional rewards are not as scarce in the Freudian economic system as this description would indicate. A fairly unlimited amount of credit exists, in resources untapped by most —in art and learning, in politics and religion—by which pleasure is replenished and new libidinal capital formed outside the home.

Utilitarian psychology led to the respectable ideal anarchism of the nineteenth century—the freedom to pursue one's pleasure so long as that pursuit did not interfere with the pleasure-seeking of others. Freud offered a less optimistic ideal, containing a harder and more internal check. It is the "education to reality," [51] or what amounts to the same thing, the restriction of pleasure, that teaches freedom and at the same time sets the limits of freedom. The reality principle does not completely supplant the pleasure principle, but it tries, through compromise, to exert discipline enough to meet the basic need for efficiency. There is a human reluctance to give up pleasures

---

* In Chapter X of the *Principles of Morals and Legislation*, Bentham argues that only ideas of pleasure and pain can serve as motives. Further, no sort of motive is in itself a bad one. "Let a man's motive be ill-will; call it even malice, envy, cruelty; it is still a kind of pleasure that is his motive; the pleasure he takes at the thought of the pain which he sees, or expects to see, his adversary undergo. Now even this wretched pleasure, taken by itself, is good: it may be faint; it may be short; it must at any rate be impure; yet while it lasts, and before any bad consequences arrive, it is as good as any other that is not more intense."

—especially those of the past—for barely acceptable and certain realities. Psychic illness signifies a clinging to dead pleasures. The neurotic is a coward about life, one who "turns away from reality because he finds it unbearable." [52] Far from advancing the ethical hedonism with which he is mistakenly charged, Freud in his psychology of pleasure indicates the futility of hedonism. Pleasure to him was just the sense of transition from an excess to a deficiency of mental energy. It was a decline in the tension of life, involving a regret as great in its way as the one involved in pain. It followed, then, that death might be the greatest pleasure, and so Freud hypostatized a "death instinct" to complement the erotic instinct. The pleasure principle might more justly be named the principle of pleasure-pain; for, conversely, pain was the transition from a feeling of deficiency to one of excess. Pleasure registers the decrease of pain, a temporary relief from the intensities of living. Freud's description of emotion in economic terms relates less to Bentham's psychology than to the Romantic meta-psychology of Schopenhauer.

Freud's analysis of pleasure must be distinguished not only from utilitarian hedonism but from the prescriptive hedonism of the post-Freudians. Karl Menninger's belief that "psychiatrists should come out squarely and courageously for hedonism as a philosophical position" finds not the faintest echo in Freud. Menninger goes on to quote Rebecca West, with whom he shares the belief that "we need no further argument in favor of taking pleasure as a standard when we consider the only alternative that faces us. If we do not live for pleasure we shall soon find ourselves living for pain. If we do not regard as sacred our own joys and the joys of others, we open the door and let into life the ugliest attribute of the human race, which is cruelty . . . the root of all other vices." If this is indeed the message which "psychoanalysts can and should give to the world," [53] then psychoanalysis has moved a long way from Freud. He understood that cruelty is itself one of the pleasures. No doubt Freud would not have been so confident as some of his followers that the pleasure of being cruel to others—which bestows other, more obvious, pleasures on oneself—would be readily relinquished if pleasure alone were the standard of value. Being an aesthetic result, increasing and decreasing dialectically in terms of the related presence of pain, pleasure is a doubtful value. Thus, contradicting hedonist theory, the Freudian psychology reveals the ephemeral quality of pleasure as an end in itself.

Like his philosophic forerunner Schopenhauer, Freud accepts the essentially contradictory character of reality and preaches a doctrine of resignation to it. Freud's credo is "to endure with resignation"; [54] thus a subtle acceptance of things as they are which changes the very condition to which one is resigned becomes the aim of Freudianism.

In promising patients help and relief through his new therapeutic method, Freud says, he was often

faced by this objection: "Why, you tell me yourself that my illness is probably connected with my circumstances and the events of my life. You cannot alter these in any way. How do you propose to help me, then?" And I have been able to make this reply: "No doubt fate would find it easier than I do to relieve you of your illness. But you will be able to convince yourself that much will be gained if we succeed in transforming your hysterical misery into common unhappiness." [55]

It is a curious sort of promise to have attracted so many followers. Common unhappiness is not an ideal toward which one can struggle enthusiastically. But then, the Freudian patient, instructed in the lore of his secret self, is not to become an enthusiast. The therapeutic effort aims at reserving our energies for everyday life instead of having them frittered away in neurosis—or in the analysis itself. Therapy prepares a mixture of detachment and forbearance, a stoic rationality of the kind Epictetus preached. The practiced ease of expected disappointment recommended by Epictetus—beginning with a broken cup, and so on ultimately to one's broken life [56]—is perhaps the best and most classical intimation of Freud's own way of coming to terms with life. To detach the individual from the most powerful lures in life, while teaching him how to pursue others less powerful and less damaging to the pursuer—these aims appear high enough in an age rightly suspicious of salvations. Freud had the tired wisdom of a universal healer for whom no disease can be wholly cured.

Freud never wanders beyond analysis into prophecy. He leaves us with the anxiety of analysis—the anxiety proper to psychological man. Fidelity may frequently be neurotic, but Freud scarcely authorizes adultery. While explaining the incest taboo as a residue of historic repressions, of course he does not sanction the cohabiting of brother and sister, mother and son. Yet if moral rules come only from cultures which legislate deviously for their own advantage, against the freedom of the individual, how can any part of conduct be taken for granted? If every limit can be seen as a limitation of personality, the question with which we may confront every opportunity is: after all, why not? While Freud never committed himself, the antinomian implications are there. And those who have interpreted Freud as advocating, for reasons of health, sexual freedom—promiscuity rather than the strain of fidelity, adultery rather than neuroses —have caught the hint, if not the intent, of his psychoanalysis.*

Freud intimates that we are ready for a new beginning; he does not actually suggest one. That there is historical accuracy reflected in this intimation we can have no doubt. Better than any other single record, the Freudian text—in its charge of cases, in its incorporation of the pathological ordinary—expresses our state of readiness, our sophisticated and much verbalized conviction that the old systems of repressive authority are enfeebled. From this perspective of depth, it is true, Freud undermines the old systems of authority. At the surface, however, this tampering with our repressions may itself foster a new dependence. The new freedom leads to a certain calculated conformity; psychoanalysis finds no more legitimate reasons for being rebellious than for being obedient. It is in this sense that Freudianism carries nihilist implications. A deliberate, detached conformity is more powerful than the old dogmatic varieties, with their exciting illusions of truth beyond matters of motive. Although it claims no validation beyond the pressure of social necessity itself, the present tyranny of psychologizing may well prove more stable than the older enforcements of guilt.

---

* See D. H. Lawrence's attack on Freud for sponsoring the violation of the incest taboo, in *Psychoanalysis and the Unconscious*.

CHAPTER TEN

THE EMERGENCE OF PSYCHOLOGICAL MAN

The important thing is not to be cured but to live with one's ailments.

—ABBÉ GALIANI TO MADAME D'ÉPINAY

IN A distinctively intimate way, psychoanalysis defends the private man against the demands made by both culture and instinct. Freud begins where G. E. Moore leaves off in the famous last chapter of *Principia Ethica* that declares personal affections and artistic pleasures the only true goods [1] in our experience. The private man needs to know how to defend his affections, for the most personal are the most easily spoiled. Psychoanalytic pedagogy is intended for the student weak in the understanding of the limited possibilities in life. Freud belongs, therefore, among those great teachers who have taken everyone as their potential subject. Seen in psychoanalytic depth, no man knows himself so well that he cannot learn something of fundamental importance from this novel enterprise in re-education. Freud speaks for the modern individual, elaborating his sense of separateness from the world and from even the most beloved objects in it. Such careful and detailed concentration on the self as Freud encourages may more often produce pedants of the inner life than virtuosi of the outer one. Yet, in default of other cures, egotism suits the age, and Freud's is only one of the most successful, and certainly the most subtle, of contemporary ideologies of self-salvation.

Calculation, Newman said, has never made a hero; but calculation can make the unheroic healthier. The essentially secular aim of the

Freudian spiritual guidance is to wean away the ego from either a heroic or a compliant attitude to the community. Here Freud differed not only from the physicians of established faiths—Catholic or other —but also from the propagandists of secular faiths, those socialists and other radicals still essentially engaged in absorbing the individual into the community. He was not impressed by the clerical strategy of confirming faith by strengthening the individual's identification with the community. Whatever flush of interior health rises on first being received back into any community of belief after the sickness of alienation is quite temporary, Freud held. The old faiths have themselves produced the sickness they still seek to cure. The psychoanalytic physician cannot therefore direct the patient to seek relief by joining "the catholic, protestant, or socialist community." What is needed is to free men from their sick communities. To emancipate man's "I" from the communal "we" is "spiritual guidance" in the best sense Freud could give to the words.[2]

Yet he also treated the neurotic as a social dilemma, as one unable to relate himself effectively to the established community. The prevailing image of psychoanalysis as reintegrating the neurotic, making him again a constructive member of society, must be studied very closely, for this does not signify that the patient gives his assent to the demands society makes upon his instinctual life; on the contrary, the successful patient has learned to withdraw from the painful tension of assent and dissent in his relation to society by relating himself more affirmatively to his depths. His newly acquired health entails a self-concern that takes precedence over social concern and encourages an attitude of ironic insight on the part of the self toward all that is not self. Thus the psychoanalyzed man is inwardly alienated even if he is often outwardly reconciled, for he is no longer defined essentially by his social relations. Psychoanalysis as a science carries an authentic alienating implication, from the breaking of the bondages of the past (advocated on the therapeutic level) to the critical appraisal of moral and religious beliefs (on the level of theory). Freud found contemptible Dostoevski's religious and political conservatism, despite his admiration for the writer's insights and experiences in the depths.* His own insights into the depths did not lead him to advocate a return to them, nor to new justifications for authoritarian codes of conduct. Rather, a less ambivalent freedom from authority is perhaps the more important motif of his doctrine, one in which authority is all the more secure.

This variety of belief in freedom makes itself felt most strongly in Freud's denial that psychoanalysis does criticize society or that it has any "concern whatsoever with . . . judgments of value." Psychoanalysis neither needs nor desires "to create a *Weltanschauung* of its own." As a branch of science, subscribing to the scientific view of the world, psychoanalysis intends to be no doctrine but only a method: "the intellectual manipulation of carefully verified observations" and the denial that any knowledge can be obtained from "intuition or inspiration." [3] Here the rational method—working upon the irrational unconscious, which Freud conceived of as undercutting the "proud superstructure of the mind" [4]—itself bespeaks a pre-eminent value. It is only just, when speaking of Freud, to speak of the humanism of his science. For after all his affirmations of the irrational, he reserves a possibility for rationality and freedom in science—understanding—itself, particularly in the method of treatment he devised: the creation of representative thought-art which, when interpreted, eases the patient's obsessions. On the one hand, then, Freud does advocate a rational reconciliation to social and cultural authority, granting that authority itself will under criticism become more reasonable; on the other hand, Freudianism supplies through its therapeutic stratagems and theoretical insights the means for a modest but nonetheless significant liberation.

---

* Freud notes that "after the most violent struggles to reconcile the instinctual demands of the individual with the claims of the community," Dostoevski "landed in the retrograde position of submission both to temporal and spiritual authority, of veneration both for the Tsar and for the God of the Christians, and of a narrow Russian nationalism—a position which lesser minds have reached with smaller effort." Indeed the point of Freud's essay on Dostoevski, from which I am quoting, is not to examine Dostoevski's artistic endowment but to find out why he changed positions—why he "threw away the chance of becoming a teacher and liberator of humanity and made himself one with their gaolers" (*Coll. Papers* V, 223). Thus, subtly, Dostoevski is identified with the position of the Grand Inquisitor.

I

Freud's emancipative intent first expressed itself in his method of treatment. By waiving the restrictions of conventional logic and prudery, the therapeutic hour provides the patient with a model refreshment. It puts an end to decorum, providing a private time in which anything may be said—indeed, in which the patient is encouraged to say everything. The analytic meeting is designed as an oasis in the desert of reticence in which the patient lives; it is much like those artificial ruins thoughtfully placed in eighteenth-century English formal gardens for the pleasure of those who wished to wander imaginatively from the beaten path.

From the patient's standpoint, the novelty of the therapeutic situation lies at once in its unique freedoms and in the accessibility of a final figure of authority. Revived facts and new fancies are definitively received by one who has contracted to be the most sympathetic of all possible listeners. The therapist listens, comprehends, does not condemn; in return, the patient has an obligation to the therapist (not a mere invitation from him) to tell all he knows in order to be told all he does not know. Talking is the patient's work. And it is hard work. Patients eager to cooperate with the analyst fail nonetheless to tell their stories with therapeutic adequacy, because, as Freud says, they consider

> them too unimportant, too stupid, too indiscreet, and so on. There are many who never learn to apply the basic rule because their fear of losing control is too great, and before they can give expression to anything they must examine it to see exactly what it is.[5]

A lifetime has been spent learning to be tactful, to achieve reticence, to avoid outbursts of emotion, to do what is proper or expedient rather than what is impulsive. All this has to be unlearned for successful free association.

Properly conducted, the analytic colloquy should be unpredictable; ideally, communication takes place between the unconscious of the analyst and that of the patient, avoiding the self-consciousness of ordinary conversations. Both analyst and patient are to relax and let the associations flow, depending as much as possible on the eruption of unpremeditated thoughts on the part of the patient, and of unscheduled interpretations on the part of the analyst. Normally our talk is selective, and not just for reasons of social propriety; it is selective in order to be efficient. Efficiency is the aim of most discourse, from the ordinary effort of rational explanation (in which one looks for some isolated cause or set of causes for an event) to the extremes of polemic and caricature (in which a few relevant considerations are stressed and others eliminated). But the Freudian treatment is characterized by its deliberate anti-efficiency. It is based on a technique for suppressing just that impulse which is normative in thought and talk when we try to cast strong light on something—the impulse to leave out, to cast other things in shadow. Rational thought, because it is selective, is not therapeutically useful. The verbal precipitates of selective thinking remain extremely valuable for self-understanding, but precisely because they are, like symptoms, guides for interpretations in terms of the interests or intentions behind them. No language is ordinary. The simplest cues may introduce the most complex roles.

The anti-efficiency of the Freudian therapy appears clearly in the extraordinary leisure with which it is conducted. Unlike the journalistic representation of events, which achieves a perfection of efficiency through its emphasis on speed, compression, and straightforwardness, the development of a psychoanalytic patient's thought takes time because he is adjured to disregard all selectivity.* The extreme leisureliness of therapy finds its correlate in a theory of mind—in particular, Freud's theory of what he deemed the crucial part of the mind, the unconscious. The timelessness and indifference to logic with which the unconscious operates are echoed in the leniency of the psychoanalytic interview. For practical reasons—lack of time and money—an individual psychoanalysis may be terminated.† Theoretically, how-

---

* We see this procedure aesthetically exploited in *Finnegans Wake*, which Joyce wrote in a poly-language of puns, attempting to recreate words in accordance with the symbolic overtones, or "free imagery," that hover about their edges.

† Freud insisted that analysis was "really interminable" no matter how regularly "in practice analyses do come to an end" (*Coll. Papers* V, 316–57).

ever, there is no end of answering. At the very least, the analysis cannot be brief. Freud likened the treatment to the play *Oedipus,* from which he drew so much in another and more famous connection. Like the drama of Sophocles, psychoanalysis has its "cunning delays" [6] in order to prolong the inquiry and thus raise the pitch of cathartic excitement. This is necessary and to be desired, for the good of the patient. "Psychological changes only come about very slowly; if they occur quickly and suddenly it is a bad sign," [7] Freud says elsewhere.

Another quality of the Freudian liberation is the interest taken in emotional recollection itself. Freud sees the therapy as withdrawing the patient from the world of "hard reality," with which he has been unable to cope—though this withdrawal is only temporary, and its purpose is to return him more realistically equipped to that very reality. During this period of therapeutic withdrawal, however, Freud sanctions all the tabooed language and the shady topics which are conventionally proscribed. Memory, daydream, fantasy are what the patient is to deal in. He has total freedom to recall. The patient tries to recapture his childhood and the nightlife of dreams and sexuality; it is chiefly this material which is analyzed, according to the emancipative dialectic, just because it is not freely discussed in the ordinary daytime world.

Memory has a peculiar and central place in Freudian theory. It is constraining, since by remembering our bondages to the past we appreciate their enormity; but it is also, Freud believed, liberating, since by remembering we understand the terrors and pleasures of the past and move toward mastering them. The tabooed thoughts are accredited, raised to the status of momentous and decisive causes, by Freud's theory of personality, not only because they are explained as part of an inexorable sequence of development, but because the patient's attention is focused on them. In therapeutic explanation the taboos dominant since childhood tend to be weakened. Even though the aims and activities of childhood have to be suppressed, superseded by "reality," a science which so values the importance of these things is plainly a liberating one.

This helps explain Freud's special interest in dreams, which he interpreted as contemporaneous fragments of the superseded child life. Dreams themselves, as Freud saw, have an ambiguously emancipative role. They indicate a kind of freedom, because they take place when there is a "slackening in the strength of the resistance." [8] He imagined sleep as the de-individualized play time of the instincts, when we cast off the burden of being individuals and vent our gross infantile wishes and anxieties in dreams. In sleep all persons become for that brief respite ciphers of identical emotions, differentiated only secondarily by constitution and traumatic accent. On the other hand, dreams are a kind of betrayal, too, because the analyst (representing the outer world) uses them to pry out the patient's secrets. On the whole, however, Freud conceded that the dream was a sanctuary for the free play of the psyche. We cannot be held responsible, Freud argues, for the thoughts expressed in our dream life.[9] Night thoughts are not our own, in the moral proprietary sense, but belong to that other self which summons us thereby to account for our day lives.

Talk is therapeutic in itself. By talking about the instincts, Freud says, we do not cause the instinctual demand to disappear—this "is impossible and not even desirable"—but we do accomplish a " 'taming' of the instinct." [10] Through talking about sexuality, we can control it, so that the healthy man can choose to express his sexual appetite and yet not be irrationally driven by it. Self-mastery being a function of self-consciousness, by making sexual desires conscious, says Freud, we gain mastery over them to a degree no system of repression can possibly equal.[11] Talk—language—is the essential medium of consciousness, and therefore the essential means of liberation.*

In psychoanalysis the individual learns to break through reticence and engage himself in a sort of confessional probing, heretofore limited to conventicle life. Freud's scientific frankness has been one of the supplementary corrosives applied to the encrusted official languages of European high culture.† That the new freedom is first

---

* Compare Marx: "All forms and products of consciousness cannot be dissolved by mental criticism, by resolution into 'self-consciousness' or transformation into 'apparitions,' 'spectres,' 'fancies,' etc., but only by the practical overthrow of the actual social relations which gave rise to this idealistic humbug" (*German Ideology* [New York, 1947], pp. 28–29).

† Out of the Vienna of Freud's lifetime came two other great critics of

of all linguistic is expressed, as I have noted earlier, in Freud's own insistence on using the word "sexual" where he might more accurately have said "erotic." To make "concessions to faintheartedness" [12] seemed to Freud an acceptance of that extraordinary dishonesty which lies dangerously near ordinary civility: "One gives way first in words, and then little by little in substance too." [13] Such concessions had exhausted the older moral vocabularies. Civilization being necessarily hypocritical, a certain terminological vulgarity, Freud calculated, was a moral imperative and a positive value. The new psychology used the plain style to debunk the innocence of childhood, the nobility of religious feelings, the objectivity of great art. It is the reaction of a naturalist doctrine, faced with the exhausted data of ethics. Nietzsche made the point concisely:

> A psychologist today shows his good taste (others may say his integrity) in this, if in anything, that he resists the shamefully moralized manner of speaking which makes all modern judgments about men and things slimy.[14]

If psychology was to be the philosophy of the future, as Nietzsche anticipated, it would have to avoid the verbal mannerisms of older moral speculations.

To be sure, one characteristic of eras of moral reform is that it becomes necessary to revise the terminology inherited from previous epochs, to withdraw the predicate of goodness from certain motives and attribute it to others. Freud's theoretical frame and clinical data converge to transmute the standard terms of ethical discourse. His zeal as a scientist leads him to a certain effrontery of expression, in which a spade is called a spade and very black. But behind this effrontery is a kind of philosophic disappointment. In the useful terms of Jeremy Bentham, Freud's dyslogy signifies the deterioration of a eulogy— that is, his clinical intention is to convince man how uncivilized he remains ("men have no business to exclude themselves [from the]

---

official languages: the brilliant literary and social critic Karl Kraus and the great and difficult philosopher Ludwig Wittgenstein. The difference is that Wittgenstein, as a critic of philosophical language, ultimately preached a verbal quietism, saying, "Whereof one cannot speak, one must be silent," while Freud, as a critic of moral language, advocated a verbal catharsis, whose motto might be "Whereof one cannot speak, one must say everything."

animal kingdom"),[15] in the light of his exaggerated claim to have overcome his instincts through civilization.

Freud's advocacy of honesty is not to be understood merely as a reaction against hypocrisy. Certainly it is not to be identified with sensationalism; Freud is very reserved. The subject of sex must be handled in "dry and direct"[16] prose, as a commonplace element in everyday life. The frankness of psychoanalysis represents a conquest of sexuality by the prosaic and communal understanding of science, rather than by the lyrical and private understanding of the individual. Freud's attitude toward sexuality must not be mistaken for romantic frankness. Actually, in his attempt to cleanse the language of sexuality of its romantic elements we see one aspect of Freud's aseptic rationalism.

II

So congenial was the stance of an emancipator that Freud could not cope with the victory that was his during the last period of his life. As he tried to ward off the easy assent of patients as itself a tactic of resistance, so Freud could not acknowledge the extent to which his own views actually had vanquished the prudery against which they were aimed. He had been prepared for a prolonged struggle of ideas: like the sick individual, he wrote, the sick society is "bound to offer us resistance."[17] Despite his general thesis that in modern times there is a crisis in the system of cultural authority, Freud never underestimated the power of religion and repression. The great Father-God had never died, despite the uninterrupted succession of voices crying out the good news.

In the matter of prudery, however, Freud's voice was actually in harmony with a swelling nineteenth-century chorus. The inhibitions which he thought characteristic of civilized society we see as one of those brief periods of contraction in the general expansion of pleasure that had been in progress since the eighteenth century set Western culture on its course of revolt against Christian ascetic standards of conduct. Even the curious Victorian period, when religion came back into fashion as the most somber moralism, was never without its contradictions. It was in 1865 that one of Freud's favorite authors,

Dickens, introduced Mr. Podsnap, with his abhorrence of anything that might bring a blush to the cheek of a young person. But in the same decade another writer whom Freud greatly admired, Zola, was publishing such frank exposures of natural impulse as *Earth* and *Fecundity*. By the 1920s, when Freud came into vogue, talk as well as literature could be improper and still respectable. Freud's reputation as an emancipator arose during the period of reaction against a Victorian prudery long since on the defensive and retreating. From our perspective, much of his culture-criticism fails precisely to grasp the "unrepressiveness" of modern culture. Public morals today, far from fitting the criteria of prudery against which Freud spoke out, are permissive, at least in terms of ease of verbal acknowledgment; images of sexuality in popular entertainment and commodities advertising are displayed straightforwardly; official mores, while never congruent with actual practice, are themselves hardly so hypocritical or so restrained as he described them. Freud was overimpressed, it now appears, with the monolithic repressiveness of culture, and unable to perceive that our own culture might become highly permissive in the sphere of private, sexual morals—the better to enforce its public repressions. The combination of a repressive political order with a permissive moral order is not unheard of in human history. And indeed, today's automatic political repressions parody the Freudian description of *private* repressive culture.

How much does the decline of prudery invalidate Freud's critique? If, as it may appear, Freud and the movement of which he is a part have already largely accomplished their emancipative task, from what now can Freud liberate us?

One persuasive answer to this question would diminish its relevance. Perhaps, as so many post-Freudians suggest, the extreme sexual repression of the Victorian era, now eased, was responsible for the role which Freud attributed to sexuality in the causation of the neuroses. Sexuality acquired a pre-eminence in his account, that is, not merely because he correctly perceived its importance, but because of the repressive method of handling its manifestations within the family during the Victorian period. Nowadays the conflict between instinct and institution may be secondary to that between the values of competition and cooperation. The Protestant ethic lingers, but it is very doubtful that it in any way dominates the expression of Western energies. The man of ambition is still with us, as in all times, but now he needs a more subtle initiative, a deeper capacity to manipulate the democracy of emotions, if he is to maintain his separate identity and significantly augment it with success. Pick up almost any post-Freudian book on our emotional condition and you will find this theme. Karen Horney's *The Neurotic Personality of Our Time* prematurely examines William H. White's *Organization Man* with his defenses cracked. Erich Fromm's *Escape from Freedom* finds American specification in David Riesman's *The Lonely Crowd*. The sexual problems of the neurotic competing for some ephemeral kudos in mid-century Manhattan are very different from the problems of the neurotic in turn-of-the-century Vienna.* History changes the expression of neurosis even if it does not change the underlying mechanisms. If Freud may be accused of biologizing the ambivalences by which all societies are constituted, the post-Freudians may sociologize them too much. The question of reconciling these biologizing and sociologizing tendencies in depth psychology has scarcely been settled, nor even fully explored. Till it is, we had better trust Freud's cheerless intuitions into the duality of all human feeling, thought, and action —whatever the style that prevails in a given historical period.

There are good reasons why sexuality is for Freud the one really profound subject matter, the demands of the instincts the most fundamental demands. A science that recognizes the instincts is a basic science, examining not this social system or that but the system of civilization as a formed thing in itself. Freud has made the greatest single contribution to the understanding of civilization—not merely to the understanding of our own. The incomparable significance of sexual life is that, "while art, religion, and the social order originated in part in a contribution from the sexual instincts," [18] civilization is also per-

---

* This is well illustrated in the most elaborate and most important of all Freud's clinical histories, the case of the "Wolf Man." When this patient, a wealthy young Russian, later became destitute, he was far from acquiring a new neurosis of the competitive-status type; rather, as Freud notes sarcastically, the old one was dissolved by the new, objective pressures. See SE XVII, 3 *et pass.*

manently opposed by sexuality. "Woe, if the sexual instincts should be set loose! The throne [of civilization] would be overturned and the [ultimate] ruler trampled under foot." [19] Yet, even in his cautious approach to sexuality as a scientific subject, Freud advanced the long-established assault on the repressions.

Sexuality has shown, for Freud and related figures of his century, a revolutionary potential somewhat diminished by the newer permissiveness in manners and speech which has followed Freud—and owes greatly to him. The idea of a sexual revolution is not new. In the late eighteenth and early nineteenth centuries, sexuality became the subject of the most advanced art and politics. The critical philosophy of industrial civilization, first put forth by Fourier and the Saint-Simonians, and after them in the literature of the "young Germans," based itself on a deliberately anti-Christian eroticism. The sexual rebellion that was linked with socialism, before the conservative Karl Marx broke the connection on the pejorative word "utopian," was closer to being geniunely revolutionary—i.e., a revolt from below—than we now can grasp, accustomed as we are by Marxism and its counterfeits to revolutions run by reason—i.e., from above. The goal of the sexual revolution was never a harmonious, classless society, but rather happier individuals freed from a false reverence for the general advantage of society. The great writers on sex, from de Sade to Lawrence, were less interested in society than in the individual, pressing in varying degrees for the freedom of the individual against the burdens of social morality.*

In the immediately pre-Christian period, when the antique world was suffering its own exhaustion, the utopian yearning had been toward something higher, for it was a period of erotic satiety and the needs of the flesh were only too well attended. In the post-Christian era—that is, the last hundred years or more—rebellion has chiefly been in the name of the flesh. The theme of liberation from a repres-

---

* For de Sade and Lawrence sexuality itself provides a utopian possibility. They assert masculine sexuality as the basis of a revolution against the prevailing feminine social order—this especially militates against political radicalism, since sex becomes an alternative to politics. Thus a new generation of Freudian-trained conservatives is rising in America. The doctrine of the revolutionary possibilities of sex is the positive side of the psychoanalytic reduction of the political radical (cf. Chapter Seven) to a special case of the neurotic.

siveness more serious than that of any merely political regime was everywhere in the haunted air of the nineteenth century—in an acutely sexed literature, in a value philosophy (Schopenhauer's) that by its interest in "values" questioned their validity, in strange political and religious movements that in the name of the future claimed to go deeper than politics and religion. With Nietzsche's *Beyond Good and Evil* the sustained attack on spiritual love and the glorification of a humanity free to live in a more sensual way came to its philosophical completion. In literature the revolutionary erotic intention emerged in the assertion of Hellenism against Hebraism, of beauty as the real object of piety—an assertion made first perhaps by Schiller, in the name of the glory that was Greece. Heine, whom Freud revered, had also taken up the indignation against a civilization too long under the shadow of the Law, and called for a rehabilitation of the flesh against the body-despising values of Christianity. In England, Swinburne watched the decline of energy and adopted an accusing tone: "Thou hast conquered, O pale Galilean; the world has grown grey from thy breath." In France, around the same time, Gautier wrote against the "Christian contempt for what is shapely and incarnate." Love was examined with a steady and detailed ferocity by literary men and philosophers, until with Freud it entered into the twentieth century under more persuasive auspices—as a science.

Yet Freud has none of the enthusiasm that characterizes the antinomian temper. Civilization, because of its discontents, was the basic problem of his psychological science. The cry for liberty did come from the instinctual depths, but Freud heard it with the cautious attention of a physician attending an eminent but dangerous patient. Sexuality for him is a force that permanently prevents any utopian transforming of the social order. Freud held no hope of transforming civilization. On the contrary, the great utopian possibility—insofar as he held to any—is whether repressive civilization can permanently tame the instincts. He took the traditional position of assuming a conflict between man's animal and spiritual nature—the spiritual being a residual quality in the transforming process of repressive civilization.

Freud felt that the sexual scarcity characteristic of all civilizations (embodied in such institutions as monogamy) concentrated a certain surplus aggressiveness in the unconscious. A freer sexuality—a juster distribution of libido, the fundamental wealth of civilization—would lower the cost of civilization itself. Such an increase of sexual rations might go far toward resolving the nervousness of modern civilized behavior. But thus to widen the range of gratification, to relocate the problem of desire in the historical variety of "objects," fails to resolve the psychological problem. Man creates his own scarcity; the aesthetic mechanics of satisfaction themselves make gratification chimerical. Any notion that Freud's doctrine of scarce satisfaction in some way reflects the economic doctrine of scarcity representative of the best social thought in his era is to render trivial Freud's point. His use of a quasi-economic metaphor to discuss sexuality gives no warrant for treating the insight frozen into this metaphor as dated. Nature still seeks a state of balance. Freud's is a theory of the equilibrium toward which the emotional life tends after every disturbance. Sexuality is subject no less completely to Freud's first law of the emotions than any other element of human existence. Only one way lies open to escape the dissatisfactions inherent in every satisfaction, and that is to grow equable. When the inner life is not easily disturbed it has achieved what is to Freud as nearly ideal a condition as he can imagine. There is something Oriental in the Freudian ethic. The "Nirvana principle" crops up, now and again, in his later writings, intimating what is entailed in mastering the balances of nature.

Short of Nirvana, if sexuality could conceivably cease to trouble man, his destructive instincts would trouble him more. His dualism allowed Freud to maintain simultaneously a psychological version of the classical liberal and radical rationalist dream, that once civilization had reached a certain level of technological productivity (read "reality adequacy") and "consumption" (read "satisfactions") the miseries of its earlier stages would drop away, and a psychological version of the equally powerful religious idea—with the redemption fantasy stripped to a minimum faith in reason. In the therapeutic encounter, reason and unreason unite to create a third force capable of mediating between the clashing instincts. But the instincts cannot be taught to abide each other; their fusion creates tension and the possibility of abrupt reversals. Besides, were aggression merely a response to the frustration of some sexual or social need, it could be resolved, or at least ameliorated, by a specifically social reform of the conditions of frustration. But an aggression that is built in, due to the presence of a "death instinct," * cannot be entirely manipulated, let alone abolished. According to this view, civilization can never resolve its nervousness, for the principle of ambivalence, more than that of integration, characterizes human nature and society. Happiness can never be achieved by the panaceas of social permissiveness or sexual plenitude. Order can never be achieved by social suppression or moral rigor. We are not unhappy because we are frustrated, Freud implies; we are frustrated because we are, first of all, unhappy combinations of conflicting desires. Civilization can, at best, reach a balance of discontents.

Here is no Swinburnian romance of free sexuality versus the moral law. Rather, Freud takes the romance out of sexuality, for romance is dependent upon taking the repressions for granted, in fact on their remaining entirely unconscious, so that they may be broken only at the price of guilt. The Freudian attitude, on the other hand, no longer takes them for granted, and therefore can no longer take sexuality as a static ideal, even against the present crippling incapacities of our erotic lives. Freud might seem to be suggesting an expansive erotic ideal. But any future sensual permissiveness is rendered suspect by what he asserts about the expansive erotic life of the past. Freud not only feared that sexual freedom might entail undesirable sacrifices in culture; he thought it itself a transient accomplishment. Love is not a final solution for Freud, but a therapeutic one. He acknowledged that the establishment of a repressive code (such as Christianity) might under certain circumstances (as during the satiety of pagan culture) prove beneficent, like an artificially induced scarcity which revives consumption after a long period of overproduction.[20] Therefore he was confident only of his analysis of our crippled condition, never of his prognosis. As a psychologist of fulfillment, Freud predicts disappointment: he sees the social value

---

* There is a significant parallel in Freud's idea, advanced in the *Three Essays,* of a primal repression prior to social inhibitions, which is set off by the instinctual process itself.

of repression, the complex nature of satisfaction. It is only in the therapeutic context—which is, after all, not life—that he rejects repression.

Freud was not hopeful; nor was he nostalgic. Retrospectively, he treasured no pagan or primitive past. He looked forward to no radically different future. Pagan antiquity had encouraged too much sensual pride and demonstrated the erotic illusion no less fully than Christianity, by encouraging spiritual pride, had demonstrated the ascetic illusion. Freud disdained permissiveness as much as asceticism; both falsely resolved the essential dualism in human experience, that very dualism between mind and flesh that produces the misery of the human condition. What man suffers from finally is no more the supremacy of spirit over flesh than of flesh over spirit; it is the dualism that hurts. Freud's own attitude toward a variety of historical dualisms, including Christianity, was always respectful, for he considered that they were but versions of a more fundamental dualism in the nature of man and in the cosmos. For this reason he never seriously entertained any utopian aspiration. Indeed, his own theory "had always been strictly dualistic and had at no time failed to recognize, alongside the sexual instincts, others to which it ascribed force enough to suppress the sexual instincts." [21] This dualism Freud described as between "sexuality" and the "ego instincts"; later he distinguished two polar instincts, love and death.* Whatever the terminology, it is important to see that—unlike the Christian or

---

* Freud thought that his version of these polar forces, which he called *Eros* and *Thanatos* and nominated as the "primal instincts," had restored the cosmology of Empedocles ("Analysis Terminable and Interminable," *Coll. Papers* V, 347–350). But what he ascribes to Empedocles is common property of the whole school of transitional thinkers passing out of the mythic stage into philosophy—Anaximander, Empedocles, Heraclitus, Parmenides, and finally Plato. Actually, among these neo-mythic cosmologies, Freud's version more resembles Anaximander's than it does that of Empedocles. (I follow here the account of Cornford in *From Religion to Philosophy*, p. 65.) "Anaximander was more purely rational than many of his successors. In later systems—notably in those of Parmenides and Empedocles—mythical associations and implications [of the love-hate, attraction-repulsion polarity] which [Anaximander] has expurgated, emerge again. In particular, we can discern that the prototype of all opposition or contrariety is the contrariety of *sex*." As late as Plato's *Timaeus*, a sexual character still clings to the great contrarieties, Form (father) and Matter (mother).

rationalist consciousness—Freud denies any permanent healing of the "derangement of communal life," of the struggle between individual interest and the economy of social demands, of the antagonism between binding and destructive forces in individual and group life. The most one can win against the eternal dualisms is a rational knowledge of their effects upon one's own life.

Perhaps it might be more accurate to see depth psychology not as an emancipation of sex but as an enfranchisement. Freud recognized that in fact the silent vote of the psychic world never had been silent. He is the Bentham of the unenfranchised unconscious; what he brought into the realm of legitimacy, he also brought to responsibility. If one cannot educate the ruled, then one must educate the rulers. This very aim, to educate the ruling ego, is a sure mark of Freud's classical liberalism. By enfranchising the uneducable populace of sexuality, Freud seeks to bring it into responsible relations with the ruling power. To the liberal political tradition, with its belief that the "two nations" could be brought together, Freud offered a supporting parallel in psychological and moral theory, for he desired, as far as possible, to bring the instinctual unconscious into the rational community. For this new art of compromise a new kind of specialist is needed, one who can take a destiny apart and put it back together again in a slightly more endurable shape.

III

Freud gives us two types of insight into the aesthetic dimension of life—art both formal and informal: the first into what I shall call its "expressive" function, and the second, its function as "self-mastery." Once we admit that a dream, poem, or symptomatic act is an "expression," there is inevitably the notion of "something" that is forced out by a pressure from within. Of course the idea that the emotions exert a psychic pressure whose expression acts therapeutically is as old as the advice about not keeping sorrow "in" but crying it "out." The Romantic poets constantly testified to the serviceability of art with respect to easing the private, and especially the sexual, passions. Rousseau confessed that *La Nouvelle Héloïse* originated in the compulsive daydreams in which he compensated for his frustrations as a lover, and Goethe observed that his youthful erotic disappointments transformed themselves into *The Sorrows of Young Werther,* which he wrote in four weeks "almost unconsciously, like a somnambulist." He felt "as if after a general confession, once more happy and free, and justified in beginning a new life." [22]

But how does the venting of painful emotions perform this thera- peutic service? In giving Freud's answer to this question, we must note the difference between his immature and mature pronounce- ments on art. The earlier Freud was too inclined to take the expres- sive function at face value, as itself curative in the way that a confession cures—in other words, as a cathartic. But as he gradually replaced the cathartic method of treating patients with the analytic, Freud's view of self-expression as basically cathartic in value was replaced by the idea that art has the function of self-mastery as well. Again, one can look to the Romantics for an anticipation of Freud's insight. The critic William Hazlitt, author of the most anguished erotic confession in English literature, the *Liber Amoris,* describes in proto-Freudian terms the capacity of art to master, by objectifying, the chaotic press of emotion.

> This is equally the origin of wit and fancy, of comedy and tragedy, of the sublime and the pathetic. . . . The Imagination, by thus embodying and turning them to shape, gives an obvious relief to the indistinct and importunate cravings of the will. . . . We do not wish the thing to be so; but we wish it to appear such as it is. For knowledge is conscious power; and the mind is no longer, in this case, the dupe, though it may be the victim of vice or folly.[23]

It is not important to inquire whether Freud read Hazlitt, but rather to note the similarity between this fairly sophisticated version of the Romantic theory of art and Freud's development of the same concept in the second chapter of *Beyond the Pleasure Principle* (1920). In the context of a discussion of children's play, which he saw implicitly as art, Freud writes:

> It is clear that in their play children repeat everything that has made a great impression on them in real life, and that in doing so they abreact the strength of the impression and, as one might put it,

make themselves masters of the situation. . . . The child passes over from the passivity of the experience to the activity of the game.

The artistic play and artistic imitation carried out by adults has essentially the same motive as the play of children, except that, unlike children's play, it is directed at an audience. That this adult play does

> not spare the spectators (for instance, in tragedy) the most painful experiences and can yet be felt by them as highly enjoyable . . . is convincing proof that, even under the dominance of the pleasure-principle, there are ways and means enough of making what is in itself unpleasurable into a subject to be recollected and worked over in the mind.[24]

The shift from expression to self-mastery as the function of play—and, by extrapolation, of art—suggests a new interpretation of catharsis.

We may compare Freud's notion of catharsis with Aristotle's. Aristotle had described catharsis as a kind of homeopathic inoculation of dangerous sentiments, through mimetic representation, in order to effect their discharge and thereby restore sentiment to bearable levels. Freud also meant by catharsis a discharge of emotion. But there are several major differences. First, whereas Aristotle was describing the experience of an audience witnessing a public spectacle, the Freudian idea of catharsis, as taking place in the privacy of the therapeutic session, united actor and audience in one person, the suffering patient; the actor is his own audience. Extended to art, this notion makes the relevant catharsis the one which the artist effects upon himself. Second, Aristotle offers no criterion for judging what the dangerous emotions are that need discharge, except to indicate that they are those which have undergone a certain excessive accumulation and must be drained off. Breuer's notion of catharsis appears to be no more than this; but in reality more is involved, as Freud was to make clear. A catharsis cannot take place with any emotion which is vented, but only with emotions toward which the patient had previously been too passive; and these emotions can be characterized even further: they involved the original feature of inhibition or repression.

In an important sense, therefore, treatment itself has an aesthetic aim: to allow the patient an expression that has been in principle repressed. The poles of the analytic situation are repression and that which remains to be expressed. Thus the Freudian analysis is focused upon an aesthetic problem—that of expression: as if we would all be artists, if only what we have to express could be free from repression. It is in this sense that the notion of a man's being natively artistic is central to Freud.

Catharsis, as the therapeutic expressiveness at which Freud understood treatment to be aiming, was, so to say, a powerful expression—itself memorable because its purpose was to empty a given memory. But Freud was dissatisfied with a merely powerful expressiveness because, although strong, it was not permanent. Catharsis remained caught within the dialectic of transience which characterizes the aesthetic process, as opposed to the intellectual one.* In consequence, Freud shifted toward a second therapeutic aim, which was an expression rather more *clear* than powerful. This shift comprises the difference between knowledge, which is at once an expression and a comprehension of the expression (analysis), and direct, acted-out, expressive presentation, which is not necessarily self-comprehending.† The cathartic method, as Freud says, "presupposed that the patient could be hypnotized, and was based on the widening of consciousness that occurs under hypnosis." [25] When Freud gave up hypnosis, this "widening of consciousness" which had made possible the "liberating" of emotion was sacrificed.[26] But the gain, Freud thought, was entirely worth while. Hypnosis had enabled the patient to evade the task of gaining insight into his mental conflicts.[27] More permanently curative than to evacuate an emotion would be to understand it; for the patient gained control not through the emptying but through the understanding of an emotion.

Thus, in therapy, Freud moved from the cathartic to the analytic explanation. Similarly, his view of art passed beyond the merely cathartic. The work of art remains, in all Freud's writings, a way

---

* Cf. the essay "On Transience" (1915) (*Coll. Papers* V, 79–82).
† Note that the technique of "psycho-drama" is a reversion from analysis to catharsis. The history of therapeutic debate since Freud describes a full circle back to catharsis.

which the artist has of responding to his own emotional burdens. But ways differ, even in the Freudian interpretation. In one view, the work of art is a safety valve, a form of exhibitionism, in which the tension accumulated by private motives is drained off in public display; but in another view, the work of art is, more positively, a means of achieving emotional stability—not weakness but self-mastery. This more sophisticated view of the artist, as having a unique activeness, is broached in a passage in the essay "The Uncanny" (1919), where Freud writes:

> In the main we adopt an unvarying passive attitude towards real experience and are subject to the influence of our physical environment. But the story-teller has a peculiarly directive influence over us; by means of the moods he can put us into, he is able to guide the current of our emotions, to dam it up in one direction and make it flow in another . . .[28]

In this second view—equally compatible with Freud's main views and closer to the truth about art, I think—the work of art is not merely a form of acceding to one's feelings; it may also be considered a means of asserting them.

Art—like intellectual activity, joking, or fun—"opens up sources of pleasure or enjoyment in our emotional life." [29] In his essay "Psychopathic Characters on the Stage" (c. 1906), Freud analyzes the drama as a means of offering the members of the audience the pleasure of identifying themselves with the hero. And the hero, in Freud's view, is always a rebel. So enjoyment of art means vicarious, or safe, rebellion—i.e., rebellion against the divine order or against society. Drama allows the spectator to imagine himself as a "great man," and to give way freely "to such suppressed impulses as a craving for freedom in religious, political, social, and sexual matters." [30] Even if the identifications promoted by art are illusory, the illusion, Freud implies, can express a critical truth about the human condition. He is usually understood to have held that art takes one farther away from, not closer to, reality. But, in this interpretation, art brings one closer to reality by releasing, as need occasions, either the rebel and blasphemer or the pietist in us all.

What I have said of art applies as well to Freud's analysis of wit.

On the one hand, humor may be pictured as a certain disguised expression of deep feeling, dodging past the sentries posted to guard against more serious expressions of the same feeling. Joking, like dreams, represents an overthrow of the mind's order and integrity. On the other hand, Freud emphasized the socially subversive tendency of joking—the significance of wit as a rebellion against authority, and of jokes as themselves an unmasking of public morality. Each of us, wrote Freud, has at times admitted the attractiveness, even the justice, of a life in which one would take what pleasure one can

and has reproached moral doctrine with only understanding how to demand without offering any compensation. Since we have ceased any longer to believe in the promise of a next world in which every renunciation will be rewarded by a satisfaction . . . 'Carpe diem' has become a serious warning.

Much joking is in the service of the exhibitionistic, aggressive, cynical, and skeptical tendencies, giving cautious notice

that the wishes and desires to men have a right to make themselves acceptable alongside of exacting and ruthless morality. . . . So long as the art of healing has not gone further in making our life safe and so long as social arrangements do no more to make it enjoyable, so long will it be impossible to stifle the voice within us that rebels against the demands of morality. Every honest man will end by making this admission, at least to himself.[31]

This analysis of joking may be extended to all types of fantasy. Fantasy may be considered not only as an escape from reality but also, more positively, as a mental reservation "reclaimed from the encroachment of the reality principle," [32] i.e., from conformity to social demands, in which the person allows himself to seek pleasure unreasonably and asocially. In sexuality, and in the products of fantasy (dreams, wit, and art) a refuge from society is created. At the same time, these activities defy society and triumph over it; they are a mode of blasphemy.

Freud's entire concern with the psychic symptom—the art of the neurotic will—has this same duality, between a conformist and a subversive meaning. On the one hand, our symptomatic life is characterized by the sublimation of feeling; on the other hand, in the more aggressive productions of wit and in the moral recklessness of dreams and in the vicarious rebellion of art, it is riotously expressive of the unclaimed possibilities of our emotional life.

In thus seeing art and humor not only as sublimations but as projections, and therefore a kind of self-treatment, Freud's view of art as always being an escape from reality takes on a double edge, a profound implication of the nascent effort to change reality. It follows that there is no progress in art. Only in art

> has the omnipotence of thought been retained in our own civilization. . . . In art alone it still happens that man, consumed by his wishes, produces something similar to the gratification of these wishes, and this playing, thanks to artistic illusion, calls forth effects as if it were something real.[33]

Reality being characterized by the progressively intensifying repressive forces of civilization, art remains behind to fulfill the permanent patterns of aspiration which have been canceled out either by the rational knowledge of reality (which comes with civilization) or by the repressive necessities of civilization itself.

Though we may doctor Freud's view in order to interpret expression as a form of self-mastery, it remains too closely tied to the *use* of art to make such an interpretation entirely acceptable. He did not believe that art—or the play of children—could be the product of superabundance and spontaneity. In Freud's view, everything in the psyche is produced for use. Play itself is a practical effort. Thus he says: "Children's play, too, is made to serve this purpose of completing and thus, as it were, annulling a passive experience by active behavior." [34] And art, too, is practical. Both in Freud's early view, that art ministers to the evacuatory need, or in his more sophisticated view, that art is a form of self-manipulation, a self-conquest of the emotions by expelling them, art is accounted for by its utility in the psychic economy. This, it is worth noting, is a feature of the most famous of all views of art as catharsis that preceded Freud's. F. L. Lucas has convincingly argued, in his splendid little book entitled *Tragedy,* that Aristotle's *Poetics* should be read as a reply to the moralizing dispraise of art by Plato. Plato had said that art encourages men to be hysterical and uncontrolled, to which Aristotle replied that poetry makes people less, not more, emotional by giving them a periodic and healthy outlet to their feelings. Against Plato's attack on art, Aristotle offered only a medical defense (the doctrine of catharsis), much as a moderate Puritan might have tried to show that wine was healthy and dancing good exercise. But we do not drink for health or dance for exercise. Nor do we go to tragedies to get rid of emotions, but rather to feel them more abundantly; to banquet is not to be purged.

The shortcomings of Freud's utilitarian view of mental symptoms may be seen clearly in his treatment of the dream-life. He sees only the dream at work, disfiguring the disguising dangerous emotions in order to protect the dreamer's sleep and/or to fulfill a wish.* The dream is just another mold into which the dream-thoughts have been poured. It is this disregard of the form of the dream as mere trappings that prevents Freud from seeing the play aspect of the dream; for play is basically a *form* rather than a content: it depends upon a certain arrangement and articulation of emotion in time, employing images and speech—in other words, upon conventions. Freud's interest—a vital one—is in elucidating the inner meaning of these conventions; he is not interested in the phenomenon of the conventionalization of meaning itself. If he were, he would see that what may be liberating in the dream is not only the fact that certain suppressed contents are allowed expression but the very fact that the sleeper's emotion is dramatized, i.e., played, in a dream. The dream is based on a certain imagination of reality (i.e., its conversion into

---

* In *The Interpretation of Dreams* Freud speaks of the dream as either a compromise disfigurement of morally reprehensible thoughts which would, if directly expressed, shock the dreamer out of sleep; or, more simply, an imaginary enactment of needs and obligations which disturb the dreamer's sleep. (E.g., we are thirsty and dream that we drink; or, we have an early appointment and, wishing to remain in bed, dream that we are already there.) In the case of art the imputation is similarly passive: the artist wards off the destructiveness of his neurotic conflict by unburdening himself in publicly acceptable fantasies. The work of art thus guards the neurosis in a twofold sense: it stabilizes rather than resolves it (having become a useful part of the artist's psyche, it is unlikely to be abandoned), but at the same time it tends to prevent the neurosis from getting any worse.

images). Dreams arise not only out of tension and distress and un-fulfillment, but also out of a spontaneous pleasure in the mind's activity. Freud says as much, in the passage already quoted:

> If we do not require our mental apparatus at the moment for supply-ing one of our indispensable satisfactions, we allow it itself to work in the direction of pleasure and we seek to derive pleasure from its own activity.[35]

But this suggestion is not developed in Freud's writings. For the most part he gives the impression that dreams are to be understood in terms of their utility—that their use is to help express anxieties which cannot otherwise be communicated.

IV

On the cultural significance of the neurotic character, Freud is entirely explicit. Neurotics are rebels out of weakness rather than strength; they witness to the inadequacies of cultural restraint. But they are unsuccessful rebels, for they pay too high a price for their revolt, and ultimately fail, turning their aggressions against them-selves. Instead of being repressed and turned inward as the neurotic is, the normal personality is active and outgoing. Expedient normal attitudes lead to some active achievement in the outer world. The brisk managerial ego of the normal personality devotes itself to ag-gression against the environment, to the practical use of objects; it does not fixate upon them. As Freud put it elsewhere: neurotic anxiety comes from a libido which has "found no employment"; there-fore, the dream, like work, has a "moralizing purpose." [36] Again, the economic metaphor discloses Freud's ideal of health as well: a fully employed libido.

In a brilliant passage Freud describes the normal attitude toward reality as one combining the best features of neurotic and psychotic attitudes:

> Neurosis does not deny the existence of reality, it merely tries to ignore it; psychosis denies it and tries to substitute something else for it. A reaction which combines features of both these is the one we call normal or "healthy"; it denies reality as little as neurosis, but then, like a psychosis, is concerned with effecting a change in it.[37]

Thus the neurotic character is the unsuccessful protestant of the emotional life; in him inwardness becomes incapacity. The normal character continues to protest, Freud implies, but is "not content . . . with establishing the alternation within itself." [38] Thus, in Freud's conception of the normal man, there is a certain echo of the Romantic idea of genius—the ideal man who attains to the self-expression that other men, intimidated by convention, weakly forgo.

As the passage just quoted suggests, Freud did not draw a sharp line between the concepts of normal and neurotic. His dictum that "we are all somewhat hysterical," [39] that the difference between so-called normality and neurosis is only a matter of degree,[40] is one of the key statements in his writings. Its meaning is threefold.

First, it declassifies human society, creating an essential democracy within the human condition. Even the Greek tragedy—the most aristocratic context—was leveled out by Freud; the unique crime of the tragic hero becomes an intention in every heart, and in the most ordinary of plots, the history of every family. Misfortune is not an exceptional possibility, occasioned by rare circumstances or monstrous characters, but is the lot of every person, something he has to pass through in his journey from infancy to old age. The aristocratic bias of the "heroic" myth is replaced, in Freud, by the democratic bias of the "scientific" myth: Oedipus *Rex* becomes Oedipus Complex, which all men live through. It is because of the suppressed tragedies of everyday life that men respond so fully to the more explicit tragedies on the stage. But this does not mean that Freud proposed a genuinely tragic view of life; he was much too realistic for that. Ordinary men compromise with their instinctual longings and become neurotic; the tragic hero, because he suffers and dies, must be presumed to have carried out his wishes in a way forbidden to most men.[41]

Secondly, to say that all men are neurotic means to imply an injunction to tolerance. At least Freud's discovery that the commonplace is saturated with the abnormal, the pathological—that psychopathology no longer deals with the exception but with the ordinary man—does something to alter established habits of moral judgment. It lightens the heavier burdens of guilt and responsibility, for many offenses can be made to appear smaller if perceived in sufficient depth.

Third, and more important, this conception of neurosis reveals the essentially ethical nature of Freud's idea of normality. Normality is not a statistical conception, for the majority is no longer normal. Normality is an ethical ideal, pitted against the actual abnormal. By another name, normality is the negative ideal of "overcoming"— whatever it is that ought to be overcome. Being essentially negative, normality is an ever-retreating ideal. An attitude of stoic calm is required for its pursuit. No one catches the normal; everyone must act as if it can be caught. Nor can the psychological man forget himself in pursuit of the normal, for his normality consists of a certain kind of self-awareness. Not least of all, the analysts themselves, Freud thought, needed to return to analysis every few years to renew their knowledge of themselves.

The psychological ideal of normality has a rather unheroic aspect. Think of a whole society dominated by psychotherapeutic ideals. Considered not from the individual's but from a sociological point of view, psychoanalysis is an expression of a popular tyranny such as not even de Tocqueville adequately imagined. Ideally, the democratic tyranny which is the typical social form of our era will not have a hierarchy of confessors and confessants. Rather, as I have pointed out in Chapter Nine, everyone must be a confessant, everyone must aspire to be a confessor. This is the meaning of the psychoanalytic re-education Freud speaks of. In the emergent democracy of the sick, everyone can to some extent play doctor to others, and none is allowed the temerity to claim that he can definitively cure or be cured. The hospital is succeeding the church and the parliament as the archetypal institution of Western culture.

What has caused this tyranny of psychology, legitimating self-concern as the highest science? In part, no doubt, it is the individual's failure to find anything else to affirm except the self. Having lost faith in the world, knowing himself too well to treat himself as an object of faith, modern man cannot be self-confident; this, in a negative way, justifies his science of self-concern. Though the world is indifferent to him, the lonely ego may here and there win something from it. For the rectitude and energetic naïveté of the man who was the ideal type during the middle-class, Protestant phase of American culture, we have substituted the character traits of husbanded energy and finessed self-consciousness. The Frank Merriwell of a psychological culture will not, like the moral athlete of Protestant culture, turn his reveries into realities. Rather, he will be mindful to keep realities from turning into reveries.

V

In this age, in which technics is invading and conquering the last enemy—man's inner life, the psyche itself—a suitable new character type has arrived on the scene: the psychological man. Three character ideals have successively dominated Western civilization: first, the ideal of the political man, formed and handed down to us from classical antiquity; second, the ideal of the religious man, formed and handed down to us from Judaism through Christianity, and dominant in the civilization of authority that preceded the Enlightenment; third, the ideal of the economic man, the very model of our liberal civilization, formed and handed down to us in the Enlightenment. This last has turned out to be a transitional type, with the shortest life-expectancy of all; out of his tenure has emerged the psychological man of the twentieth century, a child not of nature but of technology. He is not the pagan ideal, political man, for he is not committed to the public life. He is most unlike the religious man. We will recognize in the case history of psychological man the nervous habits of his father, economic man: he is anti-heroic, shrewd, carefully counting his satisfactions and dissatisfactions, studying unprofitable commitments as the sins most to be avoided. From this immediate ancestor, psychological man has constituted his own careful economy of the inner life.

The psychological man lives neither by the ideal of might nor by the ideal of right which confused his ancestors, political man and religious man. Psychological man lives by the ideal of insight—practical, experimental insight leading to the mastery of his own personality. The psychological man has withdrawn into a world always at war, where the ego is an armed force capable of achieving armistices but not peace. The prophetic egoist of Western politics and Protestant Christianity who, through the model with which he provided us, also laid down the lines along which the world was to be transformed, has been replaced by the sage, intent upon the conquest of his inner life, and, at most, like Freud, laying down the lines along which those that follow him can salvage something of their own. Turning away from the Occidental ideal of action leading toward the salvation of others besides ourselves, the psychological man has espoused the Oriental ideal of salvation through self-contemplative manipulation. Ironically, this is happening just at the historic moment when the Orient, whose westernmost outpost is Russia, has adopted the Occidental ideal of saving activity in the world. The West has attempted many successive transformations of the enemy, the world. It now chooses to move against its last enemy, the self, in an attempt to conquer it and assimilate it to the world as it is. For it is from the self that the troublesome, world-rejecting ideal of the religious man came forth.

Freudianism closes off the long-established quarrel of Western man with his own spirit. It marks the archaism of the classical legacy of political man, for the new man must live beyond reason—reason having proved no adequate guide to his safe conduct through the meaningless experience of life. It marks the repudiation of the Christian legacy of the religious man, for the new man is taught to live a little beyond conscience—conscience having proved no adequate guide to his safe conduct through life, and furthermore to have added absurd burdens of meaning to the experience of life. Finally, psychoanalysis marks the exhaustion of the liberal legacy represented historically in economic man, for now men must live with the knowledge that their dreams are by function optimistic and cannot be fulfilled. Aware at last that he is chronically ill, psychological man may nevertheless end the ancient quest of his predecessors for a healing doctrine. His experience with the latest one, Freud's, may finally teach him that every cure must expose him to new illness.

ONE STEP FURTHER

> *But why "guilt" at all? . . . And how powerful must that* Schuldgefuehl *have been, if the whole complicated, infinitely anguished story of religion grew out of that feeling. But Freud refused to go the one step further, to admit the universal objectivity of guilt. So, too, Otto Rank held that without the repression of the incest urge, civilization was unthinkable. But it did not occur to him to ask why man should have repressed the incest urge. Whatever so evidently tore man out of the context of nature was itself repressed.*
> —FREUD: THE MIND OF THE MORALIST

I intend to span twenty years in the history of my own minding of this moralist. To see what might be seen through Freud's vision faceted, toward the right conduct of our lives, was my aim in writing this book until the moment I stopped rewriting it in 1958. I conceive the theoretical enterprise, still, as ineluctably practical and moral: a matter of working through an established textual surface, cutting along discoverable lines of fracture, toward those details that show the reader some little way toward the right conduct of his own life. In this book, detail is everything.

The details latent in Freud's manifest theory are not necessarily the ones he would have noticed. For those interested, as I am, in seeing what commanding truths live in a theorist otherwise dead, I have made this Epilogue a brief reading along one line of fracture in the Freudian text, toward a certain detail unseen—rather resisted—by Freud himself. My intention was never merely to exposit manifest Freudian theory—what used to be called "dogma"*—except as its

---

* By "dogma," I mean a temporarily authoritative consensus of received interpretations, workings-through of some doctrine, toward conduct rationalized

358

resisted detail contributed to conduct newly illuminated for each of us blind beholders. To follow the many little lines of fracture in Freud's massive hardness, to see through its own intricate faceting of what is seen but darkly in every mind's eye—so much for my method and its purpose, so far as I pretend to understand them. Freud's proper influence upon me has been upon my working-through of his influence.

Next year will be the fortieth since Freud died, on 23 September 1939. In these years, Freud has died his lingering second death. The exquisitely complex silences of Freudian doctrine have been shattered in fusillades of dogmatic simplification. Those who have assaulted Freud especially in favor of sexual freedom take it as the prototype of other pistols that can be held to the head of culture. Freud's entombed genius presides over one deadly assault after another upon the living theory, or practiced detail, of that very high culture to which he could not help but belong.

---

in doctrinal terms. "Dogma" implies not only authority, but resistance to authority. Without heresy, there would have been no dogma. Without resistance, there can be no truth, in Freud's therapeutic doctrine, as I have tried to show, especially in Chapter Four. Every dogma has its term, or terms, without which nothing greatly significant can be conceived to follow; these I call "god-terms." By way of example, here follows a passage from late Freudian theory, his *New Introductory Lectures,* in which there is made out to exist something than which nothing greater can be discovered—though Freud ended by admitting he had made no further progress toward that most profound discovery. Freud says that

> Wishful impulses which have never passed beyond the id, but impressions, too, which have been sunk into the id by repression, are virtually immortal; after the passage of decades they behave as though they had just occurred. They can only be recognized as belonging to the past, can only lose their importance and be deprived of their cathexis of energy, when they have been made conscious by the work of analysis, and it is on this that the therapeutic effect of analytic treatment rests to no small extent.
>
> Again and again I have had the impression that we have made too little theoretical use of this fact, established beyond any doubt, of the unalterability by time of the repressed. This seems to offer an approach to the most profound discoveries. Nor, unfortunately, have I myself made any progress here. [SE XXII, 74]

Influenced as he was by dogmatic motives common to the scientific community of which he conceived himself a faithful member, Freud could not approach the "virtually immortal"—"unalterability by time of the repressed"—with terms other than the ones that have been so commanding in our century. All dogmas, including those expressing the authority of science, are mortal codes of immortal commands; in this stipulation, Freud was the chief dogmatist of his century.

Against the anti-Freudian dream of an erotocratic regime, the living Freud continues to know the most cautionary of all truths: that to grow healthier is not necessarily to be better. But, for his part in teaching the terminal modern neurosis of mental health, Freud must suffer his present fate. In the course of hearing us out of our rightly severe judgments against ourselves, Freud left behind a legacy of mistaken impressions—the chief of them being that he opposed all condemnatory judgments; and, in particular, that he opposed that preliminary phase of condemnation, before it is confused by facts, which he named "repression."

Freud thought repression was his crucial problem. Since this process of distancing and altering unacceptable reality was the human condition Freud did not even dream to resolve, he would have been ill at ease with "repression" as the new devil-term of our popular devotions. "Repression"—that first cause of human injustice and lack of satisfaction—what is to be done? Abolish repression! Then all will be well. When nothing further can stop Humanity from becoming perfectly developed, then the age of *libido,* successor to Holy Spirit, will have dawned.

I

Repression cannot be abolished; as like abolish the unconscious. Freud reckoned few repressions can even be explored: just those of the more obviously troubling sort, the kind no longer painful enough to keep a desire and its original object strangers one to another.

To explore the space between desire and object, Freud followed its dividing lines of pain. Precisely along those lines, a passion returns; unawareness of it begins to fail us. But then, in sickness, health may return. That very returning passion, in its morality as pain, may be conducted to a different end. In that happier end, a repression may be defeated by a certain resolutive consciousness of passion transferred, forswearings and all, to the directing figure of the therapist.

Once and again, along a path that is never straight, there appears another figure of passion transferred, first fixed in the mind's eye and then lost to direct sight. The lost sight of this other directing figure so occupies self with both the passion and the penalty of minding its absence, that both, the passion and penal pain of it, return unknown even to the most receptive knower. This "unknown,"* sovereign unconsciousness as repression, is Freud's crucial abstraction of the figure who will appear only on condition that a blind eye is turned toward it.

Direct sight of the "unknown" is always dangerous. A voraciousness of vision was no part of Freud's reckoning with repression. Never to look directly at soliciting danger is the natural beginning of wisdom. An averting of the eyes, or at least a closing of one, is the pleasure implicit in the pain of every repression.

The more deeply we see the less healthy we are; Freud could be resigned, if not content, to leave ill enough alone. All our current therapeutic pamperings of the unconscious—expectations of quick benefits from more direct contact with it—oppose Freud's cautionary wisdom. Real changes in ourselves "take place slowly; if they occur rapidly, suddenly, that is a bad sign."[1] The unconscious is an eternal enemy to be learnt from. But Freud did not propose to mold the victims of failed repression into rebels against it. To the contrary, Freud opposed suicide by the parental authority he thought represented in repressions. "Revolutionary children are not desirable from any point of view."[2] Here, in a sentence, is the Freud which his own doctrinal offspring find unacceptable as repression itself; the sentence implies the contrary view that parental authority is only one representation of repression.

There are states of mind worse than that of repression. Freud knew he was living through a general collapse of "values"; that last word, "values," is modern code for the educated belief that the central repressions, inscribed on the body as civilized nervousness, cannot hold us close enough to what they really are—the unavoidable refinements of a commanded life. Now, forty years after his first death, Freud, in his second death, signifies an inversion of his own teaching. This second, deadly Freud now teaches that repression need not be

* On the unacceptability of anything "unknown" to the modern mind, see further below, p. 377 and footnotes.

the fate of our most original desires, before they are subject to praise and blame; indeed, with this "before," baseness can be mistaken for the originality of desire.

But the essence of repression lies in a necessary turning away from direct and conscious expression of everything that is before praise and blame. A culture without repressions, if it could exist, would kill itself in closing the distances between any desire and its object. Everything thought or felt would be done, on the instant. Culture is the achievement of its unconscious distancing devices made conscious, yet indirect, in a variety of visual, acoustical, and plastic registrations. In a word, culture is repressive.

The cunning cultivated in repression, commanding intelligences unrecognized in the distortions and distances that it registers between original desire and object, may facilitate the return, by negation, of what has been repressed. In Freud's famous example, a dreamer insists that someone in his dream is "*not* my mother."[3] The psychoanalytic rule would emend this negation to: "So it *is* his mother." Negationally expressed, repressed contents seemed to Freud the credenda of consciousness vested in what is thought most incredible.

Negational—that is, modern—culture is warranted by the strangest of credulities, the one borne by those reeducated classes who believe nothing except their own endlessly shifting unbeliefs. Impiety is the latest popular piety. The canting ethic of "honesty" is heralded throughout the land. Freud has been the educator of these smart Dora's, who are not above passing the present time, into something even more self-degraded than modernity, with entertaining analyses of their endless shiftings between equally unworthy beliefs and unbeliefs. In the culture of this opening time, after Freud's closing case of modernity, every belief is the foreordained victim of an unbelief; our golem spontaneity of "impulse,"* the straw man of therapeutic cul-

---

* On "instinct" and "impulse" see Chapter Two of this book, pp. 30–34. According to Freud's usage, "impulse" and "instinct" cannot participate in any order of actual existence until they are transformed into that which limits them; those god-terms are stipulated as both a threat and the limitation of a threat. Instinct is transformed into the limit of morality. So limiting, instinct is that crucial term by which Freud maintained the distinction between desire and its opposing perfection, love. That one grows out of the other shows the power of

ture, is programmed to assert itself as the source and model of all we seek. Freud finally conjured this straw man as the "It," or *id*. Once set up, in its entirely mindless motility, then "of course . . . the id . . . knows no judgments of value: no good and evil, no morality." What could be more obvious than that "the quantitative factor . . . intimately linked to the pleasure principle, dominates all . . . processes" in the "It"?*

This is one straw man that can frighten itself. Out of this qualitative factor, fright, largely unexplored by Freud except as the anxiety that precedes repression,† there emerges the least meaningful of all Freudian conceptions: a "pure sense of guilt without any content."‡ With this phrase, Freud plunges us into the riddle of an authority ex-

---

love over desire—the morality of love. Desires have no morals. We are not polite or attentive to a glass of water when we desire it. Thirsting is not loving. Freud is entirely misunderstood when reduced to the "glass of water" theory of instinctual sexuality, or desire. There is always something splitting the condition of being in love from desire.

* "There is nothing in the id that could be compared with negation," Freud concluded (SE XXII, 74). This "nothing," without necessary form in either space or time, as the chief straw man of postmodern culture, is Freud's enemy god-term. Out of the "It," the I builds itself up. Ego is that "portion of the id which was modified by the proximity and influence of the external world" (ibid., 74). This "external world" is a representation of nothing as if it meant something. In Freudian theory, the so-called "reality principle" becomes a judgment of value.

† On repression and anxiety in Freud's theory, see his *Inhibitions, Symptoms and Anxiety*, SE XX, 160—in particular, Freud's reference to a fifth kind of resistance, "coming from the *super-ego* . . . the last to be discovered [and] also the most obscure though not always the least powerful one. It seems to originate from the sense of guilt or the need for punishment; and it opposes every move towards success, including, therefore, the patient's own recovery through analysis." The "It" Freud here repeats shows him in the condition of his chief resistance to what "It" means.

‡ Sigmund Freud, *The Origins of Psychoanalysis: Letters to Wilhelm Fliess, Drafts and Notes, 1887–1902,* ed. Marie Bonaparte, Anna Freud, and Ernst Kris, trans. Eric Mosbacher and James Strachey, with Introduction by Ernst Kris (New York: Basic Books, 1954), p. 149. (Further references to this volume are given as *Letters.*) "As to a sense of guilt, we must admit that it is in existence before the super-ego and therefore before conscience, too. At that time it is the immediate expression of fear of the external authority, a recognition of the tension between the ego and that authority" (*Civilization and It's Discontents,* SE XXI, 136). These passages (pp. 136–37) on the necessary part played in civilization by the religious sense, of guilt, are among the shortest steps Freud took toward confronting something he could not otherwise admit into his conscious, time-

ternal to, and preceding, all our moralities. Unspecified self-reproach returns unaltered with every return of the repressed. Here Freud stumbled upon what he considered the prime variety of human sickness: our insistence upon making something specific of this contentless sense of guilt.*

The prime human sickness, guilt in its pristine emptiness, seeking a content, was nothing with which Freud could wrestle—more precisely, the Nothing with which he wrestled. Of guilt as nothing specific, Freud could give no accounts except mythic, unoriginal stories of "primal" crime after crime, each set in the foundation of morality and society. Every time Freud approached the "pure sense of guilt" with the reproach of his theory, it disappeared behind the content supplied by his therapeutic myth of the first figure of authority. That content referred to an original figure of authority entirely despotic and amoral.

The myth of the first figure of authority, murdered, reappears in something as common as the death of fathers. About the common death of fathers, in its connection with the murder of authority, every mother's son is bound to suffer his own case of nerves. The case of nerves Freud suffered at the death of his father was not slight. He first reported it in a letter to his confidant Fliess. It was a

> very pretty dream I had on the night after the funeral [of his father, 25 October 1896]. I found myself in a shop where there was a notice up saying:
>
> You are requested
> to close the eyes.
>
> I recognized the place as the barber's to which I go every day. On the day of the funeral I was kept waiting, and therefore arrived at the house of mourning rather late. The family . . . took my lateness in rather bad part. The phrase on the notice-board has a double meaning. It means "one should do one's duty toward the dead" in two senses—an apology, as though I had not done my duty and my conduct

---

bound mind. (Cf., my excursus on "dogma" in the footnote on p. 358 of this book.)

* On the sickness that occurs the moment a search for meaning begins, see p. 390.

needed overlooking, and the actual duty itself. The dream was thus an outlet for the feeling of self-reproach which a death generally leaves among the survivors. . . . *

Earlier in this letter Freud had remarked how at a death the "whole past stirs within one."[4] In Chapter Six, especially, I have treated the authority of the past that stirred within Freud; in this Epilogue, I shall take one step further toward saying how that "authority" works in ways that are only apparently alterable by time.

One way to cut behind Freud's own timely questioning of authority would be to work along the same line of fracture when it reappears in another text. The Fliess line reappears in *The Interpretation of Dreams*,[5] the book with which our century began.

To say that a dream, as wish-fulfillment, must work through its means of representation, or facades, does not say clearly enough how it is used by the pure sense of guilt. Freud's guilt-line in dreams appears to have been drawn, in his interpretation of it, at least twice: once during the night before, and then again during the night after, his father's funeral. In his dream, interpreted as occurring the night before, Freud saw again

a printed notice, placard or poster—rather like the notices forbidding one to smoke in railway waiting-rooms—on which appeared either

'You are requested to close the eyes'

or

'You are requested to close an eye'.

I usually write this in the form:

'You are requested to close the/an eye(s).'

Each of these two versions had a meaning of its own and led to a different direction when the dream was interpreted. I had chosen the simplest possible ritual for the funeral, for I knew my father's own views on such ceremonies. But some other members of the family were not sympathetic to such puritanical simplicity and thought we should

---

* *Letters*, p. 171. On the hidden meaning of things seen that should not be looked at directly (for example, the sun) as "but another sublimated symbol for the father," see Freud's remarkable work on the "father-complex," *Psycho-Analytic Notes on an Autobiographical Account of a Case of Paranoia*, SE XII, 54–55.

be disgraced in the eyes of those who attended the funeral. Hence one of the versions: 'You are requested to close an eye', i.e., to 'wink at' or 'overlook'. Here it is particularly easy to see the meaning of the vagueness expressed by the 'either-or'. The dream-work failed to establish a unified wording for the dream-thoughts which could at the same time be ambiguous, and the two main lines of thought consequently began to diverge even in the manifest content of the dream.

Freud's theory was never invested* by a purer sign of his guilt than during this reported dream of a night before *and* after—a dream, after all, fulfills all possibilities and none—his father's funeral.

One possibility was closed. To keep both eyes open: that was the one thing Freud was not "requested" to do. The two versions of the line of pain by which Freud was guided in his interpretative dream, to close one or both eyes, have the same meaning: the "either-or" points us toward the necessary and determining character of Freud's sense of guilt as it appears to enliven his work.

In the sight of something superior to his ego, Freud's closed eye(s) tell us what he did not know of his own highest sensibility. That sensibility, in its negational image of looking away from something too vital for direct sight, is often disclosed uncontrolled in the work of other theorists who aim to see what is highest.† Nietzsche, for example, reticulated this image of his guilty vision into a social convention—one of those commonplace vows, made to be broken. But Nietzsche knew what it meant, than as now, to resolve, as he did on New Year's Day, 1882: *Wegsehen* sei meine einzige Verneinung!— May *looking away* be my only negation![6] Here Nietzsche describes the defining quality of negation: mind keeping secret from itself what it most wants to know.

The secret and painful resolve of mind, repression, Freud conceived

---

* What an evasive word for *besetzung* is "cathexis"; the implication of *besetzung* is of a warlike occupation or investment of an enemy position—or the filling of a vacancy and hedging it in.

† For a brief introduction to the response of meaning in "the magic of eyes," I know of nothing better than E. H. Gombrich, "Illusion and Art," in *Illusion in Nature and Art,* ed. R. L. Gregory and E. H. Gombrich (London, 1973), pp. 193–243. In particular, see p. 204 on the "sacred act . . . surrounded by strict taboos . . . of endowing a Buddha statue with eyes . . . because in painting the eyes the craftsman brings the image to life."

to be a second unconscious, both for and against its first, agonist partner, in sickness and in health: the straw man instinct or id, positive about everything—judge of nothing. From unconsciousness as a doubling of what is unknowable, Freud derived explanations for our civilized nervousness. As registrations of the affair between golem spontaneity, "instinct," and its determined friend, repression, a struggle of embraces goes on in such darkness that Freud could scarcely bear to see yet another embrace, in deepest shade—and most concerning himself.

II

In that deepest shade, Freud once thought he saw a third unconscious. This third, its range of meaning my main subject here, I see in its entitlement to be called the *repressive imperative*. By repressive imperative, I mean that authority, external to all negational recognitions of it, which splits evil and good. Authority is vested in the unalterable craving of mind for connecting oppositions—unknown and known, unconscious and conscious rejections and acceptances. The sharp division of things into dark and light characteristic of human vision gives us our first impression of authority. Call authority, dividing each of us against ourselves, the feud of what is repressive with its coda of commands (cf. Ephesians 2:15). Freud's belief, that repression operates before any idea can occur unacceptable enough to repress, implies the unalterability of authority, its priority during any occasion in which it is questioned. Often as the idea of it dies, authority is virtually immortal.

Conscious mind split from the larger unconscious, the consequent and necessary minding by conscious of unconscious ideas, speaks the secret language of power in every idea of authority. Champion of our resistances to the power of this imperative, the repressive returning, Freud was carried on the most revealing of all his passades.

> We recognize that the *Ucs.* does not coincide with the repressed; it is still true that all that is repressed is *Ucs.*, but not all that is *Ucs.* is re-

pressed. A part of the ego, too—and Heaven knows how important a part—may be *Ucs.*, undoubtedly is *Ucs.* And this *Ucs.* belonging to the ego is not latent like the *Pcs.;* for if it were, it could not be activated without becoming *Cs.*, and the process of making it conscious would not encounter such great difficulties. When we find ourselves thus confronted by the necessity of postulating a third *Ucs.*, which is not repressed, we must admit that the characteristic of being unconscious begins to lose significance for us. It becomes a quality which can have many meanings, a quality which we are unable to make, as we should have hoped to do, the basis of far-reaching and inevitable conclusions. Nevertheless, we must beware of ignoring this characteristic, for the property of being conscious or not is, in the last resort, our one beacon-light in the darkness of depth-psychology.[7]

By such a maneuver and others more mythic—all styles of cognitive avoidances, of negational recognitions, of what is called by Freud, above, the "third *Ucs.*"—the repressive imperative, being minded, becomes visible in this darkest moment of depth-psychology. Carried backwards and forwards upon his momentarily perceived paradox, of the unrepressed repressive, Freud wheeled helplessly, a virtuoso rider more commanded than commanding. Being conscious or Not: the ground of Freud's truth split beneath him. In fear, Freud retreated immediately from the third unconscious, his commanding truth. He withdrew into his inveterate talent for repressing the repressive, lest this characteristic of being take over the life of his work.

In the repressive unrepressed, Freud encountered the spiritual rule of life. That rule he could only think of as an unthinkable exception to the rule of nature—and of his theory. Yet, in this supreme denying moment of his theoretical imagination, Freud was commanded by an order of connecting oppositions that no man escapes; nor did he counsel us to try, except by maneuvers that it is the function of culture to sink into us, as character.

To survive the combined intellectualist and instinctualist assault upon the rule of incompossibility, what cannot be true together denied, we members of this emergent post-Freudian culture must learn again, through our enlistment under various registrations of the repressive unrepressed, how to narrow the range of choices otherwise open as "a cauldron of seething excitations."[8] In the reductive heat of that cauldron, no culture survives. Safely inside their culture—more precisely, the oppositional authority of a culture unsafely inside them—members of it are disposed to enact certain possibilities of behavior while refusing even to dream of others. In every culture, the best are those who know they have dreamt what the worst do.* It is unalterable authority, highly personal, repeatedly alive and inescapable, without a dead letter cluttering its code of commands, that generates this depth of character.

"Depth" is an abstraction from those unspeakably powerful immediacies of rejection and acceptance by which every man is related, as if choosing to be himself alone, at decisive moments, by the repressive imperative to itself. Mind moralizing is "a process" Freud could not help but call "unconscious." The unconscious always is in process of "*being* activated, *at the moment,* though at the *moment* we know nothing about it."[9] Moral sensibility does not need an issue of some right disgraced to be activated; Freud saw that there was something unknown and unwarranted about which it is perfectly human to feel always in the wrong.

Nothing is indifferent in the world of the repressive imperative, nothing beneath its notice of what is not to be done. Yet the repres-

---

* Freud knew who is responsible for the "evil impulses of one's dreams. . . . Obviously one must hold oneself responsible. . . . What else is one to do with them?" ("Moral Responsibility for the Content of Dreams," SE XIX, 133). That immorality should need its facades, even in dreams, gives us one relatively simple registration of the repressive imperative at work. Twenty-five years earlier, in the course of his first address to "The Moral Sense in Dreams" (1900), in *The Interpretation of Dreams* (SE IV, 66–74), Freud made parenthetical reference to one of his greatest predecessors among those who thought they saw the repressive imperative: Plato. That unsurpassed theorist understood the erotocratic nature of all tyrannies—"the reason why of old love has been called a tyrant" (*Republic* IX, 573a; Jowett transl.). Plato knew what happens in a society that encourages the cultivation of "unnecessary pleasures and desires." Then, "the wild beast in us, full-fed . . . becomes rampant and shakes off sleep to go in quest of what will gratify its own instincts. . . . [It] will cast away all shame and prudence at such moments and stick at nothing. In fantasy it will not shrink at intercourse with a mother or anyone else—man, god, or brute, or from forbidden food or any deed of blood. . . . It will go to any length of shamelessness and folly" (ibid., 571c; Cornford transl.). Then it is that the repressive imperative is said by Plato to be "asleep" (ibid.). But our ruling power never sleeps, except with one eye open. The dream, as facade, demonstrates the pure sense of guilt always at its highly composite work.

sive imperative generates a higher indifference in us all, a withdrawal from the reach of any master passion, except in the distancing condition of feeling its unutterable shame before enactment; Freud never understood this essential about his own idea of "primal repression." That "anticathexis is the sole mechanism of primal repression," that it stipulates the "process of withdrawal of libido,"* means that mastering passions are subordinate in the characterological order of the repressive itself and cannot be enthroned in absolute dominion as the Self, feasting and reveling in a world order of equally mastering passions. No society can exist, none of its very particular moralities conveyed, except through distortions and distancings of passions achieved in the repressive design of their conveyance into consciousness.

Unalterable authority, virtually immortal as moral sensibility, sinks its capacity for the higher indifference differently into every self and becomes thus individual in character. The simplest individual is an incredibly complex sensibility. In this complexity, everything truly individual grows, each in its own mystery, protected even against a culture critical of mystery. Collectivities and typologies do not exist, except as a conceptual gun held at the head of everything individual. Critical culture, in its relentless collectivizing conceptualizations, can only kill the slower and surer growths of individuality. Treated as frustrations, the protective mysteries of self no longer appear to weigh so heavily that they can slow the routine fast shuffle of stale experiences now widely cherished as "self-realization." Better not to realize

---

* Having reversed the "unpleasure-pleasure" regulation (see pp. 374–75), Freud could do no more than represent the mystery of "primal repression" in its "sole mechanism" as "anticathexis." This "*assumption* [my italics] of an *anticathexis* [Freud's italics]," which both establishes and continues every repression proper, refers to the primacy of the repressive imperative. A higher indifference is master of everything that appears to us, at any particular moment, to make all the difference in the world. On Freud's negational "Topography and Dynamics of Repression," which gives its "special characteristics" to the "system *Ucs.*," see further, SE XIV, 180–86, from which all the facets above have been cut. Now we are in a better position to see how Freud was himself being moved by the repressive imperative when he writes: "There are in this system no negation, no doubt, no degrees of certainty: all this is only introduced by the work of the censorship between the *Ucs.* and the *Pcs.* [i.e., preconscious]. *Negation is a substitute, at a higher level, for repression*" (my italics; SE XIV, 186). Here, unconsciously offered to eternal authority, is the intellectualizing symbol of rebellion: negation.

this Self, in a panic to express the fecundity of its own emptiness.

If erotocratic culture could become unauthorized enough, by beating the brains out of the mastering passion, by promoting the fecundity of emptiness, then everything could be expressed by everyone identically and nothing would remain to be expressed individually. To prevent the expression of everything is to preclude the one truly egalitarian dominion: nothingness. These preclusions are the irreducible and supreme activity of culture in its momentous detail of command, with its provision of possible disobediences and casuistries of convenience.

There is nothing static about any culture so far as it registers a code of unalterable authority. By its creation of what we are now pleased to name opposing "values" or "ideals," culture fastens its seals of disapproval upon the terrific capacity of mind to express nothing by seeking to express everything. But words such as "values" become like our "ideals"—both best engage our affection when they are lost forever and preferred that way. Our "values" and "ideals" are dead-god terms, nostalgia made to look like living moralities.

The absolute dominion of desires, the mass production of endless "needs" as the object of late modern culture, is a prescription for filling our common lives with panic and emptiness. The end of this insane condition will not much resemble our present democratic child's play with toy authorities. After this preliminary child's play, there always occurs the main event, the great game of parricide in which every man is invited to play the next egalitarian despot. Our developing erotocracy trains every man to be his own despot, toward the achievement of a character so brazen that denials of the repressive imperative will be no longer necessary. The late modern Yea is designed to carry no prohibiting Amen. Made altogether human or abstracted as "society," the repressive imperative is to be censored as something unnecessarily limiting our expressive options.

Truth, as a minding of the repressive imperative, is universally censorious. Given its compelling character, truth is less frightening to recognize in negations of it. But as this entire culture has turned negational, words reporting the censorship at work should be given inside quotation marks, as I have done above. When truth ceases to be compelling, then we know the censorship must be undoing what it has done. We stew in our own "values" and hope—rationally—for a descent of "ideals" that will make something extraordinarily true and beautiful of the endless "needs" by which life has been made into an indecent tease.

In its sociological meaning, a truth ordinarily makes things happen relentlessly against the extraordinary human capacity for expressing everything—that "everything" of which "sexuality" is the post-Freudian prototype. Repression is truth experienced negationally. The repressive imperative is truth informing every experience of its denial. To make love is not the militant sociability alternative to making war. God is not love, except as It is authority. Freud never declared himself for love and against authority. Love will not be separated from authority. To be for mortal love and against immortal authority yields a mirage within which no rectitude will ever be seen. The unbreakable link between the spirit of love and the flesh of authority is succeeded, in Freud's theory, by yet another link, equally unbreakable: between the need for punishment and the unconscious sense of guilt. True minding will not tolerate pleasures unpaid for in parallel pains. Inhibition is the price of entry into every real satisfaction. Every revolutionary child should be taught that he can live in a tolerably peaceable kingdom only if he enters in at what Jesus called the "strait gate"—and, moreover, if he acknowledges the power of the gatekeeper to shut him out for reasons that will be breached by no excuse.

Every order of actual existence, individual and collective, character and culture, derives from the recurrent splitting motion by which master passions are kept at a civilizing distance from direct enactment. Repression, not sublimation, represents the ruling power of culture.* So far as their truth goes, our arts and sciences conceal shifts in obedience—call it "freedom"; those arts and sciences try to make less painful, or at least more attractive, what they reveal of the repressive imperative. Negational acknowledgments of that apparently unknown

---

* On the meaning of "sublimation," see p. 387. See further "Toward A Theory of Culture," in *The Triumph of the Therapeutic* (New York, 1966), p. 5ff.

imperative are given in compelling evasions; resistances are self-protective only if what they acknowledge is revealed so far, and no farther, in each evasive action. Neuroses are tired resistances; they are individual expressions of a culture that is losing its secret language for mobilizing ignorant armies specially trained to clash by night—and so keep the daytime peace.

As events and artifacts of culture, these evasive nighttime actions are usually associated with another kind of action, called "symbolic." To reveal more, in more dangerously direct ways than any symbolic action allows, appears to destroy the intensely concentrated force with which repression invades every expression. Repression lets there be done on a deep but narrow front what is not to be done more broadly. Upsetting the balance, ignoring the feints, of this striking force behind expression, is a sure way to the impoverishment of expression. To reveal, in life and art, more than distancing and concealing mindfulness allows, must invite the fatigue of trench warfare. Tired as they are, neuroses express the immobility of this trench warfare against the repressive imperative. In its fundamental everyday strategy of relentless attack, the repressive imperative minds us against being merely defensive. By contrast, a neurosis is a digging-in along lines of which its defenders grow heartily tired and wish to surrender. Merely defensive, human beings may become so miserable as not to know their own misery; they refuse to know how much they know; they will not admire their own artistry in life nor admire that artistry when they see it in other lives. The neurotic does not have generous emotions. The neurotic is highly critical, not least of Freud's injunction to think uncritically.

Especially in our dreams, we know that we are all generously endowed, as if artists and scientists, with striking powers of evasion. What elaborate facades disguise the powers of moral sensibility. Even before we wake to know, for certain, that we have been dreaming, our assertions of what has been evaded are derisory: they permit us to continue asleep. Ordering as it does every actual existence, the repressive imperative never sleeps. On the contrary, we sleep to sharpen our memories of order in that imperative, to be more at ease before its oppositional command to the sleeper: "Wake."

In the night of sleep, the confusion of commanding orders seems more clear than in waking day. Command itself seems afflicted by dividing mind. Every serving man is torn by a conflict in obedience to the allied first and second officers of repressive and instinctual command. Here is a laugh: to call "freedom" the distortions and disorders that occur in mind as parallels that meet only in the necessary conflict of obedience to raising and lowering commands. Human "freedom" is an inaudible whistle to a confused dog.

Such limited visions of freedom as Freud's are admirably humane. He saw how nostalgia attacks the latest passion. In Freud, the good advice to abandon hope becomes highly specific. The compassionate alternative to a neurosis is not some impossible dream of health, but a life more artful in its self-limitation.* A neurosis is a nostalgia, some passion for what cannot be had.

Even a Caliban is so nostalgic in his morality that he wants what he cannot have, something he both likes and dislikes and imagines to be entirely unlike himself, the fair Prospero's daughter. The Freudian Caliban inside cannot have what it likes; it cannot like what it has. The Freudian Prospero dare not admit all his Caliban has lost and yearns for; knowing too much, too directly, would be to risk recovering what is better lost by the both of them together. But the repressive unrepressed brings the Caliban of desire, for its own daughter's father, dangerously near open knowledge. Then it is that love-objects of the divided self must be consciously given up. Prospero's knowing final renunciation of hope, the power-magic of his kingdom, returns him to the incompossibilities of his ordained actual existence. This exemplary return, from the kingdom of power-magic, may help us see the magistral sense Freud made, in *The Interpretation of Dreams,* when he first called his pleasure principle by its original name, the unplea-

---

* The abandonment of hope is a discipline for living every present moment in life, not some future-oriented despair of things as they are and ever shall be. "It is impossible to live artistically before one has made up one's mind to abandon hope; for hope precludes self-limitation" (S. Kierkegaard, *Either/Or* [Princeton, 1949], Vol. I, p. 240; trans. D. F. Swenson and L. M. Swenson). In *Hope Abandoned* (New York, 1974, p. 266), N. Mandelstam gives posterity this sentence: "A sense of guilt is man's greatest asset."

sure principle.* Nothing appears simpler than a renunciation. But this "Nothing" has a more complex genesis. Every psychological man must now be critical enough to know that *The Tempest* is a comedy and, moreover, that the most comical element in the play is the hidden fact that the right Duke of Milan, His Grace Prospero, is the legitimate father of that savage and deformed slave-eloquence, Caliban. It follows, therefore, that Caliban is the only child of Prospero's lawful enemy, his witch wife, Sycorax. Not only does the authority of Prospero rule but that rule hides the defiant baseness of his passions. Authority always conceals its own problems.

III

Simple-mindedness is a luxury no theorist can afford. Simplicity is an achievement of rare subtle minding. Look obediently at any order of actual existence; all reveal that none permit a simple-minded practice of what they teach—not without the complicity of mutually accusing exceptions to every rule. Both as theorist and therapist, Freud was always making exceptions; his own rigid rules of procedure shifted with each case. The second death of Freud, some forty years after his first, is a tragedy of his imagination rendered more and more remissive, the cunning of desire deified as the principle undoing what is not to be done.

Guilt may be denied; precisely so, it is the secret agent of public order. At the moment, certain noisy denials constituting our current movements of liberation from the sense of guilt have defeated the

---

* What follows may be used as one small key to the primary experience of Freud's flight from the repressive imperative that was transformed by his followers into dogma.

Freud's authorized editors, on noting the basic reversal of the god-term "*unpleasure* principle" into "*pleasure* principle," write only the following: "In his later works Freud speaks of it [i.e., the unpleasure principle] as the 'pleasure principle'" (*The Interpretation of Dreams*, SE V, Part 2, 600). The reversal is conceived, in this dogmatic footnote, as not of the slightest theoretical significance.

intense listening by which Freud communicated his lessons toward the less miserable conduct of our lives. Freud's silence accuses the post-Freudian noise. To suppose that Freud's theory and therapy can help abolish the pure sense of guilt goes beyond his own ambition. Freud never supposed he could bend the higher powers to his own or any other will. In that supposition, the "guiltless" take a further step away from acknowledging that their lives, too, are first lived in an order that is sacred.

Yet there derives from Freud's mind more than any other that fresh symbolic action, repressing the repressive, from which this century has taken its direction. So the noise of our lives rises to a pitch that deadens the senses to any messages from our own hidden existence, and this deadening we now call "culture."

Directive symbolics of hidden existence contain their own exceptions; they secretly incorporate opposing contents into themselves. No symbolic order operates without its ideology of what is interdictory. How, then, to find our way into that hidden existence to which each of us belongs in our own way? Jesus knew, no less well than his Pharisaic opponents, that culture demands a narrowing of possibilities. At the strait gate, no optional lifestyles need apply. "Narrow is the way which leadeth into life." That narrowing life is actually our graceful first, decisively opposed to and latent in the manifestly awkward second.

Each of us lives a double life, latent first and manifest second. If lived in its full simultaneity, then such a double life would find the famous "Kingdom of God" always at hand. Our "Kingdom" is no more in some future life than in the past; rather, in the virtual immortality of our double lives, that compulsive repetition which Freud saw only as neurotic.

The neurotic fact remains that few live their double lives in full simultaneity. Even those specially gifted with communicable primary imaginations, spend much of their energies trying to resist the directions set in repressive ordinances. Behind every great art, like every neurosis, there lies a deeper disobedience. Freud did not probe the deeper disobediences except in mythic form; and even to him, these myths—for example, the murder of the primal father—seemed to mock the scientific status of his thoughts. Later Freudian dogma impoverished Freud's thought in order to protect a scientific status it never had.*

The narrowing, commanded first life never appears entirely in the second as of its own right—except as the vision of someone who may well be a player of hoaxes on the second. Reports of the first life, even when themselves acutely negational, like Freud's, are usually dismissed as fantasy, hoax—or "Art." Unconscious mind is still widely considered preposterous, a paradoxical conceit of Freud's; what can this "unknown" known be except a broad joke on the spirit of strictly scientific inquiry? When science acts as if it were successive hostile penetrations of what is "unknown"—a more accurate word for Freud's intended meaning than "unconscious"†—then the history of science becomes a history of one false religiosity after another. For example: what puerile little pictures of death our newly scientized thanatologists paint. Freud had the decency to picture "Death" in its capital meaning, as a "gentleman known" not only to a certain dreamer but to Freud himself as the "great Unknown."‡

Broad as a bad joke is the way through the vale in which every man lives his more important life, first by virtue of its ordaining functions with respect to the second. A way of life functions best along its angles of division. Each *Not,* an interdict to be observed in practice along boundary lines drawn in repressive design, commands its other side. Those two sides, immediate to every issue in life, interpenetrate. Divided as they are, opposing sides come to resemble one another; they are consubstantial. No rock is so hard that it will not yield in time to water, air, something apparently soft. Cézanne colored his rocks to be

---

* Chapter One of this book ends by showing how early the label "unscientific" was affixed to Freud (p. 26).

† See *The Interpretation of Dreams,* SE V, Part 2, 528. Cf. the reference to the precise German word for unconscious in Freud's usage, "Unbewusst," in the essay "A Note on the Unconscious," in *Psycho-Analytic Notes . . . ,* SE XII, 266.

‡ This picturing of "Death as the 'great Unknown,'" in capital letters (SE V, Part 2, 472), expressed Freud's own awe, however ironically conveyed, of a "gentleman" about whom he thought much and domesticated little. That "gentleman" seemed to him, as to Job, no gentleman. Freud's rather frequent thoughts of dying have not been assimilated into the cosier visions of contemporary thanatology. The "death instinct" remains the most embarrassing god-term in the Freudian canon, even less popular than his notion that he was not a pansexualist.

consubstantial with air and vegetation.* The differing elements are indebted one to another for all that they are, in their individualities. Some debts must remain unpaid. Knowing that much about the richness of the first life, we can better tolerate the moral ambiguity of the second. Toleration of moral ambiguity, however, is nothing like the solacements of cinematic jump-cuts, those fantasy techniques by which we get through a door, or past a boundary, miraculously to appear ahead of ourselves, coming from the opposite direction. Consubstantiality is not a tricking-out of images spliced together on film. Such knowledge as we may have of the repressive in its imperatives cannot be registered on film. Here, on film, we can see the first true anti-art, entirely incompetent to frame any vision of the repressive imperative. Film is the antitheoretical art of modernity. Filmic "art" is limited entirely to representations of the second life. This gives us one reason why the theoretical culture of the book, lettered visions of the highest, cannot be put on film.

It is well known that where there is no such vision, but only television, people perish. When the first life is treated as some ancient and inhibiting superstition, or as a pathology of the second, then both eyes may open to the sight of one nothing after another. This flickering nullity sees itself on television and knows its greatest art has become the art of killing time.

---

* I owe this reading of Cézanne to the teaching of my friends and colleagues at the University of Pennsylvania, Leo Steinberg and Lawrence Gowing. "There is no such thing as [dividing] line or modeling, . . . there are only [color] contrasts," pronounced Cézanne. Gowing adds: "He lived by them. We can imagine him living among them" (Lawrence Gowing, "The Logic of Organized Sensations," in *Cézanne: The Late Work* [New York, 1977], p. 61). This "self-sufficient fabric of color contrast, which is hardly legible as form in any specific or detailed sense," stipulates Cézanne's culminating ambivalence toward sacred order realized in patches of color. Freud liked to visualize the "mental apparatus" as a "landscape of varying configuration—hill-country, plains, and chains of lakes—, with a mixed population . . . who carry on different activities. Now things might be partitioned. . . . [But] if the partitioning could be neat and clear-cut, . . . a Woodrow Wilson would be delighted by it; it would also be convenient for a lecture in a geography lesson. The probability is, however, that you will find less orderliness and more mixing, if you travel through the region" (*New Introductory Lectures*, SE XXII, 72–73). The "region" Freud travelled through was his hated god-term, the "id"—"we call it a chaos" (ibid., 73). On the delights of Mr. Wilson, as understood in the Freudian way, see my essay "14 Points on 'Wilson,' " *Encounter*, Vol. 28, No. 4 (April 1967), pp. 84–89.

Within the normative tension of leading simultaneously the acknowledged second and unacknowledged first life, human beings are left on edge. As each must lead this double life, all acquire their cases of nerve. Shakespeare noticed that canker blooms take colors no less deep than roses. All cases have their nerve in common. This universal insolence comes in a rich variety; each insolence dismisses the first life as a fantasy of the second. The risk of transgression always present within that unknown first life, sacred order, lies in the cleverness with which, in the second life, we refuse all sight of commanding truths that must derive from the first. In this confusion, our lives take on their necessary conflicts of meaning. So penetrant into the second life is the repressive imperative, our first lives minded, that it makes consubstantial with itself every dividing line, every adjoining terrain that mind's eye can possibly see.

IV

To live in sacred order is to have our obediences stretched to the breaking point by its oppositional truths. Anyone insolent enough to become a full practitioner of what he preaches, or who tries to preach what he practices—such supremely edgy moralists as Oedipus and Hamlet, to name only two—must doubt every oppositional order in the might of its hidden existence. At the same time, doubters of sacred order cannot help but recognize a command to which they submit their doubts: "I believe—Help Thou mine unbelief."

Oedipus and Hamlet, both, enacted their guilt knowledge of the truths opposing them in their own hidden existences. The Oedipal search for knowledge was a confirmation of what Oedipus knew was forbidden him to know. Hamlet challenged his sense of guilt as less daring men have been advised to cultivate their gardens: passionately. Both Oedipus and Hamlet attempted to break the repressive design of their lives; so did Freud. All succeeded only in retracing it.

Even toward the end of his career as a theoretical man, Freud never ceased to write out his hidden grievance against the sense of guilt as the agency of the sacred in its judicial function. By now no judge of sacred order, in its expressive agencies, should find, as Freud did, that

> It is a remarkable thing that the super-ego often displays a severity for which no model has been provided by the real parents, and moreover that it calls the ego to account not only for its deeds but equally for its thoughts and unexecuted intentions, of which the super-ego seems to have knowledge. This reminds me that the hero of the Oedipus legend too felt guilty for his deeds and submitted himself to self-punishment, although the coercive power of the oracle should have acquitted him of guilt in our judgment and his own.*

The censorious judgments against the censorship, made by theoretical men—for example, Oedipus, Hamlet, Nietzsche, Freud—were advances backward, crablike, toward the indifferent unity of opposites, that unity they supposed to exist "before good and evil," as the old saying should go. In life-acts, if not quite in art, "before" must be transgressive in content and demands punishment; not quite, I say, because art is not life. A picture of a horse is not a horse. The famous old horse-god is not a god but a horse using mirrors as its instrument of revolt against self-limitation.

Every revolt of Self against self-limitation invites punishment as the form of its relation to Not-self. It was for this reason that Freud equated "need for punishment" with "pure sense of guilt." The apparent lack of content in guilt is the punishment that anticipates the crime of Self, willing against Not-self. The crime of Self is concealed in suffering—Job's sort of secret—which saves all who hope to find a way out of repressive design from being merely the figures of insolence they are. As well-known adventurers up blind alleys, both Hamlet and Oedipus are saved for tragedy by their irresistible sense of guilt, by their insistence that what they suffered was the most signifying thing in their

---

* "The Internal World," in *An Outline of Psychoanalysis*, SE XXIII, 205. Freud's last account of his guilt-ridden master ideas, which he began to write in July 1938 and broke off writing that September, just a year before his death. (Cf. my distinction between the parent question and the question of parents, p. 393.) That Freud did not feel acquitted of guilt, in his own judgment, any more than did Oedipus, makes of his depth psychology a grievance procedure against the sacred no less bitter than Job's parody of the eighth Psalm (Job 7:17–21).

lives. Without that sense, they would have made themselves believe anything—anything; even that incest could be the pure therapy resolving pure guilt.

In their pure guilt, all those who suffer the sense of it feel the secret intelligence of the unrepressed repressive. With this intelligence, what is repressive directs conscious will and moral choice to function as agent, in character, of sacred order. From hidden existence derives every known existence. The success of the modern revolt against the repressive imperative can be measured by the degree to which what is now changeable as knowing life styles, sometimes called "role-playing," was once graven as character. "Character" once meant the inability to play any role except the one in which it had been cast.

Character is sacred order inscribed upon the body, sometimes in arabesques so rich in detail that they cannot be read. One clue to the reading of what is sacred in character is that its details are arranged hierarchically. In its hierarchy of enacted motifs—interdictory, remissive, and transgressive—human experience becomes moral. What is human moves vertically, up or down; the modalities of sacred order commit us to our erect postures. Yet, now more massively than when this book first appeared almost a generation ago, movements on behalf of prone positions, excusing reasons for lying down, dominate Western society. The morality of post-modernity is remissive on principle rather than in furtive practice. To abolish morality as character: that is the aim dominating all except those for whom sacred order is inscribed in the detail of their bodily motions. In such characters, to suffer and celebrate sacred order are the same, neither masochist nor sadist, but pain voided in its acceptance.

That Freud appears a remissive theorist, seeing some optional yes in the most adamant no, accounts for the closeness of his otherwise distant connections with current exemplary horrors within Freud's field of clinical interest: the erotic life of the mind. Movements such as Homosexualism, Pansexualism, Bisexualism, Transsexualism—these pilot abominations in sacred order have nothing to do with Freud. And yet Freud authorized the modernizing movement toward the abolition of character. He was the theorist crucial to the latest efforts to invert the relations between Self and Not-self.

Indeed, Freud made over into a negational faith the most illusory hope of all modernizing theories, including his own: that sacred order is finally abolished and only its affects linger. But sacred order is taking an eternity getting itself abolished. In theory, psychoanalytic therapy is interminable, but it is only so because of the interminability of that which it addresses. Because its inner connection with the survival of humanity runs along the fault line of self-respect, the repressive imperative so far survives every movement to deny it that the denials only make sense in its terms.

The shaming state of these modernizing efforts at denial is transparently obvious.* That Freud is now excommunicate from the erotocratic movements of post-modernity, in its dogmatic denials of the repressive imperative, follows from his being so near, and yet so far, from its massive jumble of inverting pieties. Post-Freudian man constructs his pieties toward what is lowering rather than raising in those hierarchies of conduct and thought which characterize our responses as life within sacred order. Shamelessness is the idealized state of things in late modernity. So far ahead, of anything we can become, have we shadows of the future tried to jump that Freud seems more the latest connoisseur of sacred order than the theorist of our latest and ugliest† inversions of it.

The charge that Freud was a connoisseur of what is virtually immortal in its artfulness is true enough. Conscientiously negational, Freud became the most influential symbolist of the return of sacred order in the twentieth century. In this compacture of the sacred and its negations, Freud drew up his agreement with the twentieth century: to check the judgmental power of the first life over the second. It would appear, by this time, safe to say why Freud failed. In its regis-

---

* Freud imagined rightly that when this "shaming state of things" had happened before, as in the period of Baal worship among the ancients of Israel, "later tendentious efforts to throw a veil" over the shaming state of things may have a certain success (*Moses and Monotheism*, SE XXIII, 124). I suspect that it is never too late for such veils to be thrown by those who take the sense of guilt as the chief thing to be brought under their pedagogic custody.

† Among the many facets of Picasso's genius, there may be one that makes him the supreme theorist of ugliness in the twentieth century. I have only the crudest, untrained sense of Picasso as a theoretical man—which he certainly was. I do see enough to see that Picasso painted and drew his denials of sacred order with a facility and courage that must dazzle even the most trained eye.

trations, the repressive imperative guarantees that failure. The higher powers meet us in the power of judgment, guilt sensed before any act. That just the most moral feel themselves condemned, that freedom from the passions is the highest passion: these register old truths beyond the acting capacity of Freud's new symbolic to do anything but repeat; repressive registrations, acceptable distortions, are the matter of Freud's true science—and of his art.

There are no limits on the range of repressive registrations. All our arts and sciences are distancings and distortions of conscious mindings, transgressive possibilities that contain a guilt no less releasing and creative than its negational theorists label as inhibiting. Creativity is a function of this inhibition. To doubt the creativity of guilt is to doubt our moral sense; to doubt our moral sense is to deny the identity of truth and beauty. I have already given the last name Freud gave to this denial: "anxiety." In their anxious arts and sciences, those who would abolish the sense of guilt suffer themselves to be heavily attended. The price we pay for their negations ·is consciousness hospitalized, culture transformed into an out-patient clinic.

Negational sharpenings in the sense of guilt herald another return of the sacred. The manic mood in Western society swings again toward depression. Freud remarked signs of a general depression at the time when Paul became the chief theorist of an earlier return of the sacred. A dull malaise and premonitions of calamity blanketed the world out of which came Christianity. That world felt sick and Christ came with healing force. To Freud's generations, other signs, less of old sickness than of newly found health, had been given; but they were not the business of this book, no more than was the playing-off of other theorists against him. There is raw material enough in Freud that continues to tell against him, as does the life act of every other theorist supreme in his vision of sacred order.

V

What tells against Freud is that he achieved greatly detailed guilt-knowledge of himself—knowledge of the most passionate kind, conducive to the second life lived inside its proper limits. Freud scrupled to tell his readers as little as he could of what he would know about himself. In that highest respect, Freud knew the uses of guilt with which faith begins. As a negational symbolist, what Freud must leave untold, in particular to our reeducated classes, is the fact that faith begins where the sense of guilt ends. Modern culture is pervaded by a sense of false guilt. At the empty center of that guilt is the inability of the educated classes to produce, on behalf of the uneducated, the last thing in good looks, some vision of happiness without tears.

Faithlessness is the Self claiming everything, including the sense of guilt, on its own behalf. Faith is the opposing Not-self recognized in all its endlessly faceted claims, as they are made against us on our behalf. It follows that not even the most faithful can have perfect faith; there are too many angles in that repressive state of being for any to see through all those lines of compacture along which sacred order bounds social order.

The fact that mind's eye must be partly blind does not mean that faith, to its own advantage, contrasts itself critically against faithlessness. Guilt sensed in its pure repressiveness need no longer pretend a superior innocence. Ignorance is never innocent. This lack of pretense is faith. The world of the faithful is never a stage; no man need be a role player. The threat of being ashamed of oneself is wisdom in fear before the act. Only in this inhibiting wisdom of fear, the knowing faith that trusts no rationalization of knowledge, does autonomous Reason, like every other autonomous "value," become too irrational and indecent for conscious consideration. The sociological test of faith is always a question of what there is, indubitably greater than anything rationalized in the course of one's second life, for which that life rightly may be given up. Decency and faith are inseparable. The decent thing is not even to consider doing what is not to be done.

Indecent rationalizing movements against culture in any form are nothing new. The rationalizing eye of mind was not sharpened yesterday. In its critical symbolism, rationalizing intellect, in search of its autonomy, was no less indecent during the regimes of King Oedipus or Prince Hamlet than it is in that of psychological man. Freud could find no greater incarnations from which to draw his theory than these two passionate rationalizers of the possibility that there is a way out of sacred order.* We mistake the power of rationalization if we think it cold. Rationalization, the autonomy of every "value" from every other, is the hottest item on which mind has ever sold itself.

Along lines so razor sharp, a great theoretical truth works its concealed way back into human consciousness: if divided at acute enough angles of criticism, dazzling the eye of faith often enough, then mind, alone, divides guilt from self-esteem. So divided in mind, connecting activities of repressive design will go subtly unrecognized: either in guilt alone or, more in the abolitionist mood, in explorations of negational self-esteem, critical of everything, culminating in a self-hatred Freud called "Oedipal." This quality of self-hatred directs the aggression of negational mindfulness. Negation of the repressive imperative is the critical force with which Freud, not alone, acknowledged that very imperative. The hubris of Oedipus consisted in seeing through his criticism of sacred order. Beyond this criticism, there is nothing but the acting out of everything perverse that is latent in criticism of sacred order.

Is there any way out of our hypercritically divided lives except into the deadly comradeship of perverse sophistications? Which gate to the privileges of simplicity? Those who become older and more backward-looking in their vision, more experienced and less afraid to live under the authority of the past, may learn again how to cut clean, simple, and short lines into apparently unfaceted reality. Freud was a great moment in the development of the cutting class. But neither Freud's nor any other critical intellectualizing can make a decisive cut through the transgressive plenitude of possibility. Therefore, in its dogma of safety in numbers, the cutting class expands at an accelerating rate. So quickly

---

* That Freud owed most to Sophocles and Shakespeare (cf. *The Interpretation of Dreams*, SE IV, Part I, 264) and least to the scientific psychology of his era shows us how dangerous scientific training can be to the mental life of the scientist when poetry is excluded from what is conceived as significant in his training. William James said this best, in the conclusion of his Gifford Lectures, *The Varieties of Religious Experience*: "Humbug is humbug, even though it bear the scientific name, and the total expression of human experience, as I view it objectively, invincibly urges me beyond the narrow 'scientific' bounds" (London, rev. ed., 1902, p. 519). Much of what passes for contemporary social Science is— Humbug. (Cf. pp. 376–77 on Freudian dogma as to humbug.)

does the cutting class reproduce itself that more and more objects must be produced for the critical slaughter; it is as if creation gave full employment to destruction.

To act out a more restrained relation to everything created takes a lifetime of preparation and a much slower rate of criticism reproducing itself. Our critical culture waits its Malthus. The privileges of simplicity are universally available, but they can only be cultivated in disciplines that recognize a decorum superior to critical intellectualizing. Decorum is a respectful treating with the consubstantialities of life locked into distancing devices so subtle that rarely are we given more than an amused hint of their inclusive workings.

What can the Freudian art of reading signs of the repressive imperative do to help retrain generations lost to the civilizing art, decorum? One source of decorum in Freud is his expectation that what will happen has already happened. Another source is in Freud's therapeutic silence, a stoic form of self-amusement. Silence expresses the honor of Freudian intellect offended at the canting hypercritical pieties of the present age. The releasing mechanisms of a culture, both square and counter, in which transgressions are considered therapeutic, may be wild psychoanalysis inflated into populist erotocracy, but Freud did not suffer gladly the wild men of his own movement, let alone those of others. He took the future out of new illusions even more enduringly than out of old, so far as the new does not repeat the old.

Once a turn again is made away from the hypercritical second life, character may become more decorous in its modesty about what can and cannot be cleaned up in the world mess, ourselves in it. Especially as our second life, the hypercritical, draws toward its close, the compacture of the first, living as it does in sacred order, can be resisted less perversely. The great pleasure of acknowledging the authority of the past is in becoming more freely obedient to returns of the sacred. Those returns have occurred before, through respectfully resistant individualities. It is this eternal recurrence of repressive unrepressed that makes us ever so lonely, even in the communion of our resistances. In its persistence, the repressive imperatively isolates each from all in the All that we are.

In the reserve, even the incommunicability, of every response to sacred order, personality is forged. There is no other way of becoming oneself, except alone in this response. Now we know how mass movements mount their appeal. The "masses" name all those who are too desperately afraid of being alone and silent, each in his own eternal moment. The silence of those moments is too easily filled by transgressive conduct arguing its right to express everything that comes to mind.

No brute expresses, as humans do, the imagination to shrink from nothing. Humans first test in imagination the possibilities of breaking through sacred order. But between image and act is the ordained space of actual existence. In that space, everything human finds its history and grows up. By "infantile," the condition of never growing up, Freud should have meant the transgressive. Except in this stipulation there is no such thing as regression, no more than there is "sublimation" —that most gentlemanly and positive sop, thrown by the negationally cultivated at everything consecrated. The fatal softness of negational culture and of its scientific studies is now papered over with academic niceties about "sublimation," the better to publish and perish with the fact that "sublimation" does not exist. "Sublimation" is to repression as Unitarianism is to Christianity: too high-minded to be true. Regression" is mind engaged in the act of lowering itself in sacred order, as if "lower" means "earlier" or more "natural."

That the unbreakable connection of self with sacred order is best seen in the sense of guilt demands a step further than intellect, naively critical of anything that takes it where it has been before, likes to take. In its purity, the sense of guilt is unnatural; it does not receive except to reject; it does not feel except to judge. Other senses are openings out; the sixth sense, of guilt, is a closing in. Every other sense participates in the sixth. To give a major example: as the eye closes, so innocence ends—too often and automatic for counting.

The repressive imperative is first expressed in splitting judgments. Every falsification of faith in this form consists in some negational surrogate of judgmental splitting—the inseparability of Marxism from its polemic in favor of general hatred, "class struggle," is one prime example of a negational surrogate.

Surrogates of faith can be so miserable that they conquer all knowledge of them. Freud called the most incommunicable misery "psychosis." To be completely ill at ease in sacred order, to reject entirely one's life in that order, is to become psychotic.* In psychosis, the first life is gravely injured, by being too far withdrawn from the second. Nervous illnesses are injuries of resistance to sacred order returning in those who wish not to mind it. Reason is capable of the most bizarre rejections, often disguised as acceptances, of sacred order. The most injurious resistances to the return of the sacred often appear most rational.

VI

Are these injuries of resistance to what is always there accidental? Freud knew better. Nothing is accidental.

Take the case of Cain. By his unrecorded chatting up of authority, in words judged not worth repeating, Cain tried to make an offer that the unrepressed repressive could not refuse; this offering was a "symbol" or "projection" of Cain's own authority. In sheer pique at the rejection of his symbolic offering (Genesis 4:3–8), Cain's way out occurs as if by accident; with malice aforethought against quite an other, Cain kills his brother. The question whether Cain attempts to marry his mother appears passed over in silence. Instrumental rationality, the forearming of ego-resistances to the repressive imperative, first came into the world by apparently accidental injury. That is how accidents happened: they appeared as premature offerings strayed casually into a mine field of action. Authority was to be taken unaware by being made an accomplice in crime after crime against its brotherhood of surrogates.

As the first taker of a step against authority so symbolic that it may be supposed to have gone along, Cain became our first critical intellectual. Critical intellect must suppose authority captive in its own sym-

---

* On the connections between the sacred and the psychotic, however dimly seen, cf. Freud's working through of Schreber's memoirs in *Psycho-Analytic Notes . . .* , SE XII, 9–82.

bolic offerings. All such offerings may be catalogued under the title "Enlightenments." Counter-Enlightenments have no chance of developing until we learn again how to produce repetitional readings of the sacred rather than symbolic offerings that aim, however unconsciously, to take over its power. Until modernity, no class has made offerings more symbolic than the religious professionals. The first critical intellectual became a missionary. He wandered the earth in search of his faith.

Cain's line of succession leads to Freud. What has been asked of critical intellect in each generation between Cain and Freud, as a question of parents in one displacement or another, is the parent question of humanity: *"Am I Thy Master or art Thou Mine?"*

One difficulty with asking the parent question is that every Thou learns to mistake itself for the I. For this mistake, the blame is not entirely thine or mine. In sacred order, nothing is simple; everything invites being interpreted—and, therefore, distanced. The repressive, in its public and shared imperative as interpretation, cannot be followed if it is always expected to be closely followed. The trained voice of conscience cannot tell the whole truth simply and yet expect it to be nothing but the truth. Trained in the arts of interpretation, conscience has the supple throat of a Baroque prima donna; it is as facile as it is disciplined. In its remissive flex, the singing voice of sacred order is too supple for us to assume there is no element of disorder in it. But authority is not interested in high intellectualizing principle; it has a passion for the practical details of conduct. In the order of actual existence, as in every great art, detail is everything—more precisely, the controlling repetition of detail is everything. Here is reason enough to follow the commandments in detail; then and only then will high and general principle follow.

In the elbow room between high principle and the details of conduct, each human being is moved, as through Keats' famous "vale of Soul-making," a certain distance from every other—until, as Keats said, "each one is personally itself."[10] Psychological man is pleased to denounce life in this vale of soul-making as "sick." Freud was psychological man enough. So he could write, even toward the close of his life, in a letter to Marie Bonaparte: "The moment one inquires about the sense or value of life one is sick, since objectively neither of them has any existence."[11] But in the vale of soul-making, no two men are sick in the same way. Each differs from the other in all that he is, in the lines of communication established the longest way round, between sacred order and self.

Psychological man is nothing if not clever and cultivated in the aggression of finding ways of travelling round the vale of soul-making. "Therapy" has become a general word describing our present distraction from the unavoidable soul-making journey. Freud prepared this great symbolic offer to take over the repressive imperative in its work. It follows that he found "the repression of aggression is the hardest part to understand."[12] He continued to think it "easy to establish the presence of 'latent' aggression, but whether it is . . . latent through repression or in some other way is not clear. What usually happens is that this aggression is latent or repressed through some counter-compensation, i.e., through an erotic cathexis. And with that one approaches the theme of ambivalency, which is still very puzzling."[13] His own ambivalencies could not cease to puzzle Freud. He resisted that parallel of aggression repressed which would reveal, in every case including his own, a traversed limit.[14] The parallel of every true aggression is that it is a transgression, some lowering move we make inside a sacred order from which there is no escape. Nothing is outside sacred order.

Everything about the manner of our being moved through the vale of soul-making makes a secret of the commanding order, transgressions included, by which humanity seizes its initiative of highly symbolic offers, so to settle the question of authority on its own terms. As the sovereign maker of symbolic offers in our century, Freud showed again the dangers inherent in publicizing surrogates as if they were the masterly thing itself. Almost forty years after his death, it is still widely believed that Freud was talking about sexuality as if it were the master passion itself and not an effort to compromise equally intolerable feelings of being nothing and being everything—that supersession of the erotic which has nothing to do with pansexualism and everything to do with the higher indifference.

Bound as he is to be unsatisfied with his own answers, any maker of symbolic offerings to the parent question risks falling into an illness un-usable in his peculiar creative act. Freud's "surplus of unsatisfied libido," the sublime hypochondriasis of his resistance theory of the sacred returning as neurosis, was bound to lead to "grief and depression."[15] Representative negations are the most defeating games anyone can play; that is why so few choose to play them. So much is at stake that most of us cannot bear to watch the game in progress; some cautionary wisdom tells us not to risk the defeat of following the game closely. Granted our tendency to I-Thou reversals, close readings of the repressive imperative in its experienced varieties of concealment would bring us dangerously near despair at any reading; the closer the reading, the greater the concealment.

How prudent of Freud to practice his despair within strict limits and artistry of expression. Freud's reticence was essential to his talking therapy. What is not to be done is expressed best in silence. Psychological men try not to remember how restricted and special the situation of therapeutic talkativeness must be, according to Freudian theory. Freud has the style to keep many a little secret from himself; after all, it is best to stop probing before the probe itself turns against the prober. An instrument against illness may infect instead. Rarely, for example, did Freud probe his relation to his mother, who boosted Freud's ego early and high enough to help him become sovereign maker of symbolic offerings in this century; no successor has appeared to inaugurate the next.

Of course, in earlier periods, some few others there have been, with ego powerful enough to express itself on behalf of its time. To those few belongs the power to make every evidence of questionable authority emerge from things that remain otherwise strictly unacknowledged. The evidence is of a special kind. It is pointed by the fact of suffering. To less powerful egos, such evidence is too painful to be made articulate. Freud trained his mind to dance on the point of pain, which for him was the point of honor in his life—not only the physical pain of his cancer but the pain that was his guilt knowledge of himself.

Dancers on the point of pain perform not least against each other. The symbolic life is highly competitive—even, for example, among those who practice some variety of the socialist symbolic. Because pain is such an unpleasant subject, those who specialize in explaining its necessity risk recurrent periods of severe rejection and loneliness. I see no reason why the quest for the historical Freud should not succeed again and again in its symbolic object of murdering him. Now he is slain as a bourgeois nihilist; in another time, other reasons will be found for this act of parricide.

That very hypertrophy of criticism, by which the character disorder of psychologizing intellectuals is best diagnosed, diagnoses their critics. Psychological men are a type that brings down to earth especially hard anyone they imagine above them. The case against Freud is bound to make a case study of him. After all, it is thanks to Freud that this case-studying type has come up from underground, where Dostoevski saw it. With post-Freudian changes in the role status of the patient, making him no more sick than his therapist, an equal among those equally seen through, Freud's turn to die has come. Freud's mind appears helpless before its own popular after-creation of the generally analytic patient.

The public debasing of analysis into ideology, psychological man justifying himself as not alone, continues to lower the tensions specific to every manifest order of hidden existence. No lowering is beneath the dignity of psychological man. His interpretative reductions of the sacred to repression derive from his most knowing humiliation: to know that nothing is really lowering.

To identify downward, so to say, is to cultivate insolence and invite humiliation. A culture declines precisely in its loss of consecrated acts. Unconsecrated by external rituals of their opposing relation, apparently clean things crawled toward filth before Freud's unblinking analytic eye. That cleanliness is next to filthiness. Consecrated acts had turned obsessive, as Freud saw in his time and place. But the difference between consecration and obsession depends upon the delicate balance of human resistances to the sacred. With one eye open and the other closed in shame, like an amateur marksman thinking his vision correct as a sharpshooter's, Freud calculated and recalculated the distances between our resistances and the truths they negate, adamantly *as if* there were forever nothing sacred between them.

A fiction such as this, sacred distances closed and what is lowering seen upside down, must prove fatal when it comes to dominate a culture. Psychological men can only reeducate themselves for the next smart job of demolition on yet another ideology of super-ego. Of all the ideological demands made in the twentieth century, the demand for analysis, in all its varieties, has been the greatest. But at this end of Freud's century, analytic ideologies have turned against themselves; they savage their own symbolics. In Freud, the savaging occurs in his reduction of the parent question to a question of parents.

Super-ego as ideology especially produces sickness because psychological men must grant the right of equal existence to every ideology. Nowadays, the arts of destruction are no longer in the hands of virtuosi. Instead of Freud's psychology with a scalpel, successor instrument to Nietzsche's philosophy with a hammer, there are masses of individual inexpert victims, practicing therapies of collective consciousness upon themselves. These victims imagine that becoming expert about themselves consists in affirming the endless senses in which they have become victims of their loneliness in sacred order. Thinking has become a grievance procedure against the heteronomy of "values." That grievance procedure is sometimes called "secularization" by sociologists of remissive religiosities. But "secularization" is as high-minded a revolt against sacred order as "sublimation." High-mindedness will not prevent the most terrible outbreaks of a violence that inverts the higher indifference. Narcissism will flower on the smallest differences. Despite its manifestos of grievances against the forms of higher authority, the movement toward secularity will be favored by the modern state. Therapies against authority serve the state's highest interest by releasing the nuclear energy of politics—namely, killing and being killed for the smallest reasons.

VII

The age of psychological man has merged into one characterized equally by its therapies and by its tortures. We are possessed by the transgressive in sacred order, as earlier fanatics were possessed—but in a different way. Psychological men are possessed by the most transgressive and original of all fantasies: that they can command themselves, which is tantamount to being uncommanded. But there is, always and everywhere, someone to obey and something to transgress. We are never uncommanded, though we may be disobedient.

The fantasy of emptiness, of being uncommanded, lacks even a reminiscence of Freud's realistic modesty when facing each acutely confused existence in sacred order. Freud was not a great healer. He was a great symbolist. His vocation was to improve upon the facts that the patient presented to him, not to transform the patient. He knew how little he could—how little he should—try to alter the repressive design of all our lives. Only compare the grandeur of Freud's modesty with the shouting puerilities of post-Freudian popular psychologizing: the latter tries to break the subtle connections between our saving sense of guilt and self-esteem. Freud preferred to leave those connections intact, whenever a reluctant abolitionist did not come to him with the connections already as if broken. The successor to the neurotic is a collector of recycled self-assertions, including modesty ploys, someone who can live in reasonable comfort with himself no matter what he does. The only guilt this successor permits himself is false guilt.

By false guilt, I mean to remark again that praise of the perverse, cultivated in the tone of every voice aggrieved enough to ask "By what authority?" Here is the questionable affect of culture transformed into patterns of grievance against the past; the prevalent ideological demand for analysis marries rancor at authority under its canopy of negations. False guilt assaults what is interdictory; this modern practice of assault trains what is transgressive to be ready for the slightest releasing occasion. To ask "By what authority?" is to train oneself in the role of symbolic despot, urging oneself to break through culture as the achievement of repressive registrations. But there is no culture except in repressive registrations.

Freud was the modern mind incarnate, split to the last on the parent question of authority. He died with his sublime hypochondriasis intact. It appears in his motto for *The Interpretation of Dreams:* "*If I cannot bend the Higher Powers, I will move the Infernal Regions.*" This passage from Virgil summarized Freud's ambivalent response to the question "*Am I Thy Master or art Thou Mine?*"

To read the parent question in Freudian style, or any other, forces acknowledgment of one important thing: that its diction is out of date. This datedness *is* the style of the parent question of our humanity, the past in its authority. All the main arguments about how to live are arguments about this style. Nothing changes except our resistances to being asked the parent question.

Neurosis is a general term for achieving a stability of releasing resistances to sacred order. That stability is what makes Freud's psychology itself great in the neurotic style of finding the Higher Powers bent. Because the Higher Powers can never be solicited by their great symbolists into lowering themselves so far that they become as they are represented, no recipe for neurotics can feed their egos. Psychosis is the illusion of Self-feeding to the point of satiety. At its therapeutic best, as a temporary undoing of the highest power, every ego-feeding recipe offers a remissive super-ego, some fizzle of an "ideal" easily sniffed out as "ideology."

To forget about general ideals and remember specific commands would make possible the action of entering one's own life in sacred order. When humans are at their best, commanded, they do not act out transgressions disguised as "optional lifestyles." By thinking ourselves, uncommanded, we are making our way to mass psychosis, a veritable anticulture. Lost in their chatter against authority, modern movements of an impossible secularization burn to take a step further, beyond neurosis into perversion. That step would take us as near as we can get to chaos. But chaos will never come. Although everything can be therapeutic for transgressives, chaos, the culture of perversion, is impossible. Equally impossible are morality without shame, faith without the pure sense of guilt, and a democracy of despotic emotions. A "prohibitive character" is "firmly attached to sacredness"[16] and to both is attached life itself, even if the modern mind wills to "know of no [rational] basis" for these attachments.[17]

So much for the impoverishment of our reasoning powers. Sacredness is an involuntary idea that is bound to emerge, however disguised and changed into visual and acoustic images.[18] The repressive imperative cannot be repressed. Mind can only fall asleep to It, by that effortless and regular avoidance in the memory of It which we may be pleased to call "rational" or "secular." Reason resists truth when it cannot acknowledge that the return of the past, in its authority, "must be called the *truth*," both eternal and historical.[19] That Freud looked away from the truth, for a final time, when it faced him in his last work, *Moses and Monotheism,* expresses the pride with which this mind would not know what it minded. Yet we must all be as we are minded. The ambivalent drive of Freud toward his final act of parricide, the murder of Moses, was also the celebration of his suicide, authority returned in symbols he could not refuse.* So the killer identified upward with his victim.

The neurotic or irrational obediences Freud analyzed were the negatives of perfectly rational perversions. In celebration of refusals to recognize that sacred order always returns, our century, which Freud began triumphantly, has ended in his defeat. The problem of the twenty-first century has already dawned upon us: it is the lowering, perverse quality of our swarming fresh enactments of old denials, of sacred order newly recognized on condition that the deeds of recognition are perverse. The last words in this book referred the reader to Freud's inauguration of our grand "new illness" as psychological men; that "new illness" was intended to be compared with older, forgotten words of judgment. For implicit in every healing doctrine which presumes to move the Infernal Regions is the judgment such grandeur elicits: immemorial wrath to come.

> *Even in the later stages of analysis one must be careful not to give a patient the solution of a symptom or the translation of a wish until he is already so close to it that he has only one short step more to make in order to get hold of the explanation for himself. In former years I often had*

---

* These failed refusals can occur in a variety of repressive registrations. For another example: Durkheim's sociology *is* his suicide, i.e., his effort to destroy the authority of his past. Especially in American culture, sociology and psychology are the stony grounds upon which post-Freudian Jewry has dashed out its brains, turning its revolts against commands into liberally discharged fizzles about "ideals."

occasion to find that the premature communication of a solution brought the treatment to an untimely end, on account not only of the resistances which it thus suddenly awakened but also of the relief which the solution brought with it.

—FREUD, "ON BEGINNING THE TREATMENT"

NOTES & INDEX

REFERENCE NOTES

TEXTS

A uniform English translation of Freud's psychological writings is currently being issued by the Hogarth Press, London, but only certain volumes had been published at the time the present work was completed. Quotations and citations from Freud's works refer, therefore, to the assorted editions listed below. Dates in parentheses following titles indicate, unless otherwise noted, the year of original publication.

I. *On Aphasia* (1891), the edition published by the Hogarth Press (London, 1953). Freud's major neurological monograph.

II. *The Complete Psychological Works of Sigmund Freud, Standard Edition* (London: Hogarth Press, 1953—; distributed in the United States by The Macmillan Company), referred to in the notes as SE with the volume number and page, for the texts of:

> *Studies on Hysteria* (with Breuer, 1895)
> *The Interpretation of Dreams* (1900) and *On Dreams* (1901)
> *Three Essays on Sexuality* (1905)
> *Jokes and Their Relation to the Unconscious* (1905)
> *Five Lectures on Psycho-Analysis* (1909), referred to in the text and notes as "Clark Lectures"
> *Leonardo da Vinci and a Memory of His Childhood* (1910), referred to as *Leonardo da Vinci*
> *Totem and Taboo* (1913)
> *Beyond the Pleasure Principle* (1920)
> *Group Psychology and the Analysis of the Ego* (1921), referred to as *Group Psychology*

and for the following case histories:

> *Fragment of an Analysis of a Case of Hysteria* (1905), referred to as "Case of 'Dora'"
> *Analysis of a Phobia in a Five-Year-Old Boy* (1909), referred to as "Case of 'Little Hans'"
> *Notes upon a Case of Obsessional Neurosis* (1909), referred to as "Case of the 'Rat Man'"
> *From the History of an Infantile Neurosis* (1919), referred to as "The 'Wolf Man' Case"
> *The Psychogenesis of a Case of Homosexuality in a Woman* (1920).

III. *Delusion and Dream in Jensen's "Gradiva"* (1906), the edition published by the Beacon Press (Boston, 1956), edited, and with an introduction, by myself.

IV. *Psychopathology of Everyday Life* (1901); the notes refer to the Brill translations in *The Basic Works of Sigmund Freud* (New York: Modern Library, 1950).

V. *Introductory Lectures on Psycho-Analysis* (1916–1917), referred to as *Introductory Lectures,* the popular edition titled *A General Introduction to Psychoanalysis* (New York: Garden City Publishing Company, 1943).

VI. The editions published in London by the Hogarth Press and the Institute of Psycho-Analysis, in the years given, have been used for:

> *The Ego and the Id* (1923)
> *An Autobiographical Study* (1925)
> *Inhibitions, Symptoms, and Anxiety* (1926)
> *The Future of an Illusion* (1928)
> *Civilization and Its Discontents* (1930)
> *New Introductory Lectures on Psycho-Analysis* (1933), referred to as *New Introductory Lectures*
> *An Outline of Psycho-Analysis* (posthumous, 1940).

W. W. Norton and Company, New York, has published American editions, in the same translation, of *An Autobiographical Study* (1952), *New Introductory Lectures* (1933), and *An Outline of Psychoanalysis* (1949); and Liveright and Company, New York, of *The Future of an Illusion* (1928).

VII. *Moses and Monotheism* (1939), the American edition (New York: Alfred A. Knopf, 1949).

VIII. *The Question of Lay Analysis* (1926), the edition published by the Imago Publishing Company (London: 1947). An American edition has been published by W. W. Norton and Company (New York: 1950).

IX. *Collected Papers of Sigmund Freud* (5 vols., London: Hogarth Press, 1949–1950), referred to in the notes as *Coll. Papers* with the volume number and page, for essays and case histories not as of that time issued in the Standard Edition.

X. *The Origins of Psychoanalysis,* edited by Ernst Kris and Anna Freud (New York: Basic Books, 1954), referred to in the notes as "Letters to Fliess." A posthumous collection of letters and manuscripts sent to Dr. Wilhelm Fliess.

NOTES

Most of the following notes document direct quotations made in the book; in some cases, additional passages which support the point are given.

CHAPTER ONE: SCIENCE AND MORAL PSYCHOLOGY

1. *An Autobiographical Study,* pp. 13, 133.
2. Cf. Jones, *The Life and Work of Sigmund Freud* (New York: Basic Books, 1953–1957), I, 348.
3. Quoted in Jones, I, 197.
4. *An Autobiographical Study,* p. 16.
5. "The Unconscious" (1915), SE XIV, 175. See also "Case of 'Dora,'" SE VII, 113.
6. *Beyond the Pleasure Principle,* SE XVIII, 60.
7. SE XI, 217. The essay is "Psychogenic Disturbance of Vision" (1910). Cf. *The Interpretation of Dreams,* SE IV, 41–42.
8. "The Resistances to Psychoanalysis," *Coll. Papers* V, 166.
9. *Studies on Hysteria,* SE II, 160.
10. "Case of 'Dora,'" SE VII, 109.
11. "Analysis Terminable and Interminable," *Coll. Papers* V, 319 *et pass.*
12. From a letter to a Gymnasium friend written in the summer of 1879, when Freud had enrolled in a course in animal experimentation. Quoted by Jones, op. cit., I, 53.
13. Recalled by his sister; see Anna Freud-Bernays, "My Brother, Sigmund Freud," *The American Mercury,* LI (November 1940).
14. Quoted by Jones, op. cit., I, 224–25.
15. Cf. "Case of 'Dora,'" SE VII, 109.
16. *An Outline of Psychoanalysis,* p. 8. Cf. pp. 46–47.
17. William James, *The Principles of Psychology* (New York: Henry Holt and Company, 1890), II, 459. James's italics.
18. *Introductory Lectures,* p. 344.
19. See Franz Alexander, *The Medical Value of Psychoanalysis* (New York: W. W. Norton and Company, 1936), pp. 180, 198.
20. *Studies on Hysteria,* SE II, 212. See also p. 263.
21. Franz Alexander, *Psychosomatic Medicine: Its Principles and Applications* (New York: W. W. Norton and Company, 1950), p. 42.
22. Cf. *Studies on Hysteria,* SE II, 203–206.
23. Jones, op. cit., I, 371.
24. Cf. R. R. Sears, *Survey of Objective Studies of Psychoanalytic Concepts* (New York: Social Science Research Council, 1951). Ethology also promises, I think, concepts and techniques of observation for the longest step yet taken toward a scientific aesthetics. The best introduction to ethology I know is Konrad Lorenz, *King Solomon's Ring* (New York: Thomas Y. Crowell Company, 1952). On instinct, see N. Tinbergen, *The Study of Instinct* (London: Oxford University Press, 1951).
25. "The Defence Neuropsychoses," *Coll. Papers,* I 75.
26. John Rickman, "Methodology and Research in Psychiatry," *British Journal of Medical Psychology,* XXIV, Part I (1951), 5.
27. *Introductory Lectures,* pp. 260–261. Freud assures us that mini-

mally such pictorial images are "useful aids to understanding . . . and . . . not to be despised." Moreover, these images "indicate an extensive approximation to actual reality."

28. *The Ego and the Id*, p. 67.
29. Cf. Jones, op. cit., II, 283.
30. Reported by Ernest Jones, op. cit., I, 21.
31. *The Interpretation of Dreams*, SE IV, 208–215.
32. *An Autobiographical Study*, p. 110; "On the History of the Psychoanalytic Movement" (1914), SE XIV, 15–16.
33. *Introductory Lectures*, p. 252; "A Difficulty in the Path of Psychoanalysis," SE XVII, 140–41; "The Resistances to Psychoanalysis" (1925), *Coll. Papers* V, 173. The source of Freud's Copernican image of himself and Darwin was

probably Haeckel. "Haeckel liked to compare Darwin's reform of biology with the reform of cosmology achieved by Copernicus three hundred years before." Cf. E. Haeckel, *Natürliche Schöpfungsgeschichte* (1868), quoted in Ernst Cassirer, *The Problem of Knowledge* (New Haven: Yale University Press, 1950), p. 160.

34. See *Beyond the Pleasure Principle*, SE XVIII, 57–58; "The Resistances to Psychoanalysis," *Coll. Papers* V, 169; *Group Psychology*, SE XVIII, 81; "Analysis Terminable and Interminable" (1937), *Coll. Papers* V, 348–50.
35. SE XIV, 36. See, further, Jones, op. cit., III, 339.
36. *New Introductory Lectures*, pp. 186–87.
37. *Coll. Papers* I, 304; see also pp. 218, 301.

CHAPTER TWO: CONFLICT AND CHARACTER

1. "Instincts and Their Vicissitudes," SE XIV, 123.
2. *Three Essays on Sexuality*, SE VII, 168. (Italics deleted.)
3. John Dewey, *Human Nature and Conduct* (New York: Modern Library), p. 87.
4. Ibid., p. 88.
5. Ibid., pp. 153–54.
6. *New Introductory Lectures*, p. 94.
7. *The Interpretation of Dreams*, SE V, 577.
8. *New Introductory Lectures*, pp. 98–99.
9. *The Interpretation of Dreams*, SE V, 613.
10. Ibid., p. 612. Cf. ibid., pp. 612–613: "everything conscious has an unconscious preliminary stage."
11. *The Ego and the Id*, p. 12.
12. Ibid., p. 13.
13. "Constructions in Analysis," *Coll. Papers* V, 359.
14. See, however, *New Introductory*

Lectures, p. 78. Where there is repression, however successful, there also must be symptoms, however subtle. "The symptom [is] the representative of the repressed in relation to the ego."

15. SE XI, 17.
16. *Studies on Hysteria*, SE II, 34–35.
17. SE XI, 16.
18. SE XI, 14. See also, "On the Psychical Mechanism of Hysterical Phenomena" (with Breuer), SE II, 6.
19. *Introductory Lectures*, pp. 250–251. Cf. ibid., p. 177.
20. Ibid., pp. 242–43.
21. There is evidence that Freud did not try to avoid the indirect influence, at least, of Plato. In 1879, at the age of twenty-three, he translated the twelfth volume of a collected edition of the writings of John Stuart Mill. The volume included Mill's essay on Grote's

Plato, in which Mill comments on the Platonic theory of anamnesis. Siegfried Bernfeld writes that Freud is reported to have said that he had been "greatly impressed by the theory of anamnesis and that he had, at one time, given it a great deal of thought." Bernfeld, "Freud's Scientific Beginning," *American Imago* VI, No. 3 (September 1949), 188.

22. *Biographia Literaria*, Ch. 6. The context is Coleridge's critique of the theory of association proposed by Locke and Hartley: were this theory true, Coleridge argues, the span of our lifetime would be divided into little bits by a despotic succession of our outward impressions and inward recollections.

23. "Case of 'Dora,'" SE VII, 18. Cf. also *Introductory Lectures*, p. 250, for another therapeutic formula, "all the gaps in the patient's memory must be filled in."

24. *Introductory Lectures*, pp. 178–179.

25. SE XI, p. 17.

26. "Constructions in Analysis," *Coll. Papers* V, 360–62.

27. *Civilization and Its Discontents*, pp. 17–18.

28. Ibid., p. 18.

29. Cf. *Three Essays*, SE VII, 172.

30. "Observations on Transference-Love" (1915), *Coll. Papers* II, 387.

31. *Civilization and Its Discontents*, p. 39.

32. "On the Sexual Theories of Children," *Coll. Papers* II, 68. In terms of his own theory, Freud ignores the possibility that the early repression of sexual curiosity may actually intensify other forms of curiosity.

33. "'Civilized' Sexual Morality and Modern Nervousness" (1908), *Coll. Papers* II, 93.

34. *The Ego and the Id*, p. 87.

35. Ibid.

36. "Character and Anal Eroticism" (1907), *Coll. Papers* II, 45–50.

37. Ibid., p. 50. See also *The Interpretation of Dreams*, SE IV, 216, on "the intimate connection between bed-wetting and the character trait of ambition." The sentence containing this phrase was added in 1914, in the fourth edition.

38. *Totem and Taboo*, SE XIII, 90. Italics mine.

39. Cf. *The Future of an Illusion*, pp. 25–42.

40. Cf. "The Case of 'Little Hans,'" SE X, 9, and "On the Sexual Theories of Children," *Coll. Papers* II, 62–63.

41. "On the Dynamics of the Transference," *Coll. Papers* II, 313.

42. "The Unconscious," SE XIV, 171.

43. *Introductory Lectures*, pp. 148, 177; "Analysis Terminable and Interminable," *Coll. Papers* V, 344; *An Outline of Psychoanalysis*, p. 28.

44. Erich Fromm, *The Forgotten Language* (New York: Rinehart and Company, 1951), p. 18.

45. *New Introductory Lectures*, p. 150 et pass. Cf., also, "Some Psychological Consequences of the Anatomical Distinction between the Sexes" (1925), *Coll. Papers* V, 191–97.

46. *Introductory Lectures*, p. 374. Cf. ibid., p. 319.

47. "The 'Uncanny,'" SE XVII, 252.

48. "The Excretory Function in Psychoanalysis and Folklore" (1913), *Coll. Papers* V, 90.

49. *Totem and Taboo*, SE XIII, 60.

50. *The Interpretation of Dreams*, SE IV, 260–61.

51. *The Question of Lay Analysis*, p. 39.

52. *The Question of Lay Analysis*, p. 14.

53. "My Contact with Josef Popper-Lynkeus" (1932), *Coll. Papers* V, 297.

54. *The Ego and the Id*, p. 30; cf.

New Introductory Lectures, p. 102.

55. "Remarks Upon the Theory and Practice of Dream Interpretation" (1923), *Coll. Papers* V, 149. Cf. *New Introductory Lectures*, pp. 81–82.

56. Cf. "The Economic Problem in Masochism," *Coll. Papers* II, 264: "The super-ego is in fact just as much a representative of the *id* as of the outer world. It originated through the introjection into the ego of the first objects of the libidinal impulses in the *id;* namely, the two parents, by which process the relation to them was desexualized."

57. *New Introductory Lectures*, p. 79.

58. "My Contact with Josef Popper-Lynkeus," *Coll. Papers* V, 297–98.

59. *New Introductory Lectures*, p. 101.

60. Ibid., p. 104.

61. *The Question of Lay Analysis*, p. 21.

62. *New Introductory Lectures*, p. 102.

63. Ibid., p. 101.

64. *New Introductory Lectures*, p. 104.

65. *The Question of Lay Analysis*, p. 46; cf. also ibid., pp. 23–26.

66. *Introductory Lectures*, p. 305.

67. "My Views on the Part Played by Sexuality in the Aetiology of the Neuroses" (1905), *Coll. Papers* I, 279. Cf. also *Introductory Lectures*, pp. 264–65; and *Delusion and Dream*, p. 76, on the "formation of symptoms by compromises between the two psychic forces struggling with each other."

68. *An Outline of Psychoanalysis*, pp. 46–47.

69. Ibid., p. 36.

70. *Introductory Lectures*, p. 290.

71. Ibid., pp. 332–33.

72. Nietzsche, *The Twilight of the Gods*, in *The Portable Nietzsche*, ed. W. Kaufmann (New York: The Viking Press, 1954), p. 477.

73. *Introductory Lectures*, p. 395. See the entire discussion, pp. 392–96.

74. *An Outline of Psychoanalysis*, p. 36.

CHAPTER THREE: THE HIDDEN SELF

1. Ernest Jones, *Life and Work*, I, 319.

2. Ibid., 319.

3. Montaigne, *Essays*, Book III, Chapter 2.

4. *The Interpretation of Dreams*, SE IV, 105.

5. Ibid., SE V, 600.

6. "Observations on 'Wild' Psycho-Analysis," SE XI, 225.

7. "Psychoanalysis and Religious Origins" (1919), *Coll. Papers* V, 93.

8. *The Interpretation of Dreams*, SE V, 603.

9. Ibid., 613. Freud's italics.

10. From "A Difficulty in the Path of Psychoanalysis" (1917), SE XVII, 143.

11. See *Coll. Papers* IV, 350–52; *Coll. Papers* V, 173; *Introductory Lectures*, p. 252.

12. *The Ego and the Id*, p. 82. Elsewhere (*New Introductory Lectures*, p. 106) Freud raised as the motto of his new pedagogy: "Where id was, there shall ego be."

13. "The Dynamics of the Transference," *Coll. Papers* II, 322.

14. See *New Introductory Lectures*, p. 78.

15. See "Recommendations on Treatment," *Coll. Papers* II, 332.

16. *Autobiographical Study*, p. 109; *New Introductory Lectures*, p. 104; *Coll. Papers* II, 264; *Coll. Papers* V, 256; *The Ego and the Id*, pp. 39, 42–46; *An Out-*

line of Psychoanalysis, p. 78.

17. *The Interpretation of Dreams*, SE IV, 263.

18. "The Case of 'Dora,' " SE VIII, 112.

19. See *Tribute to Freud*, by H.D. (New York: Pantheon Books, 1956), pp. 21–22; Joseph Wortis, *Fragments of an Analysis with Freud* (New York: Simon and Schuster, 1955), pp. 76, 155.

20. *Studies on Hysteria*, SE II, 121.

21. On the intelligent patient: "Emmy von N.," one of Freud's earliest patients (1888), "revealed an unusual degree of education and intelligence" (*Studies on Hysteria*, SE II, 49). See also *The Psychogenesis of a Case of Homosexuality in a Woman* (1920), SE XVIII, 154, where Freud speaks of his patient's remarkable "acuteness of comprehension and her lucid objectivity." Cf. SE VII, 254: "A certain measure of natural intelligence and ethical development" are required of the patient.

    "Anna O." was "markedly intelligent, with an astonishingly quick grasp of things and penetrating intuition. She possessed a powerful intellect . . . [and] great poetic and imaginative gifts" (*Studies on Hysteria*, op. cit., 21). Cf. SE XVIII, 235: Anna O. was "a person of great intelligence."

22. "The Case of 'Dora,' " SE VII, 72.

23. From "The Moses of Michelangelo" (1914), SE XIII, 222. Cf. *The Interpretation of Dreams*, SE IV, 217: "I need not explain to a Viennese the principle of the '*Gschnas*.' It consists in constructing what appear to be rare and precious objects out of trivial and preferably comic and worthless materials (for instance, in making armour out of saucepans, wisps of straw and dinner rolls)—a fa-vourite pastime at bohemian parties here in Vienna. I had observed that this is precisely what hysterical subjects do: alongside what has really happened to them, they unconsciously build up frightful or perverse imaginary events which they construct out of the most innocent and everyday material of their experience."

24. "Psychoanalysis and the Ascertaining of Truth in Courts of Law" (1906), *Coll. Papers* II, 20.

25. "Freud's Psychoanalytic Procedure" (1904), SE VII, 250.

26. "Constructions in Analysis," *Coll. Papers* V, 358.

27. Cf. *Totem and Taboo*, SE XIII, 176–77.

28. *The Interpretation of Dreams*, SE IV, 298 fn.

29. Ibid., SE IV, 96: "Every dream has a meaning, though a hidden one." Also, "Psychoanalysis and the Ascertaining of Truth in Courts of Law," *Coll. Papers* II, 20; on "the interpretation of dreams, i.e. the translation of the remembered dream-content into its hidden meaning"; and *Introductory Lectures*, p. 78.

30. *The Interpretation of Dreams*, SE V, 375. Freud is chiefly on the look-out for such puns hidden in verbal associations, the "switchwords" or "verbal bridges" crossed by the paths leading to the unconscious." Cf. "The Case of 'Dora,' " SE VII, 65 fn., 90; *Jokes and Their Relation to the Unconscious*, SE VIII, 18–20; *The Interpretation of Dreams*, SE V, 339–41.

    For a discussion of the resemblance between dreams and puns, cf. *Introductory Lectures*, pp. 210–211.

31. "Notes Upon a Case of Obsessional Neurosis" (1909) in SE X, 213–20. Cf. *The Interpretation of Dreams*, SE V, 340–41: "Words,

since they are the nodal points of numerous ideas, may be regarded as predestined to ambiguity; and the neuroses (e.g. in framing obsessions and phobias), no less than dreams, make unashamed use of the advantages thus offered by words for purposes of condensation and disguise." Cf. SE V, 471: "Every element in a dream can, for purposes of interpretation, stand for its opposite just as easily as for itself."

32. But see *Introductory Lectures*, p. 134; and *Coll. Papers* II, 58, on "the bisexual meaning of the symptom."

33. Freud tells a version of this joke in *Wit and Its Relation to the Unconscious*, p. 707.

34. From the essay on "Negation" (1925), *Coll. Papers* V, 185.

35. Ibid., 182.

36. "Case of 'Dora,' " SE VII, 57. This point was augmented in a footnote added in 1923.

37. Ibid., 58–59.

38. "Negation," op. cit., 181: "In our interpretation we take the liberty of disregarding the negation and of simply picking out the subject-matter of the association."

39. Georg Groddeck, *The Book of the It* (New York: Nervous and Mental Diseases Monograph, 1928), p. 72.

40. "Case of 'Dora,' " SE VII, 29. Cf. p. 28, where Freud declares that anyone who doesn't respond positively to an occasion for sexual excitement is neurotic. Such a person is "hysterical."

41. Ibid., 34.

42. Ibid., 62, 120 fn.

43. Ibid., 59.

44. Ibid., 104.

45. Ibid., 35.

46. *Introductory Lectures*, p. 255; "Recommendations on Treatment" (1912), *Coll. Papers* II, 332. Cf. Otto Fenichel, "Psychosomatic Method," *The Collected Papers of Otto Fenichel, First Series* (New York: W. W. Norton and Company, 1953), p. 325.

47. "Case of 'Dora,' " SE VII, 54.

48. "Case of the 'Rat Man,' " SE X, 197.

49. "On Narcissism: An Introduction" (1914), SE XIV, 96.

50. SE XVIII, 238. Cf. also "Recommendations on Treatment," op. cit., 324.

51. *The Interpretation of Dreams*, SE IV, 101–102.

52. "Recommendations on Treatment," op. cit., 324–25.

53. "Psycho-Analysis," SE XVIII, 238.

54. *The Interpretation of Dreams*, SE IV, 102.

55. Ibid., 101.

56. "Psychoanalysis and the Ascertaining of Truth in Courts of Law," *Coll. Papers* II, 18.

57. "Case of 'Dora,' " SE VII, 109.

58. Ibid., 119.

59. "Psycho-Analysis," SE XVIII, 239. Freud's italics. On the idea that one unconscious can communicate directly with another, see also Otto Fenichel's paper "Concerning Unconscious Communication" (1926), in op. cit., pp. 93–96. Cf. also *Coll. Papers* II, 125.

60. "Recommendations on Treatment," op. cit., p. 328. Perhaps the most extreme version of the demand for spontaneity, both in therapy and in esoteric theoretical discussions among therapists, is to be found in the writings of Wilhelm Reich, the most sectarian of Freud's heirs. Cf. his *Character Analysis*, third edition (New York: Orgone Press, 1949), pp. 6, 21 ff.

61. Cf. "Case of 'Dora,' " SE VII, 10; "Case of the 'Rat Man,' " SE X, 159.

62. *Psychopathology of Everyday Life*, p. 96; *New Introductory Lectures*, ix.

63. *The Interpretation of Dreams,* SE IV, 103.

64. "A Note on the Prehistory of the Technique of Psychoanalysis" (1920), SE XVIII, 263–65.

65. "Case of 'Little Hans,'" SE X, 6.

66. Ibid., 7–8.

67. Ibid., 56.

68. Ibid., 72. Freud's italics.

69. Ibid., 97.

70. Ibid., 86.

71. Ibid., 100.

72. For a simple example, see "Clark Lectures," SE XI, 23–24.

73. "Case of 'Dora,'" SE VII, 49. Cf. "Clark Lectures," SE XI, 53.

74. Ibid., 52.

75. *Introductory Lectures,* p. 247.

76. Ibid., p. 250. Cf. also, "Freud's Psychoanalytic Procedure," SE VII, 253.

77. Otto Rank, *Will Therapy and Truth and Reality* (New York: Alfred A. Knopf, Inc., 1945).

78. Edward Glover, "The Therapeutic Effect of Inexact Interpretation," *International Journal of Psychoanalysis,* XII (1931), 4, 397–411.

79. *The Interpretation of Dreams,* SE IV, 101.

80. "Psycho-Analysis," SE XVIII, 238.

81. See, for example, SE XI, 141–42, 144–45, 286, 288–89; *Coll. Papers* II, 313–14 *et pass.*

82. "On the History of the Psychoanalytic Movement," *Coll. Papers* I, SE XIV, 49.

83. "Analysis Terminable and Interminable," *Coll. Papers* V, 352.

84. "On the History of the Psychoanalytic Movement," SE XIV, 26.

85. "On Psychotherapy," ibid., 262.

86. "Recommendations on Treatment," *Coll. Papers* II, 327, 331. Cf. Otto Fenichel, "Psychoanalytic Method," op. cit., p. 327.

87. "On Psychotherapy," *Coll. Papers* I, 261–62. Freud's italics. Cf. also "Clark Lectures," SE XI, 52–53, 55–56; "'Wild' Psycho-Analysis,"

SE XI, 225–26; and the entire Lecture 19, *Introductory Lectures,* pp. 253 ff.

88. "Psychoanalysis and the Ascertaining of Truth in Courts of Law," *Coll. Papers* II, 19.

89. *Jokes and Their Relation to the Unconscious,* SE VIII, 162.

90. "Future Prospects of Psycho-Analytic Therapy," SE XI, 147. Cf., further, *New Introductory Lectures,* pp. 177–78.

91. Cf. *New Introductory Lectures,* pp. 93–94; "Case of 'Little Hans,'" SE X, 103; and the introductory note to *An Outline of Psychoanalysis.*

92. "Remarks Upon the Theory and Practice of Dream Interpretation" in *Coll. Papers* V, 142. Freud gives no concrete examples. For an instance of a confirmatory dream which apparently was not recognized as such by the analyst, see Otto Fenichel's paper, "The Appearance in a Dream of a Lost Memory," op. cit., pp. 34–38.

Cf. also "The Employment of Dream-Interpretation in Psycho-Analysis," *Coll. Papers* II, 311.

93. Ibid., V. Cf. "Future Prospects of Psychoanalytic Therapy," SE XI, 141–42: "The mechanism of our assistance is easy to understand: we give the patient the conscious anticipatory idea [the idea of what he may expect to find] and he then finds the repressed unconscious idea in himself on the basis of its similarity to the anticipatory one. This is the intellectual help which makes it easier for him to overcome the resistances between conscious and unconscious."

94. Cf. "Case of 'Dora,'" SE VII, 117, on the "sense of conviction of the validity of the connections which have been constructed during the analysis," following the resolution of the transference. Cf.,

too, a remarkable passage on the polemical intention characteristic of psychoanalysis. "For a psycho-analysis is not an impartial scientific investigation, but a therapeutic measure. Its essence is not to prove anything, but merely to alter

something. . . . The physician always gives his patient . . . the conscious anticipatory ideas by the help of which he is put in a position to recognize and to grasp the unconscious material" (SE X, 104).

Chapter Four: THE TACTICS OF INTERPRETATION

1. *The Interpretation of Dreams*, SE IV, 241–42. See also *Introductory Lectures*, p. 134.

2. Ibid., p. 241 fn. (This footnote was added in 1925.) Also ibid., SE V, 341–42, and "On the History of the Psychoanalytic Movement," SE XIV, 19. "The dreamer's associations help very little towards understanding symbols."

3. *Introductory Lectures*, pp. 134–135. "Symbols make it possible for us in certain circumstances to interpret a dream without questioning the dreamer, who indeed in any case can tell us nothing about the symbols." Cf. "On the History of the Psychoanalytic Movement," SE XIV, 19.

4. *The Interpretation of Dreams*, SE IV, 105: "In my judgment the situation is in fact more favourable in the case of *self*-observation than in that of other people." Freud's italics.

5. *Introductory Lectures*, p. 136; cf. ibid., pp. 147–48.

6. *Moses and Monotheism*, p. 156. Freud adds: "Symbolism even ignores the difference in languages" and is "probably . . . the same with all peoples."

7. *The Interpretation of Dreams*, SE IV, 111 fn.; ibid., SE V, 524–525.

8. "Case of 'Dora,' " SE VII, 10–11.

9. This is a circumstance frequently recorded by analysts since Freud. For an example, see Edward Glover, "The Therapeutic Effects of Inexact Interpretation," *Inter-*

national *Journal of Psycho-Analysis*, XII, Part 4, October 1931, pp. 397–411.

10. *Introductory Lectures*, p. 148. Cf. *The Interpretation of Dreams*, SE V, 377: one can tell the meaning of symbols and the significance of dreams best from "precisely those people who are uninitiated into psycho-analysis."

11. *Delusion and Dream*, p. 25.

12. Cf. *An Autobiographical Study*, p. 85 fn.: "There was a reason for my choosing as the title of my book not *The Dream* but *The Interpretation of Dreams*."

13. *The Interpretation of Dreams*, SE V, 608; "The Claims of Psycho-Analysis to Scientific Interest" (1913), SE XIII, 170; "Clark Lectures," SE XI, 33–34. "On the History of the Psychoanalytic Movement," SE XIV, 19.

14. *The Interpretation of Dreams*, SE IV, 136.

15. Cf. *Studies on Hysteria*, SE II, 289 (and 287–93); "Letters to Fliess," p. 172; *The Psychopathology of Everyday Life*, p. 103: "*As the architectural principle of the psychic apparatus, we may conjecture a certain stratification or structure of instances deposited in strata.*" Freud's italics.

16. *The Interpretation of Dreams*, SE IV, 219: "a succession of meanings or wish-fulfillments may be superimposed on one another, the bottom one being the fulfillment of a wish dating from earliest childhood."

17. Ibid., SE IV, 96. See for further discriminations of the terms "manifest" and "latent" content, the following: SE V, 641; SE XVIII, 241.
18. Cf. ibid., SE IV, 329–32.
19. Ibid., SE V, 340. Cf. *The Psychopathology of Everyday Life*, p. 223; *Introductory Lectures*, p. 124.
20. Erich Fromm, *The Forgotten Language* (New York: Rinehart and Company, 1951), p. 97.
21. *The Psychopathology of Everyday Life*, p. 153. Cf. ibid., p. 151: "It is impossible to think of a number, or even of a name, of one's own free will."
22. Ibid., pp. 152–53.
23. Cf. *The Interpretation of Dreams*, SE V, 522 fn. (added in 1919).
24. Ibid., SE V, 517.
25. *The Interpretation of Dreams*, SE IV, 97. See also *Introductory Lectures*, pp. 133–34.
26. Cf. *The Interpretation of Dreams*, SE IV, pp. 33–39, on the effect upon dreams of bodily sensations during sleep. See also *On Dreams*, SE V, 680–81; and *Introductory Lectures*, p. 78.
27. *The Psychogenesis of a Case of Homosexuality in a Woman* (1920), SE XVIII, 167.
28. Ibid., 168.
29. See ibid., SE V, 340.
30. Cf. "The Relation of the Poet to Day-Dreaming" (1908), *Coll. Papers* IV, 174–77.
31. Jeremy Bentham, "The Rationale of Reward," *Works*, II, 253–54.
32. Brill writes, reminiscing, that Freud, "being rationalistic . . . rebelled against being moved by something without knowing why; and as he could not discover the meaning of music, he was almost incapable of obtaining any pleasure from it." A. A. Brill, *Freud's Contribution to Psychiatry* (New York: W. W. Norton and Company, 1947), p. 27.
33. *Delusion and Dream*, p. 27. My italics.
34. *New Introductory Lectures*, p. 106. My italics.
35. *The Psychopathology of Everyday Life*, p. 227.
36. *The Interpretation of Dreams*, SE IV, 266.
37. "The Relation of the Poet to Day-Dreaming," *Coll. Papers* IV, 182.
38. *The Interpretation of Dreams*, SE V, 341; *Jokes and Their Relation to the Unconscious*, SE VIII, 179–80; *New Introductory Lectures*, p. 17: the dream "is, of course, a communication which is insufficiently communicative, because a dream is, in itself, not a social utterance; it is not a means for making oneself understood."
39. Ernst Kris, *Psychoanalytic Explorations in Art* (New York: International Universities Press, 1952), p. 167; cf. pp. 60–61, 253–257.
40. *Jokes and Their Relation to the Unconscious*, SE VIII, 96.
41. *The Interpretation of Dreams*, SE V, 578–80.
42. "My Contact with Josef Popper-Lynkeus," *Coll. Papers* V, 297.
43. *Introductory Lectures*, p. 38.
44. "The Moses of Michelangelo," SE XIII, 212. Freud's italics.
45. Ibid., 221–30.
46. Ibid., 235–36.
47. Ibid., 235.
48. *The Interpretation of Dreams*, SE IV, 219 fn. (added in 1914).
49. *Introductory Lectures*, p. 121. For more on this painting and on the psychoanalytic interpretation of art, see Alexander Grinstein, "A Psychoanalytic Study of Schwind's 'Dream of a Prisoner,'" *American Imago*, VIII (1951), 65–91.
50. SE XIV, 324.
51. "The Moses of Michelangelo," SE XIII, 229–30.
52. *Leonardo da Vinci*, SE XI, 133.
53. "Dostoyevsky and Parricide" (1928), *Coll. Papers* V, 223.

54. Ibid., 222.
55. Ibid., 237.
56. Cf. "Case of 'Dora,'" SE VII, 78, 91: the symptom both "betrays and conceals."
57. The Interpretation of Dreams, SE IV, 281.
58. William Hazlitt, "On Poetry in General" (1818), in The Great Critics, ed. Smith and Parks (New York: W. W. Norton and Company, 1939), p. 700.
59. The Interpretation of Dreams, SE V, 592; On Dreams, SE V, 640.
60. The Interpretation of Dreams, SE IV, 284.
61. Ibid., 314.
62. "Psycho-Analysis" (1923), SE XVIII, 242.
63. The Interpretation of Dreams, SE IV, 99; cf. ibid., 103–104.
64. Ibid., 49.
65. "Dostoyevsky and Parricide," Coll. Papers V, 233. "Instead of punishing himself, he got himself punished by his father's deputy."
66. "Psychoanalysis and the Ascertaining of Truth in Courts of Law," Coll. Papers II, 20. Freud says: Critics "accuse us . . . of playing with words."
67. Cf. Coll. Papers IV, 258.
68. Cf. "Dostoyevsky and Parricide," Coll. Papers V, 222, 224; Leonardo da Vinci, SE XI, 120; "The

Moses of Michelangelo," SE XIII, 211; "The Claims of Psycho-Analysis to Scientific Interest," SE XIII, 187.
69. "The Theme of the Three Caskets," Coll. Papers IV, 246.
70. The Interpretation of Dreams, SE V, 341.
71. Introductory Lectures, p. 133. Cf. On Dreams, SE V, 384–85.
72. Introductory Lectures, pp. 133–134.
73. Ibid., p. 137.
74. "Die Menscheit hat ja gewusst, dass si Geist hat; ich musst ihr zeigen, dass es auch Tribe gibt." Freud is reported to have made this remark on the occasion of his seventieth birthday, on May 7, 1936, to Ludwig Binswanger, the Swiss psychiatrist and existentialist. Cf. L. Binswanger, "Freud und die Verfassung der Klinische Psychiatrie," Schweitzer Archiv für Neurologie und Psychiatrie, (Zurich, 1936), vol. XXXVII, No. 12, 177. Cf. also "The Psycho-Analytic Movement," Coll. Papers I, 354, where Freud accuses Adler of sounding a "few of Culture's harmonics in the symphony of life . . . while the daemonic forces of the instinct-melody have once more passed unheard."

CHAPTER FIVE: SEXUALITY AND DOMINATION

1. "The Resistances to Psychoanalysis," Coll. Papers V, 169.
2. Civilization and Its Discontents, p. 74.
3. Three Essays, SE VII, 229.
4. Ibid., p. 160.
5. Ibid., pp. 145–46 fn. (added in 1915).
6. This is the main point of the first of the Three Essays, pp. 135–72. Cf. also Introductory Lectures, pp. 282–84: ". . . facts of the kind just described naturally tend to

diminish the gulf beween normal and perverse sexuality."
7. Ibid., p. 146 fn.
8. Ibid., pp. 135–36.
9. Group Psychology, SE XVIII, 91.
10. Cf., for example, "Obsessions and Phobias" (1895), Coll. Papers I, 130–31. A reference to masturbation as the cause of a neurosis (more accurately, the cause is the renunciation of "the autoerotic gratification") occurs as late as 1909. Cf. "General Remarks on

Hysterical Attacks" (1909), *Coll. Papers* II, 102; for an alternative explanation see *Coll. Papers* I, 158.

11. "The Aetiology of Hysteria," *Coll. Papers* I, 198. Cf. *Studies on Hysteria*, SE II, 275 (the seducing governess); *Coll. Papers* I, 157, 198, 203; and *Three Essays*, SE VII, 148 (on the sexual abuse of children by teachers and servants).

12. From " 'Wild' Psycho-Analysis," SE XI, 222–23. "In psychoanalysis the concept of what is sexual . . . goes lower and also higher than its popular sense. This extension is justified genetically; we reckon as belonging to 'sexual life' all the activities of the tender feeling, . . . even when those impulses have become inhibited in regard to their original sexual aim or have exchanged this aim for another which is no longer sexual."

13. "The Dynamics of the Transference," *Coll. Papers* II, 319.

14. "The Resistances to Psychoanalysis," *Coll. Papers* V, 169. Cf. "Predisposition to Obsessional Neurosis," *Coll. Papers* II, 129: "Psychoanalysis stands or falls by the recognition of the sexual component-impulses, of the erotogenic zones, and by the consequent expansion of the idea of the "sexual function" as opposed to the narrower one of a "genital function."

15. *Group Psychology*, SE XVIII, 91.

16. Ibid. Cf. the preface to the 4th edition of the *Three Essays*, where Freud again associates "the enlarged sexuality of psycho-analysis . . . with the Eros of the divine Plato" (SE VII, 134).

17. From "On the Universal Tendency to Debasement in the Sphere of Love" (1912), SE XI, 183.

18. Ibid., 215. Cf. SE VII, 31. On the correct intuitions built into the erotic life of antiquity as distinguished from our own, cf. SE VII, p. 149 fn. (added in 1910).

19. "On the Sexual Theories of Children," *Coll. Papers* II, 69. Cf. *Three Essays*, SE VII, 196, on the sadistic view of sexual intercourse; and "The 'Wolf Man' Case," SE XVII, 45 fn: observing coitus "cannot fail to produce" upon a child "the impression of being a sadistic act." Freud's italics.

20. Ibid., 70.

21. *Three Essays*, SE VII, 209.

22. Ibid., p. 211.

23. Ibid.

24. Ibid., p. 150.

25. Ibid., pp. 145–46 fn. (added in 1915). Cf. p. 148 on the original bisexuality: "The sexual instinct and the sexual object are merely soldered together. . . . The sexual instinct is in the first instance independent of its object; nor is its origin likely to be due to its object's attractions."

26. *New Introductory Lectures*, p. 127. Italics mine.

27. *Jokes and Their Relation to the Unconscious*, SE VIII, 111.

28. "The Economic Problem in Masochism" (1924) in *Coll. Papers* II, 259.

29. Cf. "On Narcissism: An Introduction" (1914), in *Coll. Papers* IV, 41.

30. *Beyond the Pleasure Principle*, SE XVIII, 57–58. Freud quotes the myth retold in Plato's *Symposium*.

31. "The Most Prevalent Form of Degradation in Erotic Life," *Coll. Papers* IV, 204–205. (This distinction is first broached in the *Three Essays*, SE VII, 200). Cf. also *Group Psychology*, SE XVIII, 111.

32. Ibid., p. 205.

33. Ibid., p. 206.

34. Bronislaw Malinowski, *Sex and Repression in Savage Society*

(New York: Harcourt, Brace and Company, 1927), p. 158.

35. *Group Psychology*, SE XVIII, 107.

36. Ibid., p. 127.

37. "The Most Prevalent Form of Degradation in Erotic Life," op. cit., 207.

38. Ibid., pp. 208–209.

39. Ibid., pp. 209–10. Psychic impotence characterizes "the erotic life of civilized people."

40. Ibid., pp. 208, 210.

41. Ibid., p. 210.

42. "Types of Neurotic Nosogenesis" (1912), in *Coll. Papers* II, 113. The tenses, although confused, are given as in the text.

43. "The Most Prevalent Form of Degradation in Erotic Life," op. cit., 204.

44. *Three Essays*, SE VII, 150.

45. Ibid., p. 161.

46. *Three Essays*, op. cit., p. 149. Italics mine.

47. "Observations on 'Wild' Psycho-Analysis," *Coll. Papers* II, 299.

48. "The Most Prevalent Form of Degradation in Erotic Life," op. cit., p. 214.

49. Ibid., pp. 213–15.

50. "A Special Type of Object-Choice," op. cit., p. 200.

51. Ibid., p. 197.

52. *Three Essays*, op. cit., p. 149. For sexuality as a total clue to the rest of the person, cf. ibid., 161: "Manifest abnormality in the other relations of life can invariably be shown to have a background of abnormal sexual conduct." Cf. also Ferenczi, *Sex in Psychoanalysis*, p. 17, on the "prefigurativeness of sexuality" for the rest of the psychical behavior; and Brill, op. cit., p. 77. Also *Coll. Papers* II, 93: in a normal sexual life, no neurosis is possible; therefore, normality is defined by normal sexuality (the genital character).

53. "On Beginning the Treatment" (1913) *Coll. Papers* II, 360. Analysis depends on emotionally attaching the patient to the physician. "Therefore until a powerful transference is established the first explanation should be withheld" (ibid., p. 365).

54. *Introductory Lectures*, p. 387.

55. "Some Character-Types Met with in Psycho-Analytic Work" (1915), SE XIV, 312. Cf. *Introductory Lectures*, p. 387: the patient is only capable of being influenced intellectually "in so far as he is capable of investing objects with libido."

56. "Thoughts for the Times on War and Death" (1915), in *Coll. Papers* IV, 303. Cf. *General Introduction*, p. 258.

57. "Discussion of Lay Analysis," *Coll. Papers* V, 210. Cf. *Introductory Lectures*, p. 387.

58. "Recollection, Repetition, and Working Through" (1914), *Coll. Papers* II, 374.

59. "The Dynamics of the Transference" (1912), *Coll. Papers* II, 313.

60. "Observations on Transference-Love" (1915), *Coll. Papers* II, 379.

61. Ibid., p. 380.

62. Ibid., p. 382. "Behind moral prescriptions," Freud tells us, is "the source of them, namely . . . utility." Because it is therapeutically useful to avoid involvement with "the infatuated women," but not "on the score of conventional morality," the analyst must renounce his own "love-transference."

63. Ibid., p. 381.

64. Ibid., p. 381. Thus "the resistance acts as an *agent provocateur*," offering an erotic compromise which would serve to vindicate the repressions (ibid.).

65. "On the History of the Psycho-analytic Movement," SE XIV, 49.

66. *Introductory Lectures*, p. 386. Now "all the patient's symptoms

have abandoned their original significance and have adapted themselves to a new meaning"—that of transference.

67. "Observations on Transference-Love," *Coll. Papers* II, 389.
68. "The Dynamics of the Transference," op. cit., p. 316.
69. Ibid., p. 383.
70. Ibid., pp. 384–85.
71. "On Beginning the Treatment, etc.," *Coll. Papers* II, 359.
72. Ibid., p. 379.
73. Ibid., p. 357.
74. "Recollection, Repetition, and Working Through," op. cit., 373.
75. Cf. "The Passing of the Oedipus-Complex" (1924), *Coll. Papers* II, 275: "The Oedipus-complex in the girl is far simpler, less equivocal, than that of the little possessor of a penis; in my experience it seldom goes beyond the wish to take the mother's place, the feminine attitude towards the father."
76. *Outline of Psycho-Analysis*, pp. 13, 62. The little girl's disappointing realization that she has no penis has "permanent" and limiting effects "upon the development of her character." Cf. *New Introductory Lectures*, p. 169: "Nature has paid less careful attention to the demands of the female function than to those of masculinity." Also "Some Psychological Consequences of the Anatomical Distinction between the Sexes" (1925), *Coll. Papers* V, 192.
77. *Introductory Lectures*, p. 309. Cf. Helene Deutsch, *The Psychology of Woman* (New York: Grune & Stratton, 1944), I, 290.
78. *New Introductory Lectures*, p. 173.
79. Ibid., pp. 173–74.
80. Ibid., p. 173.
81. "Analysis Terminable and Interminable" (1937), *Coll. Papers* V, 356. Cf. p. 63: "If we ask an analyst . . . for a penis."
82. *Introductory Lectures*, pp. 139, 145.
83. Ibid., p. 138. See, for example, Otto Fenichel, "Die Symbolische Gleichung: Madohen-Phallus," *Internationale Zeitschrift für Psychoanalyse*, Vol. 22 (1936), 299–315.
84. Ibid., p. 138.
85. Ibid., p. 139. "The complicated *topography* of the female sexual *organs* accounts for their often being represented by a *landscape* with rocks, woods and water, whilst the imposing *mechanism* of the male sexual *apparatus* lends it to symbolization by all kinds of complicated and indescribable *machinery*." (My italics.) These rocks and trees, ordinarily thought of by Freud as male symbols, if put in the context of a landscape, symbolized parts of the female anatomy. Cf. ibid., 149: "Weapons and tools in general stand for the male, and materials and things worked on for the female."
86. See Ernest Jones, *Psycho-Analysis*, 4th edition (New York, 1929), p. 145.
87. *General Introduction*, p. 169: "All objects capable of elongation are symbols of the male organ."
88. "Analysis Terminable and Interminable," op. cit., p. 357.
89. *Introductory Lectures*, p. 141.
90. Ibid., pp. 133–50.
91. *Introductory Lectures*, p. 138.
92. Karl Abraham, *Dreams and Myths* (New York: 1913), p. 17.
93. Otto Rank and Hanns Sachs, *The Significance of Psychoanalysis for the Mental Sciences* (New York: 1916), p. 57. Cf. *Coll. Papers* IV, 427, on the tree-trunk as a phallic symbol.
94. *The Interpretation of Dreams*, SE V, 355; *Introductory Lectures*, p. 143: "The Occurrence in Dreams of Material from Fairy-Tales" (1913), *Coll. Papers* IV, 237 fn.

95. *New Introductory Lectures,* p. 145.

96. "The Taboo of Virginity" (1910), SE XI, 198–99. Cf. *The Interpretation of Dreams,* SE IV, 299, where Freud detects in a dream a strong concern over "the danger" of one of his sons "coming to grief over a woman."

97. "Medusa's Head" (1922), in SE XVIII, 273–74. Cf. the *New Introductory Lectures,* p. 37, on the "phallic mother" whom one fears, and who is symbolized in dreams and fairy tales by the spider.

98. *New Introductory Lectures,* pp. 171–72.

99. *The Interpretation of Dreams,* SE IV, 204.

100. "The Theme of the Three Caskets" (1913), *Coll. Papers* IV, 256.

101. Ibid.

102. *The Interpretation of Dreams,* SE V, 453. (Italics deleted.) Here it is not possible to distinguish Freud from Jung. Jung, too, admired the psychological profundity of *She.* See his essay, "Marriage as a Psychological Relationship" (1925), in Vol. 17 of the English *Collected Works of C. G. Jung.*

Generally speaking, however, the romantic polarity of the sexes is far more explicit and prepossessing in Jung's writings. Freud could never have written the supremely anti-rationalist essay "Women in Europe" (1927), pp. 164–88 of the *Contributions to Analytical Psychology* (London: 1928). Here Jung writes: ". . . How is a man to write about woman, his exact opposite? . . . For woman stands just where man's shadow falls" (p. 164). Jung speaks of the "unconsciousness and indefiniteness of the woman" (p. 168). And: "It is woman's outstanding characteristic that she can do everything for the love of a man. . . . The love of a thing is man's prerogative" (p. 169). "Woman is far more 'psychological' than man. For the most part he contents himself with 'logic' simply. Everything 'psychical,' 'unconscious,' etc. is antithetic to him" (p. 178).

On Jung's notion of the *anima,* "the fundamentally unconscious . . . eternal image of women" which "every man carries within him," see *Coll. Works,* Vol. 17, pp. 198–99; and *Psychological Types* (1920), pp. 594–99.

103. " 'Civilized' Sexual Morality and Modern Nervousness" (1908), *Coll. Papers* II, 94.

104. See Viola Klein, *The Feminine Character, History of an Ideology* (London: 1946).

105. Cf. the best book in English on the subject: Walter Kaufmann, *Nietzsche* (Princeton: Princeton University Press, 1950), pp. 19, 63: "Nietzsche's writings contain many all-too-human judgments —especially about women—but these are philosophically irrelevant. . . . The unjust and unquestioned prejudices of a philosopher may be of interest to the historian as well as to the psychologist; but Nietzsche's prejudices about women need not greatly concern the philosopher."

106. *Civilization and Its Discontents,* p. 73. Cf. also *The Ego and the Id,* p. 50: "The male sex has taken the lead in developing . . . these moral acquisitions [religion, moral restraint, social feeling]; and . . . they have then been transmitted to women by cross-inheritance."

107. "Psychogenic Disturbance of Vision" (1910), SE XI, 109, 215.

108. *Moses and Monotheism,* p. 186. Cf. *Coll. Papers* V, 286. Cf. SE XI, 190.

109. *New Introductory Lectures*, pp. 172–73.
110. *Moses and Monotheism*, pp. 155, 158.
111. *New Introductory Lectures*, Lecture XXXIII, pp. 144–74.
112. Cf. *Group Psychology*, SE XVIII, 78. "What [the group] demands of its heroes is strength, or even violence. It wants to be ruled and oppressed and to fear its masters."
113. *Psychopathology of Everyday Life*, p. 101.
114. *Three Essays*, SE VII, 220 fn. (added in 1915). Ibid., 141–43.

CHAPTER SIX: THE AUTHORITY OF THE PAST

1. *Inhibitions, Symptoms and Anxiety*, p. 75.
2. Cf. Carl-Gustav Carus, *Symbolik der menschlichen Gestalt* (Leipzig, 1853, 1858) XXX; Freud had both editions in his library, now housed at the New York State Psychiatric Institute; Hughlings Jackson, *The Croonian Lectures* (London: Royal College of Physicians, 1884); T. A. Ribot, *Diseases of Memory*, trans. W. H. Smith (New York: 1882); Pierre Janet, *L'Automisme psychologique: essais de psychologie expérimentale sur les formes inférieures de l'activité humaine* (Paris: 1889); Moritz Lazarus and H. Steinthal, *Einleitende Gedanken über Völkerpsychologie* (Berlin: 1859).

For a brilliant survey of this entire development, see "Der Aufbau der Personlichkeit," in Gottfried Benn, *Essays* (Wiesbaden: 1951), pp. 71–90.
3. *The Interpretation of Dreams*, SE V, 548–49.
4. *The Question of Lay Analysis*, p. 71.
5. *Moses and Monotheism*, p. 128.
6. *The Question of Lay Analysis*, pp. 96–97.
7. *Totem and Taboo*, SE XIII, 88. Cf. ibid., 77. As early as 1750 the French philosopher Turgot asserted that the advance of our knowledge of nature proceeded by a gradual emancipation from those anthropomorphic concepts which first led humans to interpret natural phenomena after their own image, as animated by minds like their own. This idea was later to become a leading theme in the positivist philosophy of history, and the earliest stage of thinking it described was first called "fetishism," and then "anthropomorphism" and "animism."
8. Ibid., p. 90. My italics.
9. *Moses and Monotheism*, p. 186.
10. "Why War?" (1932), *Coll. Papers* V, 286.
11. G. Stanley Hall, *Life and Confessions of a Psychologist* (New York: D. Appleton and Company, 1927), p. 359. Hall, with James J. Putnam, was one of Freud's first sponsors in America, and was president of Clark University when Freud delivered his lectures there in 1909. Hall ended as a very respectful critic, but a critic nonetheless. What the Freudians thought man needed was more and more rational consciousness. Hall agreed. "True," he writes, in the introductory chapter of his autobiography, "consciousness is in itself in many ways, and to a far larger extent than we have ever dreamed before, remedial" (p. 12). But then he suggests an alternative remedy, one the Freudians have treated as part of the disease. Hall continues: "But it is the motives of shame and shocked modesty which I believe are the chief curative

agents." Here is a serious, indeed Christian, rejoinder to Freud's rationalism, according to which what men need nowadays may be not more consciousness, but more guilt.

12. *Totem and Taboo*, SE XIII, 161.
13. "Constructions in Analysis" (1937), *Coll. Papers* V, 370.
14. *Group Psychology*, SE XVIII, 122.
15. *Moses and Monotheism*, p. 159.
16. *Group Psychology*, SE XVIII, 123.
17. *Totem and Taboo*, SE XIII, 144.
18. *Moses and Monotheism*, p. 129.
19. *Civilization and Its Discontents*, p. 59.
20. Ibid., pp. 51–52. In his conjectural prototypes of work and first cultural possessions, Freud presumes a universal facility in perceiving subjective spatial analogies. The uses of a tool to form and shape materials, he says, are regularly "animized" as the relation of male to female. With regard to the infantile impulse to extinguish fire with a stream of urine, Freud asserted that "the legends we possess . . . and in the later fables of Gulliver in Lilliput and Rabelais' Gargantua . . . leave no doubt that flames shooting upwards like tongues were originally felt to have a phallic sense." As he symbolically equated penis with flame, from the grossest abstraction of maleness, he similarly inferred that dwellings, hearths, and all other spaces of enclosure —on the analogy of the womb— are female. Cf. *Coll. Papers* V, 288–94.
21. "Constructions in Analysis," *Coll. Papers* V, 363.
22. *Moses and Monotheism*, pp. 204–205.
23. Ibid., pp. 157–61.
24. Ibid., pp. 204–205.
25. "Analysis Terminable and Inter-

minable," *Coll. Papers* V, 343. Cf. *Totem and Taboo*, SE XIII, 158: "Without the assumption of a collective mind, which makes it possible to neglect the interruptions of mental acts caused by the extinction of the individual, social psychology in general cannot exist."
26. The remarkable, curious Lamarckianism of Samuel Butler can best be documented from his *Notebooks* (ed. Henry Festing Jones, London: 1912). On pp. 57–59: "The connection between memory and heredity is so close that there is no reason for regarding the two as generically different." And further, "all forms of reproduction . . . are based directly or indirectly upon memory." See also Butler's book *Life and Habit* (London: 1910) esp. Chap. XI: "Instinct as Inherited Memory."
27. *Moses and Monotheism*, p. 209.
28. Ibid., p. 208.
29. Ibid., p. 201.
30. William James, *The Principles of Psychology*, Vol. II (New York: 1890), p. 678. James's italics.
31. *Moses and Monotheism*, p. 126.
32. *Introductory Lectures*, p. 387.
33. *Civilization and Its Discontents*, pp. 23–24.
34. *Group Psychology*, SE XVIII, 135
35. "Why War?" *Coll. Papers* V, 283.
36. J. W. von Goethe, "Briefe an Frau Stein," 8 June, 1787, in *Goethes Briefe* (Leipzig: 1923), Vol. VIII, pp. 252 ff.
37. *Group Psychology*, SE XVIII, 122.
38. Ibid., pp. 135–37.
39. "Psychoanalysis," SE XVIII, 242.
40. *Introductory Lectures*, p. 134.
41. *The Interpretation of Dreams*, SE V, 352.
42. Ibid., 352 fn. Darwin had "actions" not "things" in mind when discussing the origin of symbolism.
43. *Moses and Monotheism*, p. 205.

44. Ibid., p. 113.
45. Ibid., p. 114.
46. *Totem and Taboo*, SE XIII, 28–29.
47. *Moses and Monotheism*, p. 108.
48. Ibid., p. 109.
49. "Obsessive Acts and Religious Practices" (1907), *Coll. Papers* II, 25, 33.
50. G. W. F. Hegel, *The Philosophy of History* (rev. ed.; New York: 1900), pp. 31–32.
51. Karl Marx, *Capital* (Chicago: 1906), I, 648.
52. *Moses and Monotheism*, p. 200.
53. *Beyond the Pleasure Principle*, SE XVIII, 49. Cf. "The Libido Theory," SE XVIII, 258.
54. *Moses and Monotheism*, p. 198.
55. *The Future of an Illusion*, p. 8.

CHAPTER SEVEN: POLITICS AND THE INDIVIDUAL

1. *Moses and Monotheism*, p. 129.
2. *Totem and Taboo*, SE XIII, 148.
3. Ibid.
4. Ibid., p. 22.
5. Ibid., p. 123. Frazer, quoted by Freud.
6. Ibid. Frazer, quoted by Freud.
7. Cf. ibid., p. 30.
8. Ibid., pp. 33–34.
9. "Some Character-Types Met with in Psycho-Analytic Work" (1913), SE XIV, 314–15.
10. *Group Psychology*, SE XVIII, 93.
11. Jones, *The Life and Work of Sigmund Freud*, I, 184.
12. *Group Psychology*, op. cit., p. 79.
13. Ibid., p. 88.
14. Ibid., p. 115.
15. Ibid., p. 114.
16. Ibid., p. 89.
17. Ibid., p. 92.
18. Ibid., p. 102.
19. Ibid., p. 101.
20. Ibid., p. 103.
21. Ibid., p. 92.
22. *The Ego and the Id*, p. 63.
23. *Group Psychology*, SE XVIII, 114.
24. Ibid., p. 97.
25. Ibid., p. 127.
26. *Totem and Taboo*, SE XIII, 89.
27. *Three Essays*, SE VII, 150. Freud's italics.
28. *Group Psychology*, op. cit., 123–124.
29. Ibid., p. 123.
30. *Totem and Taboo*, SE XIII, 49–50. Freud notes that "the variety of outcomes of a conflict of this kind," between hostility and veneration, in the relation between rulers and ruled can be traced to the "situation of emotional ambivalence."
31. *Civilization and Its Discontents*, p. 93.
32. *Totem and Taboo*, op. cit., p. 50.
33. Harold D. Lasswell, *Power and Personality* (New York: W. W. Norton and Company, 1948), p. 146.
34. Ibid., p. 200.
35. Ibid., p. 197.
36. *The Psychopathology of Politics* in *The Political Writings of Harold D. Lasswell* (Glencoe, Ill.: Free Press, 1951), pp. 75–76.
37. *The Future of an Illusion*, p. 13.
38. *New Introductory Lectures*, p. 231.
39. "Why War?" (1932), *Coll. Papers* V, 284.
40. *New Introductory Lectures*, p. 231.
41. *Group Psychology*, SE XVIII, 79.
42. *Introductory Lectures*, p. 295.
43. Ibid.
44. *Group Psychology*, op. cit., p. 135.
45. "Thoughts for the Times on War and Death," SE XIV, 299.
46. Ibid., p. 288. Freud's italics.
47. *Totem and Taboo*, SE XIII, 36.

48. "Thoughts for the Times on War and Death," op. cit., 279.
49. Ibid., p. 296.
50. Ibid. Freud's italics.
51. Ibid., p. 295.
52. *Group Psychology*, SE XIII, 69.
53. Lawrence S. Kubie, "Authority and Freedom: Some Insights from Psychoanalysis," *The Journal of Religious Thought*, Vol. IX, No. 1, Autumn–Winter, 1952–1953, pp. 40–47.

CHAPTER EIGHT: THE RELIGION OF THE FATHERS

1. Quoted by A. A. Brill, *Freud's Contribution to Psychiatry* (New York: W. W. Norton and Company, 1944), pp. 195–96.
2. See Ernest Jones, op. cit., pp. 64, 145–46. For evidence from Freud's own dreams, see *The Interpretation of Dreams*, SE IV, 136 *et seq.*
3. "My Contact with Josef Popper-Lynkeus" (1932), *Coll. Papers* V, 301.
4. "A Religious Experience" (1928), *Coll. Papers* V, 244.
5. *The Interpretation of Dreams*, SE IV, 196.
6. Cf. ibid., SE V, 447–48.
7. *The Interpretation of Dreams*, SE IV, 136 ff. The dream of the uncle with the yellow beard. Cf. ibid., 216.
8. Ibid., 197.
9. Ibid., SE V, 427–29.
10. *The Future of an Illusion*, p. 66.
11. Ernest Jones, op. cit., p. 31.
12. *Moses and Monotheism*, p. 181.
13. *The Future of an Illusion*, p. 57.
14. Matthew Arnold, *Last Essays on Church and Religion* (London: 1877), vii–viii.
15. *The Future of an Illusion*, p. 42.
16. *Civilization and Its Discontents*, pp. 7–9. Rolland is not mentioned by name in the text.
17. *Beyond the Pleasure Principle*, SE XVIII, 57–58.
18. Cf. the concluding passage of *Civilization and Its Discontents*, p. 144, on the two "immortal adversaries," Eros and Thanatos; and *Coll. Papers* V, 346.
19. *Moses and Monotheism*, p. 142.
20. "The Economic Problem in Masochism," *Coll. Papers* II, 258.
21. "Obsessive Acts and Religious Practices," *Coll. Papers* II, 25.
22. In *Die Menschenopfer der alter Hebraer.* Cf. also the work of Ghillany's friend Daumler.
23. *Totem and Taboo*, SE XIII, 72.
24. "The Economic Problem in Masochism," op. cit., 265.
25. Ibid., p. 267.
26. *Totem and Taboo*, SE XIII, 145.
27. Ibid., pp. 144–46.
28. *Civilization and Its Discontents*, p. 121.
29. *The Future of an Illusion*, p. 18.
30. *Totem and Taboo*, SE XIII, 159.
31. *Civilization and Its Discontents*, p. 132.
32. *The Future of an Illusion*, p. 66. Cf. also "The Economic Problems in Masochism," *Coll. Papers* II, p. 266.
33. Ibid., p. 66–67.
34. "The Economic Problem in Masochism," op. cit., p. 266.
35. Nietzsche "on the Pale Criminal" is mentioned in *Coll. Papers* IV, 342–44.
36. "The Economic Problem in Masochism," op. cit., pp. 266–67. For another discussion of crime from a sense of guilt, see *The Ego and the Id*, p. 76. Concept of guilt is prior to the concept of crime, *Totem and Taboo*, op. cit., p. 159.
37. *Totem and Taboo*, op. cit., p. 156.
38. The metaphor of psychoanalysis as pedagogy is one of the most significant Freud uses. See, e.g., *The Future of an Illusion*, p. 14.

39. "The Economic Problem of Masochism," op. cit., p. 267.
40. *Civilization and Its Discontents*, p. 93.
41. *Moses and Monotheism*, p. 173.
42. Ibid., pp. 166, 168.
43. See especially the sub-section on "The Great Man," ibid., pp. 168–175.
44. Ibid., p. 142. Like Christianity, the founding of Mohammedanism is also "an abbreviated repetition of the Jewish one" (ibid., p. 146). Both successor religions, according to Freud, lack the heroic suffering and achievement, the "lofty heights of spirituality to which the Jewish religion had soared" (ibid., p. 139).
45. Ibid., p. 142.
46. *The Future of an Illusion*, p. 34. Cf. ibid., p. 67.
47. Frazer's argument is tortuous, and I have simplified it. The preface and pp. 65–70 of Vol. I of *The Golden Bough* sum it up best.

Nevertheless, if the association is not made pejorative then a great deal can be said for the erasing of Frazer's distinction between magic and religion. No one has been able to find the culture in which magic in fact preceded religion. It was in order to guard the notion of religion from the pejorative rationalist association with primitive culture that Frazer insisted on an original distinction. Thus his anthropology saved "religion" for beliefs in personal divine beings, or charismatic moral teachers. But religious experience plainly attached to all sorts of impersonal forces and to intuitions of sacred orders beyond the social and natural. Thus, in Freud's sense, the breaking of a taboo established mythically is at once magical and religious. Here Freud does well not to follow Frazer. Nevertheless the ethical religions of the West to which Freud attends are not simply tangles of myth and magic. They are founded religions, with charismatic moral virtuosi of high rational capacity as their founders. This makes a great deal of difference in the psychology of religion, and partly justifies Frazer's distinction of religion, although not in terms of successive spooks.

48. Frazer, *The Golden Bough*, 2nd edition, Vol. I, XX. Cf. also p. 70.
49. "Case of the 'Wolf Man,'" SE XVII, 115.
50. "A Neurosis of Demoniacal Possession in the Seventeenth Century" (1923), *Coll. Papers* IV, 436.
51. "The Future of Psycho-Analytic Therapy," SE XI, 146.
52. "Case of the 'Wolf Man,'" SE XVII, 114–15.
53. A. R. Radcliffe-Brown, *Structure and Function in Primitive Society*, (Glencoe, Ill.: Free Press, 1952), p. 149.
54. *The Future of an Illusion*, pp. 76–77.
55. Ibid., p. 77.
56. "Lines of Advance in Psycho-Analytic Therapy," SE XVII, 168.
57. *The Future of an Illusion*, p. 86.
58. Ibid., p. 92.
59. Ibid., pp. 60–69.
60. Ibid., pp. 61, 91.
61. Arthur Schopenhauer, *Essays*, tr. T. Bailey Saunders (New York: A. L. Burt Company, n.d.), p. 213.
62. Ibid., p. 220. Schopenhauer's italics.
63. *The Future of an Illusion*, pp. 68–69, 76, 93, 95.
64. Ibid., pp. 77–78.

Chapter Nine: THE ETHIC OF HONESTY

1. "Psychoanalysis," SE XVIII, 252. Cf. the last chapter, *New Introductory Lectures.*
2. "The Resistances to Psychoanalysis," *Coll. Papers* V, 168.
3. "Postscript to a Discussion on Lay Analysis," *Coll. Papers* V, 208.
4. Letter of April 2, 1896, "Letters to Fliess," p. 162: "I was never really interested in therapy." Cf. letter of April 2, 1896, to Fliess, and letter of Jan. 1, 1896, in "Letters to Fliess," p. 141.
5. *The Question of Lay Analysis,* p. 77.
6. "Postscript to a Discussion on Lay Analysis," *Coll. Papers* V, 210.
7. See *Coll. Papers* II, 351–53.
8. *The Question of Lay Analysis,* pp. 78–79.
9. "The Future Prospects of Psychoanalytic Therapy," SE XI, 146.
10. " 'Civilized' Sexual Morality and Modern Nervousness," *Coll. Papers* II, 77–80.
11. Ibid., 77.
12. Cf. ibid., 80. (Also SE XIV, 281 *et pass.*)
13. Ibid., 90.
14. Quoted, Ernest Jones, op. cit., I, 190.
15. Ibid., 191.
16. " 'Civilized' Sexual Morality and Modern Nervousness," *Coll. Papers* II, 99.
17. "Thoughts for the Times on War and Death," SE XIV, 291.
18. Ibid., 277–78.
19. Ibid., 285.
20. Ibid., 277.
21. Ibid., 289–90.
22. Ibid., 291.
23. Ibid., 284.
24. Ibid., 299.
25. "Why War?" *Coll. Papers* V, 284.
26. "Thoughts for the Times on War and Death," SE XIV, 285.
27. Ibid., 299.
28. Ibid., 291.
29. George Orwell, "Diaries," *World Review* Memorial Number, quoted in Wyndham Lewis, *The Writer and the Absolute* (London: 1952), p. 181. Even David Hume, in an age when culture was felt less oppressively, inclined to think that "interruptions" (Freud would have said eruptions) in "the periods of learning, were they not attended with such destruction of ancient books and the records of history, would be rather favorable to the arts and sciences by breaking the progress of authority and dethroning the tyrannical usurpers over human reason. In this particular, they have the same influence as interruptions [i.e., revolutions] in political governments and societies." At least Hume knew what wars do: they destroy ancient books and the records of history. (David Hume, "Of the Rise and Progress of the Arts and Sciences," *Essays,* London, 1882, I, 184.)
30. "The Resistances to Psychoanalysis" (1925), *Coll. Papers* V, 170. (Cf. *Coll. Papers* II, 99; SE XIV, 284.)
31. Ibid., 171. My italics.
32. "On Beginning the Treatment, etc.," *Coll. Papers* II, 355.
33. "The Future Prospects of Psycho-Analytic Therapy," SE XI, 149.
34. "A Special Type of Choice of Object Made by Men," SE XI, 170.
35. "The Future Prospects of Psycho-Analytic Therapy," SE XI, 148–149.
36. Ibid., 148.
37. Ibid.
38. "On Beginning the Treatment," *Coll. Papers* II, 355, 356 fn.

39. Ibid.
40. Freud compares analysis with the confessional in *An Outlet of Psychoanalysis*, p. 37.
41. Papal speech, quoted in *The New York Times*, pp. 1, 18, April 6, 1953.
42. "The Future Prospects of Psycho-Analytic Therapy," SE XI, 150.
43. Ibid., 148.
44. Ibid., 150.
45. Ibid.
46. Bernard Groethuysen, *Les Origines de l'esprit bourgeois en France* (Paris: 1928), p. 288. My translation.
47. Thomas Carlyle, *Heroes and Hero Worship* (Cambridge: Cambridge University Press, 1907), p. 172.
48. "The Future Prospects of Psycho-Analytic Therapy," SE XI, 150.
49. "Thoughts for the Times on War and Death," SE XIV, 288.
50. Ibid., 284–85.
51. *The Future of an Illusion*, p. 86.
52. "Formulations Regarding the Two Principles in Mental Functioning" (1911), *Coll. Papers* IV, 13.
53. Karl Menninger, "Present Trends in Psychoanalytic Theory and Practice," *The Yearbook of Psychoanalysis*, Vol. I, Sander Lorand, ed. (New York: 1945), pp. 89–93.
54. *The Future of an Illusion*, p. 86.
55. *Studies on Hysteria*, SE II, 305.
56. See, on Epictetus, T. R. Glover, *The Conflict of Religions in the Early Roman Empire* (London: 1909), p. 51.

CHAPTER TEN: THE EMERGENCE OF PSYCHOLOGICAL MAN

1. G. E. Moore, *Principia Ethica* (Cambridge: Cambridge University Press, 1903), Ch. 6.
2. "Postscript to a Discussion on Lay Analysis," *Coll. Papers* V, 211–12.
3. *New Introductory Lectures*, pp. 232, 202–203.
4. "Psychoanalysis and Religious Origins," *Coll. Papers* V, 94.
5. Otto Fenichel, *The Psychoanalytic Theory of Neurosis* (New York: W. W. Norton and Company, 1945), p. 24.
6. *The Interpretation of Dreams*, SE IV, 262.
7. *New Introductory Lectures*, p. 200.
8. *Delusion and Dream*, p. 86.
9. See "Moral Responsibility for the Content of Dreams" (1925), *Coll. Papers* V, 154–57.
10. "Analysis Terminable and Interminable," *Coll. Papers* V, 326.
11. "Psychoanalysis," SE XVIII, 252.
12. *Group Psychology*, SE XVIII, 91.
13. Ibid.
14. Nietzsche, *The Genealogy of Morals*, Third Essay, Section 19.
15. "Why War?" *Coll. Papers* V, 274.
16. Cf. SE VII, 48.
17. "The Future Prospects of Psychoanalytic Therapy," SE XI, 147.
18. "The Resistances to Psychoanalysis," *Coll. Papers* V, 169.
19. Ibid., p. 170.
20. Cf. *Three Essays*, SE VII, 149 fn., on the difference between the love life of antiquity and our own.
21. "The Resistances to Psychoanalysis," *Coll. Papers* V, 169.
22. *Dichtung und Wahrheit*. Quoted by M. H. Abrams, *The Mirror and the Lamp* (New York: Oxford University Press, 1953), p. 142. Cf. "Letters to Fliess," p. 208.
23. William Hazlitt, "On Poetry in General," *Complete Works*, V, 7–8.
24. *Beyond the Pleasure Principle*, SE XVIII, 16–17.
25. SE VII, 249.
26. Ibid., p. 250.
27. Cf. "Psychical Treatment," op. cit., p. 297.

28. "The Uncanny," SE XVII, 251.
29. "Psychopathic Characters on the Stage," SE VII, 305.
30. Ibid., p. 306.
31. *Jokes and Their Relation to the Unconscious*, SE VIII, 109–10.
32. Cf. discussion in *Introductory Lectures*, p. 325.
33. *Totem and Taboo*, SE XIII, 90.
34. "Female Sexuality," *Coll. Papers* V, 264.
35. *Jokes and Their Relation to the Unconscious*, SE VIII, 95–96. In his Introduction to this same work, however, Freud gives a clue to his meaning, when he refers to the "aesthetic attitude" as "playful," and as asking nothing of the object.

36. *The Interpretation of Dreams*, SE IV, 244.
37. "The Loss of Reality in Neurosis and Psychosis," *Coll. Papers* II, 279.
38. Ibid., pp. 279–80.
39. *Three Essays*, SE VII, 171: Freud cites Moebius, who said "with justice that we are all to some extent hysterics."
40. Cf. "Analysis Terminable and Interminable," *Coll. Papers* V, 337: "Every normal person is only approximately normal: his ego resembles that of the psychotic in one point or another, in a greater or lesser degree. . . ."
41. Cf. *Totem and Taboo*, SE XIII, 156.

Epilogue: ONE STEP FURTHER

1. *New Introductory Lectures*, SE XXII, 156. Cf. Chapter Ten of this book, p. 334.
2. Ibid., p. 151. Cf. Chapter Seven of this book, p. 223.
3. *Negation*, SE XIX, 235; Freud's italics.
4. *Psycho-Analytic Notes on an Autobiographical Account of a Case of Paranoia*, SE XII, 170.
5. *The Interpretation of Dreams*, SE IV, Part 1, 317–18.
6. Friedrich Nietzsche, *Gesammelte Werke*, Vol. XII, "Die Fröhliche Wissenschaft" (Munich: Musarion Verlag München, 1924), § 276, p. 201; Nietzsche's italics.
7. *The Ego and the Id*, SE XIX, 18.
8. *New Introductory Lectures*, SE XXII, 73.
9. Ibid., 40; *being*, my italics; *at the*

moment, Freud's italics.
10. *The Letters of John Keats*, ed. Maurice Buxton Forman (London and New York: Oxford University Press, 1948), p. 336.
11. Ernest Jones, *The Life and Work of Sigmund Freud*, Vol. 3, *The Last Phase, 1919–1939* (New York: Basic Books, 1957), p. 465.
12. Ibid.
13. Ibid.
14. See further, Deuteronomy 17 and 18, and Romans 1:18–32.
15. Jones, *op. cit.*, p. 465.
16. *Moses and Monotheism*, SE XXIII, 120.
17. Ibid.
18. *The Interpretation of Dreams*, SE IV, Part 1, 103.
19. *Moses and Monotheism*, SE XXIII, 130; Freud's italics.

INDEX

Authors are cited for all written works except those of Freud

Abel, murder of, 195
Abel, Karl, 78n.
Abraham, Karl, 23, 178, 284
Abraham, myth of, 195
Adaptation, Dewey's view of, 32
Addison, Joseph, 88
Adler, Alfred, 20, 26, 33, 53; conception of masculine protest, 181; Lamarckianism, 200, 202
Adolescence, 211n.
Adultery, 163
Aeschylus, 207
Affection, 158
Agape, 152–53
Aggression: inevitability of, 342–43; in libidinal development, 46–47n; repression of, 390; universal, 274
Agrippa, 43
Alexander, Franz, 14–15; quoted, 15
Ambiguity, *see* Language
Ambivalence, 54–55; toward leaders, 239; primal, 223
Amenhotep IV, 280
America: Freud's attitude toward, 307; Jews in, 262, 269; psychoanalysis in, 302–303
Amnesia, 38
Anal stage, 45, 46
Analysis, *see* Psychoanalysis
Analysis of emotion, contrasted to catharsis, 348–49
"Analysis Terminable and Interminable," 10, 53n.
Analyst, *see* Psychoanalyst
Anamnesis, 41, 362
Anaximander, 344n.
Andreas-Salome, Lou, 121
Anima, 29
Animals, memory of, 40; personality of, 19
Animism, 377
Animistic phase, in social development, 47
"Anna O.," 11, 39–40, 73, 74, 94, 367

Anthropology: influence of upon Freud, 192–93, 198–99, 205–207; and study of religion, 270; *see also* Primitives *and* Myth
Anthropomorphism, 377
Anticathexis, 370, 370n.
Anti-Semitism, 229n., 285
Anxiety, 62n., 106, 363, 363n., 383
Aphasia, 18
Appropriation, 53n.
Aristophanes, 148
Aristotle, 49, 347, 352; quoted, 16
Arnold, Matthew, quoted, 264–65
Art: antiart, 378; as confession, 132; disobedience in, 376; and dreaming, 118–22; emotive statement of, 123; expressive function of, 345–53; filmic, 378; function of, 126; as hoax, 377; hostility to, 120–21; as projection, 349–53; spontaneity of, 88–89, 91; standards of, 139–40; as time-killer, 378; unreality of, 380
Artist, 119, 120; ego regression of, 124; intention of, 127, 139; neurotic conflict of, 352n.; as sensualist, 184 and unconscious sources, 121
Asceticism, 344
Associations, 76
Atkinson, J. J., 189
Aton, religion of, 209, 280, 281
Augustine, St., 166
Authenticity, as existentialist criterion, 321
Authoritarian Personality, The, 242
Authority: as accomplice in crime, 388; of analyst, 97–101; concealed, 375, 391; of culture, 369, 371; experiment in types of, 19; external to morality, 363–64; first, 364; and idea of God, 264; individual in character, 370; and modern movements, 395; murder of, 364, 365, 385, 386, 396n.; parental, 361, 394, 395; of the past, 365, 385, 386, 396; personal,

425